Aaron Kleman
April 24, 2019
eBay

To Loot
My Life
Clean

Thomas Wolfe

Maxwell Perkins

To Loot
My Life
Clean

The Thomas Wolfe–
Maxwell Perkins
Correspondence

EDITED BY
MATTHEW J. BRUCCOLI
AND PARK BUCKER

UNIVERSITY OF SOUTH CAROLINA PRESS

Published in Columbia, South Carolina, by the
University of South Carolina Press

Manufactured in the United States of America

04   03   02   01   00   5   4   3   2   1

Library of Congress Cataloging-in-Publication Data

Wolfe, Thomas, 1900–1938.
    To loot my life clean : the Thomas Wolfe—Maxwell Perkins correspondence /
Matthew J. Bruccoli and Park Bucker, eds.
    p.   cm.
    Includes bibliographical references and index.
    ISBN 1-57003-355-2 (alk. paper)
    1. Wolfe, Thomas, 1900–1938—Correspondence. 2. Perkins, Maxwell E. (Maxwell
Evarts), 1884–1947—Correspondence. 3. Novelists, American—20th century—
Correspondence. 4. Book editors—United States—Correspondence. 5. Editors—
United States—Correspondence. I. Perkins, Maxwell E. (Maxwell Evarts),
1884–1947. II. Bruccoli, Matthew Joseph, 1931– III. Bucker, Park. IV. Title.
PS3545.O337 Z493   2000
813'.52—dc21   00-009542

Frontispiece: Thomas Wolfe with the manuscripts and typescripts for *Of Time and the
River* in 1934 (courtesy of the Thomas Wolfe Collection, North Carolina Collection,
University of North Carolina Library–Chapel Hill); Maxwell Perkins at the time he
began working with Thomas Wolfe.

To Judith S. Baughman

I want, much more than I have ever in this first draught, to loot my life clean, if possible of every memory which a buried life and the thousand faces of forgotten time could awaken and to weave it into <u>Antaeus</u> like a great densely woven web.

Thomas Wolfe (April 1933)

If it were not true that you, for instance, should write as you see, feel, and think, then a writer would be of no importance, and books merely things for amusement. And since I have always thought that there could be nothing so important as a book can be, and some are, I could not help but think as you do.

Maxwell Perkins (16 January 1937)

Contents

List of Illustrations   xi

Acknowledgments   xiii

Introduction: Thomas Wolfe and the House of Scribner   xv

Editorial Note   xxv

Chronology   xxvii

THE LETTERS   1

Appendix 1: Undatable Letters   277

Appendix 2: Unmailed Wolfe Letters   279

Appendix 3: Maxwell Perkins's Biographical Observations on Thomas Wolfe   305

Appendix 4: Errors and Inconsistencies in the Published Text of
    Look Homeward, Angel   313

Appendix 5: Scribners Alterations Lists for *Of Time and the River*   329

Background Readings   333

Index   335

Illustrations

Thomas Wolfe with the manuscripts and typescripts for *Of Time and the River* in 1934   Frontispiece

Maxwell Perkins at the time he began working with Thomas Wolfe, and Wolfe with manuscripts and typescripts   Frontispiece

The contract for *Look Homeward, Angel*   6–7

The announcement of *Look Homeward, Angel* in the Scribners Fall 1929 catalogue   10

The dust jacket for *Look Homeward, Angel*   30

Catalogue copy for *Look Homeward, Angel* six months after publication   31

A page from the Scribners Spring 1931 catalogue   72

Wolfe's account at Scribners as of 5 June 1931   88

Wolfe's revised galley proof for "The Web of Earth" in *Scribner's Magazine*   96

Salesman's dummy for *K–19* novel   100

Catalogue announcement for *K–19*   101

The announcement for *Of Time and the River* in the Scribners catalogue   122

Perkins's draft of a contract with Wolfe for a collection of short stories   127

The dedication printed in *Of Time and the River*   130

The dust jacket for *Of Time and the River*   132

A full-page advertisement for *Of Time and the River*   135

Two postcards from Wolfe to Perkins   151

The Scribners Fall 1935 catalogue entry for the still-untitled *From Death to Morning*   155

The dust jacket for *From Death to Morning*, the only short-story collection Wolfe published in his lifetime   185

The dust jacket for *The Story of a Novel*   187

A bill for the excess cost of Wolfe's proof alterations   189

Perkins's initial response to Wolfe's announcement that he intended
to leave Scribners   201

Wolfe's annotated copy of his letter summarizing relations with Perkins
and the House of Scribner   224

John Hall Wheelock, editor at Scribners   230

The last letter   272–273

Perkins in his office   275

Acknowledgments

The late Paul Gitlin, administrator for the estate of Thomas Wolfe; Charles Scribner III; and William L. Joyce, Associate University Librarian for Rare Books and Special Collections at Princeton University Library, granted permissions for this publication. Catherine Fry, Director of the University of South Carolina Press, supported this project.

In Columbia, South Carolina, the editors wish to thank: Arlyn Bruccoli; Judith S. Baughman; Nancy Chesnutt; Ken DeBarry; Robert F. Moss; Robert Newman, Chairman of the English Department at the University of South Carolina; and the staff at the University of South Carolina Press (Barry Blose, Barbara Brannon, Patricia Callahan, and George Lang).

This volume was facilitated by the library staffs at Princeton University (John Delaney, Don C. Skemer, John S. Weeren, and AnnaLee Pauls) and the Houghton Library at Harvard University (Leslie A. Morris, Susan Halpert, Jennie Rathbun, Melanie Wisner, and Virginia Smyers). Assistance was also provided by: Ted Mitchell, Thomas Wolfe Memorial; Alice R. Cotten, Reference Historian, and Robert G. Anthony, Jr., Curator, North Carolina Collection, University of North Carolina Library–Chapel Hill; Noel Kinnamon; Alexa Selph; Aldo Magi; Clara Stites; Robert Cowley; and Lydia Zelaya, Simon & Schuster.

Introduction

Thomas Wolfe and the House of Scribner

> The editorial relation between us, which began—it seems to
> me—so hopefully, and for me so wonderfully, has now lost its
> initial substance. It has become a myth—and what is worse than
> that, an untrue myth—and it seems to me that both of us are
> victims of that myth.
>
> TW to MP from an unmailed fragment (November 1936)

Thomas Wolfe's friendship with his editor Maxwell Perkins is the most celebrated—
and the most mythologized—author/editor relationship in American literature.
Wolfe's reliance on and ultimate rejection of Perkins's guidance continues to be the
subject of literary argument. According to the popular version of this story, Wolfe
was an undisciplined writer whose exuberant, overwritten prose could only be published through a collaboration with his editor. Perkins is portrayed as a controlling
editor-father to Wolfe, the child-writer, from whom words flowed unhindered and
unexamined. Ostensibly because critics charged that he could not complete a novel
without his editor's help, Wolfe formally severed his professional relationship with
Perkins and the House of Scribner in 1937. The real story is not that simple.

Through the evidence provided by this correspondence the truth of the
Wolfe/Perkins relationship can be separated from more than seventy years of gossip
and anecdotes. The letters between a writer and his publisher can reveal both the
aesthetic and economic pressures under which the professional author must oper-
ate. William Charvat explains in *The Profession of Authorship* (1968, 1992) that "the
problem of a professional writer is not identical with that of the literary artist; but
when a literary artist is also a professional writer, he cannot solve the problems of
the one function without reference to the other."[1] The letters published here document Wolfe's artistic and professional problems and demonstrate how Perkins, serving as both editor and friend, aided Wolfe in solving them. They set the record
straight. Only by considering the entire author/editor/publisher correspondence
can Wolfe's literary career and his complex relationship with Scribner be properly
assessed.

Elizabeth Nowell's *The Letters of Thomas Wolfe* (1956) publishes seventy-five
letters from Wolfe to Scribners personnel (fifty-one letters to Perkins); John Hall
Wheelock's *Editor to Author: The Letters of Maxwell Perkins* (1950) publishes eight-

---

1. *The Profession of Authorship in America: 1800–1870: The Papers of William Charvat*, ed. Matthew J. Bruccoli. (Columbus: Ohio State University Press, 1968), p. 3.

een letters from Perkins to Wolfe. Of the present volume's 251 letters between Wolfe and the House of Scribner, two-thirds have never before been published.

Wolfe, more than other members of Perkins's stable of writers, regarded the House of Scribner as his literary home and was proud to be associated with such an eminent and well-established firm. He used the Scribner accounting office as his bank; his mailing address was 597 Fifth Avenue, the Scribner Building. Wolfe's relationship with Scribner extended beyond his friendship with Perkins, and this volume collects the correspondence between Wolfe and other Scribner employees—particularly editor John Hall Wheelock, who was responsible for shepherding all of Wolfe's Scribners books through the press: their correspondence reveals how the author grew to trust Wheelock's literary judgment. While writing his second novel, Wolfe excised episodes from his work in progress to be published as short stories in *Scribner's Magazine.* The revision of these stories is recorded in Wolfe's correspondence with magazine editor Alfred Dashiell. Wolfe also enjoyed a friendly relationship with the firm's president, Charles Scribner III.

Maxwell Perkins is the most acclaimed book editor of the twentieth century. During the 1920s and 1930s he presided over the greatest cadre of writers associated with one editor in the history of American publishing: F. Scott Fitzgerald, Ernest Hemingway, Thomas Wolfe, Ring Lardner, Marjorie Kinnan Rawlings, and, briefly, Erskine Caldwell, J. P. Marquand, and Zora Neale Hurston, were all Perkins authors. He built an impressive roster of female writers, including Taylor Caldwell, Caroline Gordon, Nancy Hale, and Marcia Davenport. Perkins enjoyed warm relationships with many of his authors.[2] When he joined Scribners in 1910 as advertising manager, the firm was a highly respected conservative house, the publishers of Edith Wharton, John Galsworthy, George Santayana, and Theodore Roosevelt. In 1914 Perkins became an editor. He displayed an ability to discover young talent and a willingness to take risks—staking his job on the publication of Fitzgerald's first novel, *This Side of Paradise* (1920). Throughout his career, Perkins encouraged exciting, unconventional, and even uncommercial writing. Under his stewardship as editor in chief, Scribners published classic American novels. He edited such masterpieces as *The Great Gatsby, The Sun Also Rises, A Farewell to Arms, Look Homeward, Angel, Tender Is the Night, Of Time and the River,* and *For Whom the Bell Tolls.* He also edited Rawlings's *The Yearling,* Lardner's *How to Write Short Stories,* Erskine Caldwell's *Tobacco Road,* Thomas Boyd's *Through the Wheat,* the Philo Vance mysteries by Willard Huntington Wright (S. S. Van Dine), the Civil War histories of

---

2. MP's correspondence with his writers has been collected in four previous volumes: *Dear Scott/Dear Max: The Fitzgerald-Perkins Correspondence,* ed. John Kuehl and Jackson R. Bryer (New York: Scribners, 1971); *Ring around Max: The Correspondence of Ring Lardner & Max Perkins,* ed. Clifford M. Caruthers. (DeKalb: Northern Illinois University Press, 1973); *The Only Thing That Counts: The Ernest Hemingway/Maxwell Perkins Correspondence 1925–1947,* ed. Matthew J. Bruccoli with the assistance of Robert W. Trogdon (New York: Scribners, 1996); and *Max and Marjorie: The Correspondence Between Maxwell E. Perkins and Marjorie Kinnan Rawlings,* ed. Rodger L. Tarr (Gainesville: University of Florida Press, 1999). MP's letters to various writers are collected in *Editor to Author: The Letters of Maxwell E. Perkins,* ed. John Hall Wheelock (New York: Scribners, 1950).

Douglas Southall Freeman, and Winston Churchill's five-volume history *The World Crisis*. When he died in 1947, Perkins was reading the typescript of Alan Paton's *Cry, the Beloved Country* and early drafts of James Jones's *From Here to Eternity*.

Perkins was not a line-editor—an editor concerned with sentence structure, grammar, or usage—as the many typographical errors in Scribners books edited by him indicate. His editorial contributions lay primarily in suggesting revisions in structure and/or character presentation. Perkins refused to impose his will on an author. In a 1921 letter to Fitzgerald, the editor warned: "Don't *ever* defer to my judgment. You won't on any vital point I know, and I should be ashamed, if it were possible to have made you; for a writer of any account must speak solely for himself."[3] On 16 January 1937 Perkins stated this belief to Wolfe: "I believe the writer, anyway, should always be the final judge, and I meant you to be so. I have always held to that position and have sometimes seen books hurt thereby, but at least as often helped. 'The book belongs to the author.'"

Perkins's level of editorial involvement depended upon an author's needs. Fitzgerald solicited his opinions. After reading a draft of *The Great Gatsby* Perkins criticized the revelation of Gatsby's biography, and he advised Fitzgerald, "I thought you might find ways to let the truth of some of his claims like 'Oxford' and his army career come out bit by bit in the course of the actual narrative."[4] The author followed his editor's advice. Hemingway required, and accepted, little direction. Perkins's greatest editorial, and personal, involvement was with Wolfe. The editor's structural skills proved especially useful with Wolfe's episodic fiction.

When "O Lost"—the original title of *Look Homeward, Angel*—was sent to Scribners, it began with Wolfe's "NOTE FOR THE PUBLISHER'S READER," in which the author asked for "a little honest help" in making his lengthy novel publishable. Early in 1929 Perkins accepted the novel only if "it might be worked into a form publishable by us." Contrary to the generally accepted myth that Perkins collaborated with Wolfe to make the huge, unpublishable mess of "O Lost" publishable as *Look Homeward, Angel* (1929), this is what the editor did: moved one major episode, Gant's homecoming, from Book II to Book I; recommended the cutting of 60,000 words (22% of the work); and advised Wolfe to write connecting passages bridging the cuts.[5] Perkins wrote nothing that went into the book. Although the novel was not a best-seller, it gradually attracted widespread acclaim. Wolfe readily adopted his editor as his literary father. On Christmas Eve 1929 Wolfe wrote Perkins: "Young men sometimes believe in the existence of heroic figures, and wiser than themselves, to whom they can turn for an answer to all their vexation and grief. Later, they must discover that such answers have to come out of their own hearts; but the powerful desire to believe in such figures persists. You are for me such a figure: you are one of the rocks to which my life is anchored."

Perkins's greatest editorial achievement—and the primary basis for the Wolfe/Perkins apocrypha—was his work with Wolfe on the author's second novel,

3. *Editor to Author,* p. 30.
4. *Dear Scott/Dear Max,* p. 84.
5. The complete novel *O Lost,* has been edited by Matthew J. Bruccoli and Arlyn Bruccoli (Columbia: University of South Carolina Press, 2000).

Of Time and the River (1935). Wolfe struggled with the manuscript for three years before reluctantly submitting a draft to Perkins in April 1933. The result was a "gigantic" manuscript described by Wolfe as "twice the length of *War and Peace*."[6] In *The Story of a Novel* (1936), Wolfe's confessional book-length essay about the composition of *Of Time and the River,* the author credits Perkins with identifying two separate story cycles within the narrative, and encouraging him to focus on the one that chronicled Eugene Gant's "period of wandering and hunger" rather than his love affair with Esther Jack (modeled on Wolfe's lover-patron Aline Bernstein). The author also admitted that he needed Perkins's help in reducing the novel's length. For most of 1934 Perkins and Wolfe met regularly to work on the novel. Perkins did not write a word of Wolfe's book, but rather offered suggestions for possible connections among episodes. Wolfe revised on his own. The Wolfe/Perkins letters do not record their discussions during these meetings; the two men worked at night in Perkins's office and had no need to correspond. Perkins described his working relationship with Wolfe to journalist Peter Munro Jack. Written less than two weeks after Wolfe's death, the letter documents the extent to which the editor participated in Wolfe's fiction:

> Tom's physical size symbolized his difficulty.- He was out of scale with the world not only in that respect, but in respect to <u>time</u> and to space. I always thought that at bottom he did have a sense of form, and some of the things he wrote like "Web of Earth" showed it. Not a word in that was ever changed. If Tom could have taken ten years to a novel, I think he might have mastered the form. But the trouble was not so much the practical problems, at least in the case of "Of Time and the River" but of the state of depression that Tom would get into from the prolonged struggle with the material. It seemed to me that "Of Time and the River" must be got out at any cost because Tom was frantic at the time he brought it to me, which was about a year before it was published. But there was one thing that happened which ought to be told, and which shows that Tom really did know where he was going. There were many places in that book which needed to be connected. Tom recognized this perfectly well,- some of them were concerned with episodes which he had shrunk from writing. One was his father's death. When we came to that point I said to him that this must be put in, but that since Eugene was at Harvard and only went home on news of his father's death, and since the current of the book was the course of Eugene's career, he need only tell how the news came, and how he went home, and how it all affected him, a matter perhaps of 5,000 words. So Tom said he would do that. We worked here every night. The next night he came in with some thousands of words about the doctor, as I remember it, and I protested against this. It seemed to me that it was extraneous, and Tom agreed and meant to do what we discussed. But the next night he came back with some thousands of words about, perhaps,

6. *The Story of a Novel* (New York: Scribners, 1936), p. 76.

his sister's Helen's life in Asheville at that time,- you will remember how it was in the book. I said, "Tom, this is fine, but it is not what you ought to be doing." And Tom again agreed. But then he began to get into his father's illness, and I just laughed at the whole matter and said, "Really, this does not seem to me to be essential to the book and we ought to get forward, but it is so good that we must keep it, and you ought to go on and do it.- And so he did. And there are so many people who think that all that death of Gant is as fine as anything, and certainly it is magnificent. But Tom really knew where he was going there, and nothing could stop him from going, even his own apparent willingness to go somewhere else. I think this was a very significant incident, In a large sense Tom knew all about it.- His great enemy was time. He always felt that he did not have time enough.[7]

Wolfe dedicated *Of Time and the River* to Perkins, praising his friend as "A BRAVE AND HONEST MAN, WHO STUCK TO THE WRITER OF THIS BOOK THROUGH TIMES OF BITTER HOPELESSNESS AND DOUBT AND WOULD NOT LET HIM GIVE IN TO HIS OWN DESPAIR." In a dictated oral history, Wheelock described the novel's dedication to Perkins as the determining factor in Wolfe's ultimate decision to leave Scribners:

Tom wrote this absurd dedication. I said to Tom, "Now look—you can't. You'll make yourself ridiculous. Don't do this, Tom. Think it over. Cut it down. You've got four pages here—cut it down to four lines, if you can."

Oh, he was furious with me. He had this overwhelming emotion, and he wanted to articulate it.

I did get it down—I think to about 18 lines but even so, I knew it was fatal. Max knew it would be, too. Or at least, I suggested to him, "Why can't you tell Tom that you can't accept anything in the dedication except just 'To my friend Maxwell Perkins'?"[8]

In *The Story of a Novel* Wolfe elaborated on his personal relationship with Perkins, "a man of immense and patient wisdom and a gentle but unyielding fortitude."[9] In the essay Wolfe described writing the novel as a warlike struggle with his own "secret darkness" through which Perkins encouraged him: "My friend, the editor, has likened his own function at this painful time to that of a man who is trying to hang onto the fin of a plunging whale, but hang on he did, and it is to his tenacity that I owe my final release."[10] In 1933 Perkins did inject himself into Wolfe's composition process by ending it; he took the novel away from Wolfe. Wolfe

7. 29 September 1938, PUL. MP wrote the letter to Jack in admiration of his tribute to Wolfe: "Remembering Thomas Wolfe," *The New York Times Book Review,* 2 October 1938.

8. Columbia University Oral History Collection.

9. *Story of a Novel,* pp. 55–56.

10. Ibid., pp. 56–57.

remembered: "[Perkins] called me to his home and calmly informed me that my book was finished. I could only look at him with stunned surprise, and finally I could only tell him out of the depth of my own hopelessness, that he was mistaken, that the book was not finished, that it could never be completed that I could write no more. He answered with the same quiet finality that the book was finished whether I knew it or not."[11] Perkins regarded Wolfe's writing as novels separated by single published volumes. Yet Wolf's fiction cannot be isolated by arbitrary boundaries. All his fiction is one lifelong novel. Perkins did not "finish" a book by taking the manuscript away from Wolfe; he interrupted a work-in-progress.

Wolfe's public acknowledgment of debt and gratitude to an editor gave his detractors grounds to question the author's artistic independence. In "Genius Is Not Enough," Bernard De Voto's review of *The Story of a Novel,* the influential critic attacked Wolfe's reliance on Perkins: "The most flagrant evidence of his incompleteness is the fact that, so far, one indispensable part of the artist has existed not in Mr. Wolfe but in Maxwell Perkins."[12] This charge marked a turning point in Wolfe's growing unhappiness with Scribners. In an unmailed letter to Perkins, Wolfe charged De Voto with destroying their editorial relationship in his "venomous" charge that "there exists at Scribner's an 'assembly line' that must fit the great dismembered portions of my manuscript together into a semblance of unity, that I am unable to perform these functions of an artist for myself."[13] Wolfe's insecurities, self-doubt, and suspicions could not withstand such an attack on his life's work. Once other pressures—such as lawsuits—came to bear on Wolfe, a break with Scribners became unavoidable.

As an autobiographical writer, Wolfe inevitably came to include in his material his experiences with Charles Scribner's Sons. Wolfe's intention to fictionalize the publishing house alarmed Perkins, who feared that many of the confidences he had shared with Wolfe would be revealed. Wolfe regarded the editor's attempts to dissuade him from writing about Scribners as a personal attack on his artistic freedom. He could not understand why anyone should fear inclusion in his fiction. Wolfe claimed his characters as "my people," full of "variety and madness." He expressed great affection for all their excesses; they "could make an epic," he wrote.[14] Some people were not pleased to be depicted in Wolfe's fiction, making the author vulnerable to charges of libel. In 1936 Wolfe's Brooklyn landlady filed a lawsuit against him, claiming that she and her family had been maligned in "No Door," the opening story in Wolfe's collection *From Death to Morning* (1935). Although their contract with Wolfe did not require it, Scribners agreed to share the monetary liability with Wolfe, but only if he agreed to settle the lawsuit. Perkins and Charles Scribner III believed that otherwise the lawsuit would consume all of Wolfe's energies. The author viewed such legal threats as blackmail that endangered his livelihood and that should be vigorously fought on principle. Wolfe never forgave the publishing firm for pressuring him to settle the suit.

11. Ibid., p. 74.
12. *Saturday Review of Literature,* 25 April 1936, 4.
13. Harvard.
14. "Note for the Publisher's Reader," p. 2

In 1937 Wolfe formally severed his ties to the House of Scribner and signed with the House of Harper. On 19 November Wolfe wrote Perkins about the break: "Like you, I am puzzled and bewildered about what has happened, but in conclusion can offer this: - that maybe for me the editor and the friend got too close together and perhaps I got the two relations mixed." Perkins provided his own assessment of Wolfe's determination to leave Scribners in a 1938 letter to Marjorie Kinnan Rawlings: "[T]here were these three elements in it: the libel suit which he always strangely thought we got him into, although it seemed to us that he got us into it, and we had to pay for it; the desire which was very strong, to use us as material in a book,- and this may have been the largest influence upon him; and also a really fine and subconscious desire which I sensed, to tear himself loose from a state of dependence which he had got into toward us, and which wasn't right."[15]

Wolfe's fictional depiction of Perkins did not appear until the posthumously published novel *You Can't Go Home Again* (Harper, 1940). The author casts Charles Scribner's Sons as James Rodney & Co. and Maxwell Evarts Perkins as Foxhall Morton Edwards. Fox Edwards is the only "real friend" of George Webber, Wolfe's fictional surrogate. Webber recalls that he and Edwards "spent many hours together, wonderful hours of endless talk, so free and full that it combed the universe and bound the two of them together in bonds of closest friendship."[16] In an episode titled "The Fox" Wolfe openly describes his filial feelings for Perkins: "The older man was not merely a friend but father to the younger. Webber, the hot-blooded Southerner, with his large capacity for sentiment and affection, had lost his own father many years before and now had found a substitute in Edwards. And Edwards, the reserved New Englander, with his deep sense of family and inheritance, had always wanted a son but had five daughters, and as time went on he made of George a kind of foster son. Thus each, without quite knowing that he did it, performed an act of spiritual adoption."[17] The novel ends with an extended letter to Fox in which George recounts their relationship. He ascribes "the root of trouble and the seed of severance" to a difference in philosophy: "[T]here is our strange paradox: it seems to me that in the orbit of our world you are the North Pole, I the South—so much in balance, in agreement—and yet, dear Fox, the whole world lies between."[18] According to George, Fox believed in man's inherent and unchangeable tragedy. Webber intellectually accepts Edwards's fatalism but resists it emotionally: "Man was born to live, to suffer, and to die, and what befalls him is a tragic lot. There is no denying this in the final end. *But we must, dear Fox, deny it all along the way.*"[19] Perkins, appointed by Wolfe as his literary executor, could have suppressed the author's fictional portrayal of him but did not.

In *Why Write a Novel* (1943) John Woodford distorted the Wolfe/Perkins legend by charging that "one American editor's pride and joy today is that he threw a lot of the immortal work of Thomas Wolfe into the waste basket."[20] In a 17 June

15. *Max and Marjorie*, pp. 331–32.
16. *You Can't Go Home Again*, p. 437.
17. Ibid., p. 437.
18. Ibid., pp. 734–35.
19. Ibid., p. 737.
20. Hollywood: Murray & Gee, p. 166.

1943 letter to Woodford, Perkins countered that "nothing was ever taken from Tom's writings without his full consent. When he could go no further with 'Of Time and the River,' he brought it to me and asked me to help him, and I did it with very great reluctance and anxiety. Tom *demanded* help, He *had* to have it." Perkins concluded his letter: "Editors aren't much, and can't be. They can only help a writer realize himself, and they can ruin him if he's pliable, as Tom was not."[21] Some critics, operating under the mistaken belief that Perkins "threw out" Wolfe's words, have accused Perkins of not throwing out enough of Wolfe's prose. In 1930 Fitzgerald dismissed such criticisms against Wolfe, writing Perkins that "He strikes me as a man who should be left alone as to length, if he has to be published in five volumes."[22] But later Fitzgerald and Wolfe engaged in a Flaubert/Zola debate, arguing the literary merits of Flaubert's novel of selection versus Zola's novel of inclusion. In 1937 Fitzgerald urged Wolfe to "cultivate an alter ego" that could temper or counterbalance his emotional excesses: "[O]ften people who live at a high pitch often don't get their way emotionally at the important moment because it doesn't stand out in relief. . . . Repression itself has a value."[23]

As the father of five daughters, Perkins regarded his male writers—particularly the triumvirate of Fitzgerald, Hemingway, and Wolfe—as surrogate sons. He encouraged them to meet and correspond with each other. The three authors wrote of themselves as sibling rivals. In 1934 Fitzgerald observed, "What family resemblance there is between we three as writers is the attempt that crops up in our fiction from time to time to recapture the exact feel of a moment in time and space exemplified by people rather than by things . . . an attempt at a mature memory of a deep experience."[24] Among the three writers Perkins's most intense, and most painful, relationship was with Wolfe. In 1938 Fitzgerald wrote Perkins: "What a time you've had with your sons, Max—Ernest gone to Spain, me gone to Hollywood, Tom Wolfe reverting to an artistic hill-billy."[25] In his oral history Wheelock commented on Wolfe's break with Scribners and Perkins: "Tom wounded Max almost mortally. I think Max died of a broken heart in a sense, because this is a man he'd helped the most, and Tom was the man who turned on him. We found in Max's death—he died while he was still an editor—we found the terrible letters that Tom had written and that Max was too ashamed to put in the Scribners files because of what they said."[26]

On 15 September 1938 Thomas Wolfe died in Baltimore of tuberculosis meningitis. The last letter Wolfe wrote—in which he anticipates his death—was a letter of reconciliation addressed to Maxwell Perkins. After Wolfe's death, Perkins wired the author's family: "MY FRIENDSHIP WITH TOM WAS ONE OF THE GREATEST

21. *Editor to Author,* p. 228.

22. *F. Scott Fitzgerald, A Life in Letters,* ed. Matthew J. Bruccoli with the assistance of Judith S. Baughman (New York: Scribners, 1994), p. 200.

23. Ibid., p. 332.

24. *Dear Scott/Dear Max,* pp. 203–4.

25. Fitzgerald, *A Life in Letters,* p. 360.

26. Columbia University Oral History Collection.

THINGS IN MY LIFE."[27] The other two members of the Scribner triumvirate wrote Perkins letters of condolence.

From Fitzgerald: "I feel like writing to you about Tom as to a relation of his, for I know how deeply his death must have touched you, how you were so entwined with his literary career and the affection you had for him . . . . that great, pulsing, vital frame quiet at last. There is a great hush after him."[28]

From Hemingway: "I should have written you a long time ago how sorry I was about old Tom. But I knew you would know it and it never does any good to discuss casualties. You must have had a hell of a time with it all. That was a good letter he wrote. . . . Remember if anything happens to me I think just as much of you as Tom Wolfe even if I can't put it so well."[29]

Other good editors could have provided Wolfe with guidance as well as Perkins. What made the Wolfe/Perkins relationship extraordinary was the strength of Perkins's personal and professional commitments to Wolfe. Perkins won the admiration, trust, and affection of his authors because he truly believed that literature is "the only thing that counts."[30] Few editors share this conviction. It resulted in all the books Wolfe published in his lifetime. Readers have Wolfe because he had Perkins.

P. B.

27. MP to Fred Wolfe, 11 September 1938.

28. *Dear Scott/Dear Max*, p. 249.

29. Ernest Hemingway, *Ernest Hemingway: Selected Letters, 1917–1961*, ed. Carlos Baker (New York: Scribners, 1981), p. 473.

30. *The Only Thing That Counts*, p. 224.

Editorial Note

This volume assembles 63 letters from Thomas Wolfe to Perkins, 67 from Maxwell Perkins to Wolfe, and 105 between Wolfe and other Scribners personnel—of which 71 are Wolfe/John Hall Wheelock letters. The letters are published in their entirety. Except for six unlocated items taken from *The Letters of Thomas Wolfe,* ed. Elizabeth Nowell (New York: Scribners, 1956), all other letters are transcribed from an extant original or carbon copy. The identifications for these documents are ALS (autograph letter signed), AL (autograph letter without signature), TLS (typed letter signed), TL (typed letter without signature), TS (typescript), CC (carbon copy), CCS (carbon copy signed). All letters have been independently transcribed from the originals. No editorial emendations have been made in the texts of the letters, except for silent correction of obvious typographical errors—strikeovers, transpositions, or misspacings.

Transcribing Thomas Wolfe's holograph documents requires many decisions: his periods and commas are generally indistinguishable, as are his colons and semicolons; he wrote certain words in a personal shorthand ("ming" for "morning," "Suday" for "Sunday," "friedly" for "friendly"); he wrote various dash lengths, which may not have been intentional. The punctuation provided here represents editorial judgment calls; the condensed words are printed as intended; the dashes have been regularized to em-dashes unless a long dash seems deliberate and meaningful. Bracketed words represent the editors' best guess; empty brackets indicate the editors' inability to decipher a word. The principal problem in Perkins's holograph letters is the capitalization of the letter 'Y' at the beginning of words—almost certainly without significance; these have been lowercased, except at the start of a sentence. The footnotes provide necessary information; they are not discursive.

Each letter has four items of data in its headnote:

To/From [if required]   *Description and location of the document*
Assigned Date [if required]   *Address* [if required]

The following location symbols are used: PUL (Princeton University Library), Harvard (Houghton Library Reading Room), UNC (University of North Carolina–Chapel Hill), and HRHRC (Harry Ransom Humanities Research Center at the University of Texas–Austin).

Dates that are on the originals are transcribed as part of the letters. The reader is to assume that the return address on a letter from Perkins or other Scribners staff is the Scribner Building at 597 Fifth Avenue, unless otherwise stipulated.

Chronology

20 September 1884	Birth of Maxwell Perkins.
3 October 1900	Birth of Thomas Wolfe.
February 1910	MP joins Scribner as advertising manager.
1911	John Hall Wheelock joins Scribner.
1914	MP becomes an editor.
March 1928	TW completes *Look Homeward, Angel*, then titled "O Lost."
May 1928	Madeleine Boyd becomes TW's literary agent.
22 October 1928	MP expresses interest in publishing "O Lost" after it had been rejected by three publishers.
2 January 1929	TW and MP meet for the first time.
9 January 1929	TW signs contract with Scribner to publish "O Lost."
Spring 1929	TW revises "O Lost" and changes title to *Look Homeward, Angel*.
August 1929	"Angel on the Porch," an episode from *Look Homeward, Angel*, appears in *Scribner's Magazine*.
18 October 1929	Publication of *Look Homeward, Angel*.
March 1930	TW awarded Guggenheim Fellowship.
9 May 1930	TW sails for Europe.
14 July 1930	British publication of *Look Homeward, Angel*.
4 March 1931	TW arrives in New York.
11 March 1931	TW settles in Brooklyn.
January 1932	TW learns of agent Madeleine Boyd's misappropriation of foreign royalties.
April 1932	"A Portrait of Bascom Hawke" appears in *Scribner's Magazine* and is selected cowinner of the magazine's Short Novel Prize.
Summer 1932	Scribner issues a salesman's dummy of TW's "K-19" but cancels publication when MP convinces TW that the book would be harmful to the author's reputation.
26 September 1932	MP named editor in chief and vice president of Scribners.
July 1932	"The Web of Earth" appears in *Scribner's Magazine*.
15 April 1933	TW submits lengthy manuscript of "The October Fair" (later retitled *Of Time and the River*) to MP.
May 1933	"The Train and the City" appears in *Scribner's Magazine*.
June 1933	"Death, the Proud Brother" appears in *Scribner's Magazine*.
July 1933	"No Door" appears in *Scribner's Magazine*.
12 July 1933	TW signs contract for *Of Time and the River* calling for fall publication.
14 December 1933	TW delivers draft of *Of Time and the River* to MP.

January–June 1934	With MP's assistance, TW revises novel.
February 1934	"The Four Lost Men" appears in *Scribner's Magazine*.
May 1934	"The Sun and the Rain" appears in *Scribner's Magazine*.
August 1934	"The House of the Far and Lost" appears in *Scribner's Magazine*.
November 1934	"Dark in the Forest, Strange as Time" appears in *Scribner's Magazine*.
26 December 1934	TW signs contract for *From Death to Morning*.
January 1935	*Of Time and the River* goes to press.
January 1935	"One of the Girls in Our Party" appears in *Scribner's Magazine*.
2 March 1935	TW sails for Europe.
8 March 1935	Publication of *Of Time and the River*, which TW dedicates to MP.
May 1935	Madeleine Boyd files suit against TW for agent's commissions and royalties.
June 1935	"Gulliver, The Story of a Tall Man" appears in *Scribner's Magazine*.
4 July 1935	TW returns to New York from Europe; MP meets him at the dock.
19 August 1935	British publication of *Of Time and the River*.
October 1935	TW revises short stories for *From Death to Morning*.
14 November 1935	Publication of *From Death to Morning*.
16 March 1936	British publication of *From Death to Morning*.
21 April 1936	Publication of *The Story of a Novel*.
25 April 1936	In his review of *The Story of a Novel* Bernard De Voto attacks TW's literary dependence on MP.
23 June 1936	At MP's urging, TW settles Madeleine Boyd's suit.
23 July 1936	TW sails for Europe.
24 September 1936	TW returns to New York.
November 1936	TW and Scribner sued for libel by Marjorie Dorman over "No Door" in *From Death to Morning*.
9 November 1936	British publication of *The Story of a Novel*.
January 1937	In two letters mailed to MP, TW severs his relationship with Scribners.
7 February 1937	TW reluctantly settles Dorman libel suit at urging of MP and Charles Scribner III.
June 1937	"Oktoberfest" appears in *Scribner's Magazine*.
31 December 1937	TW signs contract with Harper.
8 February 1938	TW wins lawsuit against Muredach Dooher to reclaim consigned manuscripts; MP and TW meet for the last time, and MP testifies for TW.
12 August 1938	From hospital in Seattle TW writes his last letter, addressed to MP.

15 September 1938	TW dies at Johns Hopkins of tuberculosis meningitis. TW's will names MP as his literary executor.
17 June 1947	MP dies in Connecticut of pleurisy and pneumonia.

To Loot
My Life
Clean

The Letters

Late March 1928   *TS, 4 pp., PUL*

NOTE FOR THE PUBLISHER'S READER[1]

This book, by my estimate, is from 250,000 to 280,000 words long.[2] A book of this length from an unknown writer no doubt is rashly experimental, and shows his ignorance of the mechanics of publishing. That is true: this is my first book.

But I believe it would be unfair to assume that because this is a very long book it is too long a book. A revision would, I think, shorten it somewhat. But I do not believe any amount of revision would make it a short book. It could be shortened by scenes, by pages, by thousands of words. But it could not be shortened by half, or a third, or a quarter.

There are some pages here which were compelled by a need for fullness of expression, and which had importance when the book was written not because they made part of its essential substance, but because, by setting them forth, the mind was released for its basic work of creation. These pages have done their work of catharsis, and may now be excised. But their excision would not make a short book.

It does not seem to me that the book is overwritten. Whatever comes out of it must come out block by block and not sentence by sentence. Generally, I do not believe the writing to be wordy, prolix, or redundant. And separate scenes are told with as much brevity and economy as possible. But the book covers the life of a large family intensively for a period of twenty years, and in rapid summary for fifty years. And the book tries to describe not only the visible outer lives of all these people, but even more their buried lives.

The book may be lacking in plot but it is not lacking in plan. The plan is rigid and densely woven. There are two essential movements—one outward and one downward. The outward movement describes the effort of a child, a boy, and a youth for release, freedom, and loneliness in new lands. The movement of experience is duplicated by a series of widening concentric circles, three of which are represented by the three parts of the book. The downward movement is represented by a constant excavation into the buried life of a group of people, and describes the cyclic curve of a family's life-genesis, union, decay, and dissolution.

To me, who was joined so passionately with the people in this book, it seemed that they were the greatest people I had ever known and the texture of their lives the richest and strangest; and discounting the distortion of judgment that my nearness to them would cause, I think they would seem extraordinary to anyone. If I could get my magnificent people on paper as they were, if I could get down something of their strangeness and richness in my book, I believed that no one would object to my 250,000 words; or, that if my pages swarmed with this rich life, few would damn an inept manner and accuse me of not knowing the technique for making a book, as practiced by Balzac, or Flaubert, or Hardy, or Gide. If I have failed to get any of this opulence into my book, the fault lies not in my people—who could make an epic—but in me.

But that is what I wanted to do and tried to do. This book was written in simpleness and nakedness of soul. When I began to write the book twenty months ago I got back something of a child's innocency and wonder. You may question this later when you come to the dirty words. But the dirty words can come out quickly—if the book has any chance of publication, they will come out without conscience or compunction. For the rest, I wrote it innocently and passionately. It has in it much that to me is painful and ugly, but, without sentimentality or dishonesty, it seems to me, because I am a romantic, that pain has an inevitable fruition in beauty. And the book has in it sin and terror and darkness—ugly dry lusts, cruelty, a strong sexual hunger of a child—the dark, the evil, the forbidden. But I believe it has many other things as well, and I wrote it with strong joy, without counting the costs, for I was sure at the time that the whole of my intention—which was to come simply and unsparingly to naked life, and to tell all of my story without affectation or lewdness—would be apparent. At that time I believed it was possible to write of all things, so long as it was honestly done. So far as I know there is not a nasty scene in the book,- but there are the dirty words, and always a casual and unimpeded vision of everything.

When I wrote the book I seized with delight everything that would give it color and richness. All the variety and madness of my people—the leper taint, the cruel waste, the dark flowering evil of life I wrote about with as much exultancy as health, sanity, joy.

It is, of course, obvious that the book is "autobiographical." But, in a literal sense, it is probably no more autobiographical than Gulliver's Travels. There is scarcely a scene that has its base in literal fact. The book is a fiction—it is loaded with invention: story, fantasy, vision. But it is a fiction that is, I believe, more true than fact—a fiction that grew out of a life completely digested in my spirit, a fiction which telescopes, condenses, and objectifies all the random or incompleted gestures of life—which tries to comprehend people, in short, not by telling what people did, but what they should have done. The most literal and autobiographical part of the book, therefore, is its picture of the buried life. The most exact thing in it is its fantasy—its picture of a child's soul.

I have never called this book a novel. To me it is a book such as all men may have in them. It is a book made out of my life, and it represents my vision of life to my twentieth year.

What merit it has I do not know. It sometimes seems to me that it presents a strange and deep picture of American life—one that I have never seen elsewhere; and that I may have some hope of publication. I do not know; I am very close to it. I want to find out about it, and to be told by someone else about it.

I am assured that this book will have a good reading by an intelligent person in a publishing house. I have written all this, not to propitiate you, for I have no peddling instinct, but entreat you, if you spend the many hours necessary for a careful reading, to spend a little more time in giving me an opinion. If it is not a good book, why? If parts are good and parts bad, what are they? If it is not publishable, could it be made so? Out of the great welter of manuscripts that you must read, does this one seem distinguished by any excellence, interest, superior merit?

I need a little honest help. If you are interested enough to finish the book, won't you give it to me?

1. TW's explanatory note was included with the TS of *O Lost* that was submitted to publishers.

2. The length of *O Lost* has become inflated. TW's estimate is accurate; the typescript is approximately 275,000 words.

CC, 2 pp., PUL

Oct. 22, 1928

Dear Mr. Wolfe:

Mrs. Ernest Boyd[1] left with us some weeks ago, the manuscript of your novel, "O Lost." I do not know whether it would be possible to work out a plan by which it might be worked into a form publishable by us, but I do know that setting the practical aspects of the matter aside, it is a very remarkable thing, and that no editor could read it without being excited by it, and filled with admiration by many passages in it, and sections of it.

Your letter that came with it,[2] shows that you realize what difficulties it presents, so that I need not enlarge upon this side of the question. What we should like to know is whether you will be in New York in a fairly near future, when we can see you and discuss the manuscript. We should certainly look forward to such an interview with very great interest.

Ever truly yours,
[Maxwell Perkins]

1. New York literary agent Madeleine Boyd (1885?–1972). Boyd wrote MP on 18 October providing TW's Munich address.

2. "Note for the Publisher's Reader."

ALS, 7 pp., PUL

Vienna, Saturday Nov 17, 1928

Dear Mr Perkins: Your letter of October 22 which was addressed to Munich, was sent on to me here. I have been in Budapest for several weeks and came here last night. I got your letter at Cook's[1] this morning.

Mrs Ernest Boyd wrote me a few weeks ago that she was coming abroad, and said that you had my book. I wrote her to Paris but have not heard from her yet.

I can't tell you how good your letter has made me feel. Your words of praise have filled me with hope, and are worth more than their weight in diamonds to me. Sometimes, I suppose, praise does more harm than good, but this time it was badly needed, whether deserved or not.—I came abroad over four months ago determined to put the other book out of my mind, and to get to work on a new one. Instead, I have filled one note book after another, my head is swarming with ideas—but I have written nothing that looks like a book yet. In Munich I did write thirty or forty thousand words; then I got my head and my nose broken, and began to have things happen thick and fast with a great many people, including the police. I have learned to read German fairly well, and have learned something of their multitudinous books. But I had indigestion from seeing and trying to take in too much, and I was depressed at my failure to settle down to work. Now I feel better. I have decided to come back to New York in December, and I shall come to see you very soon after my arrival.

I have not looked at my book since I gave a copy to Mrs. Boyd—at the time I realized the justice of all people said—particularly the impossibility of printing it in its present form and length. But at that time I was "written out" on it—I could not go back and revise. Now I believe I can come back to it with a much fresher and more critical feeling.—I have no right to expect others to do for me what I should do for myself, but, although I am able to criticize wordiness and over-abundance in others, I am not able practically to criticize it in myself. The business of selection, and of revision is simply hell for me—my efforts to cut out 50000 words may sometimes result in my adding 75000.

—As for the obscene passages and the dirty words, I know perfectly well that no publisher could print them. Yet, I swear to you, it all seemed to me very easy and practical when I wrote them.—But already I have begun to write a long letter to you, when all I should do is to thank you for your letter and say when I am coming back Then the other things can come out when I see you.

But your letter has given me new hope for the book—I have honestly always felt that there are parts of it of which I need not be ashamed, and which might justify some more abiding form. I want you to know that you have no very stiff necked person to deal with as regards the book—I shall probably agree with most of the criticisms, although I hope that my own eagerness and hopefulness will not lead me into a weak acquiescence to everything.

I want the direct criticism and advice of an older and more critical person. I wonder if at Scribners I can find Someone who is interested enough to talk over the whole huge Monster with me—part by part. Most people will say "it's too long," "its got to be cut," "parts have to come out," and so on—but obviously this is no great help to the poor wretch who has done the deed, and who knows all this, without always knowing how he's going to remedy it.

I am sorry that Mrs Boyd sent you the letter that I wrote for the Reader. She said it was a very foolish letter, but added cheerfully that I would learn as I grow older. I wish I had so much faith. I told her to tear the letter out of the binding;[2] but if it indicated to you that I did realize some of the difficulties, perhaps it was of some use. And I realize the difficulties more than ever now.

I am looking forward to meeting you, and I am still youthful enough to hope that something may come of it. It will be a strange thing indeed to me if at last I shall manage to make a connection with such a firm as Scribner's which, in my profound ignorance of all publishing matters, I had always thought vaguely was a solid and somewhat conservative house. But it may be that I am a conservative and at bottom very correct person. If this is true, I assure you I will have no very great heartache over it, although once it might have caused me trouble. At any rate, I believe I am through with firing off pistols just for the fun of seeing people jump— my new book has gone along for 40000 words without improprieties of language— and I have not tried for this result.

Please forgive my use of the pencil—in Vienna papers and pen and ink, as well as many other things that abound in our own fortunate country, are doled out bit by bit under guard. I hope you are able to make out my scrawl which is more than many people do—and that you will not forget about me before I come back.

Cordially Yours
Thomas Wolfe

My address in New York is The Harvard Club—I get my mail there. Here in Vienna, at Thomas Cook's,[1] but as I'm going to Italy in a week, I shall probably have no more mail before I get home[3]

1. Thomas Cook and Sons, travel agency.
2. The ribbon copy for *O Lost* submitted to Scribners does not survive; presumably it was in several binders.
3. TW ended his first draft of this letter, mistakenly addressed to "Mr. Peters," with "Is there someone on Scribner's staff who might be interested enough in my book to *argue* with me? On many points I am sure he would not have to argue at all. But it would be wrong for me to say 'Yes, sir,' to everything in a spirit of a weak agreement" (*The Notebooks of Thomas Wolfe,* ed. Richard S. Kennedy and Paschal Reeves [Chapel Hill: University of North Carolina Press, 1970], p. 243).

CC, 1 p., PUL

Dec. 7, 1928

Dear Mr. Wolfe:

Thanks very much indeed for your letter of November 19th. I look forward impatiently to seeing you, and I hope you will call up as soon as you conveniently can after reading this. Then we can have a talk.

Ever sincerely yours,
[Maxwell Perkins]

Memorandum of Agreement, *made this* — ninth — *day of* January 1929

between THOMAS WOLFE

of New York City, N.Y., — — — *hereinafter called "the* AUTHOR,"

and CHARLES SCRIBNER'S SONS, *of New York City, N. Y., hereinafter called "the*

PUBLISHERS." *Said* — — Thomas Wolfe — — *being the* AUTHOR

and PROPRIETOR *of a work entitled:* ~~O LOST~~ *published as* → LOOK HOMEWARD, ANGEL,

in consideration of the covenants and stipulations hereinafter contained, and agreed to be per-
formed by the PUBLISHERS, *grants and guarantees to said* PUBLISHERS *and their successors the*
in the United States and Canada after first serialization
exclusive right to publish the said work in all forms, during the terms of copyright and renewals
thereof, hereby covenanting with said PUBLISHERS *that he is the sole* AUTHOR *and*
PROPRIETOR *of said work.*

    Said AUTHOR *hereby authorizes said* PUBLISHERS *to take out the copyright on said*
work, and further guarantees to said PUBLISHERS *that the said work is in no way whatever a*
violation of any copyright belonging to any other party, and that it contains nothing of a scandal-
ous or libelous character; and that he *and* his *legal representatives shall and will hold*
harmless the said PUBLISHERS *from all suits, and all manner of claims and proceedings which*
may be taken on the ground that said work is such violation or contains anything scandalous or
libelous; and he *further hereby authorizes said* PUBLISHERS *to defend at law any and all*
suits and proceedings which may be taken or had against them for infringement of any other copy-
right or for libel, scandal, or any other injurious or hurtful matter or thing contained in or
alleged or claimed to be contained in or caused by said work, and pay to said PUBLISHERS *such*
reasonable costs, disbursements, expenses, and counsel fees as they may incur in such defense.

    Said PUBLISHERS, *in consideration of the right herein granted and of the guarantees*
aforesaid, agree to publish said work at their own expense, in such style and manner as they
shall deem most expedient, and to pay said AUTHOR, *or — his — legal representatives,*
TEN (10) ————————————— *per cent. on their Trade-List (retail) price, cloth style, for*
the first Two Thousand (2000) copies of said work sold by them in the United States
and FIFTEEN (15) per cent. for all copies sold thereafter.
Provided, nevertheless, that one-half the above named royalty shall be paid on all copies sold out-
side the United States; and provided that no percentage whatever shall be paid on any copies
destroyed by fire or water, or sold at or below cost, or given away for the purpose of aiding the
sale of said work.

    It is further agreed that the profits arising from any publication of said work, during
the period covered by this agreement, in other than book form shall be divided equally between said
PUBLISHERS *and said* AUTHOR.

The contract for *Look Homeward Angel,* which provided for a royalty of 25 cents per copy on the first two thousand copies of the $2.50 volume and 37 cents thereafter. (Princeton University Library).

Expenses incurred for alterations in type or plates, exceeding twenty per cent. of the cost of composition and electrotyping said work, are to be charged to the AUTHOR's account.

The first statement shall not be rendered until six months after date of publication; and thereafter statements shall be rendered semi-annually, on the AUTHOR's application therefor, in the months of February and August; settlements to be made in cash, four months after date of statement.

If, on the expiration of **five** years from date of publication, or at any time thereafter, the demand for said work should not, in the opinion of said PUBLISHERS, be sufficient to render its publication profitable, then, upon written notice by said PUBLISHERS to said AUTHOR, this contract shall cease and determine; and thereupon said AUTHOR shall have the right, at **his** option, to take from said PUBLISHERS, at cost, whatever copies of said work they may then have on hand; or, failing to take said copies at cost, then said PUBLISHERS shall have the right to dispose of the copies on hand as they may see fit, free from any percentage or royalty, and to cancel this contract.

Provided, also, that if, at any time during the continuance of this agreement, said work shall become unsalable in the ordinary channels of trade, said PUBLISHERS shall have the right to dispose of any copies on hand paying to said AUTHOR — **fifteen (15)** — per cent. of the net amount received therefor, in lieu of the percentage hereinbefore prescribed.

Said Publishers shall pay to said Author the Sum of FIVE HUNDRED ($500.) DOLLARS (the receipt of which is hereby acknowledged) as an advance payment on the royalty account, said amount to be reimbursed to said Publishers from the first monies accruing under said royalties.

All monies due under this contract shall be paid to Mrs. Ernest Boyd, 131 East 19th Street, New York City, as representative of said author, and her receipt shall be a valid discharge for all said monies.

In consideration of the mutuality of this contract, the aforesaid parties agree to all its provisions, and in testimony thereof affix their signatures and seals.

Witness to signature of
Thomas Wolfe

Madeline Boyd

Thomas Wolfe

Witness to signature of
Charles Scribner's Sons

N. J. Watson

Charles Scribner's Sons
G Charles Scribner
Chairman

{ L. S. }

CC, 2 pp., PUL

Jan. 8, 1929

Dear Mr. Wolfe:

This is to tell you that we have formally considered "O Lost" and shall be delighted to publish it on the basis of a 10% royalty on the first 2,000 copies and of 15% thereafter;- and as soon as we hear that the terms suit you, we shall send a cheque for five hundred dollars as an advance. The question of terms would naturally be taken up with Mrs. Boyd who brought us the book and acts as literary agent. I'd be glad to get into touch with her if she's in New York, or you might do it;- or if she's out of reach, we could make the terms dependent on her approval, which I hardly doubt she would give, and send you the advance immediately. You could simply give us a note accepting provisionally.

Ever sincerely yours,
[Maxwell Perkins]

ALS, 4 pp., PUL
Harvard Club letterhead

Jan 9, 1929

Dear Mr Perkins: I got your letter this morning and I have just come from a talk with Mrs Madeleine Boyd, my literary agent.

I am very happy to accept the terms you offer me for the publication of my book, O Lost. Mrs Boyd is also entirely satisfied.

I am already at work on the changes and revisions proposed in the book, and I shall deliver to you the new beginning some time next week.[1]

Although this should be only a business letter I must tell you that I look forward with joy and hope to my connection with Scribner's. To-day—the day of your letter—is a very grand day in my life. I think of my relation to Scribner's thus far with affection and loyalty, and I hope this marks the beginning of a long association that they will not have cause to regret. I have a tremendous lot to learn, but I believe I shall go ahead with it; and I know that there is far better work in me than I have yet done.

If you have any communication for me before I see you next, you can reach me at 27 West 15th Street (2nd Floor Rear).

Faithfully Yours,
Thomas Wolfe

1. This letter followed TW's first meeting with MP.

CC, 1 p., PUL

Jan. 11, 1929

Dear Mr. Wolfe:

I sent the contract and check to Mrs. Boyd yesterday. She said she would immediately get in touch with you. I look forward eagerly to seeing the first section of the revised manuscript. You can certainly be sure that your novel will have the greatest personal support and interest in this establishment. Many thanks for your letter.

Ever sincerely yours,
[Maxwell Perkins]

CC, 1 p., PUL

March 28, 1929

Dear Mr. Wolfe:

I am writing you in order to avoid disturbing you by phone in case you are still doing your sleeping by day. I want to arrange to go over the manuscript thus far, in order to show cuts I would like to suggest, and to consider others;- and this might take an hour or two.

Besides, we ought to get on now as rapidly as we possibly can with the book.[1]

Ever sincerely yours,
[Maxwell Perkins]

1. On 12 April MP wrote Madeleine Boyd: "We are making progress with Wolfe's book. I believe we shall soon have it short enough to be got into one volume form. And the more I see of it, the more I think of it" (PUL).

TO: John Hall Wheelock[1]

ALS, 3 pp., PUL
Hotel Bellevue letterhead, Boston

Tuesday July 16, 1929

Dear Mr Wheelock: My address will be Ocean Point, Maine, Boothbay Harbor, Care of Mrs Jessie Benge, Snow Cottage.[2] Somewhat complicated, but if you have proofs for me send them there I'm going up to-day and glad to be out of the city.

I noticed the enclosed cartoon in the Boston Herald this morning, and think it was probably inspired by Scribners' Magazine-Hemingway affair.[3] Dashiell[4] is making a collection—if you think it would interest him please send it down.

CHARLES SCRIBNER'S SONS

Look Homeward, Angel
BY THOMAS WOLFE $2.50

This novel is a strange and deep picture of American life, the cyclic curve of a large family—genesis, union, disintegration. It touches not only their visible, outer lives, but explores their buried lives as well.

The rich variety of its characters and the freedom of their portrayal give it a vividness seldom matched in fiction. The early pages are dominated by the lusty, Gargantuan figure of Oliver Gant, in whose stone-cutter's shop stood the angel of Carrara marble that was the secret symbol of his buried life. Then there is Eliza, his wife, stubborn with the patience of avarice, and their odd brood of children—Frank, with all the taints of his heredity; Helen, slapping her father out of his drunkenness; Luke, who quivers with wild laughter; Ben, bitter, secretive, attractive, aloof in his brief life, aloof in his death; and the youngest, Eugene, the stranger who never ceases to view life with something of a child's innocency and wonder. It is Eugene's life thread which the author weaves ever more firmly into the fabric of his novel, writing with sweeping intensity and moments of free beauty.

The announcement of *Look Homeward, Angel* in the Scribners Fall 1929 catalogue

I went out to the Arnold Arboretum yesterday—it was very beautiful, but the birds were inciting one another to lust, in a lewd and uncensored manner, all over the place.

Yours faithfully,
Wolfe.

1. John Hall Wheelock (1886–1978) was the editor at Scribners responsible for seeing *O Lost* through the press; he was also a respected poet. Since MP was indifferent to proofreading, Wheelock's editorial role in TW's books became increasingly important.

2. TW's landlady.

3. The June and July issues of *Scribner's Magazine* with the first two installments of *A Farewell to Arms* were banned in Boston for their alleged obscenity. On 16 July the *Boston Herald* published a twelve-panel cartoon, "A Policeman Looks at Literature," by Carl Rose.

4. Alfred Dashiell (1901–1970) was editor of *Scribner's Magazine*.

FROM: *John Hall Wheelock*   *CCS, 5 pp., PUL*

July 17, 1929

Dear Wolfe:

I hope you don't mind my omitting the "Mr.," and that you will do the same in writing me. I was very glad to get your note of the 16th this morning, giving your complete address. Thanks so much for the cartoon from the Boston Herald, which was undoubtedly inspired by Scribner's Magazine, as you surmise - and which I have passed on to Mr. Dashiell. I am surprised that the Boston authorities haven't looked into the moral situations which seem to be prevailing in the Arnold Arbore-tum, according to your ornithological report.

I have good news and bad news for you. The good news being that your story is out in the August number of Scribner's,[1] and that I will ask the Magazine to send you your copies to the new address. In the back of the Magazine you will find a brief write-up about your work, and also what seems to me an excellent picture of your-self. The bad news is that some seventy-five pages of your manuscript have been mislaid in some way, so that I am obliged to send you proof of galleys 79 to 100, inclusive, without the original copy.[2]

These galleys go forward to your new address to-day by first-class post[3] I have read them most carefully and I think you will understand my various corrections and suggestions. They will require of course a most careful reading by yourself.

Please note that I have deleted, on galley 80, several sections which it seems best to omit. You and Mr. Perkins had agreed to omit these sections, when you went over the manuscript, but in some way the printer set them up. I think nothing is lost by their omission. In the same way I have deleted one or two phrases in other places.

Is there any danger of confusion through the use of the names "Sheba," "Horty" and "Miss Amy"?[4]

I have looked up and verified all your quotations, so you need not worry about these.

I wish I had time and space to tell you how my enthusiasm grows with the proofreading. I must content myself with the less gracious act of pointing out what seems to me a defect. If you do not agree with me, kindly disregard my criticism. It seems to me that the section beginning in the middle of galley 87 and running to Chapter 25, is too long. This is the section dealing with the conversation between George Graves and Eugene, and is full of literary allusions, very skilfully interwoven with the story. It is one of the best parts of the book but it loses by being too much prolonged. You don't want the reader to get, for a moment, the impression that the author is conscious of his own skill and virtuosity; and I am afraid this will be the feeling aroused if this section runs on as long as it now does. Won't you consider this, and if you agree indicate such parts as you wish omitted?

You have not yet returned to me revised galleys 71 and 72, together with their foul galleys; nor have you returned galleys 72 to 78, inclusive, together with copy thereto. I have received here page proof covering the first 70 galleys, which is to say about 250 pages, but as this page proof covers only revised galleys, which had very very few changes and as I am following page proof most carefully myself, I felt it was not necessary to trouble you with them.

The printer was a little bit upset by the very lengthy insertion which you made on one of our revised galleys. I don't suppose it is likely that you'll be making another of this kind. It is of course desirable to do as little of this as possible, on account of the expense and delay involved.

This is a tiresome letter, but I do hope with all my heart that you're going to have a fine rest and a happy time, too, up in Maine.

As ever, dear Wolfe,
Yours sincerely,
<u>J.H.W.</u>

To
Mr. Thomas Wolfe
c/o Mrs. Jessie Benge
Boothbay Harbor, Maine.
Snow Cottage, Ocean Point.

1. "An Angel on the Porch," an episode from *Look Homeward, Angel,* was published in *Scribner's Magazine* to generate interest in the forthcoming novel.

2. None of the galley proofs for *Look Homeward, Angel* survive.

3. Galleys do not survive.

4. Sheba in *Look Homeward, Angel* was Hortense (or Horty) in "O Lost"; Amy in *Look Homeward, Angel* was Emma in "O Lost."

TO: *John Hall Wheelock*   ALS, 1 p., PUL
c. *17 July 1929*

Dear Mr Wheelock: Will you look over Galley <u>62</u>? I have written in a paragraph to soften the harsh impression one gets of Leonard (where he beats the little boys), and I include Margaret, his wife, who seconds him out of love and loyalty—I did this on the idea that "misery loves company." Do with it what you like.

My address is Ocean Point, Maine, C.W. Snow Cottage, care of Mrs Jessie Benge. There is also a general P.O. address, which should also be given—I believe it is Boothbay Harbor, but not sure. Will let you know

Yours,
Thomas Wolfe

And thanks again for   Final Galleys 57, 58
your pains and labor   missing

TO: *John Hall Wheelock*   *ALS, 16 pp., PUL*

Ocean Point, Maine July 19, 1929

Dear Mr Wheelock: Don't mind if I call you "mister" at present, but you must please not do it to me. I no longer have the slightest feeling of stiffness or diffidence toward you, I have on the contrary the warmest and gratefullest feeling toward you and Mr Perkins, but I could no more call you Wheelock than I could call him Perkins. Alone in my mind I know that I am now a man in years, and as I face my work alone I come pretty close at times to naked terror, naked nothing, I know that no one can help me or guide me or put me right—that's my job. Perhaps that is why in my personal relations with people I cling to the old child's belief—that there are older people who are wiser and stronger, and who can help me.—I am far from being melancholy—I am more full of strength and power and hope than I have been in years—I have in me at the present time several books, all of which are full of life and variety, and rich detail. If I can only put down finally the great disease and distress of my spirit—which is to take in more of life than one man can hold—I can go on to do good work—because all men are certainly bound by this limit and I believe my chance to learn and experience, and my power of absorption are as good as those of most men. I feel packed to the lips with rich ore, in this wild, and lovely place, all America stretches below me like a vast plain, the million forms that repeat themselves in the city, and that torture us so by their confusion and number, have been fused into a calmer temper—I am filled with a kind of tragic joy; I want to tear myself open and show my friends all that I think I have. I am so anxious to lay all my wares out on the table—when one thing that I have done is praised, to say: You have not seen 1/10 or 1/20 of what is in me. Just wait" Then I am tortured when I have talked to people that I have seemed too exuberant, too full of wild energy—I go away thinking they have this simple picture in two or three colors of me, when there are a thousand sombre and obscure shadings that have not been shown. I am full of affection and hope for this first book, but when you and Mr Perkins have praised it I have been stirred with the desire to do something far better—I will, I must show these men what is in me! Hence, again, we come to those reasons that make me say "mister" to some people—the spirit of the young man is thirsty for real praise, for admiration of his works: the creative impulse, which has such complex associations, may have roots as simple and powerful as this one.

It would be inexact to say that I feel that whatever I do is by its doing right—in my own life I am trying for greater balance sanity, kindness to other people—but when I write at present I want to wrench the most remote and terrible things in myself and others—whatever scruples and restraints from the traditional morality I have—and I have many—vanish under the one surpassing urge to make everything blaze with light, to get intensity and denseness into everything!—Thus when I write, my own lusts, fears, hatreds, jealousies—all that is base or mean—I drag up with strong joy, as well perhaps as better qualities, feeling not how bad these things may be, but what magnificent life this is, how little all else is by comparison. This is of course the most colossal egotism—but how else do people create? not surely, by telling themselves they are dull, and their affairs petty or mean? what profit is in that, or where's the improvement? In short there are moments when I work when I feel that no one else is a quarter my power and richness—my baseness is better than their nobility, my sores more interesting than their health—etc, that, one way or another, I am a fine young fellow and a great man. I know you will not despise me for this confession—there are people all around, especially the critics, who would rail and sneer at this, but under their silly little pretenses of modesty and cynical urbanity they are nasty little mountains of egotism—I merely work in this way, by feeling when things are going well that I am something tremendous like a God, but as a person I am no longer insolent or proud at heart, I feel on the contrary a constant sense of inferiority, often to people I am in no wise inferior to. Professor Babbitt[1] at Harvard could figure all this out in 40 seconds by his patented quack's system, and have all my various romantic diseases healed with a half dozen [tickets] of his own manufacture—but his brand of "classicism" is so much more romantic than my wildest romanticism that by comparison Plato might have begot me out of Lesbia.

I cannot tell you how moved I was by your letter—by its length, its patience and care; it is a symbol of my entire relation with you and Mr Perkins—I could not a year ago have thought it possible that such good luck was in store for me—a connection with such men, and such a house, and editing and criticism as painstaking and intelligent as I have had.

I should have once said that it was like a child's fantasy come true, but I know this is not exact—a child's dream is swollen with so much false magnificence that much in life seems stale and disappointing to the young man. But a slow and powerful joy is awaking in me as I come to see that life has real wonder that is more strange and marrowy than our fictions. Consider this: I was a little boy born among great mountains from obscure people, I saw strange and beautiful things when I was a child, I dreamed constantly of wonderful far off things and cities—and when I grew up I went away and saw them I was a poor boy who grew up in anarchy—I said that one day I should go to Harvard, and I went. People who make jokes about Harvard would make a joke about this, but it was not a joke to that boy—it was magic—and the journey must first be viewed from its beginning. I read and dreamed about strange foreign cities—I grew up and went to see them, I met people in them, I wandered from place to place by myself, I had wonderful adventures in them. When I was 16 or 18 I hoped,—I dreamed, I did not dare to speak the hope, that someday I would write a book that men would read—now I have written a book, and a great publishing house is printing it, and men who have seen it have been moved by it and praised it. Seven months ago I came to Vienna from Budapest after months of wandering about in Europe: I had a scar on my head and a broken nose, I found there a letter from Scribners. Now I am writing this from a little cottage on the wild coast of Maine—the sky is grey and full of creaking gulls, the Atlantic sweeps in in a long grey surge. I have eaten delicious foods and drunk glorious wines in many countries; I have read thousands of noble books in several languages; I have known and enjoyed beautiful women, have loved and been loved by one or two.

Fools will sneer "How romantic!"—I tell you merely what you will easily agree to—this is not romantic, this is only a bald statement of a few facts in a single ordinary life. No man can say that there is a single garnishment or distortion of fact here—whoever chooses to believe there is no wonder and no richness here is only stupidly and stubbornly hugging fantoms of sterility. No—what one comes to realize is that there is a reasonable hope that one may cherish in life that makes it well worth living—and that the childish pessimist who denies this is as lying and dishonest a rogue as the cheap ready-made optimist—and that, indeed, of the two brands of rascals, the merchant who deals in Pollyanna optimism is a better man than he whose stock-in-trade is snivelling drivelly Pollyanna pessimism. The spirit that feels from its mothers womb the tragic [underweft] of life, and never sees the End as different from what it is, is all the more certain that sunlight is not made of fog, wine of vinegar, good meat of sawdust, and a womans lovely body of nitrogen, decaying excrement, and muddy water. To hell with such lying drivel—why do we put up with it?

I know that it is good to eat, to drink, to sleep, to fish, to swim, to run, to travel to strange cities, to ride on land, sea, and in the air upon great machines, to love a woman, to try to make a beautiful thing—all such as consider such occupations "futile," let them go bury themselves in the earth and get eaten by worms to see if that is less futile   However, these despisers of life who are so indifferent to living, are the first ones to cry out and hunt the doctor when they have bellyaches

There is an island in this lovely little harbor—I can look out on it from the porch of my cottage. It is covered by a magnificent forest of spruce trees, and a little cottage is tucked away in a clearing under three mighty trees at one end. One end of the island (where this house is) looks in on the bay and on the little cottages along the shore, the other end fronts the open Atlantic. Now I fantasy about buying this island (which has 15 or 20 acres), and so strange is possibility that one day perhaps I shall. Several weeks ago when I knew I was coming to Maine I began to think about islands. Presently I saw myself owning one, living on one, putting off from the mainland (a decrepit old wharf) with my servant, in a little motor boat stocked with provisions—to the minutest detail I saw this place, even to the spring house where butter and milk and rounds of beef should be stored. This scene became a part of my dream—however blurred the actual details have become, I cannot say, the picture remains vivid, only the island I dreamed about has become this one here—I am unable to distinguish one from the other, so imperceptibly have the two fused (even to the rotten old wharf from which I fish)

In a child's dreams the essential thing happens—it is this that makes <u>wonder</u>— the long vacancies between the <u>flare</u> of reality are left out; he is, for example, on a great ship going to a strange country, the voyage ends, and the very next moment the ship is sailing into a harbor, he sets foot not on land, but on Paris, London,

Venice. I am living in such a [place]—there is the harbor, with wooded islands in it, a little shore road that winds around by the waters edge, and all the little cottages, with tidy yards, bright flowers. Then immediately there is the ocean. I had ceased until recent years to believe there could be such scenes; and even now it does not seem real. I thought there would be preludes to the sea. But there are not. The other night I walked along the road. The little farmhouses slept below the moon, the gnarled apple trees full of apples getting ripe leaned over the hedges, and on the walls the wild wood lilies grew. You would not say along that road the sea was there, behind the houses, behind the fir trees, and the hedges, and the apples getting ripe, and yet you round a bend, and the sea is there. I thought there would be vast length-enings into the sea, slow stoppages of land and rock, drear marshy vacancies, slow lapse and waste relinquishment of earth, but when you round the bend of the road the sea is there—he has entered at one stride into the land—this union of the vast and lonely with the little houses, the land, the little harbor, made a great music in me. I could not tell you all it meant, but it was like Milton standing by a little door. And I thought that if one came into this place on a ship from open sea it would be with the suddenness of a dream.

To unspin all the meanings in these things would take too long—and my let-ter is much too long already

I got the proof sent with your letter—through galley 100. I am sending off to you this afternoon the few galleys I had before—through 78 (including foul galleys for 71, 72) I am sorry the printer was upset by my one long insertion—I do not think it will happen again: I did it here to round out one detail in Leonard's life—much that showed the man in a favorable light had previously been cut, and I though it proper to add a little here. But I shall not do this again. I note carefully all you say—I shall study the boys-going-away-from-school scene, and cut where I can. I am sorry to know it is still too long—Mr Perkins suggested a very large cut out of it, which was made—I have a much fresher mind for it now, and will per-haps find more. I shall certainly send all the proofs I now have (through 100) back to you by Tuesday of next week—they should reach you Thursday. I still have ten or eleven days in this lovely place—that is, until a good week from next Tuesday—you would therefore have time to send me more. I propose to go to Canada when I leave here, for a week, and return to New York before August 10. It would be good if I had proof to take with me.

You gave me a great start when you said 75 pages of ms. had been lost, but on re-reading, as I understand your letter, it seems that we already have galley proofs for these pages—even if we haven't there is at Scribners a complete copy of the orig-inal mss. besides the one Mr Perkins and I cut. Of course what revisions were made in these 75 p. I don't know. It is a thrilling shock to know that you have already page proof for 70 galleys—of course I am excited and anxious to see them. I await eagerly the copies of the magazine with my story and the piece about my work—What's the use of acting coy and modestly restrained when you don't feel that way!

This is another day—a glorious blue-white cold sparkling day. Forgive the long letter, the personal rhapsodies—I have victimized you by making you the target. My next letter will come with the proof and be strictly concerned with business. I fish, read, and write here.

Faithfully Yours, Tom Wolfe

1. Irving Babbitt (1865–1933), Harvard professor of French, denounced both romanticism and naturalism.

FROM: John Hall Wheelock   *CCS, 2 pp., PUL*

July 19, 1929

Dear Wolfe:

I am sending along to-day by first-class mail galleys 101 to 108, inclusive. I have given these galleys a most careful reading and have left a few questions for you to decide. As we are now planning to go from galleys direct into page proofs we ought to decide these questions definitely and finally in the galleys. With these galleys I also send along the original manuscript which they cover.

I am still waiting for revised galleys 71 and 72 with their foul galleys, which you took away with you, and galleys 72 to 78, inclusive, with manuscript therefor, which you also took away with you. I hope that my letter of the 17th and also galleys 79 to 100, inclusive, reached you safely.

In returning galleys and manuscript, or galleys and foul galleys, it may save time to address them directly to me and to send them by first-class mail.

I hope you are having a good time and only wish that we could let you forget the cares and annoyances of proof-reading. However, if we press forward determinedly and cheerfully now, the thing will be done in a surprisingly short time. As far as I have been able to find out there are only about sixty more galleys to follow.

With all sorts of good wishes, dear Wolfe,
Yours sincerely,
J.H.W.

To
Mr. Thomas Wolfe
Boothbay Harbor, Maine
c/o Mrs. Jessie Benge, Snow Cottage, Ocean Point

TO: John Hall Wheelock   *ALS, 2 pp., PUL*
c. 20 July 1929   *Boothbay Harbor, Maine*

Mr Wheelock:—Saturday afternoon 4:30

I got your second installment of proof today through (I believe) galley 108. No time for extended comment now—trying to get this off on last mail today—but believe all my corrections clear.

This is galleys 71–78 inclusive (which I brought here with me) along with foul galley 71 72, and mss for, I believe, this section.

Note—galley 73—<u>bawdy</u>-<u>house</u> for <u>whore</u>-house galley 73—<u>Dalliance</u> under difficulties for <u>Concupiscence</u> under diff. <u>Note</u> galley 75; deletion of <u>delightful</u> (do what you think best here Galley 76—deletion of [<u>Sliding</u>] <u>kiss and</u> (do what you like here)

I'll send the new stuff back to you Monday

Yours,
Wolfe

➥

TO: *John Hall Wheelock*   *ALS, 7 pp., PUL*
1929

Monday, July 22

Dear Mr Wheelock: I am sending you galleys 79–90—it was for this section (79–100 that the mss., you say, has been lost. Will you please urge the printer again to try to recover it?—there are several places here that cause me difficulty. Naturally, without the mss. I cannot remember word for word the original, but it seems to me that there are omissions in several places that are not covered by the cuts Mr Perkins and I made. The most important of these is at the beginning of the boys-going-from-school Scene which you say should be cut still more. Mr Perkins and I took out a big chunk, but there is now a confusing jump that nullifies the meaning of several speeches (you have pointed out one of these) I have tried to patch it up as well as I could.

The name <u>Sheba</u> should always be used for ~~Horty~~, and the name <u>Amy</u> for ~~Emma~~—you mentioned this in your first letter and I have tried to correct wherever I found the old names.

I do not remember what Mr Perkins and I did on <u>galley 80</u>—where you have made a cut It does not seem to me that what happens here is more likely to give offense than many other things that remain—as an alternative I have cut out parts of it, and I submit the result to your decision. If it still seems best to cut it all, please do so. (Cut)

Will you look over the titles of the German books on Galley 85 and correct mistakes in grammar—i.e. is it <u>Der</u> or <u>Die</u> Zerbrochene Krug? etc.[1]

—As I read over the proofs again, I become more worried.—There is a reference, for example, by one of the boys in the coming-from-school scene to <u>Mrs Van Zeck</u>, the wife of a lung specialist—but the whole section describing her as she leaves a store has been omitted. I cannot recall making this cut with Mr P. As to further cuts in this scene I will do what I can—but it seems to me that conversation between the two boys, which you say is too long, has been cut down to very little—

JULY 1929 / 19

what you <u>do</u> have is the undertakers scene, the W. J. Bryan scene, the Old Man Avery Scene, the Village Idiot Scene, the Old Colonel Pettingrew Scene, the Men Discussing the War Scene—all of which it seems to me are good.—But I'll do what I can—In view of the gaps I have discovered I think I shall send you by this mail only 79–90—I shall send the rest on as soon as I can do something to fill up the holes—I do hope people will not look on this section as a mere stunt—I really don't know what to do about cutting it—it is not a stunt, a great deal of the town is presented in short order. I'm going to send you galleys to 90 without further delay—I want you to go over the going-from-school scene and if you see cuts make them. I shall cut where I can in the last part of the scene

This is all for the present, I'm sorry to cause you all this trouble—but, as I think you know, deeply grateful.

At times, getting this book in shape seems to me like putting corsets on an elephant.—The next one will be no bigger than a camel at the most I'll send more tomorrow.

Yours Faithfully,
Wolfe

1. Wheelock was fluent in German.

∽

TO: *John Hall Wheelock*   *ALS, 7 pp., PUL*

Dear Mr Wheelock: I am sending you herewith the proofs from galley 91–100, which I have now gone over carefully. In spite of your advice to shorten this section (that part dealing with boys coming from school) I am afraid I have lengthened it a little. This was necessary because of certain omissions and gaps which it seemed to me, either the printer had caused, or Mr Perkins and I had failed to consider when we made cuts. I have written in the omitted segment on Mrs Van Zeck, somewhat shorter, I think, than it first was—I have had to pin this to the proof, for want of space and indicate the place where it is to be inserted. I have also written in various themes from poetry at places where it seemed to me there was a vacancy—this was the mood and temper with which the scene started—the inwoven poetry—and it seemed to me it should be continued.—Now, Mr Wheelock, I have not willingly run counter to your advice on this section—I am simply not able intelligently to select between what I have left. I should be troubled to think this is too long— please consider it again as carefully as you can and, if it seems best make cuts where you think they are needed.

Although the Van Zeck bit means extra work for the printer, I think it might take precedence over some other things in the scene for several reasons: First, it is war time, a discussion of the war, the Allies, the "ancestral voices prophesying war" comes right after—the womans German name, her position, wealth, etc—opens vistas and implications that may be interesting. Second, the boys mention her in their speeches—the whole may suggest how varied (not how uniform) may be the pattern of race, culture, background, etc. even in a small town. Please verify, if you can, my quotations—The "Nur wer die (?) Sehnsucht kennt," etc is Goethe.

"Drink to me only with thine (?) eyes," and the Keats 'O for a draught of vintage' (I think its "Ode to Autumn"—not sure) On Galley 93, I restored a sentence you had struck out and changed the words I thought objectionable—if you still find it too strong, cut it out. (nozzles cut for end-tips, for example)

On galley 94, I added a sentence "Having arranged to meet her" (Mrs Pert)—etc for a scene between Ben and Mrs Pert which I cannot remember having been cut.

—There was originally a burlesque of the English war-books on galley 94—was this omitted in the cuts?—I have added a line here to sum up what remains.

This is all for the present, I now have left eight galleys, which I shall try to get off to you to-morrow.

I am leaving here, I think, Saturday or Sunday. Do not send any more proofs after Thursday. If I get more before then I shall return them all corrected to you before I leave. My present plan is to go to Portland and to take train or ship for Canada. I'll let you know. If I go there I shall stay a week. I'll give you my address and also tell you when I am coming back to New York. Naturally I want to finish with the proofs now as quickly as possible.

Thanks again for your great care and patience.

Yours faithfully,
Tom Wolfe

Tuesday Afternoon
July 23, 1929

TO: John Hall Wheelock   *PUL*

Dear Mr Wheelock:

Just sent off galleys 91–100—found at P.O. a package of proof addressed to Thomas Boyd[1]—it is my stuff all right, through galley 115, but did you by any chance, through this very understandable error, send any more of my stuff to the real Thomas Boyd?

Ocean Point,   Yours Faithfully,
Maine   Thomas Wolfe
July 23, 1929

1. Thomas Boyd (1898-1935) was a Scribners author and no relation to Madeleine Boyd.

FROM: John Hall Wheelock   *CCS, 6 pp., PUL*

July 23, 1929

Dear Wolfe:

I was greatly delighted and touched by your fine letter of July 19. I wish I could answer it as it deserves to be answered, but the rather unusual pressure in the office just now, which means that I have to work every evening as well, makes the writing of letters a luxury beyond my reach at the moment.

I think you know that both Mr. Perkins and myself have the greatest admiration for your genius and an almost fatherly solicitude for the fortunes of your work in the world. Now that we have come to know you through our meetings together in the office, we count you with pride among those friends for whom we have real affection. I'm afraid years do not bring always the feeling of greater wisdom and assurance, but if we can be of any help by virtue of our longer experience in the work-a-day world, you know that you may look to us for it.

I am so glad to see that you are happy at Ocean Point and that you feel the exhilaration which one has always, I think, in the presence of the sea. Some day I shall present you with a book of mine containing some poems about the sea. I was sea-born, just as Eugene was hill-born.

Now to business. With your permission I'm not going to show you the 256 pages that we have. There were hardly any corrections in the revised galleys and I have checked up all that there were most carefully. I think you have enough on your hands now, and that any further kind of proof will only be confusing and distracting. Page proof after this will be made direct from original galleys, and this page proof we will want you to see.

I received this morning corrected galleys 73 to 78, inclusive, also corrected revised galleys 71 and 72, also manuscript and foul galleys. All of these have been carefully attended to. I also received corrected galleys 79 to 90. I have a confession: the manuscript covering these galleys was lost by myself in a taxi-cab, together with original printer's set of proofs. I had read all the galleys of this set except one, and I can assure you that no part of the manuscript was omitted from the galleys except one or two places which you and Mr. Perkins had decided to omit. Of this I can be absolutely positive, as I went over the whole manuscript with the galleys before it was lost. I am terribly sorry.

You must follow your own judgement entirely in the matter of cutting the boys-going-from-school scene. You need not worry about the correctness of quoted lines or of words in foreign languages, as I will take care of all of that here; but you must watch very carefully the names of your characters, for I may slip up on these now and then.

I'm sorry, but since you leave the matter to us, it still seems best to cut the passage on galley 80, as we originally had done. This passage doesn't add anything more to what has already been said, and in our opinion it would be likely to cause trouble.[1]

I sent you yesterday galleys 109 to 115, inclusive, together with manuscript.

Now, my dear Wolfe, I can write no more but this letter brings you all sorts of good wishes. If my communications seem dry and matter-of-fact, please know that I am not really so by nature, but that I'm working under terrible pressure here just now during the absence of Mr. Perkins.

As ever,
Yours sincerely,
J.H.W.

To
Mr. Thomas Wolfe
  c/o Mrs. Jessie Benge,
Snow Cottage, Ocean Point
Boothbay Harbor, Maine

P.S. Please excuse this hurriedly-written note, dear Wolfe.

J.H.W.

1. In the absence of galleys it is impossible to identify this passage.

FROM: John Hall Wheelock   *CCS, 3 pp., PUL*

July 24, 1929

Dear Wolfe:

I sent forward this morning galleys 116 to 125, inclusive, and I plan to send forward early to-morrow galleys 126 to 131, inclusive. I have of course given all these galleys a most careful reading.

In the meantime I have received from the press galleys 132 to 140, inclusive, and the balance of 40 galleys or so will probably reach me within the next week. As I understand it you leave for Canada on the 30th, and I want to get you all the proof I can before that time. You will, won't you, keep me advised as to your address as you move - that is, if you are going to be long enough in any one place to receive further proof. I should like very much to get the galley proof through with as little delay as possible. Correcting the page proof is largely a matter of making sure that the corrections in the galleys were properly transferred to the page proofs, and that no new errors crept in in the process; seeing that the folios, running heads, margins, etc., are in order - and such details can well be taken care of by the publisher. The galleys, on the other hand, do demand a most careful reading by the author.

Mrs. Ernest Boyd sails for Ireland to-morrow on the "Westphalia," and I am sending her all the proof we have of your book. She plans to be in London for some time, where she has a considerable acquaintance among the better publishers, and it is our hope that she may be able to find a suitable English publisher for "Look Homeward, Angel."

I have reread, several times, your very fine letter of July 19. It gives a remarkably vivid impression of your present mood and environment, as well as a sort of panorama of the past, and it is permeated by a certain positive quality which is to me one of the finest elements in your work: its great love of things, discernible even in the midst of the most bitter satire or ridicule. I hope you are enjoying yourself in the country.

With all goods wishes,
Yours sincerely,
J.H.W.

To
Mr. Thomas Wolfe
Boothbay Harbor,
Maine

TO: *John Hall Wheelock* *ALS, 2 pp., PUL*

Dear Mr Wheelock: Thanks for your letter which came this morning. It was not in the least short and formal, as you suggested—it was a very friendly and cheering letter, and I was happy to get it I quite understand how pressed you are at present—and I don't expect long letters or anything more than bare instructions.

I am sending you galleys 101–108 today—this leaves me 109–115, which Ill send tomorrow. That is all the proof I have at present—I hope more comes. It is safe to send me proof up to Thursday night. I am leaving here Saturday or Sunday. I shall be back in New York in a week or 10 days from then—if it is possible to give you an address to which proof may be sent during that time, I'll do so.

There was very little to do in this batch of stuff—I made the corrections you indicated, and made two small insertions which I thought added to the picture—but follow your own judgment and cut them if you think best.

It's quite all right about the lost mss—my uneasy feeling about omissions was only a phantom of my mind, and your assurance that everything is in dispels it.

I am enclosing an editorial from this mornings Boston Herald which seems to have gone emphatically pro-Scribner.[1] Dashiell's clipping bureau will probably send him this, but perhaps not.—I do not think there is anything more to be said about the proof that has not already been said, or that is not evident from the galleys.

Yours faithfully,
Tom Wolfe

Ocean Point, Maine,
Wed. July 24, '29

P.S. I'll get your sea-poems and read them when I come back to New York

1. On 29 July the newspaper published an unsigned editorial, "Cheapening Boston," criticizing the censoring of *Scribner's Magazine.*

FROM: John Hall Wheelock   *CC, 1 p., PUL*

July 25, 1929

Dear Wolfe:

Thanks for your postal of the 24th. We have not sent any mail to Thomas Boyd for some time: it was simply a case of the girl writing "Thomas" and continuing "Boyd," through force of habit. I am awfully sorry it happened even although, as it was, no harm was done.

I received this morning corrected galleys 91 to 100, inclusive, together with your note. I am sending off to-day galleys 132 to 139, inclusive, together with the manuscript; but I will send nothing more to your present address, but will wait for word from you as to where further proof should be sent.

With ever so many good wishes,

Yours sincerely,

TO: John Hall Wheelock   *ALS, 4 pp., PUL*
25 July 1929   *Ocean Point*

Dear Mr Wheelock: I am sending you herewith galleys 109–115. Galleys 116–125, with mss, and with a letter from you arrived this morning. Most of the corrections in today's batch have already been indicated by you—I think all corrections are plain. Usually when you suggest words or phrases for others that you consider of dubious meaning, I accept your revision, but once or twice I have stuck to my own. For example the other day for my 'The world [or the earth] shook to the <u>stamp</u> of marching men,' you suggested <u>to the tread</u>—on thinking it over I decided that <u>to the stamp</u> more nearly got my meaning. You have done glorious work on the <u>adverbs</u>—I get red in the face when I see them coming, and when they come, they come in schools and shoals. I hope my versions here are satisfactory.

Thanks for your splendid letter—the news about Mrs Boyd is very exciting: she is a shrewd and energetic woman, and knows many people. I am glad you are letting her have proofs, I wish it were possible to give her proofs for the whole book since some of the best of it, I think, comes in the closing chapters—Ben's death, etc. It would be a grand thing if a good English publisher did it.—I am very happy at the way the proofs are coming in. I shall get today's batch off to you tomorrow, and shall return all that I get hereafter in this place before I leave I, too, am very anxious to get the galleys corrected and see it in page-proof. If I get to Canada I shall try to wire you my address—perhaps, under these circumstances, I will not go, but if I do, I will not be out of touch with the book more than a week.

As I have said I do not think you had better send proofs <u>here</u> after Thursday, although it would be safe up to Thursday evening (from N.Y.)

I am glad you liked my letter—it was written on impulse and I did not think until later how busy you are, and how little time you must have now for correspondence of this sort. Your own letters lift me tremendously—I hope in some way my book will deserve the labor you have put upon it.

Faithfully Yours,
Tom Wolfe

I do hope there is time for the dedication—I have one that I want very much to use. If you need it now let me know.—I think perhaps I may have to use one of Scribners old envelopes for todays proofs

TO: John Hall Wheelock   *ALS, 2 pp., PUL*

Friday, July 26,
1929

Dear Mr. Wheelock: I am sending you with this letter galleys 116–125—two other sets of galleys that you mention in your letter that I got this morning have just been given to me: 126–131, 132–139. I'll send them back corrected before I leave here. I send you a wire Monday telling you what my next address will be, or whether I'm coming back to New York now.

There was very little to do on 116–125—I think I have made all necessary changes and corrections, including names. Bought the new copy of Scribner's—terribly excited to see my story, picture, and the piece about me.

Everyone has been most fair and generous.

Faithfully yours,
Tom Wolfe

TO: John Hall Wheelock   *ALS, 2 pp., PUL*
1929

Ocean Point, Me. Saturday
July 27

Dear Mr Wheelock:

Here are galleys 126–131. I found very little to do here, but please note on galley 127—several lines you said should come out—I modified them until I thought objectionable part was cut—I thought the trouble lay in "fifty cents one time, a dollar another" etc—If it is not all right now, cut it out.

I am leaving here Monday morning and going to Portsmouth N.H. for a day—after that may go to Canada, but will wire you. At any rate, I shall send you on Monday all the remaining galleys, with mss—132–139.

Faithfully Yours,
Tom Wolfe

Delighted to be so near the end. Thanks ever so much for the way you've handled this

TO: *John Hall Wheelock*   *ALS, 2 pp., PUL*
                                          Hotel Westminster letterhead, Boston

Tuesday, July 30
Dear Mr Wheelock: I am sending you with this letter Galleys 132–139. There were very few corrections to make in this lot and nothing, I think that requires explanation.

I am going to Montreal tomorrow morning—I do not yet know what my address there will be but if there is one to which proofs may safely be sent I'll let you know at once. At any rate, I shall be away only a few days—a week at longest. After that I shall return to New York for the rest of the summer. Hope this finds you enduring the heat well

Faithfully Yours,
Tom Wolfe.

TO: *John Hall Wheelock*   *Telegram, PUL*
1 August 1929   *Montreal*

HERE UNTIL SATURDAY SEND PROOFS CORONA HOTEL GUY STREET MONTREAL
          THOMAS WOLFE

FROM: *John Hall Wheelock*   *Wire draft, 1 p., PUL*

August 2, 1929
Thomas Wolfe, Corona Hotel, Guy Street Montreal, Canada.
Too late to get proof to you by Saturday. Will hold and await your instructions. Now have proof complete. Many good wishes
Wheelock

TO: John Hall Wheelock   *ALS, 2 pp., PUL*
                                        Corona Hotel letterhead, Montreal

Aug 3, 1929

Dear Mr Wheelock: I got your telegram this morning. I am going on to Quebec tonight and think I shall be back in New York Wednesday. Under these circumstances I think you had better keep what proofs you have on hand until my return. I am sorry my telegram came too late—I sent it from this hotel <u>Thursday</u> afternoon and was told it would be delivered within an hour—I thought this would leave plenty of time to get the proof. Did you get the last set of galleys—132–139—sent on from Boston? I am very anxious to get back now to finish the galleys, and regret causing you this delay.

My trip has done me lots of good. I have drunk plenty of ale and beer here, but no whiskey. I am very fat and must go on a diet. I hope this finds you well, and that you have not suffered from the hot weather in New York.

Faithfully Yours,
Tom Wolfe

FROM: John Hall Wheelock   *CCS, 2 pp., PUL*

August 29, 1929

Dear Wolfe:

I am sending along proof of front matter and I think the quotation looks very well on the title page.[1] The dedication page looks a bit overloaded, but will be improved I think if we move the stanza from Donne to the lower right-hand corner.[2]

I showed Mr. Perkins the "To the Reader" and he feels very strongly that the phrase "at the suggestion of his editors," ought to be deleted, also the final paragraph.[3] The first suggests that the editors felt the book to be autobiographical; which is bad. The second, Mr. Perkins thought and I agree with him, takes away a little from the clear-cut impression the first three paragraphs.

In case I don't see you again before my vacation, I want to tell you how much I have enjoyed our talks and the work of the book. It is a really magnificent book and I hope it may not take too long for your readers to discover this.

With many good wishes, dear Wolfe, I am

Yours sincerely,
J.H.W.

To
Mr. Thomas Wolfe
27 West 15th Street,
New York

1. The title-page epigraph reads: "'At one time the earth was probably a white-hot sphere like the sun.'—Tarr and McMurry." Scribners omitted Wolfe's epigraph beginning in the 1952 *Modern Standard Authors* series edition.

In the early 1900s Ralph S. Tarr and Frank M. McMurry wrote geographies for secondary schools. In his own copy of Tarr and McMurry's *A Complete Geography* (New York: Macmillan, 1908) Wolfe underlined the book's first sentence: "At one time the earth was probably a white-hot sphere like the sun; but in time the outside cooled to a crust of solid rock" (p. 1).

Cf. "It was like going back to school again in September and getting some joy and hope out of the book-lists that the teacher gave you the first day, and then the feel and look and smell of the new geography" (*The Web and the Rock*, p. 104).

2. "Then, as all my soules bee,
    Emparadise'd in you, (in whom alone
    I understand, and grow and see,)
    The rafters of my body, bone
    Being still with you, the Muscle, Sinew, and Veine,
    Which tile this house, will come again."
        Stanza 5 of John Donne's "A Valediction: Of My Name, in the Window."

TW dedicated the novel "To A.B." Aline Bernstein (1881–1955) and TW met on the *Olympic* ocean liner in 1925. Some eighteen years older than he, Bernstein was a successful stage designer married to a wealthy stockbroker. She became TW's lover and patron, encouraging and partly supporting him through the writing of *Look Homeward, Angel*.

3. Draft unlocated.

∽

Postcard, PUL

1929

Asheville, N.C. Sept 14

Dear Mr Perkins: I have had a very remarkable visit down here—the town is full of kindness and good will and rooting and boosting for the book. My family knows what it's all about, and I think is pleased about it—and also a little apprehensive. We get one another crazy—I've been here a week and I'm about ready for a padded cell. But no one's to blame. It's a strange situation, and God knows what will happen. I'll be glad when its over. Hope to see you next week in New York.

Cordially—Tom Wolfe

∽

FROM: Charles Scribner's Sons[1]

CC, 2 pp., PUL

Dec. 18, 1929

Dear Mr. Wolfe:

We are deeply interested in your writing, and have confidence in your future, and we wish to cooperate with you so far as possible toward the production of a new novel. We think you would be able to write it to much greater advantage if you were free from the necessity of earning money at the same time, and we should be glad to undertake to pay you, as an advance on the earnings of the next novel, forty-five hundred dollars ($4500) in installments, at the rate of two hundred and fifty dollars ($250) a month, beginning with February first.

We should be glad to draw up a contract with regard to your next novel whenever you desire, but presumably about February first, which would embody this agreement. We only defer drawing this contract because it is unnecessary so far as we are concerned, since this letter is binding, and also because when February first comes there may be some reason why you would rather have the arrangement made differently in some respect. For the present, however, this letter may stand as a definite agreement.

Ever sincerely yours,

1. The letter bears no signature but the formal tone suggests Charles Scribner III as the author. *Look Homeward, Angel* was published 18 October. On 6 November MP reported to Madeleine Boyd: "We printed an edition of something over five thousand, and we are now printing another edition of three thousand;- although we have only sold so far, 2,600 copies. . . . We did submit it to the Book of the Month Club, but they did not think well of it" (PUL).

ALS, 5 pp., PUL
Harvard Club letterhead

New York, Dec 24, 1929

Dear Mr Perkins: One year ago I had little hope for my work, and I did not know you. What has happened since may seem to be only a modest success to many people; but to me it is touched with strangeness and wonder. It is a miracle.

You are now mixed with my book in such a way that I can never separate the two of you. I can no longer think clearly of the time I wrote it, but rather of the time when you first talked to me about it, and when you worked upon it. My mind has always seen people more clearly than events or things—the name "Scribners" naturally makes a warm glow in my heart, but you are chiefly "Scribners" to me: you have done what I had ceased to believe one person could do for another—you have created liberty and hope for me.

Young men sometimes believe in the existence of heroic figures, and wiser than themselves, to whom they can turn for an answer to all their vexation and grief. Later, they must discover that such answers have to come out of their own hearts; but the powerful desire to believe in such figures persists. You are for me such a figure: you are one of the rocks to which my life is anchored.

I have taken the publication of my first book very hard—all the happy and successful part of it as well as the unhappy part: a great deal of the glory and joy and glamour with which in my fantasy I surrounded such an event has vanished. But,

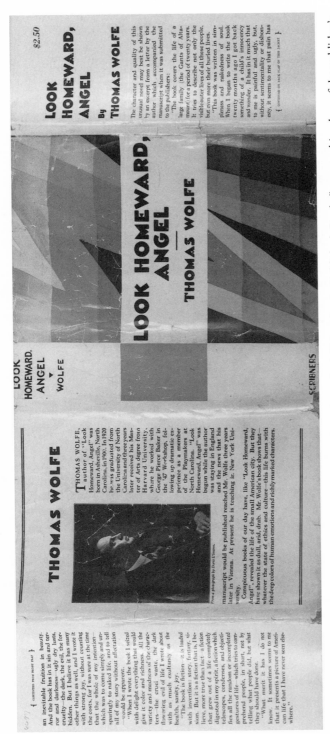

The dust jacket for Wolfe's first novel, on which an excerpt from the author's "Note for the Publisher's Reader" appeared in place of the publisher's usual flap copy.

Look Homeward, Angel
BY THOMAS WOLFE
Third large printing $2.50

This amazing book was published on October 18th, 1929, at the very height of the season, when books by famous "names" were pouring from the presses in numbers sufficient to swamp the average first novel. But here was an exception. Without special promotion it became overnight the talk of literary New York. In two weeks time it was in its second large printing. Two weeks more made a third big printing necessary. The universality of its appeal, the magnificent breadth of its canvas and the writer's opulent handling of his theme make it one of those few novels whose sale is not bounded by the imaginary limits of any set season.

© *From a photograph by Doris Ullman*

"Here is a novel of the sort one is too seldom privileged to welcome. It is a book of great drive and vigor, of profound originality, of rich and varying color. Its material is the material of every-day life, its scene is a small provincial Southern city, its characters are the ordinary persons who come and go in our daily lives. 'Look Homeward, Angel' is as interesting and powerful a book as has ever been made out of the drab circumstances of provincial American life. Assuredly, this is a book to be savored slowly and reread, and the final decision upon it, in all probability, rests with another generation than ours."—MARGARET WALLACE in the *New York Times Book Review*.

"'Look Homeward, Angel' has the good, rich, buoyant health of those roaring Elizabethan tales of Nash and Greene. It breathes the vigor of youth, bawdy, profane, soaring, depressed—but alive and real and full of meaning. It rushes full-bodied with its finely drawn characters through a life which is without falseness or artificiality or circumscribed etiquette."—*Richmond Times-Dispatch*.

"Its glowing beauty has made other books dwindle to shadows before it. The more we consider it the more amazing it becomes. . . . It is a book in which pain and pleasure, beauty and horror are endlessly intermingled, a book in which life and the fullness thereof are depicted with a lusty honesty."
—*Toledo Times*.

"It is a rich, positive grappling with life, a remembrance of things past untinged by the shadow of regret, of one who has found his youthful experiences full of savor. No more sensuous novel has been written in the United States."
—JOHN CHAMBERLAIN in *The Bookman*.

[37]

Six months after the publication of *Look Homeward, Angel,* the Scribners Spring 1930 catalogue celebrated the strong reception of the novel.

as usual, life and reality supplant the imaginary thing with another glory that is finer and more substantial than the visionary one

I should have counted this past year a great one, if it had allowed me only to know about you. I am honored to think I may call you my friend, and I wish to send to you on Christmas Day this statement of my loyal affection.

Faithfully Yours,
Thomas Wolfe.
Dec 24, 1929

ALS, 3 pp., Harvard

Dec 27 '29

Dear Wolfe:—I'm mighty glad you feel as you do,—except for a sense of not deserving it. I hope anyway that there could be no serious thought of obligation between us but, as a matter of convenience in speech, I would point out that even if you really 'owed' me a great deal it would be cancelled by what I owe you.—The whole episode, from receipt of Ms. up to now was for me a most happy, interesting, + exciting one.

Come in soon,— + bring the story. What you last told me of the October Fair[1] made me eager to have you get to it,—it gave me a real glimpse into the quality + character of it

Ever yours,
Maxwell Perkins

1. TW's proposed second novel was never published although some of the material was recycled in later volumes.

CC, 1 p., PUL

May 1, 1930

Dear Wolfe:

I am enclosing herewith our check for two hundred and fifty dollars ($250) because I believe you want us to do this until you begin to get Guggenheim money;- but if you do not, just return it.

I hope you will come in soon. Could you come up for lunch on Friday,- that is, the day on which this reaches you?

Ever yours,
[Maxwell Perkins]

ALS, 4 pp., HRHRC

S.S. Volendam
Saturday May 17 1930

Dear Mr Perkins: The ship is stopping at Plymouth tomorrow—I wanted to write you a line or two so that it would get off on an early boat. The voyage has been very quiet and uneventful—I have done little except eat and sleep and prowl all over the boat. I have had a good rest, and am now ready to get off. I am going to Paris Monday morning directly from Boulogne. I shall write you from there and let you know future plans. My address is The Guaranty Trust Company, Paris. Please write me there if you have occasion and also if you have time for a note now and then. I shall try to keep you informed regularly.

I feel like a man faced with a great test, who is confident of his power to meet it, and yet thinks of it with a pounding heart and with some speculation. I am impatient to get at my book: I know it will be good if I have power to put it on paper as I have thought it out. One thing is certain—I have not used up my nervous vitality: I am prowling around the decks like an animal. I am restless to get off. I have talked to all the passengers, and already I have violent likes and prejudices

I miss Scribner's and seeing you all very much—I think of you all with the warmest and most affectionate feeling. During the last year the place has become a part of my life and habit.

I wish I could tell you how magnificent a great ship at sea is, or of the glory and beauty of the sea and the sky, which are always different. We are nearing the coast of England, the days are much longer, and we have begun to pass tramps and steamers outward bound for America. All day the gulls have been sweeping over the water: I look forward with the greatest excitement to seeing land tomorrow: it has never failed to touch me very deeply.

I can't write a good letter on ship—the movement, the tremble of the engines, and the creaking of the wood destroy concentration. I'll write later from Paris. Good-bye for the present, and health and happiness

With my best and warmest wishes,
Tom Wolfe

TLS, 3 pp., Harvard

June 3, 1930

Dear Wolfe:

I was mighty glad to get a letter from you. We all miss you greatly and I expect to miss you more this summer.- There aren't many people who take pleasure in walking, and there are fewer with whom I take pleasure in drinking. Everything is much as usual here except that the fiction market which was bad enough as things were, has been rendered still worse by the Doubleday announcement that they are to publish new novels at one dollar. I am glad you worked hard and we were able to get out "Look Homeward Angel" before this collapse came.

When you get down to work, just do the work the best you can. Don't ever think about the public, or the critics, or any of those things. You are a born writer if there ever was one, and have no need to worry about whether this new book will be as good as the "Angel" and that sort of thing. If you simply can get yourself into it, as you can, it <u>will</u> be as good. I doubt if you will really think of any of the extrinsic matters when you are at work, but if you did, that might make it less good.

There are two people I hope you may see,- Scott Fitzgerald and John Galsworthy.[1] I dare say the Heinemann[2] crowd will see you see Galsworthy, and I hope you will see that you see Scott. I know you would have a grand time together. I meant to have written him that you were likely to turn up, but never did it.- If you need any introduction you can tell him that I was extremely anxious that you should look him up,- but the fact is you won't need any introduction, for he will know all about the "Angel" and will be eager to see you.

I shall write more when there is more to be said.

Ever yours,
Maxwell Perkins

1. (1867–1933), British novelist published by Scribners.
2. William Heinemann, Ltd., London publisher of *Look Homeward, Angel.*

FROM: John Hall Wheelock   *TLS, 4 pp., Harvard*

June 5, 1930

Dear Tom:

I was awfully glad to get your steamer note dated May 17, and to know that you had a good trip over and felt the benefit of the rest.

We all miss you here very much and I don't have the pleasure of looking forward to a possible interlude and respite from work during the afternoon—when we occasionally used to discuss everything from poetry to the high price of liquor. Which reminds me, by the way, that Marjorie Allen Seiffert[1] came to town last week and threw another of her parties. Louise Bogan and her husband, Raymond Holden,[2] were there and several other writers, poets or novelists—not to forget your old arch-foe Bill Benét.[3] I thought you'd be glad to know that Mrs. Seiffert spoke with very great enthusiasm of your book. You will remember that she didn't write you about it at the time. She admitted that she'd been a bit prejudiced against the book at first by the vast amount of it and its overwhelming force. She now says, however, that it is very clear to her that it's a book of the first rank and she's quite won over to the poetry of it. Bill Benét spoke of you with interest and friendliness—so you see there are no hard feelings over your little tiff about modern poets. Needless to say, every one was pretty tight before the evening was over, but it wasn't as late a party as last year.

I have very little news of interest, dear Tom. My life, as you know, does not abound in dramatic incident nor, at the moment, in any spiritual activity that is communicable. My sister is to be married on Wednesday to a very nice chap whom we are all very fond of, and for the present I am playing the part of a sort of mother-chaperon-brother all rolled into one. She asked to be remembered to you whenever I wrote.

At the office things move in their usual steady and methodical fashion. Max receives as many visitors as ever, and Meyer evinces as little outer enthusiasm as possible.[4] Dunn is up to his ears in manuscripts, many of them very long, but reports nothing at all likely to give him such a thrill of discovery as he experienced when he first stumbled across "O Lost!"[5]

Dear Tom, I won't try to write any more just now except to say that I believe you are going to have a bully time and get a lot of fine work done. All you have to do is to give yourself a certain amount of isolation and solitude, whether you want to or not, and the rest will follow by itself. Whatever you do, don't think of your writing as something difficult or a feat that has to be reachieved. Your writing is the most natural thing in the world, much like your breathing, and will be what it is by virtue of what you are, rather than any effort that you try to make.

I wish you were here and were going to drop in for lunch. We'd go over to 63[6] and have some of their excellent calves' liver. At least I can send you all sorts of good wishes and I'll think of you very often.

> As ever, dear Tom,
> Your friend,
> Jack

To Mr. Thomas Wolfe,
c/o Guaranty Trust Company,
4 Place de la Concorde,
Paris, France.

1. Poet published by Scribners.
2. Louise Bogan (1897–1970), poet and Scribners author; Raymond Holden (1894–1972), poet and mystery writer under the pseudonym Richard Peckham.
3. William Rose Benét (1886–1950) was the editor of the *Saturday Review of Literature*. TW insulted Benét and his wife poet Elinor Wylie at a 1927 Greenwich Village party.
4. Wallace Meyer was an editor at Scribners.
5. Charles F. Dunn (1875–1962), first reader at Scribners, was the first advocate in the house for "O Lost."
6. Manhattan restaurant.

TO: *John Hall Wheelock*   *ALS, 22 pp., PUL*
24 June 1930   *Guaranty Trust letterhead, Paris*

Everything moves, everything moves, changes, goes on from place to place—
and of the women of the everlasting earth[1]

Dear Jack: Thanks very much for your fine letter—I can't tell you how touched and
grateful I was. I'm not going to write you a long one now—I'll do that later when
things have settled a little more. Briefly, this has happened: I have been in Paris
almost all the time since I landed with the exception of a few days in Rouen—this
not because I love Paris, but because after two weeks of casting around, moving
from one hotel to the other, I suddenly decided that we spend too much of our lives
looking for ideal conditions to work in, and that what we are after is an ideal condition of the soul which almost never comes. So I got tired and disgusted with
myself went to a little hotel—not very French, I'm afraid, but very touristy—and
set to work. I've been doing five or six hours a day for almost two weeks now—the
weather is hot and sticky, but I sweat and work—its the only cure I've found for the
bloody hurting inside me. Dear Jack, its been so bad I can't tell you about it: I feel
all bloody inside me—but have faith in me, everything's going to be all right. What
do you know about it? I am writing a book so filled with the most unspeakable
desire, longing, and love for my own country and ten thousand things in it—that I
have to laugh at times to think what the Mencken[2] crowd and all the other crowds
are going to say about it. But I can't help it—if I have ever written anything with
utter conviction it is this—dear Jack, I <u>know</u> that I know what some of our great
woe and sickness as a people is now, because that woe is in me—it is rooted in
myself, but by God Jack, I have not written a word directly about myself yet God
knows what Maxwell Perkins will say when he sees it, but I've just finished the first
section of the first part—it is called <u>Antaeus</u>,[3] and it is as if I had become a voice for
the experience of a race: It begins "Of wandering forever and the earth again"—and
by God, Jack, I believe I've got it—the two things that haunt and hurt us—the eternal wandering, moving, questing, loneliness, homesickness, and the desire of the
soul for a home, peace, fixity, repose. In Antaeus, in a dozen short scenes, told in
their own language, we see people of all sorts <u>constantly in movement</u>, going somewhere, haunted by it—and by God, Jack, it's the <u>truth</u> about them—I saw it as a
child, I've seen it ever since, I see it here in their poor damned haunted eyes:—Well
there are these scenes—a woman telling of the river—the ever-moving river—coming through the levee at night, and of the crippled girl clinging to the limb, of the
oak, and of then how she feels the house break loose and go with the tide, then of
being on the roof-top with Furman and the children, and of other houses and people—tragedy, pity, humor, bravery, and the great wild savagery of American nature;
then the pioneer telling of "the perty little gal" he liked, but moving on because the
wilderness was getting too crowded; then the hoboes waiting quietly at evening by
the water tower for the coming of the fast express; then a rich American girl moving on from husband to husband, from drink to dope to opium, from white lovers

to black ones, from New York to Paris to California; then the engineer at the throttle of the fast train; then a modest poor little couple from 123d St—the woman earning living by painting lampshades, the man an impractical good-for-nothing temporarily employed in a filling station—cruising in their cheap little car through Virginia and Kentucky in autumn—all filled with details of motor camps, where you can get a shack for $1.00 a night, and of "lovely meals" out of cans—whole cost $0.36—etc; then a school teacher from Ohio taking University Art Pilgrimage No. 36 writing back home "—didn't get your letter till we got to Florence . . . stayed in Prague 3 days but rained whole time we were there, so didnt get to see much, etc," then Lee coming through Virginia in the night on his great white horse; then the skull of a pioneer in the desert, a rusted gun stock and a horses skull; then a Harry's New York Bar American saying "Jesus! What a country! I been back one time in seven years. That was enough. . . . Me, I'm a Frenchman. See? But talking, telling, cursing, until he drinks himself into a stupor—then a bum, a natural wanderer who has been everywhere; then a Boston woman and her husband who have come to France to live—"Francis always felt he wanted to do a little writing. . . . we felt the atmosphere is so much better here for that kind of thing; then a Jew named Greenberg, who made his pile in New York and who now lives in France having changed his name to Montvert, and of course feels no homesickness at all, save what is natural to 4000 years of wandering—and more, and more, and more! Then amid all this you get the thing that does not change, the fixed principle, <u>the female principle</u>—the <u>earth again</u>—and, by God, Jack, I know <u>this is true</u> also. They want love, the earth, a home fixity—you get the mother and the lover—as the book goes on, and you see this incessant change, movement, unrest, and the great train with the wanderers rushing through the night outside you get the eternal silent waiting earth that does not change, and the two women, going to bed upon it, working in their gardens upon it, dreaming, longing, calling for men to return upon it. And down below in the mighty earth, you get the bones of the pioneers, all of the dust now trembling to the great trains wheel, the dust that lived, suffered, died, and is now buried, pointing 80 ways across 3000 miles of earth—and deeper than all, eternal and enduring, "the elm trees thread the bones of buried lovers" Through it all is poetry—the enormous rivers of the nation [drinking] the earth away at night, the vast rich [stamina] of night time in America, the lights, the smells, the thunder of the train—the savage summers, the [fierce] winters, the floods, the blizzards—all, all! and finally the great soft galloping of the horses of sleep! Mr Perkins may say that the first part is too much like a poem—but Jack, I've got it [loaded] with these stories of the wanderings of real people in their own talk, and by God, Jack, a <u>real unified</u> single story opens up almost at once and gathers and grows from then on. The chapter after Antaeus is called at present <u>Early October</u>, and begins "October is the richest of the seasons"—it tells about the great barns loaded with harvest, the mown fields, the burning leaves, a dog barking at sunset, the smell of supper cooking in the kitchen—Oct is full of richness, a thousand things, then a section begins 'October is the time for all returning'—(which is true, Jack)—it tells how exiles and wanderers think of home again, of how the last tourists come back on great ships, of how the old bums shiver in their ragged collars as the newspaper behind the Public Library is blown around their feet, and of how they think of going South; it tells of the summer girls who have gone back home from the resorts; of the deserted beaches; of people lying in their beds at night thinking "Summer has come and gone—has come and gone"—then in the frosty dark and silence, they hear the thunder of the great trains. Then the October of a persons life—the core, the richness, the harvest, and the sadness of the end of youth.

By God, Jack, I'm just a poor bloody homesick critter, but when I think of my book sometimes I have the pride of a poet and a master of man's fate. Don't sigh and shake your head and think this is a welter of drivel—I've slapped these things down wildly in my haste but I tell you, Jack, this book is <u>not</u> incoherent—it has a beautiful plan and a poetic logic if I am only true to it. <u>I have not</u> told you the thousandth part of it; but I hope you can see and believe in the truth and worth of it— and then if you do, please pray for me, dear Jack, to do my best and utmost, and to write the kind of book I want to write. In case you should doubt my condition, I am perfectly sober as I write this, it is a hot day, and I am now going back to my little room to work like hell. I have really not told you <u>about</u> my book—all this has been [coming] in the sweat and heat of the last few days, and this letter, however crazy, has made things clearer for me. I shall not leave Paris until I finish that first section—then I'm going like a shot to Switzerland, I think. I wont waste time moving about—I have a horror of moving now at all. Reeves,[4] the English publisher was here, took me around to see Aldington, Michael Arlen,[5] and other lit. lights—I was so unhappy at the time I have not been back since—although they [were] very nice. Reeves wants me to come to England and stay with him, the book is coming out there next month, but I've a horror of reading more reviews—I don't want to do anything more about it. Hope and pray for me, dear Jack—write me soon and talk to me. I've said nothing about you, forgive me, I'll write you a regular letter later.

With love and best wishes to everyone.

Tom Wolfe

Write me <u>here</u>—the mail will be sent on

Dear Jack—I'm sending this on a day or two later—I guess I've really started—six hours a day, kid
June 24, 1930

This is my schedule if you can call such a way of living a schedule—up at noon, to Bank for mail, write letters, have lunch, (and bottle of wine!), buy a book—go home and work from four or five until 10 at night. Then out to eat, walk—back at midnight or one o'clock read—work until three or four

1. Written above letterhead.
2. H. L. Mencken (1880–1956), literary critic and editor of *American Mercury*.

3. "Antaeus, or A Memory of Earth" was intended as a prologue for "October Fair." "Antaeus" was suspended on MP's advice and later rewritten for *Of Time and the River*. See *Antaeus, or A Memory of Earth*, ed. Ted Mitchell (n.p.: David Strange, Thomas Wolfe Society, 1996).

Antaeus, son of Earth (Gaea) and Sea (Poseidon), was the Libyan wrestler who was unbeatable when he remained in contact with the earth; Heracles defeated Antaeus by lifting him off the ground. For TW, Antaeus represented the themes of wandering and the search for a father.

4. A. S. Frere-Reeves (1892–1984), editor at Heinemann.

5. Richard Aldington (1892–1962), British imagist poet and novelist; Michael Arlen (1895–1956), British society novelist.

TLS, 2 pp., Harvard

July 1, 1930

Dear Wolfe:

I hope you will write soon, but not if it means any let-up in the writing of the book. That is the big thing for all of us. I have hopes for a vacation for the month of August, so write before then if you can, just to say how things are going.

We came across a very good manuscript the other day, and curiously enough it begins with an episode similar to the death of Ben, though by no means so fine. It is the story of the effect of the death of the father of a family, a really remarkable piece of work, slightly impaired by the influence of Mr. Arlen.[1]

Aiken won the Pulitzer prize for poetry, since you left I think,- and this had a good effect on the sale of his book, doubled it, in fact.[2] Perhaps this happened before you left, but it pleased me so much that he should have got this recognition, and the resulting sale, that it is still in my mind, and that makes me speak of it.

Business,- of course, is rotten, but there are small orders right along for "The Angel."

Hoping to hear from you, and to see you before so very long, I am,

Ever yours,
Maxwell Perkins

1. *This Our Exile* by David Burnham (New York: Scribners, 1931).
2. *Selected Poems* by Conrad Aiken (New York and London: Scribners, 1929).

ALS, 17 pp., PUL
Guaranty Trust letterhead, Paris

July 1, 1930

Dear Mr. Perkins: I have a long letter under way to you, but I shall probably not send it until I have left Paris. The main news is that I have been at work for several weeks, and have worked every day except last Sunday, when I met Scott Fitzgerald for the first time. He called me up at my hotel and I went out to his apartment for lunch: we spent the rest of the afternoon together talking and drinking—a good deal of both—and I finally left him at the Ritz Bar. He was getting ready to go back to Switzerland where he has been for several weeks, and had come up to close up his apartment and take his little girl back with him. He told me that Mrs Fitzgerald has been very sick—a bad nervous breakdown—and he has her in a sanitarium at Geneva. He spoke of his new book and said he was working on it: he was very friendly and generous, and I liked him, and think he has a great deal of talent, and I hope he gets that book done soon.[1] I think we got along very well—we had quite an argument about America: I said we were a homesick people, and belonged to the earth and land we came from as much or more as any country I knew about—he said we were not, that we were not a country, that he had no feeling for the land he came from. "Nevertheless," as Galileo said, "it moves" We do, and they are all homesick or past having any feeling about anything.

I have missed America more this time than ever: maybe its because all my conviction, the tone and conviction of my new book is filled with this feeling, which once I would have been ashamed to admit. I notice that the Americans who live here live with one another for the most part, and the French exist for them as waiters, taxi drivers, etc—yet most of them will tell you all about the French, and their minute characteristics. I have been absolutely alone for several weeks—Fitzgerald was the first American I had talked to for some time, but yesterday I was here in the bank, and in walked Jim Boyd:[2] I was so surprised and happy I could not speak for a moment—we went out to lunch together and spent the rest of the day together. He has been quite sick with the sinus trouble, as you know. We went to see a doctor, and I waited below: this doctor made no examination and gave no verdict, but is sending him to a specialist. I hope they do something for him—he is a fine fellow, and I like him enormously. We went to a nice cafe and drank beer and talked over the American soil and what we were going to do for literature while Mrs Boyd shopped around town: later we all drove out to the Bois and through it to a nice little restaurant out of town on the banks of the Seine—we had a good quiet dinner there and came back. I think Jim enjoyed it, and I am going to meet them again tonight. It has done me a great deal of good to see them—I don't know if this enforced loneliness is good for one, certainly it is very bitter medicine, but everyone needs a period of hermitage and isolation and one is forced to think a great deal about his work. Mr Reeves, the English publisher was over here a few weeks back and took me around to see a lot of celebrated people—he was very friendly and generous, and wants me to come to England to stay with him: my book is coming out there July 14, but I am not going—I do not want to read any more reviews or hear any more about it now: I want to do the new one. I am going to Switzerland—I have several places in mind but must go and see them—I would have gone long ago, but I did not want to move fast when I had started. I do not know how long I shall stay over here, but I shall stay until I have done the first part of my book, and can bring it back with me. It is going to be a very long book, I am afraid, but there is no way out of it: you cant write the book I want to write in 200 pages. It has four parts, its whole title is The October Fair, and the names of the four parts are ① Antaeus; ② The Fast Express; ③ Faust and Helen; ④ The October Fair.³ I am working on the part called Antaeus now which is like a symphony of many voices run through with the beginning thread of story that continues through the book. I propose to bring back to America with me the parts called Antaeus and The Fast Express (all these names are tentative and if you don't like them we'll get others. The book is a grand book if I have character and talent enough to do it as I have conceived it. The book has to do with what seem to me two of the profoundest impulses in man—Wordsworth, in one of his poems "To a Skylark," I think—calls it "heaven and home"—and I called it in the first line of my book "Of wandering forever and the earth again"—

By "the earth again"—I mean simply the everlasting earth, a home, a place for the heart to come to, and earthly mortal love, the love of a woman, who, it seems to me belongs to the earth and is a force opposed to that other great force that makes men wander, that makes them search, that makes them lonely, and that makes both hate and love their loneliness.

You may ask what all this has to do with America—it is true it has to do with the whole universe—but it is as true of the enormous and lonely land that we inhabit as any land I know of, and more so, it seems to me.

I hope this does not seem wild and idiotic to you, I have been unable to tell you much about it here, but I will in greater detail later. I ask you to remember that in the first part—Antaeus—the part of many voices, everything moves, everything moves across the enormous earth, except the earth itself, and except for the voices of the women crying out "Dont go! Stay! Return, return!"—the woman floating down the river in flood on her housetop with her husband and family (I finished that scene the other day and I think it is a good one—the whole scene told in the woman's homely speech moves to the rhythm of the great river—yet the scene has pungent and humorous talk in it, and I think does not ring false—you understand that the river is in her brain in her thought in her speech, and at the very end, lying in her tent at night while a new house is being built where the old one was—for he refuses to go up on high ground back beyond the river where nothing moves, she hears him waken beside her—he thinks she is asleep—she knows he is listening to the river, to the whistles of the boats upon the river, that he wants to be out there upon the river, that he could go floating on forever down the river. And she hates the river, but all of its sounds are in her brain, she cannot escape it

. . . "All of my life is flowing like the river, all of my life is passing like the river, I think and dream and talk just like the river as it goes by me, by me, by me, to the sea."

Does it sound idiotic? I don't think so if you could see the whole; it is full of rich detail, sounds and talk. I will not tell you any more now,—this letter is too long and I have had no lunch—the river woman is only one thing—there are hoboes waiting for the coming of the fast express at sun down by the water tower and the old clay railway cut; there's a backwoods pioneer who is fascinated by "a perty little gal" and goes "courtin her"; there's a little couple from the Bronx riding through Virginia in their cheap car and spending the night at "motor camps"; there's a Paris-American drunk from Harry's New York Bar who says "Jesus! what a country!" and talks about it (America) constantly; there's a woman riding home to the Middle West from Prague—she is on a tour—there is Robert E. Lee coming through Virginia on his white horse—I'll tell you all about it later. Everything moves except the earth and the voices of the women crying out against [wandering]!

I miss seeing you and Scribners more than I can say. I hope I can do a good book for you and for myself and for the whole damn family. Please hope and pull for me and write me when you can. Excuse this long scrawl. I hope this finds you well and enjoying the summer, and also that you get a good vacation. Jim Boyd and I will think of you every time we drink a glass of beer and wish that you were here just for an hour or so to share it. I send everyone my best and warmest wishes.

Faithfully Yours,
Tom Wolfe

Don't tell any one where I am or where I'm going unless you think they have some business to find out. Tell them you don't know where I am (if anyone asks) but that mail will get to me if sent to The Guaranty Trust Co, Paris.

1. *Tender Is the Night* was published in 1934.
2. James Boyd (1888–1944), Scribners novelist.
3. This projected four-part work was not published; sections of it were salvaged for *Of Time and the River, The Web and the Rock,* and *You Can't Go Home Again.*

⌒

TO: *John Hall Wheelock*　　　　　*Postcard of unidentified theatre, Dijon, PUL*
Early July 1930　　　　　　　　　　　　　　　　　*Dijon*

Dear Jack: I got 14 closely typed pages from a man in Brooklyn the other day filled with two or three thousand alleged mistakes in grammar, wording, printing, proofreading, and usage in my book.[1] It amused me, it made me mad, and it also worried me a little. I'm going to send it on to you for your opinion. Hope this finds you well—Tom Wolfe

1. See Appendix 4.

⌒

　　　　　　　　　　　　　　　Postcard of Monument Piron, Dijon, PUL
Early July 1930　　　　　　　　　　　　　　　　　*Dijon*

Dear Mr Perkins: I am on my way to Switzerland and I hope to a good book. I saw Dashiell for two or three days in Paris—we were together a great deal. Im alone in the wilderness now—nobody knows my address—but I think its going to be all right Hope this finds you well.

Tom Wolfe

ALS, 39 pp., PUL
Hotel Lorius letterhead, Montreux, Switzerland

July 17,
1930

Dear Mr Perkins: Your letter was sent on here from Paris, and I got it this morning. I suppose by now you have the letter I sent you from Paris several weeks ago. I have been here five or six days. I came down from Paris and stopped off at Dijon for two days. A few days after I wrote you, I believe, Fritz Dashiell came to Paris and found me one morning in the Guaranty Trust Co—together with Mrs Dashiell we spent two or three days together, visited one or two museums, and did some very fancy eating. Every time we went to a new place we wished you were there. I think I told you I saw Scott Fitzgerald and Jim Boyd. I was with Jim for a day or two—after that I did not see him: before he left Paris he wrote me, he had had another attack of sinus trouble and was off for Mont 'Dore.'[1]

The other night at the Casino here I was sitting on the terrace when I saw Scott Fitzgerald and a friend of his, a young man I met in Paris. I called to them, they came over and sat with me: later we gambled at roulette and I won 15 francs—then Scott took us to a night club here. This sounds much gayer than it is: there is very little to do here, and I think I saw all the night life there is on that occasion. Later Scott and his friend drove back to Vevey, a village a mile or two from here on the lake: they are staying there. They asked me to come over to dine with them, but I am not going: I do not think I am very good company to people at present. It would be very easy for me to start swilling liquor at present but I am <u>not</u> going to do it. I am here to get work done, and in the next three months, I am going to see whether I am a bum or a man. I shall not try to conceal from you the fact that at times now I have hard sledding: my life is divided between just two things;—thought of my book, and thought of an event in my life which is now, <u>objectivally</u>, finished.[2] I do not write any more to anyone concerned in that event—I received several letters, but since none have come for some time I assume no more will come. I have been entirely alone since I left New York, save for these casual meetings I have told you about: Something in me hates being alone like death, and something in me cherishes it: I have always felt that somehow, out of this bitter solitude, some fruit must come. I lose faith in myself with people. When I am with someone like Scott I feel that I am morose and sullen—and violent in my speech and movement part of the time—later I feel that I have repelled them.

Physically my life is very good. My nerves are very steady, I drink beer and wine, mostly beer, I do not think to excess, and I have come to what is, I am sure, one of the most beautiful spots in the world. I am staying at a quiet and excellent hotel here; have a very comfortable room with a writing desk and a stone balcony that looks out on the lake of Geneva, and on a garden below filled with rich trees and grass and brilliant flowers. On all sides of the lake the mountains soar up: everything begins to climb immediately, this little town is built in three or four shelving terraces, and runs along the lake shore. Something in me wants to get up and see places, the country is full of incredibly beautiful places, but also something says 'stay here and work.'

That, in a way, is what my book is about. I hope in these hasty scrawls I have been able to communicate the idea of my book, and that it seems clear and good to you. I told you that the book begins with "of wandering forever, and the earth again," and that these two opposing elements seem to me to be fundamental in people. I have learned this in my own life, and I believe I am at last beginning to have a proper use of a writer's material: for it seems to me he ought to see in what has happened to him the elements of the universal experience. In my own life my desire has fought between a hunger for isolation, forgetting away, for seeking new lands, and a desire for home, for permanence, for a piece of this earth fenced in and lived on and private to oneself, and for a person or persons to love and possess. This is badly put, but I think it expresses a desire that all people have. I think the desire for wandering is more common to men, and for fixity and a piece of the earth to women, but I know these things are rooted in most people. I think you have sometimes been puzzled when I have talked to you about parts of this book—about the train as it thunders through the dark, and about the love for another person—to see how they could be reconciled or fit into the general scheme of a story, but I think you can get some idea of it now: the great train pounding at the rails is rushing across the everlasting and silent earth—here the two ideas of wandering and eternal repose—and the characters, on the train, and on the land, again illustrate this. Also, the love theme, the male and female love, represent this again: please do not think I am hammering this in in the book. I let it speak for itself—I am giving you a kind of key.

There is no doubt at all what the book is about, what course it will take, and I think the seething process, the final set of combinations, has been reached. I regret to report to you that the book will be very long, probably longer than the first one, but I think that each of its four parts makes a story in itself and, if good enough, might be printed as such. I have been reading your favorite book, War and Peace— it is a magnificent and gigantic work—if we are going to worship anything let it be something like this: I notice in this book that the personal story is interwoven with the universal—you get the stories of private individuals, particularly of members of Tolstoy's own family, and you get the whole tremendous panorama of nations, and of Russia. This is the way a great writer uses his material, this is the way in which every good work is "autobiographical"—and I am not ashamed to follow this in my book. The four parts of the book as they now stand are: ① Antaeus or Immortal Earth (Title to be chosen from one of these)

② Antaeus or The Fast Express

③ Faust and Helen (?)

④ The October Fair.

—I do not think <u>Immortal Earth</u> or <u>The Immortal Earth</u> is a bad title; and if you are not keen upon <u>The Fast Express</u>—we might call part I <u>Immortal Earth</u>— and Part II <u>Antaeus</u>—since in part I the idea of eternal movement, of wandering and the earth, of flight and repose is more manifest, and in Part II, even though we have the fast train, the idea of redoubling and renewing our strength by contact with the earth (Antaeus) is more evident.

Now, the general movement of the book is from the universal to the individual: in Part I <u>The Immortal Earth</u> (?), we have a symphony of many voices (I described this briefly in my other letter) through which the thread of the particular story begins to run. I think this can be done with entire clearness and unity: we have a character called David (chapter II is called <u>The Song of David</u>) but this character appears at first only as a window, an eye, a wandering seer: he performs at first exactly the same function as the epic minstrel in some old popular epic like Beowulf—who makes us very briefly conscious of his presence from time to time by saying "I have heard," or "it has been told me." Thus in Part I, in the chapter called <u>The River</u>, the woman telling the story of the river in flood refers to him once by name, in the chapter Pioneers, O Pioneers, we understand that David is a member of an American family, two or three hundred of whose members are buried in different parts of the American earth, and we get the stories and wanderings of some of these people; in the letter of the tourist from Prague he is referred to by name; in the chapter On the Rails we know that he is on the train, although the story is that of the engineer; in the chapter <u>The Bums at Sunset</u>[3] we know he has seen them waiting for the train at the water-tower; in the chapter called The Congo, the wandering negro who goes crazy and kills people and is finally killed by the posse as he crosses a creek is known to David, the boy—etc.[4]

So much for some of the general movement: now among the twenty Chapters of this first part is interspersed the first elements of the particular story—the figure of David remains almost entirely a window, but begins to emerge as an individual from what is told about him by other people—and by the way all these episodes, even the general ones—Pioneers, O Pioneers, The Congo, etc—give flashes of his life—but in this first part, not to tell about him, but to tell about his country, the seed that produced him, etc. It will be seen in the particular story that the desire and longing of David is also the desire and longing of the race—"wandering forever and the earth again"—these half dozen chapters, moreover, are concerned with the <u>female</u> thing: the idea of the earth, fructification, and repose—these half dozen chapters interspersed among the twenty are almost entirely about women and told in the language of women: the mother, the mistress, and the child—sometimes all included in one person, some times found separately in different women

Now, if you will follow me a little farther in this, here is another development. I have said that wandering seems to me to be more of a male thing, and the fructification of the earth more a female thing—I don't think there can be much argument about this, as immediately we think of the pioneers, the explorers, the

Crusaders, the Elizabethan mariners, etc. I am making an extensive use of old myths in my book, although I never tell the reader this: you know already that I am using the Heracles (in my book the City is Heracles) and Antaeus myth; and you know that the lords of fructification and the earth are almost always women: Maya in the Eastern legends; Demeter in the Greek; Ceres in Latin, etc.

Now I hope you dont get dizzy in all this, or think I am carrying the thing to absurdity: all intense conviction has elements of the fanatic and the absurd in it, but they are saved by our belief and our passion: Contained in the book like a kernel from the beginning, but unrevealed until much later is the idea of a man's quest for his father: the idea becomes very early apparent that when a man returns he returns always to the female principle—he returns, I hope this not disgusting, to the womb of earthly creation—to the earth itself, to a woman, to fixity. But I dare go so far as to believe that the other pole—the pole of wandering is not only—a masculine thing, but that in some way it represents the quest of a man for his father—I dare mention to you the wandering of Christ upon this earth, the wanderings of Paul, the quests of the Crusaders, the wanderings of the Ancient Mariner who makes his confession to the Wedding Guest—please don't laugh:

"The moment that his face I see

I know the man that must hear me,

To him my tale I teach."

I could mention also a dozen myths, legends, or historical examples, but you can supply them quite as well for yourself. Suffice it to say that this last theme—the quest of a man for his father—does not become fully revealed until the very end of the book: under the present plan I have called the final chapter of the fourth and last part (The October Fair), Telemachus.

Now, briefly, in the first part on which I am now at work (to be called Antaeus or The Immortal Earth.) I want to construct my story on the model of the old folk epic: Beowulf, for example. I want the character of David to be the epic minstrel who sings of the experience of his race, and I want to do this with eloquence, with passion and with simplicity. I want my book to be poetry—that is I want it to be drenched in a poetic vision of life: I believe at this moment in the truth and the passion of what I have to say, and I hope, in spite of this fast scrawl, I have been able to make parts of it clear to you, and to show you it has a coherent plan and purpose.

In the first chapter of the first part (after the prelude)—the first chapter is called The Ship—I think I have done a good piece of writing: I tell about the sea and the earth—I tell why they are different—of the sea's eternal movement, and the earths eternal repose. I tell why men go to sea, and why they have made harbours at the end; I tell why a ship is always called "she"; I tell of the look in the eyes of men when the last land fades out of sight, and when land comes first in view again; I tell of the earth; I describe the great ship, and the people on it—and, so help me, when I am through, I am proud of that ship and of man, who built her, who is so strong because he is so weak, who is so great because he is so small, who is so brave because he is so full of fear—who can face the horror of the ocean and see there in that unending purposeless waste the answer to his existence—I <u>insist</u>, by the way, in my book that men are wise, and that we all know we are lost, that we are damned together—and that man's greatness comes in knowing this and then making myths; like soldiers going into battle who will whore and carouse to the last minute, nor have any talk of death and slaughter.

Well, I have almost written you a book, and I hope you have stayed awake thus far. I don't know if it makes sense or not, but I think it does: remember, although this letter is very heavy, that my book, as I plan it will be full of richness, talk and humor—please write me and tell me if all this has meant anything to you, and what you think of it. Please don't talk about it to other people. Write me as often as you can, if only a note. We like to get letters when we are in a strange land.

Please forgive me for talking so much about myself and my book. I hope I can do a good piece of work, and that any little personal distress does not get the best of me—I do not think it will.

One final thing: please understand—I think you do—that my new book will make use of experience, things I have known and felt, as the first one did—but that now I have created fables and legends and that there will be no question of identification (certainly not in the first two parts) as there was in the first. The David I have referred to is part of me, as indeed are several other characters, but nothing like, in appearance or anything else, what people think me) this is very naive and foolish, and for God's sake keep it to yourself: in making the character of David, I have made him out of the <u>inside</u> of me, of what I have always believed the inside was like: he is about five feet nine, with the long arms and the prowl of an ape, and a little angel in his face—he is part beast, part spirit—a mixture of the ape and the angel—there is a touch of the monster in him)

But no matter about this—at first he is the bard and, I pray God, that is what I can be. Please write me soon I'll tell you how things come

Yours Faithfully, Tom Wolfe

P.S. My book came out in England last Monday, July 14. I hope it goes well and gets good notices, but I have instructed them not to send any reviews—I can't be bothered by it now. Some <u>kind</u> friend probably will send reviews, but I hope for the best.

My address will continue to be The Guaranty Trust Co, Paris I hope you have a nice vacation and get a good rest.

1. Mont-Dore, spa in south-central France.
2. TW is referring to his relationship with Aline Bernstein.
3. Published as a story in *Vanity Fair*, October 1935.
4. The Congo story was published as "The Child by Tiger" in *The Saturday Evening Post*, 11 September 1937. The David character was not retained in *Of Time and the River*.

FROM: John Hall Wheelock   *TLS, 4 pp., Harvard*

July 23, 1930

Dear Tom:

A day or so ago I got your postal card telling of the man in Brooklyn who sent you fourteen closely-typed pages listing two or three thousand alleged mistakes in "Look Homeward Angel." I hope you will send it on to me so that it can be checked up here.[1] I don't doubt that one of the tribe who make a profession of this sort of thing could find a great many errors, typographical and other, if he went over the book with a fine-tooth comb; but then this much could be said of any book, however carefully edited. Unless author and publisher are willing and prepared to devote the rest of their natural lives to the ideal of absolute letter-perfection as regards every semicolon and spacing, there must always be errors.

I was awfully glad, dear Tom, to get your fine long letter of June 24, which I would have answered long ago had it not been for pressure of work and other events. Your daily schedule in Paris sounds good to me and I am tempted to cast off all responsibilities and follow you over.

Of course the tremendous and exciting thing in your letter is the news about the new book - the fact that it is going forward, that you are working on it, and that it is growing from day to day. What you tell me about it stirs me deeply and I can see from the tone of your letter and the mood out of which it is written, that you have got started. Nothing can stop you now I think. There is only one way for a man to work and that is his own natural way, without thinking much about it, and above all without the slightest regard for what others might or will think. You'll always have to pour out your work at white heat, great slags of it, and shape it up afterwards when the more critical part of your mind is clear. At the same time I don't doubt that your experience with "Look Homeward Angel" will stand you in good stead and that you'll find yourself able to rein in a little more as you go along.

One of the sad things about a daily job is that one hasn't the time even to write letters to one's friends - I mean real letters, like the one you have written me. Perhaps you can tell from this how much your letter meant to me. I know that a great book is in process and if there's anything more cheering to know about than that, I have yet to discover it. In many ways, too, it now seems that your going abroad has given you just the right setting for the sort of thing you're trying to say. It brings all these feelings to a focus, to a poignancy which I am sure is nearly unbearable but which will be reflected magnificently in your story.

Dear Tom, we all miss you. We speak of you very often and I have even imagined, on occasions, that I heard your voice in the outer office. I wish it might have been so.

Max is away for a few days and I'm kept pretty busy. We've had some very hot weather but, as you know, the hotter it gets the better I like it. I must have a dash of nigger blood.

All sorts of good wishes, dear Tom.

> As ever,
> Your friend,
> Jack.

P.S. I hope the "Angel" goes well in England. I've read one splendid review so far, but based upon the American edition.

1. TW sent the list because it is now in the Scribner Archives at Princeton. See Appendix 4. None of the errors or inconsistencies was emended in the plates of the first edition.

ALS, 8 pp., Harvard
Harvard Club letterhead

Tuesday July 30th, 1930

Dear Wolfe:—

I had to go to Baltimore for two weeks for medical purposes—not serious. I was never better except my nose which it was thought an expert could improve— + I took with me your letter meaning to answer it there at leisure. It was hardly ever less than 100 + for three days 104 in the shade; + never a drop of rain. The ink in the ink wells coagulated + caked on the pens;— + the hotel stenographer was "overcome" + went to the seashore, + so I came back, letter unwritten, today, + found another letter. Don't think I ever worry about the book.—All you say of it interests me deeply, + in fact excites my imagination. It sounds like a very Leviathan of a book as you describe it, now lying in the depths of your consciousness; + I believe you are the man who can draw out such a Leviathan. So far as I can judge—by a sort of instinct—all you say of your plan + intention is right + true.—But chasten yourself. You know your danger, the rarer sort, comes from lack of restraint. Your talent seems to me a truly great one, + that sort requires to be disciplined + curbed. Length itself is so important as with the first book,—though there is a limit to a volume + I think you'd gain by the compression needed to subscribe to it.—By keeping that always in your mind.

I wish you were here,—that we might now cool ourselves with a long Tom Collins. When will you be here? Baltimore I liked much. I tramped the entire city from waterfront to Druid Hill Park. There seemed to be a sort of kindly preciousness about it,—quite different from the tone of Philadelphia which I hate,— + from that of N.Y. which I like.

I'm glad you saw Scott, but he's in trouble: Zelda is still very seriously ill in a nervous breakdown.[1] I don't know how it will end. Scott is blameable I know for what has come to Zelda, in a sense. But he's a brave man to face trouble as he does, always facing it squarely.—no self-deceptions.

Everything goes on well in the office. Will James "Lone Cowboy"—his autobiography—was taken for August by the Book of the Month Club. It should be a great success, as Van Dine's "Scarab" was this spring,[2]—So in spite of bad business conditions we make out reasonably well.

Ever yours,
Maxwell Perkins

1. Zelda Fitzgerald (1900–1948) was being treated for schizophrenia in a Swiss clinic.
2. *The Scarab Murder Case* by S. S. Van Dine, the pseudonym for Willard Huntington Wright (1888–1939).

ALS, 24 pp., PUL
Hotel Lorius letterhead, Montreux, Switzerland

July 31, 1930

Dear Mr Perkins: Please forgive me for flooding you with letters, but I think the news I send will interest you. I told you before that my book came out in England July 14—I wrote Frere Reeves and told him not to send me any reviews as I am working on a new one; but this morning he sent me a great batch of clippings (20 or more) and a long letter in which he was quite enthusiastic—he said that the book, in spite of its high price on account of its length (10'6d instead of the usual 7'6d), was selling at the rate of 1000 copies every 4 days: if this is true, it is selling faster in England than in America; he also sent one of their advertisements from The <u>Observer</u> (I am sending it to you along with one or two clippings of which I have duplicates: I'll send you the rest a little later) I've read all the clippings over briefly, and they seem to me mighty good—four or five got in some nasty cracks about formlessness and filth, but all were favorable and some of them said things that made my head swim (as good, it seems to me, as the best we had in America) I hope he didn't hand-pick them, to spare my feelings, but he seems to have most of the big ones <u>The Times</u>, <u>The Sunday Times</u>, <u>The Times Literary Supplement</u>, <u>The Sunday Referee</u>, <u>The Morning Post</u>, <u>The Evening Standard</u>, <u>The Evening Telegraph</u>, <u>The Daily Mail</u> etc. I want to send you Richard Aldington's review in <u>The Sunday Referee</u> later (it made me dizzy), but I am sending you today <u>The Times Literary Supplement</u> which Frere Reeves says is the most important in England—it sounds pretty swell to me: please read it and tell me what you think I suppose the book has stopped selling in America: do you think it would be a good idea to print some of these English things (in an ad. under some such heading as <u>What The English are Saying</u>)—do you think it would make some of the snobs buy the book?

I am sending you one of the Heinemann ads together with The Times Supplement—later I'll send the others: do what you think best about it, and write me. I suppose I'm jumping too fast at conclusions—but if this <u>1000</u> every 4 days business keeps up a few weeks I'll have nothing to complain of. I think Frere Reeves and Heinemann have done a mighty fine job. I am an American but I have more English blood in me than the English royal family. They were my heroes, my mighty poets when I was a child, I was so hurt and bitter about them when I saw them after the war—but I cannot deny to you that it would make me happy if the people who invented the language I use liked my work. I do not think there is one God-damned ounce of snobbishness in this! I am very lonely here, but I work; there's nothing else to do. I think if I see it through it will be very good—I am all alone, and sometimes I doubt: do you think I'll ever amount to anything. I read Shakespeare, Racine, the English poets—and The Bible. I have not read the Bible since I was a child—it is the most magnificent book that was ever written: when Walter Scott was dying he called for "The Book," and they asked "What book?" and he said "There is only one"—and it is true. It is richer and grander than Shakespeare even, and everything else looks sick beside it: in the last three days I have read Ecclesiastes and The Song of Solomon several times: they belong to the mightiest poetry that was ever writ-ten—and the narrative passages in the Old Testament—stories like the life of King David, Ruth and Boaz, Esther and Ahasuerus, etc,—make the narrative style of any modern novelist look puny. I am soaking in it, and for the first part of The Octo-ber Fair, which I am calling The Immortal Earth I have chosen this verse from the great book of Ecclesiastes as a title page legend: "One generation passeth away, and another generation cometh: but the earth abideth forever." I am sorry to say that this verse comes immediately before the verse Hemingway used: "The sun also ariseth—" etc; and people will say I have imitated him, but it can't be helped, it is chance, and this is the verse I want.

I am now at work on a section of The Immortal Earth which has the curious title of The Good Child's River—I like the title and hope you will too when you see the story: it is complete in itself, and very long—a short book—and I will send it to you when it's finished. I'm excited about Frere Reeves clippings and letter, and I'm going to take a little trip this afternoon: I'm going to catch a train in a few min-utes + go to the neighboring town of Lausanne and see if there are any pretty girls or women. I am very lusty, the air, the mountains, the quiet, and the very dull very healthy food has filled me with a vitality I was afraid I'd lost; I wish you were here + we could take a walk together—please write me when you can. I am very lonely, but I really think we must have some of it now: I am distressed by some letters + cables from America which say that people are surely to find me if I do not answer at once; I hope to God I can do a good piece—in Ecclesiastes a great passage says: the Fool foldeth his hands and eateth his flesh—and that is what the little sneering Futility—People the world over are doing—I think the Bible has very probably said everything. With their bitter sterile thirst for failure in New York, people, some peo-ple, are waiting with bitter smiles for my ruin and wreck: I will tell you honestly I do [blot] know if they are right or wrong. I myself am in in the process of seeing, but I think the bastards are wrong, and we shall see Nor do I want any little chat-tering ape to talk to me of "nonsense" and "persecution manias"—I say, by God, that they are sterile and that they stink and that they await man's ruin, and that we shall call them loudly by their bestial and abominable names—Here is what I say: I know the waste, the ruin, the tragedy and the defeat of living—but I love life ten thousand times better than death, I had rather draw my breath in agony than not to draw my breath at all, I had rather live than die—and whoever says that is not

<u>faith</u> nor <u>belief</u>—Van Wyck Brooks and all the rest of them, can shove it up their lousy useless posteriors[1]

I have noticed about these dull bastards wherever I've seen them, that they will insist that nothing matters but take great pains to get in out of the rain: nothing really matters, but they will pick out the easiest chair to set their lazy tails in; they are sure there is no good living; but you'll find them on hand at meal time—they could eat their way across the Pampas from Buenos Aires to Rio de Janeiro without even pausing to take a breath.

Write me when you can. I am glad you got a good manuscript, but I hope you won't forget me or cease [blot] my friend. I hope this finds you well and enjoying your vacation. I wish we could drink a big bottle of wine together.

Faithfully yours,
Tom Wolfe

—P.S.—About these people both in England or America who say "This is not a great book" or "great art" or "a work of genius"—I have never said it was; but why should they be so hard and exacting on a young man's book, when they are willing to slobber over any amount of dirty trash:—even Van Doren[2] told me how lucky I was to get so much reputation out of one book, as if the vilest rubbish doesn't get ten times more everywhere you turn. Why have things got to be made so unfair and hard for me?—in addition to my personal troubles, I have to listen to 8000 Jeremiahs yelling "Wait and see . . . We will be pleasantly surprised of course if he amounts to anything, but" etc It makes me vomit! Sometimes I think everyone in the world is that way—their idea of helping you is to kick you in the face: if you survive its because you have been trampled by adversity + they've really done you a good turn. Why shouldnt people in America buy more copies of my book than they have bought? Why should I be so damned humble before them, when they will rush out and buy trash by Wilder[3] or some one else by the millions? Please write to me soon.

1. Literary historian Van Wyck Brooks (1886–1963) was MP's close friend from boyhood and college. Brooks claimed that certain nineteenth-century American writers had been damaged by the lack of cultural values in American life.
2. Critic and historian Carl Van Doren (1885–1950).
3. Thornton Wilder's novel *The Woman of Andros* (1930) was a popular success.

ALS, 8 pp., UNC
Harvard Club letterhead

Aug 8<u>th</u> 1930

Dear Wolfe:—

I'd already seen the English reviews,— + read them with delight. We shall have to make use of them, + also of the fact of the English sale. You should be pleased about them because of two things:—the English have a prejudice against American books still, which gives more meaning to their praise; + their relative remoteness from the scenes + conditions you write about gives them a greater perspective, similar to that given by the passage of time. Another thing.—They are (I think) less perceptive of originality than we.

All these things taken together give their opinion great interest, but the truth is, the Angel—I was looking at the Eng. edition today—bears the marks of astonishing talent, at least, on any page you open at. If they hadn't seen it I'd have thought that surely Old England was done. I'd like to hear from Galsworthy about it.

For God's sake don't think about these people you tell of who would be glad if the new book were not so good. They would only be the jealous people, + of no possible consequence. Why do you bother about them? Make the book what you want it to be. It will be a struggle with such a theme but if you master it— + barring outside complications you will—it will be one of the great books.—How eagerly I shall read the chapter you will send separately that you tell of. How soon will that be? Make it soon if you can.

This I began in N.Y. + could not finish because train time came. I know the bible is grand— + Ecclesiastes seems to say it all. The greatest single piece of writing in the world. I was reading the bible much in Baltimore,—The Gideon Society having put one in my room. Do you remember Melville on Ecclesiastes in Moby Dick, I think? Anyhow the philosophy of it pervades Moby Dick.

––––––

Well, write me when you feel like it, but never by way of an answer. The book is the thing. And remember, I'd rather read any fragment of it you might care to send than even Don Quixhote which I'm reading again, + as if I'd never done it before.

I dined last night with Copeland of Harvard,[1] at Walpole N.H. 30 miles from here. He is so much interested in you on account of your story in Scribners;—for The Angel he said was set in type too small of antique eyes. He said the story alone was enough to convince him of the truth of what I said

––––––

Maybe it's good for your work to be lonely.—But I know it's not fun: I was lonely for sixteen days in Baltimore

Always yours,
Maxwell Perkins

1. Charles Townsend Copeland (1860–1952), Boylston Professor of Rhetoric.

TO: *John Hall Wheelock*   *ALS, 6 pp., PUL*
                              Grand Hotel Bellevue letterhead

Geneva, Aug 18, 1930

Dear Jack: Thanks very much for your good letter. There is very little that I can say to you now, except that ① I have stopped writing and do not want ever to write again. The place that I had found to stay—Montreux—did not remain private very long: ② Fitzgerald told a woman in Paris where I was, and she cabled the news to America—I have had all kinds of letters and cables speaking of death and agony, from people who are perfectly well, and leading a comfortable and luxurious life among their friends at home. In addition, one of Mrs Boyd's "young men" descended upon me, or upon Montreux, and began to pry around. This, of course, may be accident, but too many accidents of this sort have happened.

③ The English edition has been a catastrophe: some of the reviews were good, but some have said things that I shall never be able to forget—dirty, unfair, distorted, and full of mockery. I asked the publisher not to send any reviews, but he did all the same—he even wrote a special letter to send a very bad one, from which he said he got no satisfaction. Nevertheless the book is selling fast and they continue to advertise. All I want now is money—enough to keep me until I get things straight again. It is amusing to see the flood of letters and telegrams I began to get from "old friends" who were "simply dying to see me" when the first good reviews came out in England—it is even more amusing to see how the silence of death has settled upon these same people recently—I want to vomit, I should like to vomit until the thought and memory of them is gone from me forever.

There is no life in this world worth living, there is no air worth breathing, there is nothing but agony and the drawing of the breath in nausea and labor until I get the best of this tumult and sickness inside me. I have behaved all right since I came here—I have lived by myself for almost 4 months now and I have made no enemies: people have charged me and my work with bombast, rant, and noisiness—but save for this letter to you I have lived alone, and held my tongue, and kept my peace: how many of them can say the same? What reward in the world can compensate the man who tries to create something: my book caused hate and rancour at home, venom and malice among literary tricksters in New York, and mockery and abuse over here. I hoped that that book, with all its imperfections, would mark a beginning; instead it has marked an ending. Life is not worth the pounding I have taken both from public and private sources these last two years. But if there is some other life, and I am sure there is, I am going to find it. I am not yet 30, and if these things have not devoured me, I shall find a way out yet. I have loved life and hated death, and I still do.

I have cut off all mail by wiring Paris, and I am going to stay alone for some time to come. I know that that is the only way. Write me if you can   The address is The Guaranty Trust Co, Paris. I hope this finds you well and that you get a good vacation

Ever yours,
Tom Wolfe

ALS, 2 pp., PUL
Grand Hotel Bellevue letterhead

<u>Geneva Aug 18, 1930</u>

Dear Mr Perkins: Will you please have Mr Darrow[1] send me, at his convenience, a statement of whatever money is due me? I shall not write any more books and since I must begin to make other plans for the future, I should like to know how much money I will have. I want to thank you and Scribner's very sincerely for your kindness to me, and I shall hope Someday to resume and continue a friendship which has meant a great deal to me.

I hope this finds you well, and entirely recovered from the trouble that took you to Baltimore. Please get a good vacation and a rest away from the heat and confusion of New York.

Yours Faithfully,

Tom Wolfe.

I have just stopped all mail by telegraph, but my mail will be held for me at the Guaranty Trust Co, Paris, and that will be my address.

1. Whitney Darrow, chief financial officer for Charles Scribner's Sons.

CC, 2 pp., PUL

Aug. 28, 1930

Dear Tom:

If I really believed you would be able to stand by your decision, your letter would be a great blow to me. I cannot believe it, though. If anyone were ever destined to write, that one is you. As for the English reviews, I saw one from an important source which was adverse,- though it recognized the high talent displayed. It argued that the book was at fault because it was chaotic and that the function of an artist is to impose <u>order</u>. That was the only review that could be called unfavorable, and as I say, it recognized that the book showed great talent. Otherwise the reviews—and I must have seen all the really important ones—were very fine.

For heaven's sake write me again. I am sending you herewith a royalty report showing the money due.

Always and anxiously yours,

[Maxwell Perkins]

FROM: John Hall Wheelock   *CCS, 6 pp., PUL*

August 28, 1930

Dear Tom:

I was distressed and saddened by your letter of August 18, but at the same time I could not help being pleased that you have sufficient confidence in me to unburden yourself thus frankly as to a real friend, which I hope I am. Although the bitterness and vehemence of your letter was something of a shock, I must confess that I was not entirely surprised. As we get older there are fewer and fewer things that surprise us. Then, too, I have some understanding of the excitements, sufferings, and nauseas to which the man who is trying to do the almost impossible is subject.

I'm awfully sorry, dear Tom, that you have been bothered by all these people and I can sympathize with your feeling—at having your privacy broken into this way. It sometimes does seem as if privacy and solitude were conditions which have been permanently lost for any of us. There is nothing quite so depressing—almost degrading—as the constant intrusion upon one's state of mind by well-meaning and otherwise-disposed "friends." Can't you make another move, in great secrecy, and escape all this sort of thing, for a while at least?

I find it more difficult to feel with you in your decision not to write any more, and if I really believed this decision to be final and not the reaction from a mood, I should be more than unhappy. You are one of the few men of genius writing in English to-day. I am not saying that there are no faults in your first book; doubtless there are many which might be pointed out by careful analysis; but they are all faults which are the reverse of great qualities, qualities very rare to-day, such as vigor, profusion and vitality. Your book has had a remarkable reception in this country and has moved thousands of people. At the age of thirty you have taken your place among the best writers of our day, and have all the future before you in which to discipline your art and progress to even finer things. Your book is doing excellently in England, from all reports, and had a review in the London Times which might be considered flattering from any source, but from this particular source (usually so captious towards American work) amounts to superlative praise.[1] Why in God's name should you allow yourself to be cast down by a few unintelligent or prejudiced English reviews? The greatest writers of all periods have been subjected to just this sort of thing but have had the courage and the serenity to come through it and to weigh it for what it is worth, which isn't much. I hardly think you will go the way of Keats, you are built of more vigorous stuff, without forfeiting any of his sensitiveness. It would certainly be a tragedy if the forces of ignorance and second-rate criticism were going to prove stronger than the creative energy of our best men. Yet your confession would seem to imply that such was the situation. I know this frame of mind will be very temporary with you.

I think you will need only one thing, Tom, and that is isolation from the artificial world of letters—not from the actual world. Don't receive any reviews; don't read any reviews; don't see any literary or writing people; enjoy life as you go along and devote a part of your time to regular work on your new novel, proceeding with it serenely or stormily as the mood may take you, but in absolute nonchalance where the opinions of literary critics are concerned.

Dear Tom, isn't it a grand thing to be a poet or a writer and you are both! Surely you must realize the tremendous impression that your book has made, both here and in England, and is destined to make in other countries too (we received yesterday an interested letter from a German publisher). Yet even if your book had had the most unfriendly reception, or had fallen absolutely flat, you ought not be prevented from going forward with what you had in mind. There will be moods of depression and even despair, but then you can't expect to achieve anything as important and as fine as a really good book without suffering on the way. I wish we could have a good talk; it would be so much more satisfactory than a letter. I shall be thinking of you very often during my vacation at the seashore, and hoping that things are a little less oppressive.

Many good wishes to you, dear Tom. As ever,

Yours,

J.H.W.

To Mr. Thomas Wolfe,
c/o Guaranty Trust Company,
4 Place de la Concorde,
Paris, France.

1. The unsigned review praises *Look Homeward, Angel* as "a most remarkable manifestation, for here we have a talent of such torrential energy as has not been seen in English literature for a long time" (*London Times*, 22 July 1930, p. 19).

TLS, 4 pp., Harvard

Sept. 10, 1930

Dear Tom:

I wrote you very hurriedly at the end of August: I was then on the edge of a ten days' vacation which is now ended. I hoped when I got back there might be another letter telling me you felt differently than in your last, and I have had that letter on my mind ever since you wrote it. I could not clearly make out why you had come to your decision, and surely you will have to change it;- but certainly there never was a man who had made more of an impression on the best judges with a single book, and at so early an age. Certainly you ought not to be affected by a few unfavorable reviews—even apart from the overwhelming number of extremely and excitedly enthusiastic reviews.- By the way, Scott Fitzgerald wrote me how much better things were with him now;- but most of his letter was taken up with you. I daresay it would be a good thing if you could avoid him at present, but he was immensely impressed with you, and with the book,- and however you may regard him as a writer, he is certainly a very sensitive and sure judge of writers.- Not that there is any further need of confirmation with respect to you. There is no doubt of your very great possibilities,- nor for that matter of the great accomplishment of the "Angel."

Somewhere, perhaps to Jack, you referred to a young man of our friend Madeleine's having run you down and taken observations. I daresay this was not pleasant, but I have seen the letter he wrote her—she came in with it—and it was extremely interesting. He also has great admiration for you, and he quoted some of your sayings which I could recognize as authentic, and which were extremely discerning. There was one about Scott.

It seems rather futile to write this letter in view of your having stopped all communications. I hope somehow it will break through to you. If you do not write me some good news pretty soon, I shall have to start out on a spying expedition myself. You know it has been said before that one has to pay somehow for everything one has or gets, and I can see that among your penalties are attacks of despair,- as they have been among the penalties great writers have generally had to pay for their talent.

Please do write me.

Always your friend,
Maxwell Perkins

⌒⌒

TO: *Maxwell Perkins*   *Cable, PUL*
13 September 1930   *Freiburg, Germany*

WORKING AGAIN EXCUSE LETTER WRITING YOU
    TOM ROLFE

⌒⌒

TLS, 1 p., Harvard

Sept. 27, 1930

Dear Tom:

For Heaven's sake send us some word. I got your cable which said you were writing,- and said you were working. But no letter has come, and I am as worried again as I was before. I wish you would come back here now and live in the country. I could show you some fine country that would suit you. Please do write me the moment you get this. Send some word if only a postcard.

Ever yours,
Maxwell Perkins

Cable draft, 1 p., PUL

Oct. 8, 1930

Mr. Thomas Wolfe
Guaranty Trust Co.
Paris France
How are you Please write
Max

Cable, PUL
London

14 October 1930

ESTABLISHED SMALL FLAT HERE ALONE IN HOUSE OLD WOMAN
LOOK AFTER ME SEEING NOONE BELIEVE BOOK FINALLY COMING
EXCITED TOO EARLY TO SAY LETTER FOLLOWS GUARPAMAL LON-
DON[1] FAITHFULLY.
    TOM.

1. Cable address for the Guaranty Trust Co., 50 Pall Mall.

ALS, 7 pp., PUL

London, S. W. 1   The Guaranty Trust Co.   50 Pall Mall
Dear Mr Perkins: I am writing you a separate letter telling you what there is to be
told at present about myself. This concerns another matter. Two swindling New
York dentists are trying to extort $525 from me for two weeks incompetent and
shoddy work. I left instructions with Mr Darrow to pay them, but fortunately told
him not to go beyond $200 which I thought would leave a big surplus. Now these
dentists are threatening ominous things if I do not pay in full at once. I have written them courteously telling them I have not money enough to pay such a bill, and
have never had (one of them had just come back from his vacation when I left, business was bad, I think he intended me to pay for it)
    In letters to Mr Darrow they are threatening to "put the matter in the hands
of their Paris representative"—why Paris, I dont know: I don't live there + have no
connection there. I am assured here in London that they can touch nothing in
Europe—letter of credit, personal belongings. Now I have been worried enough—
I am not trying to avoid payment of any just debt, but I tell you this thing is an
abomination: one man has charged $285 for seeing me five times and doing an
incompetent piece of work. If I have any money in America—i.e. at Scribner's—I
want it to be protected against these people by any means possible. I do not know
the law, but I know that I have the right to dispose of my money as I see fit and I

am therefore sending you a separate statement in which I make over to you any money that is due me. These people are trying to get money from me that I cannot afford to lose, I left enough to pay them amply, the thing is a cheat. Let's don't let them do it: please get my money made over to you if that is necessary to protect it—you could let me have it as I need it. I would not bother you, but they would not be able to touch it. I wish to God I could have a little peace—I am writing you a long letter. I shall finish that book, so help me God, and if agony and loneliness can make a book, it will be good. You are the only person in the world that I can turn to—I am a solitary and an exile, people in comfortable homes surrounded by friends, may sneer, but its the simple God's truth. The weather here is like a sodden blanket of wet grey, misery is on the faces of the poor, the King opened parliament today, there is only one thrilling and interesting place in the world—and that is America, but I am not [cast] down, and I will do the book. Only now, now, is the time they must not bother me. I am writing you a long letter—I cannot begin to tell you how I miss seeing you, it is unfair to make you the goat this way

Faithfully Tom Wolfe—75, Ebury St

I, Thomas Wolfe, hereby instruct Charles Scribner's Sons, Publishers, to pay over to my friend Maxwell Evarts Perkins all money that is due to me, or will be due to me, from the publication of any work of mine; Said money to be used, administered, and governed by Maxwell Evarts Perkins as he sees fit

Thomas Wolfe
Oct 27, 1930

TO: Alfred Dashiell   ALS, 20 pp., PUL
November 1930

London—The Guaranty Trust Co. 50 Pall Mall

Dear Fritz: Please forgive me for not having answered your fine long letter before—I have done very little letter writing of any sort to anyone for some time: at one time I wanted to take my pen in hand and "tell you all about it," but telling you all about it seems such a long and complicated business just now that I must wait until I see you, and then I hope they are still running that German place and that I can talk eloquently until I see signs of fatigue and care on your face.

I have been here in this great cit-ee for about two months. I have a bally little digs on Ebury Street (hyah, hyah!) and for over five weeks I have been working like the son-of-a-bitch many charming but mis-guided bastards consider me. November—lovely London November—soft, wet, woolly, steamy, screamy, shitty November—is here: if you have ever contemplated horror and weariness, if you have ever thought of such jolly subjects as misery, damnation, and death, if you have ever wanted to curse God and die, you have really known nothing but a spirit of rollicking comedy, a child's happy prattle—you have not known London in November. You draw your breath in agony and despair, you walk the leaden air as if you were forcing your way step by step through a ponderous, resisting, and soul-destroy-ing mush: it soaks into your skin, your legs, your bowels, it gets into your heart, it is a grey mucousy substance in which you smother in ennui and dull horror as if you are slowly drawing in some ocean of obscene and unspeakable substance: if, in addition to this, you are invited to a Sunday afternoon tea in a detached "villa" belonging to a literary architect in St. Johns Wood, a gent who has written a novel that was well spoken of, and who wears grey-looking glasses on his grey looking face, if you meet there his wife who also has glasses and a grey face, and their little child, also with glasses, if you drink the weak tea and eat the cold Sunday night lamb, if you hear Mama telling the infant the quaintest cunningest bedtime story—all about a character named Oyjee-Boyjee—Mama invented him and each night he must do the <u>very dullest</u> thing you can think of ("it's really awfully hard," Mama said, "to think of a dull thing every night"—to which I made no reply)—if, I say, you have gone through this, and talked about Art and Life by the cheerful fumes of the gas burner by which London warms itself, if you have sat in the parlour reeking with its grave damp chill, if then you go out in the steaming air into a street of vil-las, catch your bus, and ride home through vast areas of drab brick, lightened by an occasional pub in which you see a few sodden wretches mournfully ruminant over a glass of bitter beer—if you have gone through this, then, my boy, you will smite your brow, and rend your flesh to see the blood come, and cry, "O woe is me! O misery!," and your guts will ache with passion for the Happy Land, the beautiful glorious country with the bright Sunday evening wink of the Chop Suey signs, the roar of the elevated, the sounds of the radio, the homelike jolly glow of the deli-catessen stores, and the peaceful noise of millions of Jews in the Bronx slowly turn-ing the 237 pages of the New York Sunday Times. Thank God you live in the beautiful and interesting place where all these things are accessible; and also thank God for the great Sounds that roar across America, the howl and sighing at the eaves, the lash and din of it at the corners, the bite and sparkle of the air, the sharp color of October, the baying of the great boats in the harbor, the thunder of the great trains in the night—the exulting and joy that grips your guts and makes you cry out—and when you see some bastard who tells you lies about Europe, and worse lies about America, when you see some fool who wants to leave the most interesting and glorious place on earth to live here—remember what I have told you: spit in his face—no, piss on him instead, for the carcass of such a lying degen-erate must not be dignified by spittle from the lips of an honest man.

I have been shy and silent before these liars and fools far too long—I have eaten crow and swallowed my pride for ten years before the wastelanders, the lost gener-ationers, the bitter-bitters, the futility people, and all other cheap literary fakes sick-lied o'er with a pale cast of Stein-shit[1]—but now I will hold my tongue no longer: I know what I know, and I have learned it with blood and sweat. I have lived alone in a foreign land until I could not sleep for thinking of the sights and sounds and colors—the whole intolerable memory of America—its violence, savagery, immen-sity, beauty, ugliness, and glory—and I tell you I know it as if it were my child, as if it had been distilled from my blood and marrow: I know it from the look and smell of the railway ties to the thousand sounds and odours of the wilderness—and

I tell you I had rather have ten years more of life there than fifty years of continental weak tea and smothering in this woolly and lethargic air, than a hundred years of shitty expatriatism: you have seen them in Paris sitting on their rumps around the cafe tables and pretending to know France and Europe—they know nothing, and as for the superior European "culture" some of them profess their love for—how many of them do you think give one good God damn for it: they do not know either Europe or France their life is a vile cardboard affair, the French hate and despise them and they know it—but they are like pimps who will endure slaps, insults, and mockery so long as they can have their whore. I tell you this "living abroad" business is bloody balls: I know something about Europe. I have gone alone and known some of the Europeans—at least I know more of their language, literature, and ways of living than most of our Paris friends—and I have heard all their stale jargon—that we are "not a country," that we are base and mean, that there is no glory, dignity, or beauty in our life, that we are Puritans, Babbitts, Rotarians, etc, etc—but these people know nothing of anything, they have read it all in books—and they know less than nothing of America: I tell you we have got to live in our own country and be what we are, and that no one who has ever known and felt America can find living in Europe as interesting or beautiful.

I am certainly not bitter against Europe at the present time and in spite of my violent attack on English dulness, I have an enormous liking and sympathy for them—they have been most kind and friendly this time, I do not go out often, but there are a few people I can go to see and talk to, which is a comfort after many months of being alone. There are also other blessings: I have the top two floors of a tiny little house on Ebury Street, it is nicely furnished, and I am completely alone in it at night; also I have a char-woman who cooks for me, brings her darling tea in his little beddy, coddles and coaxes him, and is in fact a perfect priceless damned Kohinoor—all, house, woman, etc for £3,14s a week. I stay in from 6 oclock on, read, eat the meal she has left for me, or cook one of my own, brew vast quantities of tea and coffee and at midnight—the present hour—when all outside is quiet save for the massive footfalls of the bobby, and a few gay dogs reeling home from the American talkies—I set to work and work—with time off for tea, coffee, or beer until broad daybreak. Then I see life awaken in a London street—which is one of the nicest things I have seen: I see the light come on the yellow walls and the smoking brick, the milk wagon comes through with the milkman making a funny cry, and I hear the sound of a horse in the empty street—a sound that makes me think of a thousand mornings in American streets. Then the housemaids come out and scrub, the shops open, the noise begins. I light the "geyser,"[2] have a bath, and go to bed, where my charwoman finds me, brings me tea and toast, all gossip to her pet about the movie she saw last night

Farewell, dear Fritz: Someday, some faroff future day, Tommy is coming sailing home again, and then I will tell you all about it. There is no joy in the world comparable to the cessation of intolerable pain—sometimes I think that is what joy is the way you feel, how beautiful and glorious life is, after the tooth stops aching—and that is what it will be like when I come home again: the most exultant, the most glorious, the most incredibly magnificent experience in the modern world is the voyage to America, and I pity the poor wretches who will never know it. If you speak of me to anyone, for God's sake do not communicate any of this letter to people who would use it to mock at and injure me: I mean the futility boys and girls, the sterility lasses, the elegant mockers, the American T. S. Elioters—they are a low but vilely cunning lot of bastards and they will not see their cheap little stock in trade—I mean the what-is-the-use-we-are-a-doomed-generation-life-here-is-a-barren-desert-we-can-do-nothing—they will not see their little business cursed without a hissing and jeering retaliation: it is all they have, and even vermin will bare their teeth and bite if their stale cheese is menaced, even bawds and pimps will fight to protect the commerce of the drab who feeds them.

You know that I am no Polly-anna now, or that I think God's in his heaven. I don't, and I agree with Ecclesiastes that the saddest day of a man's life is the day of his birth—but after that, I think the next saddest day is the day of his death. I have had some bad times recently, but I think I shall always love life and hate death, and I believe that is an article of faith. The futility people hate life, and love death, and yet they will not die; and I loathe them for it. Observe carefully: you will find that the man who kills himself is almost always the man who loves life well. The futility-people do not kill themselves: they wear rubbers and are afraid of colds. The waste-lander does not waste himself: it is the lover of life who wastes himself, who loves life so dearly that he will not hoard it, whose belief in life is so great that he will not save his own: I mean Christ and Coleridge and Socrates and Dostoievsky and Jeb Stuart and David Crockett. My! how the boys would snicker if they could hear that!

Goodbye for the present, Fritz. We'll drink beer again at Weber's some happy day, and we'll be a couple of damned tourists together, and we'll stand on the bridges of Paris at midnight again, and remember the voices of men in Virginia, and the smell of the tar in the streets. Give my love to Corey, and tell Max Perkins that I will really write him—if I could only say in a letter all I want to say to him!—and that I am really working, and sometimes I am full of joy and hope about it, and other times depression, but that I shall finish it (when, I don't know) and that it will have to have in it the things that are bursting in my heart and mind. Forgive this long and violent letter, I did not mean to write it myself when I started, remember me to the folks at Scribners, and love again and good wishes to you and the family. I have Scotch blood in me, and often I see spooks: there is a happy land, there is a good life, and better times are coming for all men of good will.   Yours Ever, Tom Wolfe

1. Gertrude Stein (1874–1946), modernist American writer who influenced expatriate writers.

2. Hot water heater.

TLS, 3 pp., Harvard

Nov. 12, 1930

Dear Tom:

I have your letter about the bill, but don't worry over it.- We investigated the party and found that he was supposed to be highly reputable, but very high priced.- But now we are trying to effect some kind of a compromise. But anyhow, you are making too much of it, I think. I do not believe for a moment that they have any Paris representative who could do anything, or any other foreign representative. Let the thing ride if you like, and it will be fixed up when you get back some way. Come back with the novel finished and that amount of money will seem trifling. I enclose herewith some remarks about the "Angel" by Mr. Sinclair Lewis, who recently wrote to congratulate us on publishing it. When they interviewed him about getting the Nobel prize, he immediately began to talk about your book, and only mentioned one or two others at all. We put out what he said in an ad.[1]

When are you likely to come back? Everything goes on here well enough in spite of the extremely severe business depression. A man in our cashier's department took away sixty-one thousand of our dollars and lost all of them in the stock market. Ernest Hemingway, motoring in Montana at night, went off the road in the glare of an approaching car and down into a gulley, and came out with a very badly broken arm. Dos Passos was with him, but not hurt; but Ernest has been suffering a great deal in a hospital in Billings. I suppose you saw that the election all went the right way in respect to prohibition, and in other respects too, from my point of view.[2]

Always yours,
Maxwell Perkins

1. On 6 November 1930 *The New York Times* quoted Lewis: "I don't see why he should not be one of the greatest world writers. His work is so deep and spacious that it deals with the whole of life" (p. 27 from metropolitan edition). Scribners issued the quote on a wrap-around band for *Look Homeward, Angel.*
2. In the 1930 election Democrats gained control of the House of Representatives and eight seats in the Senate.

TLS, 3 pp., Harvard

Dec. 4, 1930

Dear Tom:

When you write again—and may it be soon—tell me when you think you may come home. We all want greatly to see you, but you may decide to stay the full year and finish everything completely.- If so we shall be patient.

The Colums[1] have gone to France, but after a little they are to be in England, and as soon as I have their address (they have only just sailed), I am going to send them yours, for I know you would enjoy talking to them immensely, and that only good could come of it.- And by the way, Mrs. Colum in particular is a tremendous admirer of your book.

I have seen Kang every now and then, in the course of getting along with "The Grass Roof."[2] He always asks about you, and I tell him what I can. His book is very fine, with a quality of its own. He has completely finished with the proof now, and it won't be so very long before we shall have copies. I shall send one to you though he is sure to do it himself.

Jim Boyd, I hear, is now back in Southern Pines after a very very bad summer with sinus.- And even now he has not got the best of it, though some good seems to have been accomplished by a French physician. I guess you must have seen him before he was anything like his worst which was mighty bad.

I told you about Hemingway's accident.- He is still in the hospital, in fact in bed.

Asheville, as you prophesied, seems to be absolutely flatened out.- They cannot even pay those on the city payroll, according to reports.- But nobody over here is so very far from ruin apparently. Jack complains that you said you were writing him, and never did it.- But do let someone here hear from you when you can.- And may all go well with you.

Always yours,
Maxwell Perkins

1. Padraic (1881–1972) and Mary Colum (1884–1957), critics who were friends of MP.

2. *The Grass Roof* (Scribners, 1931) by Younghill Kang (1903–1972). TW met Kang while both worked in the English Department at New York University and introduced him to MP.

ALS, 34 pp., PUL

London, Tues Dec 9
1930

Dear Mr Perkins: I am sure this is a bad year and that all the bad news is coming at once—there is only three weeks more of it, and then things, I know, will get better. For one thing, some time next year I hope to come home again and end this some-times ghastly pain of homesickness. I am working like hell and I hope it will be worth something when I get it down. Before I go on with the letter I want to get something off my mind: my family have suffered the most terrible calamities—they have simply been wiped out. Mabel and Ralph[1] (that is my sister) have been sold out in Asheville, they have lost everything they had, every piece of property, every cent of money, and he has lost his job: they are at present living in Washington where he is trying to earn a $50 a week commission salary; my other sister's big fam-ily have been for the most part out of work, and my brother Fred has been struggling to keep them up. In addition he has had to quit his job because there is no business—things in the South are in a horrible hell of a shape, and the last calamity I read of was that the leading bank at Asheville where I am afraid they had some money has smashed. Now these people are too good and too proud to ask for anything—their letters have been full of courage and cheerfulness, but they are simply wiped out. Two or three months ago from Paris, when I thought my profits on the English publication were much greater than they turned out to be, I wrote Fred and told him for God's sake to let me know if he needed money and I would let him have what I could. He wrote me the other day and assured me none of them is in actual want for food or clothing—thank God for that!—then he asked me, if I really had the money, would I let him have $500 for a year—he sent along some damned document giving me security, 8% interest, etc—of course, I won't have the damned thing, nor a penny's interest; I tore it up.

Mr Perkins, I know its a bad year for everyone, but <u>if I've got it there</u> at Scribner's, or even if I haven't got it, for God's sake get that money for the boy, and I will work my fingers to the bone: if it comes to a question of these damned lying cheating swine of dentists and my own people, <u>I want my people to have the money</u>: please understand my people have not asked me for a damned penny, and my brother wrote me only when I had written him and assured him that I could spare the money and would not forgive him if they needed it and would not speak—at that time I thought I would have more—but no matter: if I am able to help these people now it is a Godsend for me, and if I don't do it I shall regret it bitterly as long as I live. I think you understand how much joy it gives me to think I may be of a little help now in time of trouble—we have always stood together in trouble before, and I don't want to fail them now. There is no question about Fred paying me back someday—he would do that if he had to mortgage his right arm—but even if he never did it would be all right and I dont want his damned notes or mortgages or interest. He has never asked me nor anyone else for anything before, and he has got everybody's burden on him now, I know he would not ask unless he were hard pressed—I wrote him the other day and told him not to worry, that I could afford it and it wouldn't pinch me, and that I would get you to send him $500— <u>please</u> do this for me, and I will make it up to you somehow: I'm a young man and I have never failed anyone yet to whom I was indebted—I don't mean these low cunning bastards of dentists, and it will be a damned shame if these rich unscrupulous swindlers get my money while my family is down and out: if its a question of deciding between the two of them, send my brother the money, and let the dentists go to hell and sue me—I'll tell you more about these fine lads later, and what a dentist here says about it.

Now don't get worried and think I'm going to flop on you and be a sponge— I'll make this $500 up to you in extra work and sweat: I can't promise to write a good or a great book or even one that will sell, but if that fails, I'll make it up to you in some other way. There's money in me somewhere if I'm put to it—I've always believed I could make it if I had to. I want you to know this: I believe I have acted decently and honestly to everyone—certainly I have tried to—if you hear scurrilous and slanderous stories about me, about any action of mine, about anything to do with me spread by any of the ten million envenomed and reptilian Madame B——ds[2] who walk the streets of this earth full of hate, malice, and poison, put them down as lies: I have been in a hell of a jam this last year or so, and during the last six or eight months I have sweated out blood and agony—but <u>I have behaved all right</u>: I have done what I thought I had to do, and what people asked me to do, I have never betrayed or deserted anyone—in the end, if anyone gets betrayed or deserted it will be me. I have done the best I could, I have done some things badly, but please understand that I have behaved all right: if anyone thinks I have not let him come forward and say so to my face—otherwise let them hold their tongues in fairness, and someday they will know I have been square. You know me much better now than any of these people, you know what a nest of lies and venom New York is, for God's sake make any judgment or opinion on me for yourself, and out of our own relation— you are my friend, and one of the two or three people that I would not let any one in the world say a word against, so until I get back at least don't listen to opinions and judgments from <u>people who</u> don't know a God damned thing about me, whether Scott Fitzgerald, Madame B, or anyone else.[3]—Please dont be alarmed at all this, or think I've gone suddenly mad—there's so much I want to say to you and so little I can say in a letter that part of it comes in convulsions and bursts—I seem to have to spend a maddening amount of time talking about dentists, and making foolish answers—I should like to tell you about the book, but I'll have to write another letter But here is the title, at any rate, and it seems to me to be a good and beautiful title and to say what I want it to say—if anything about it puzzles you I'll try to interpret all of it for you next time. Here it is:

<u>The</u> <u>October</u> <u>Fair</u>
<u>or</u>
<u>Time and the River</u>: <u>a Vision</u>:
Italics { The Son, The Lover, and The Wanderer;
{ The Child, The Mistress, and The Woman;
{ The Sea, The City, and The Earth.

"one generation passeth away,
and another generation cometh;
but the earth abideth for ever"

for title
page

Part One

<u>ANTAEUS</u>

"Who knoweth the spirit of man that goeth upward, and the spirit of the beast that goeth downward to the earth?"[4]—(small italics for title page of <u>Antaeus</u>)

(If this <u>argument</u> seems bad or inadvisable we wont use it. It gives a kind of key)

Argument: of the Libyan giant, the brother of Polyphemus, the one eyed, and the son of Gaea and Poseidon, whom he hath never seen, and through his father, the grandson of Cronos and Rhea, whom he remembereth. He contendeth with all who seek to pass him by, he searcheth alway for his father, he crieth out: "Art thou my father? Is it thou?" And he wrestleth with that man, and he riseth from each fall with strength redoubled, for his strength cometh up out of the earth, which is his mother. Then cometh against him Heracles, who contendeth with him, who discovereth the secret of his strength, who lifteth him from the earth whence his might ariseth, and subdueth him. But from afar now, in his agony, he heareth the sound of his fathers foot: he will be saved for his father cometh!

Now, don't get alarmed at all this and think I'm writing a Greek Myth. All of this is never mentioned once the Story gets under way, but it is a magnificent fable, and I have soaked myself in it over a year now: it says what I want to say, and it gives the most magnificent plot and unity to my book. The only other way in which the Antaeus legend is mentioned directly is in the titles to the various parts which are, tentatively, at present—① Antaeus, ② Heracles, (or Faust and Helen), ③ Poseidon

To give you the key to all these symbols and people—Antaeus of course, is a real person, that he is in me but he is <u>not</u> me as the fellow in the first book was supposed to be—he is to me what Hamlet or Faust may have been to their authors—Thank God, I have begun to create in the way I want to—it is more completely <u>autobiographic</u> than anything I have ever thought of, much <u>more</u> than the first one—but it is also completely <u>fictitious</u>—nobody can identify me with Antaeus—whose real name is David Hawke, but who is called Monkey Hawke—except to say. "He has put himself into this character." It is a magnificent story, it makes use of all the things I have seen and known about, and it is like a fable—The other symbols are:

Heracles, who is the City: Poseidon, who is the Sea, eternal wandering, eternal change, eternal movement—but who is also a real person (<u>never</u> called Poseidon) of course, the father of Monkey Hawke, whom he has never seen, and whom, I have decided he shall never see, but who is near him at the end of the book, and who saves him (the idea that hangs over the book from first to last is that every man is searching for his father)—It is immensely long, I am bringing the Antaeus (which has two parts back home with me) and parts of the second—the City scenes are already written. The woman in various forms, at different times, is Gaea, Helen, or Demeter—but these things are never told you, and the story itself is direct and simple, given shape by this legend, and by the idea I told you—but it is also tremendously varied—it gives the histories of my people and it reconstructs old time—the idea of time—the lost and forgotten moments of peoples lives, the strange brown light of old time (i.e—America, say, in 1893—photographs of people coming across Brooklyn Bridge, the ships of the Hamburg American packet co, baseball players with moustaches, men coming home to lunch at noon in small towns, red barns, old circus posters) and many other phases of time is over all the book. I'd like to tell you of a chapter I'm now writing in the Second part of <u>Antaeus</u>—the chapter is called Cronos and Rhea (or perhaps simply <u>Time and the River</u>—that means <u>Mem-</u>

<u>ory and Change</u>)—my conviction is that a native has the whole consciousness of his people and nation in him—that he knows everything about it—every sight sound and memory of the people—don't get worried: I think this is going to be all right—you see, I <u>know</u> now past any denial, that <u>that</u> is what being an American or being anything means: it is not a government, or the Revolutionary War, or the Monroe doctrine—it is the ten million seconds and moments of your life—the shapes you see, the sounds you hear, the food you eat, the colour and texture of the earth you live in—I tell you <u>this</u> is what it is, and this is what homesickness is, and by God I'm the world's champion authority on the subject at present. <u>Cronos and Rhea</u> occurs on board an Atlantic liner—all the Americans returning home—and the whole intolerable memory of exile and nostalgia comes with it: it begins like a chant—first the smashing enormous music of the American names—first the names of the state—California, Texas, Oregon, Nebraska, Idaho, and the Two Dakotas—then the names of the Indian tribes—the Pawnees, the Cherokees, the Seminoles, the Penobscots, the Tuscaroras, etc—then the names of railways—the Pennsylvania, the Baltimore and Ohio, the Great Northwestern, the Rock Island, the Santa Fe, etc—then the names of the railway millionaires—the Vanderbilts, the Astors, the Harrimans; then the names of the great hoboes—Oakland Red, Fargo Pete, Dixie Joe, Iron Mike, Nigger Dick, the Jersey Dutchman etc—(the names of some of the great wanderers i.e)—then the great names of the rivers (the rivers and the sea standing for movement and wandering against the fixity of the earth)—the Monongahela, the Rappahannock, the Colorado, the Tennessee, the Rio Grande, the Missouri—when I get to the Mississippi I start the first of the stories of wandering and return—the woman floating down the river with her husband in flood time tells it, it is good—the whole thing is this pattern of meaning and narration—don't get alarmed, I think it's all right and fits in perfectly, I have plenty of straight story anyway I have told you too much and too little—I have had to scrawl this down and haven't time to explain dozens of things—but please dont be worried—its not anarchy, its a perfectly unified but enormous plan. I want to write again and tell you some more, especially about the last scene in Poseidon—it is the only fabulous scene in the book, he never sees his father but he hears the sound of his foot the thunder of horses on a beach (Poseidon and his horses) the moon drives out of clouds, he sees a print of a foot that can belong only to his father since it is like his own, the sea surges across the beach and erases the print, he cries out <u>Father</u> and from the sea far out, and faint upon the wind, a great voice answers "My Son!" That is briefly the end as I see it—but cant tell you anything about it now—the rest of the story is natural and wrought out of human experience—Polyphemus, by the way, the one eyed brother of Antaeus, represents the principle of sterility that hates life—i.e. waste landerism, futility-ism, one-eyedism (also a character in the book)

I don't know whether you can make anything out of this or not—I have worked all night it is 10:30 oclock as I finish this on the morning of Tues Dec 9, there is a fog outside that you can cut, you can't see across the street, I am dog tired—I want to come home when I know I have this thing by the well known balls—write me if you think its a good idea, but say nothing to anyone.

I'm a week late with this letter, I don't want my brother to suffer—<u>please</u> Mr

Perkins send him $500 at once if you can—address <u>Fred W. Wolfe, 48 Spruce Street Asheville North Carolina</u>—get it to him before Christmas   I'm writing you about dentists—but don't pay them if my brother has to suffer.

I'm sending this out right away to be mailed. I hope this finds you well, I'd like to be able to see and talk to you.

As Ever Faithfully,
Tom Wolfe

The Guaranty Trust Co
50 Pall Mall
London

<u>Address again</u>

Fred W. Wolfe
48 Spruce St
Asheville
N. C.

Don't tell anyone about this letter—If I've talked foolishness I'd rather keep it between us—at ten in the morning after being up all night you're not sane.

1. Mabel Wolfe Wheaton and Ralph Wheaton.
2. Literary agent Madeleine Boyd had placed *Look Homeward, Angel* with Scribners; after TW discharged her over mishandling of his royalties, she incurred his permanent enmity by claiming continuing commissions on his work.
3. In his notebooks for 1930–1931, TW recorded his interpretation of MP's motivation for arranging a meeting between TW and Fitzgerald:

> I will tell you a little story:
> There was once a young man who came to have a feeling of great trust and devotion for an older man. He thought that this older man had created liberty and hope for him. He thought that this older man was brave and loyal. Then he found that this older man had sent him to a drunken and malicious fellow, who tried to injure and hurt his work in every way possible. He found moreover that this older man had sent him to this drunk in order to get the drunk's "opinion" of him. That is the real end of the story (*Notebooks*, p. 511).

4. Eccelsiastes 3:21.

TLS, 2 pp., Harvard

Dec. 23, 1930

Dear Tom:

Delighted to get letters even though they do not sound very happy.- Better come back soon and spend an evening with me at "63." I certainly look forward to that time, however distant. Fred has already received his five hundred, and that is why I am writing this note, for I am too rushed to say much more.

I do not understand all this talk about M.B. and F.S.F., but I am not in a position to listen to what anybody says, having formed my own opinion for good with respect to T.W.

Every time you write about the book, I get as excited as I did when I began "The Angel." I wish to thunder you would come back with the ms.

Always yours,
Maxwell Perkins

TO: *John Hall Wheelock*
December 1930

Christmas card, PUL
London

Dear Jack: I owe you a letter, or two letters—Ill write after the New Years—I am writing like a madman but whether its good or bad I don't know—I am a tissue of bright blood and agony. I miss ten thousand things about America, so much that it hurts!—its like an abscess! I shall have a quarter of a million or 300000 words ready for your inspection by next Fall—whether good or bad words I don't know I've got cold and fever from this sodden wet wool of steaming and unutterable dreariness that they call a climate—I pity the poor dreary bastards who for the most part populate these isles, the poor whining, worn out creatures as I would pity some blind [sucking] sea creature that leeches to the body of great fish below the sea—enough has happened to me, I'll tell you about it, and at present I'm in great demand with the Russians—too great demand for I don't know when I may come home and find sinister faces lurking in the hallways. I have no friends, I trust as friends not even three or four people in the world but there are millions of people who want to pry in and feed off young blood and marrow.

The main thing is to work in the face of all manner of disaster—if we can do that we we save ourselves—I believe in a much better and more beautiful life than these people know about, I am willing to spend my life finding it.

Good luck and love, dear Jack, and a happy Christmas
Tom Wolfe

FROM: *John Hall Wheelock*

TLS, 3 pp., Harvard

December 24, 1930

Dear Tom:

It is fine to have your Christmas card with the brief letter upon it. For Heaven's sake don't feel that you "owe" me any letters. I know what it is to be hard at work and any time off that you have ought to be spent in other ways than writing letters. The best news I've heard for some time is that the book is coming along and that

A Farewell to Arms by Ernest Hemingway 7th large printing $2.50	Sinclair Lewis, in his Nobel Prize acceptance address, said: "Ernest Hemingway, educated by the most intense experience, disciplined by his own high standards, an authentic artist whose home is in the whole of life."
"Thomas Wolfe, whose only novel, 'Look Homeward, Angel,' is worthy to be compared with the best of our literary productions, a gargantuan creature with a great gusto of life."	Look Homeward, Angel by Thomas Wolfe 5th large printing $2.50

A page from the Scribners Spring 1931 catalogue exploiting Sinclair Lewis's 1930 Nobel Prize acceptance speech.

you will have the "first quarter of a million words" ready for us in the fall. It's going to be a grand book.

What you have to say about the citizens of the isles where you are now residing hit me in the right spot, coming on top of several rather arrogant letters from English authors. They certainly have no high opinion of us, but thank God we're beginning to lose some of our provincial humility.

As you probably know, "Look Homeward Angel" is selling right along, though not heavily. Sinclair Lewis's very high praise has been widely quoted, of course, and we have made a special band which now goes over the jackets of all copies, bearing this quotation from his speech before the Swedish Academy. I hope the book keeps up in England.

I'm writing this the day before Christmas; a light snow is falling and the city is crowded with shoppers. New York has never seemed more attractive than during the past month - in spite of the many signs of unemployment and poverty. I wish you were here and we could go out to lunch together and have a talk over a glass of wine. All sorts of good wishes to you, dear Tom, for the New Year and affectionate greetings from your friend,

Jack.

P.S. Had lunch with André Maurois[1] the other day, and told him about "Look Homeward, Angel." He hadn't read it, so I sent him a copy at his request. Marjorie Seiffert asked to be remembered to you when I wrote.

J.

1. André Maurois (1885–1967), author of best-selling biographies.

TO: Maxwell Perkins   *Christmas card, PUL*
Late December 1930   *London*

Begin here
I wish you a happy and joyful Christmas—my [   ] is not as happy as last year's,
but, by God, I believe I thrive on adversity: I am not going to be beaten because I
won't be beaten—Now is the time to see what is in me—you will never lose a penny
on me—my family must be helped: you should have the other letter by now asking
you to send $500 to my brother Fred. I am thinking of sending $100 to my mother
and $100 [   ] to Mabel if I have it, I may cable you. Don't let the damned den-
tists get the money if you can help it—a dentist here told me it was a fraud and a
swindle—he said they had extracted a tooth needlessly in order to put in expensive
work, he said it was a such a despicable thing to frighten people with threats of sudden death and terrible diseases—he said it was a low-down thing Don't pay them,
but don't let them hold responsible a woman named Aline Bernstein—she is a fine
woman but she wrote me a little note telling me she was absolutely broke and
couldn't be held responsible There is no question of that, there must be no question
of it, all she did was to give me their name, and I think she called up for me, they
wrote her to get my address but I cant see that she is any way responsible—if those
conniving scoundrels by some slimy trick of law can hold her so, we must pay: but
get Whitney Darrow to write her a note, or please write her yourself, explaining the
situation—assure her she will have to pay nothing, but that I am concerned the
[   ] is outrageously unfair and a cheat, and ask her not to do anything please to
embarrass us unless she is herself in trouble with them. Her address is

The Civic	And here is
Repertory	just a little
Theatre, New York City.	space to say God
	bless you and good
	luck this Christmas

I have been down for two days with cold and fever, and I am, driven frantic by these
things, but I take a vindictive pleasure in doing my 5 hours or more a day—I'll be
God damned if I'll be done in by these bastards—dentists, [   ], or anything else.
                                    Tom Wolfe

Forgive me all this trouble I'm causing you—stay with me—I'll make money [   ]
books, articles, stories or in some way—believe in me

TO: Whitney Darrow   *Cable, PUL*
5 January 1931   *London*

PLEASE CABLE TWOHUNDRED FIFTY GUARPAMAL LONDON
    TOM WOLFE.

ALS, 20 pp., PUL

London Jan 7
1931

Dear Mr Perkins: Thanks for your letter + for sending Fred that money—I'll never forget it. I have written you another enormous letter full of plans and intentions, but as usual it's not yet completed. But here's the idea briefly: I'm simply living with the book, sometimes I go out over a day, sometimes not at all. I went to Paris for a few days but worried about it all the time I'm going to work on it now here till I drop—about six weeks more, I think—then I'm coming home. Don't say anything to anyone about my coming back! I want to be in my own terrible, confused, distorted unhappy country—its the place for me. I am wild about the way time has gone—I can't lose any more. If I get back home by March 1st—I want to be going full blast again by March 10th or 15th I can't waste more time than that. That will give me several months before Fall and I'll work like hell. This is a hell of a lot to ask—but I don't want to lose the time if I can help it—can you get someone to find me two rooms, a bath, and a gas stove in a place that's quiet—they ought to be cheaper now because of hard times. I don't know whether New York's a good place or not, I probably ought to get out of it, but I cant go chasing around the country now looking places up. You mentioned country near you once—I'd like that or a place in New York where I could look at the River (I mean the East River—I'd thought of Brooklyn). You mentioned boarding houses once near you—I don't think boarding houses would work: I stay up all night and I don't think I can change It must be a place where I've got my own place and can do as I damned please—doesn't have to be up to date, but quiet and free. I notice there are ap't houses in the country outside N.Y. now—a good American idea. It's a lot to ask—particularly since you're rushed—but I'll stand by anything you do: there's a good competent friendly sort of boy downstairs with Miss Devoy—name of Kissenburger (or something like that)—don't you suppose he could do something for me. Seems I ought to get something for $60 or $70 a month—could this be done? I've got a little furniture somewhere—bed, chairs, table etc—but forget where I stored them: person in N.Y. knows address

When I come back I want to see you and go to that speakeasy again—but I'm not going to see anyone else: I mean this—otherwise, I'm done for—no parties, no going out, no literary people—nothing but obscurity and work. It's the only game for me, I shall never be a damned literary-party monkey again, I'm a poor dumb simple bloke—but I will not fail you! I don't mean by that that I'll write a good book, but it ought to be good if I've any good left in me—I know that the book is right   When I came back from Paris the other day I sat down and worked for 12 hours—wrote 4500 words—most I've ever done: its a damned fool thing to do, been paying for it ever since.

In what I said about M. B. and F. S. F. I meant nothing against Scott: he made me mad once or twice and he knows it, but everything you said about him is true: he is a very generous and at heart a very kind and sensitive person, and also a man of talent.

If you are less rushed now than you were could you let me know about this room business I want to come back 3ᵈ class on a fast boat—Bremen or Europa—and get to it There are many wonderful places, things, books, people etc to be known about, but I've got to get on with this now. I'm getting thin and have lost my belly, Thank God! but I'll be still thinner before I'm through. I went to see just two people in Paris—name of Gorman¹—you must know them Man I think means well, but woman vicious and foolish: they had called me up in London and asked me to come to see them in Paris—prophetic soul suspected one of three things: it turned out to be all three—on one side a man says "I believe you know so and so, my sister in law's cousin in N.Y"—on another "I believe you know so-and-so my cousin in London"—then knowing snickers and chuckles when I admitted knowing it; and from the front this Gorman trollop "When will your book be finished? How many words have you written? What's it all about? etc." I wanted to vomit, and I did later, got out as quick as I could—she knows your friend Mrs Colum and I wish I could see and talk to Mrs Colum, but alone—not with this harpy around. You may think I'm bitter and suspicious—well, I am, and I ought to be: these people are envenomed and sterile, they want to cause you pain and sterility, they have not an ounce of decent friendliness, they are liars and fools and frauds. I say now, <u>Goddam them to hell</u>! both abroad and in New York, which means the whole gossip business. Mr Perkins, I'm going to be all right, because I'm desperate and at work, and unless I die of tea, cigarettes, and the gas fire (I'm drinking very little) I'll heal myself of other troubles, but I mean to say now and forevermore to these people: Your sterility is dullness, your despair is dreariness—there is joy in the world and I know what it is and I shall fight to keep it and believe in it. I grind my teeth when I think how we have been cheated and intimidated by these people—we have been secretly filled with horror and weariness by waste-landism, but we have stood for it because we thought these exalted people were bitter and wise and had some truth and beauty to offer—well, they haven't a damned thing, and they lie: they are a dreary false set of bastards—I know how the kid feels on his first trip as he lies in his dark berth in the Pullman and hears the beautiful woman below stirring her lovely legs between the sheets,—and by God, the kid is everlastingly right, and the others are dreary frauds, and I shall say so down to the last remote and unspeakable detail. America is joy—it is richness and joy—and Mencken + all those people were right but they went after the wrong things—it is not "Puritanism"—but it is everything that denies life and joy—whether the Methodist Bishops and the Comstocks² or the T.S. Elioters—I mean the thing we've got to hate, the terrible enigma and puzzle of America, is the thing that makes men burn wheat on the prairies while men are starving for bread in N.Y.; it is the thing that makes people eat trash in drug stores and "Shoppes" when the country is groaning with the most magnificent food in the world The real impulse of America is rich, beautiful, spacious, humorous, earthly—full of joy—we must hate all that denies it! The moving pictures, by the way, are all right—just as the dime novels are all right—they are much more all right than the "Art Theatre" and the Atlantic Monthly—I'll tell you why when I see you.

I love all the good times I've ever had, and I've had thousands: do you know when I had a good time—when we used to go to that speakeasy and have a few good drinks of that strong gin, and then attack those great steaks with a ravenous hunger: later we would walk all over New York or take the ferry to Staten Island. To me that is joy: you are a little older and more restrained but I think you had a good time, too. There was nothing false about that, we lied about nothing in enjoying it. I do not know what truth is but I know that Joy is Truth—and we must hate all that denies it, we must carry our hatred against heaven if it denies it—I mean we must hate the dreary skies, the reeking air the choking fogs that make these poor devils spew and cough just as much as we must hate those other fogs that get into the brain and the spirit. I am a desperate character—desperate not to anyone but myself—but I feel I stand on the edge of destruction of life and glory; I may destroy myself, but I am much [   ] about this now, and I may come through to the good life: I am a religious and believing person, I am still discovering my religion and belief, but I know they are good, and sometimes in these letters I have tried to tell you a little of it.

Well—can you write me about the room business, and if you think it can be done, wont you write me anyway and say "Come on," even if nothing has been found at present. The little man Reeves, the publisher, tried to be nice to me here, but he is crazier than I am—he got cracked up in the war and has crazy spells—he got me down to his place in Surrey when I first came, and went into mad raving fits of hate against the Americans, although they've done everything for him—Double-days own Heinemann and old man D.[3] worships Reeves—it is not fair! Also, suggested I was making love to his wife—came around here drunk and read passages from bible to me about committing adultery with wife's friend: it's a damned lie and he knows it, but he wanted to believe it in order to enjoy pain—I hate this thing in life too. The wife is lovely, healthy beautiful girl who loves him, he has treated her shockingly, and told me other night coming up from Folkestone (I met him on boat coming back from Paris) that she has now left him. I don't wonder! What a lot of messed-up stupid living there is! I believe something can be done about it, and I'm going to try!

Write me soon—thanks with all my heart for sending Fred money, and for all else. The Sinclair Lewis thing was wonderful and generous but also a little frightening. I must be myself and do my best—that's all we can do. Good luck, good health, happy New Year. It will be good to see you. Tom Wolfe

1. Herbert Gorman (1873–1954), James Joyce critic and biographer.
2. Anthony Comstock (1844–1915), secretary of the New York Society for the Suppression of Vice, sought to ban the sale of what he regarded as obscene books.
3. Publisher Frank Nelson Doubleday (1862–1934).

ALS, 47 pp., PUL

London, Jan 19
1931

Dear Mr Perkins: You ask me to write to you and then I inundate you with long letters. But I have tried not to be too difficult or too much trouble: if you are willing to take the trouble with me now you may help me do something that will keep me forever.

I want you to help me to do a very few simple physical things: I want to come back to my country in another month or so without anyone but yourself knowing about it; I want to find a quiet place to live in, and to live and work there in almost complete isolation for <u>at least</u> three months; during that time I should like to see and talk to you whenever you have time for it, and if there are a few simple kind and perfectly un-literary people that I could meet, I should like to meet them. Do you think it would be possible to do these things? It is of vital importance to me now that this should be so—I ask you humbly and earnestly to help me if you can. The isolation and privacy should certainly not be hard to get: I have achieved them almost perfectly here in England—some people say you cannot in America, as long as there is some little rag and bone of reputation + scandal that the curs can gnaw at—but I say that you can, and I'm going to have them. The reason I want to see one or two people is because I like people and need them, and this solitude has begun to prey upon me, I talk to myself, and when I sleep my mind continues to function with a kind of horrible comatose intelligence. I hear strange sounds and noises from my youth, and from America. I hear the million strange and secret sounds of Time.

Once you told me of a member of your family who had been "sort of wild" but who had now come through, chiefly, I believe because of your mother's intelligence and subtlety in dealing with him. Forgive me for mentioning this, but I mention it now because you told me you had never tried to find too definitely or exactly what he had done, because that kind of knowledge about a person embarassed you. But I think you do find out about a person more indirectly—sometimes I have talked to you about things I knew about by using a hypothetical way of speech.

—i.e. "If a certain person did so and so and if a person did so-and-so-what—" etc. But I suppose you know the two very ancient jokes about the young fellow who was suffering from one of the <u>physical</u> diseases of love, and who went to see his physician about it:

"I have a friend"—he began "All right, son.". the doctor said, "take your friend out of your pants and we'll look at him"—or that other one who craftily asked his doctor "if it was possible for a man to get a venereal disease in a W. C."—"Yes, but thats a hell of a place to take a woman."[1]

You cant lie to your doctor, and you ought not to beat about the bush with your physician, and at the present moment, I am asking you to try to be my physician—I am not asking you to cure me of my sickness, because you can't do that, I must do it myself, but I am very earnestly asking you to help me to do certain things that will make my cure easier and less painful, at the present time, I am convalescent, but, as you know, in convalescence, you have occasional periods of relapse when everything sinks—vitality, hope, strength—and it is then that the patient must fight like hell. Well, I am a good boy and I have fought like hell. I am not using simply an extended metaphor about this convalescence business, I'm speaking literally—just as the diseases of the spirit are much more terrible than the diseases of the flesh, so their cure is more painful and difficult. I have just passed through a two day period of relapse, which has been attended by fever and fits of vomiting (physical facts, this time). This relapse was caused by the visit of one of those bubonic rats of the spirit who live by the destruction of others and who exist in such great numbers in New York.

So, here, bluntly and directly, is the cause of my present trouble, which I think you may help me with: When I was twenty-four years old I met a woman who was almost forty and I fell in love with her. I can not tell you here the long and complicated story of my relations with this woman—they extended over a period of five years, they began with me lightly and exultantly—at first I was a young fellow who had got an elegant and fashionable woman for a mistress, and I was pleased about it; then, without knowing how, when, or why, I was desperately in love with the woman, then the thought of her began to posess and dominate every moment of my life, I wanted to own, posess, and devour her; I became insanely jealous; I began to get horribly sick inside: and then all physical love, desire, passion ended completely—but I still loved the woman, I could not endure her loving anyone else or having physical relations with anyone else, and my madness and jealousy ate at me like a poison, like all horrible sterility and barrenness. Twice I got away from New York and came abroad in an effort to end it, but when I came back I would resume my life with the woman again. I can not say much about her here—and I am saying not one word of criticism of her, the woman always swore she loved me and no one else, she always insisted on her fidelity, and certainly she must have felt some strong passion, because for years she would come every day, and stay with me, cook for me, and do many lovely and beautiful things.

The anatomy of jealousy is the most complicated and tortuous anatomy on earth: to find its causes, to explore its sources is more difficult and mysterious than it was for the ancients to probe the sources of the Nile: people usually attribute to it one cause, but comes from a terrible and bewildering complication of causes; there is usually in it the feeling of inferiority, induced by some terrible shame, distrust, and humiliation of the past; there is in it also the horrible doubt that arises in the conflict of fact and ideal belief—it is true, for example, that not war, Darwin, or science has destroyed the ancient conception of God, so much as has the life of the modern city: the inhuman scenery, the stony architecture, and the vast hordes of swarming maggots—crawling, pawing, cursing, cheating, pushing, betraying, dying or living, swearing or pleading!—the spectacle of the subway rush hour, for example, is sufficient to destroy all ideas of man's personal destiny, his personal conversations with God, his personal importance and salvation So it is with the other Ideal Beliefs—the beliefs in Courage, Honor, Faithfulness, and Love—in that great stain of crawling filth which is the city's life—that stain which is so horrible and yet has so much beauty in it—we see the infinite repetitions of lust, cruelty, and sterility, of hatred, defeat, and darkness, of gouging and killing!—We see, moreover, the horrible chemistry of flesh, of millions of pounds and tons of flesh; we see flesh soothed, or irritated, or maddened, or appeased in a million different patterns daily, and our belief fails: how can one memory live here where a million memories pass before us in a second? How can one face be cherished and remembered out of the million faces? How can one grief, one joy, endure among ten million griefs and joys? How, finally, can love endure here?—where treason can be consummated in 30 seconds? How can faith live, where a million faiths have died? If we surrender to this despair we are lost—the end of it all is futility and death—at its cheapest, gin-party Van Vechtenism² or Madeleine Boydism, which is not sinister as it wants to be, only cheap—as if the Saturday Evening Post had suddenly turned nasty; at its worst it probably results in the death of such a man as your friend, Mr. Brooks But here is the situation: I came away finally, over eight months ago. I did not want to come, but I yielded to what her friends wanted for her, and what it seemed to me would be best: I wrote her from the boat, but since then I have not written her. The woman wrote and cabled me often during the first four months, and then, quite properly, stopped. I cannot tell you what distress and torment these letters + cables caused me—I would get letters signed in her blood, and cables which said she was going to die Finally, about 3 mos. ago I got a cable which said:

"No word from you. Life impossible. Desperate Cannot go on living like this Are you willing to accept the consequences?" For a few days, I thought I would go mad. But I did not write or cable. Each day I would go for mail in the most horrible state of nerves, wondering if I should see some cable which carried the dreadful news. I longed for <u>no</u> news and I hoped for <u>some</u> news—but nothing came, and that was almost worse than ever. I imagined that she had died or killed herself, and that her embittered and griefstricken friends and family were saying nothing to me. I began to read the American papers for news. I would buy the filthy rag they print in Paris—the Herald—and be afraid each day that it would contain news of her death by leaping from a window, I began to read the horrible mortuary columns of The New York Times, looking first in that dense double column of names for one that began with <u>B</u>

But then, in the theatrical columns of that same paper, at just about the date when I feared this tragic act had happened, I read an account of a great success she had scored in the theatre,³ I met a man who asked me if I knew her, and said he had seen her, looking very radiant and happy at a "party" in New York several weeks before, other people wrote me telling me how well happy and prosperous she was looking, in Paris people would seek out café tables next to me and the women, whom I did not know, would begin discussing the lady and me, hinting new interests for her very loudly so that I would not lose the benefit, and finally about a month ago (the middle of December) her cables began again: there had been two months silence, during which she had scored a great success—perhaps that had worn off again: anyway she had decided to begin dying again and I had done it. She said she was "desperate, hold out your hand to me in my hour of need. Impossible to face new year, I stood by you in bad years why have you deserted me? I love you and am faithful unto death, pain I bear too great to endure"—etc, etc. There were

8 or 10 of these messages: I felt the most enormous relief to know she was still alive + kicking, I cabled back, I asked her if it was fair to cable such messages when I was alone in a foreign land trying to write, I told her not to speak of hard years, that mine was harder than this, that I had no money, that her dentists + my family were getting it, and that if I didnt get peace and quiet to work now I was done for. She cabled that her family had "lost everything"—it pleases her to feel poor now, but while my family is living in actual want, hers is living in an expensive hotel apartment, they have two cars and a magnificent house in the country, and her sister is abroad now stopping at the Ritz in London. If this is poverty, then God knows what you would call what millions of people in America are enduring this winter. Her sister came to see me here in London, her sister hates me, but was unable to keep away out of bitter curiosity to see how I felt and how I was standing up under this hammering. Her sister made several shifty and hinting remarks about her, in order to draw me out, and of course I talked with complete frankness and honesty: I was too agitated and too horribly nervous to attempt concealment—I told this woman that it could not possibly be news to her that I had been in love with her sister and that she had been my mistress, I told her this could not possibly have gone on for years, with the woman coming to my place day after day without the family knowing it— at this she began to hedge and evade, saying she had suspected things, but that they knew nothing—in spite of the fact that a cable from the woman a few days before had said they knew all about it. Her sister at first, before these avowals of mine, had said she had been worried and upset and they knew something was wrong: now she said she had never been happier or calmer or more joyful and successful than this Fall: I then asked if her sister was a woman whose word could be believed—she said "yes"—and I demanded why, then, I should be driven mad by these cables threatening death, misery, and destruction. To this she made no reply but presently she said I must not take these things "too seriously"—that her sister was an "emotional woman" and might "think she meant these things" for five minutes or so, but that they were really not important. If this is true, I think it is one of the vilest and basest things I have ever heard, and to believe that a person that I have loved so dearly, and who has professed her love, faithfulness and faith for me so often, could deliberately and trivially do this ruinous and damnable thing to a young man without influence or money who is leading a desperately lonely life abroad, trying to get on with his work—this may strike her friends as an amusing thing, but I hope to God it seems to you to be a vile, cruel, and cowardly act. You may wonder why I come to you with this: my answer is that if I cannot come to you with it, there is no one in the world I can come to. I can not tell you what horrible pain and suffering this thing has caused me: I would wake up in the morning with a feeling of nausea in my guts, and my horror and fear would grow all day long until I went to the bank for mail— later, I would sometimes have to vomit from physical sickness. When her sister left the other night I vomited for two hours, I have lost two days on account of it, but tonight I am getting to my work again. But I am all right in spite of this weakness; during the past 3 mos (a little more) that I have been in this place I have written over 100000 words on my book—I have made myself work some time in the most ghastly state—but I have worked—and it has taken guts. I am a brave man, and I

like myself: I am a good fellow, and I shall always like myself for what I did here, and I hope you like me, too, for I honor and respect you, and I believe you can help me to save myself. Also, I tell you this: I want to save not only myself, but by doing so, to save something else that is part of me, and without which no one can be saved; I mean my utter and absolute belief in love and in human excellence. No matter what breach of faith, truth, or honesty this woman may be guilty of, I want to come out of this thing with a feeling of love and belief in her—I remember full well countless acts of beauty, loveliness, and tenderness in this woman, there is the most enormous beauty and loveliness in her yet, and if she has learned craft, cunning, and treachery from these rats of the spirit—that is a matter for grief and pity rather than hate. But in this, the most passionate and devastating event of my life, I shall not be devoured at the end by hatred and bitterness and finally by cynicism and indifference. That is what the rats of the soul would like to see, it fits into all the trashiness of Sinister Van Vechtenism, etc—the young fellow who comes to New York, falls in love with a worldly and experienced woman, is made a fool of, and then either destroys himself or becomes one of the rats' club, eagerly awaiting the delightful entry of another visitor into the Spider's Parlor. But this is not going to happen to me—I think, during the early years of this affair, her friends were quite amused at the spectacle of a kid of 24 going around like a madman, eaten up with love and desperation, getting drunk and violent over a woman of 40. But I broke the rules of the game by doing a piece of work that had some little success; at this, their amusement turned to venom, they said I was making the woman unhappy, how badly I treated her, etc—and now, it seems, they are willing to do any dirty trick to destroy my work for the future—if my next book is no good, I assure you they will be immensely pleased; they will then say it is because I left her, etc.

Don't put this down simply to the suspicion and distrust of which I am accused. I admit that I am suspicious and distrustful but, in view of what I have seen during the past five or six years,—I think it is a God damned sane and solid principle to live by. I dont think I have ever mistrusted a man or woman who deserved to be trusted, and if I have lived almost entirely alone, these past eight or ten months it is because it was the only way I knew of meeting this thing. A man who has been sick and is convalescent must "lay low"—he can't play on football teams. In this solitude at present is my power and my way of healing myself—they hate me for it, they can not get at me: her sister venomously remarked that it was "unnatural" to stay away from people like this, but I think staying away from people who make you vomit, and who hate life and love sterility is very natural: certainly if staying away from Paris Americans, and New York parties is unnatural I shall remain so now to the end of my days. But it is not a fair fight. These people talk of fairness, but they are rich, cunning, and powerful—they are a hundred against one, and I have no money nor influence. I have given this woman six of the best years of my life— madness, passion, good, bad—she had it all. Now, it is a rotten thing to try to ruin me when I must go on and use the little success I have gained. I have been fair— the one boastful thing I ever heard this woman say was that "she always got what she wanted in the end"—her sister repeated it the other day: I think it is a bad thing for anyone to say, it indicates something not to be trusted in people—if, by gentleness, sweetness, tears—by any means—she consciously "gets her way," it is bad and miserable in the end. You can "get your way" with people, but you can not "get your way" with life—she must grow old and die. Also, she has failed this time with me! I shall feel much more dreadful pain over this thing, but I am through. If I go back to her now, I am done for—it means real death—but I shall never go back, and I think she knows it. There are two courses left: one is a deep and abiding love and friendship, and the kind of relation I would like with her—I think this is possible and I am going to try to achieve it. The other to which her friends may counsel her is poison—the desire to "get back," to "show me," to see that rotten and malicious stories reach my ears, to launch out on new loves, to wound me through base trickery, and to [bring] the thing before me all they can. Also, to write lying letters and cables. If this is done, it will be a filthy thing, but I will not be made filthy by it; I am alone now, if I am brave and decent and have faith, and work, all will be well. I <u>must</u> not die. But I need help—such help as a man may hope to receive from a friend,—I turn to you for it now. You know how warmly and gratefully I feel toward Scribner's, but you are the only person there I can turn to. Mr Darrow is a good fellow but he calls me "Tom" when he gets an order for the book, and nods curtly when there are none. Dashiell does not know me and has no belief or faith in my work.

As for Jack, I have the warmest and deepest feeling for him: he is a kind + sensitive man, but he believes more in my defeat than in victory, he says he expects my next book to be good but I think he may rather expect a crash. I like Jack enormously, but I cannot take this to him I turn to you because I feel health and sanity and fortitude in you: try to help me to get away from this loneliness and to find a place in my own country where I can talk to a few people. Pain and sterility does not kill me, but it makes me vomit, and I cannot work while I am vomiting If this is a frenzied appeal, understand that it is also a real and earnest one. I cannot tell you one tenth or one hundredth of this story, but, so help me God, I have told you the truth, I cannot begin to tell you the horrible pain and despair I have suffered over this.

The rats will say that "it serves him right" but, Mr. Perkins, I have never done anything to deserve this, I have never let anyone down, and at the end I have tried to do the best I could for this woman I do not really mistrust people, in my heart I trust and believe in them, and I have trust and belief left in this woman even now, and I believe the beautiful part of her will win through in the end. Surely you cannot misunderstand what I have said in this letter; it is plain enough. I am in deep trouble, so deep that I may not get out of it, and I need a friend, I am not putting anything off on anyone, no one can say I have ever tried to get other people to live for me. Your last letter was only a note—well, write me another note: you need not discuss this letter, but if you understand my trouble, say simply that you do, and that you will try to help me.

I wish to God there were someone in the world who thought enough of me to go to see the woman, to ask her now to give me a decent chance for peace and hope in which to do my work. If she has an atom of the love and faith she protests, surely to God she does not want to ruin me now: I do not believe, if someone talked to her, that she would deny the things she has said to me, or have written these letters and cables—surely she is not so base as to lie about that.

Whatever else she has done or wants to do now I can not help, and I have given to this thing all the feeling I have in me—there's no more left. But at any rate, if she will not be my friend, and love me as a friend, she can at least give me a chance to do my work and get some joy and tranquility back into my heart again. I must not be smashed this way at thirty—for God's sake, stand by me now, and I will be all right. The woman is surrounded by friends, wealth, success, luxury—she has a family—I can expect no help from these people: they will not only refuse to help, they will lie, cheat, and aid in anything that will cause me distress and failure. I swear to you that I have told the truth, and for God's sake do not think this is only a long speech: I am in terrible trouble, and I need a friend. This is the first appeal of this sort I have ever made. I do not know what to do, where to turn, but I want to live in my own country, and I want to forget this horrible business entirely. Someday, when we are both I hope, better and calmer, I trust I can see her again and be her friend.

You said that my letters sounded "unhappy." I hope this makes the reason plainer. Write me, please.

Tom Wolfe.

Mr Perkins, if I said anything here that I should not have said, be generous and lenient with me: I want to do what is decent and fair, and if I have spoken bitterly of this woman, please try to understand that she is a very wonderful woman, and I love her dearly, but she must get through this baseness of passion and the flesh which make people do terrible things. I know that there is in this world an excellence that will not compromise and some day I shall find it—when it says "love" it means it, when it says "forever" it does not mean four months—it will not talk of desperation and death unless it means those things, and the end of it will not be ruin and bitterness, but life and beauty.

Now, I shall get on with my work. But write me soon.

Would you like a foreigner's account of Merry England as it is today? They have reached the second stage of degeneration, I know a dozen people in and out—and an interesting variety of lives it is:

① A Russian doctor, naturalized Englishman, an abortionist, who writes doctors stories. For 2 hrs in the afternoon the ladies come here in droves—what he has told me about it is highly interesting, as is the man

② Mrs Lavis—my charwoman—she comes, cooks for me, looks after me, and loves me dearly for 14 shillings a week.[4] She is a good soul, and I know all about her sisters, cousins, aunts—the amazing story of her father—her own early life—and her whole philosophy, which is most curious and I think the same as that of the poor people all over England

③ A woman who is a spiritualist and spook writer in Chelsea—she is the daughter of the late Professor Darden[5]—the gatherings at her house are very curious

④ A nurse in a "crazy house" at Basingstoke—her tales of the inmates and the conditions there

⑤ A girl who is an alcoholic—merry Eng. again

⑥ A publisher and his wife and a rich old American who lives with them.

⑦ The English wife of one of the great Russian Soviet Commissary's—this lady I understand has given me an undeserved notoriety[6]

⑧ The Hampstead Heath literary people and the present standard of sexual mawrals in merry England—which the boastful say is lower than at any time since the Restoration: in my opinion the Restoration was not in it.

⑨ Various Russian women, divorced ladies, cooks, bottlewashers, Piccadilly tarts, etc, etc.

No, I have not been entirely blind: the story of this little house in Ebury street and what comes in and out of it day by day might be interesting!

1. This joke appears in "O Lost," chapter 12, but was deleted from *Look Homeward, Angel.*

2. Carl Van Vechten (1880–1964) wrote novels about sophisticated New Yorkers, one of which was titled *Parties* (1930).

3. Bernstein designed the sets for *Grand Hotel* (1931) by Vicki Baum (1888–1960).

4. She inspired the character Daisy Purvis in "'E, A Recollection," *The New Yorker,* 17 July 1937.

5. Unidentified.

6. Ivy Litvinoff, with thom TW had a brief affair. See *Notebooks,* p. 530.

ALS, 6 pp., Harvard
MP's New Canaan letterhead

January 31st 1931

Dear Tom:—To begin with I'll do anything you ask of me, + any reluctance will come only from lack of confidence in my ability to do good.—But I should be glad that you did feel that you wanted to ask me. I look forward to your return.—If you're in N.Y. in the Summer it will be a great thing for me. I'm generally horribly lonely. There are people enough, but none I care really to see. I'll count on <u>some</u> of your company anyway.

As to the other matter, I had gathered of course that things were bad in some such way, but not that they were so bad as they are. Heaven knows how it would go with me in such a situation, but <u>may</u> you get strength some where to stick it out. I'm certain you took the right course in going away.—No one could think otherwise. As for <u>me</u>, I can only feel angry with <u>her</u>. She maybe really fine, but there is an Egotism in women beyond any known in men, + they infuriate me.—But I know I'm prejudiced against them. Did any one of them ever admit that she was in the wrong about anything! I know you've been in hell. I'm no good at suffering myself + so it's hard to encourage others to it. But I'm dead sure you've done right + you must stand it for the sake of everything, if you can.

I hope you'll see the Colums if they go to London in July, as they've planned. You'll find no fault in Mollie. You'll enjoy them both. They see things as you do + believe in the things you believe in. Please see them a lot + talk freely to them.

They're real, true people who know what solid ground is. Wholesome people, quite undamaged by the people you write about + the cheap cocktail parties + all. Mollie wrote about having heard of you in Paris. They thought well of you there.

I had a nice note from Fred for the check. I wrote him he must come in if ever he comes to N.Y. I'd like to see him. Everything is very bad all over the country, + Hoover does whatever he can, it almost seems, to make it worse.—But there are some slight signs of improvement. My oldest daughter, a Freshman at Smith, wrote me that she knew she had flunked her first Mid Year.[1] She had had two days to study for it but didn't: she began to to read Look Homeward Angel + could think of nothing else til long after she finished it. They all have read it or are reading it up there. Really it's far more a man's book.

As for the room: let me know a week before you sail. I'll get you one if you want though you probably wont like it. I'd say it better be in N.Y. unless youre sure you'd want the country. Then I could bring you out here + we could ride around + walk + you could see how it is. It's fine country + a good town too, but in the Summer its full of city people + rather 'fashionable,' as they used to say. If the Colum's come back here to live it would be better. I don't know if they ever will.

Well, I'm sorry things are so bad. It's a rotten shame. I wish I'd been through the like of it.—Then I could preach. You've started right so stick to it. That's easy to say! My great hope is some day to see you walk in with a ms. two or three feet thick.

Yours Always,
Maxwell Perkins

1. Bertha Perkins Frothingham.

24 February 1931

Cable, PUL
London

SAILING EUROPA THURSDAY NEED NO HELP NOW CAN HELP MYSELF MOST WORK SIX MONTHS ALONE BEST WISHES.
TOM WOLFE.

FROM: John Hall Wheelock   *CCS, 2 pp., PUL*

March 26, 1931

Dear Tom:

What the — — has happened to you? My secretary won't allow me to write out the words. I had a glimpse of you it seems to me about two weeks ago when you got back and since then no sign. I hope this means you're hard at work.

I'm kept pretty busy at the moment because Max, as you probably know, is away for a week or ten days. I don't think he wanted to go off much this time, as he had many irons in the fire here, but he'll probably be back sometime next week: possibly Monday. I've been reading plenty of manuscripts and have received calls from a good many authors, particularly "poets." One of them tried to read me his entire manuscript the other day and I was wondering why it is so difficult to be firm under these circumstances. Probably because I sympathize with the poor wretch.

When you have nothing better to do, don't forget your old friends at Scribners. Can't we have lunch together some day, dear Tom? If I've broken in upon a period of solitude and work, please forgive me.

As ever,
Your friend.
J.H.W.

To
Mr. Thomas Wolfe,
40 Verandah Place,
Brooklyn, New York

⌁

FROM: *John Hall Wheelock*   *CCS, 1 p., PUL*

April 2, 1931

Dear Tom:

As you know, we have a tentative date for dinner and a walk on Wednesday evening, April 8. I find I can't manage it that night and I am hastening to let you know so that you can make your plans. How about Sunday evening, April 12? You will probably be in before then and we can fix up the time. Sunday evening is a good one for me because I usually feel more human than I do on week days.

I hope all goes well, dear Tom. Max got back this morning and asked after you. Please forgive this hurried line.

As ever,
J.H.W.

To
Mr. Thomas Wolfe,
40 Verandah Place
Brooklyn, New York

⌁

CC, 1 p., PUL

April 3, 1931

Dear Tom:

I have just got back, and I hope you will soon be in.- I knew you were to come in last night, but I could not wait long enough. Let me know of any day we can have lunch.

Always yours,
[Maxwell Perkins]

Typed wire draft, 1 p., PUL

April 9, 1931

Mr. Thomas Wolfe
40 Verandah Place
Brooklyn, N.Y.
Could you call me up this afternoon
Maxwell Perkins

FROM: John Hall Wheelock

CCS, 2 pp., PUL

April 17, 1931

Dear Tom:

How about our date for Sunday evening? Unless your plans have been changed in the meantime, I understand that we are to meet in front of the statue of Civic Virtue at City Hall, at six o'clock, and will then walk across Brooklyn Bridge, dining in that Borough. I hope we don& get lost in Brooklyn. My experiences there, in that respect, have not been very reassuring. Avenues and streets seem to follow the Einstein theory of space curving back on itself. It is said, you know, that it's the only place in the world where a man can see the back of his own head going around a corner - and that in the prohibition era.

But to come down from these lofty problems, if Sunday for any reason proves inconvenient, give me a ring here or at the house, Rhinelander 4 - 3476, as otherwise I shall be standing in front of the statue of Civic Virtue.

I hope all goes well, dear Tom, and am looking forward to being with you. If Sunday won't do we'll make another date, but I hope to see you then.

As ever,
J.H.W.

To
Mr. Thomas Wolfe
40 Verandah Place
Brooklyn, New York.

TO: *Alfred Dashiell*

Postmarked 8 August 1931

Postcard of Monument Rock,
Eagle Island, Maine, PUL
Orrs Island, Maine

Dear Fritz: I'm cooked with sunburn from head to foot—it hurts something awful. I'm taking my meals at a boarding house and the crowd of boarders is the same as it always was—they sit on the porch and rock—they never change—Hope you're well—T.W.

CC, 1 p., PUL

August 27, 1931

Dear Tom:

I think you ought to make every conceivable effort to have your manuscript completely finished by the end of September. I meant to speak of this when we were last together. I hope you will come in soon and tell me what you think you can do.

Always yours,

[Maxwell Perkins]

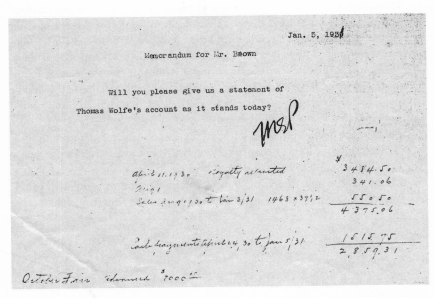

Wolfe's account at Scribners as of 5 June 1931, showing that *Look Homeward, Angel* had earned a total of $4,375.06. Wolfe received a thousand-dollar advance for a second novel, "The October Fair," which was not published (Princeton University Library).

ALS, 23 pp., PUL
Brooklyn

1931

Saturday—Aug 29

Dear Max: Thanks for your note which came this morning. I am glad you wrote me because I have some definite idea of when you expect to see my book, and I can say some things about it that I wanted to say. You say you think I ought to make every conceivable effort to have the manuscript completely finished by the end of September. I know you are not joking and that you mean <u>this</u> September, and not September four, five, or fifteen years from now. Well, there is no remote or possible chance that I will have a completed ms. of anything that resembles a book this September, and whether I have anything that I would be willing to show anyone next September, or any succeeding one for the next 150 years is at present a matter of the extremest and most painful doubt to me.[1]

I realize that it has been almost two years since my first book was published and that you might reasonably hope that I have something ready by this time. But I haven't. I believe that you are my true friend and, aside from any possible business interest, are disappointed because what hope you had in me has been weakened or dispelled. I want you to know that I feel the deepest regret on this account, but I assure you the most bitter disappointment is what I feel at present in myself. I don't want you to misunderstand me, or think that, aside from you and a few other people whose friendship has meant a great deal for me, I care one good God-damn of a drunken sailors curse whether I have "disappointed" the world of bilge-and-hogwash-writers, Boyds,[2] Cohns,[3] or any of the other literary rubbish of sniffers, whiffers and puny, poisonous apes. If what I am about to lose because of my failure to produce was, as I once believed, something beautiful and valuable—I mean a feeling of deep and fine respect in life for the talent of someone who can create a worthy thing—then my regret at the loss of something so precious would be great. But do you really think that after what I have seen during the past 18 months I would cling very desperately to this 'stinking' remnant of a rotten bush, or any longer feel any sense of deference or responsibility to swine who make you sign books to their profit even while you break bread with them, who insolently command you to produce a book and "be sure you make it good or you are done for," who taunt and goad you by telling you to take care since "other writers are getting ahead of you," who try to degrade your life to a dirty, vulgar, grinning, servile, competitive little monkey's life—do you think I am losing anything so wonderful here that I can't bear the loss? You must know that I don't care a damn for all this now—I want you to know, Max, that the only thing I do care for now is whether I have lost the faith I once had in myself, whether I have lost the power I once felt in me, whether I have anything at all left—who once had no doubt that I had a treasury—that would justify me in going on. Do you think anything else matters to me? I have been a fool and a jack-ass—cheapened myself by making talks at their filthy clubs and giving interviews, but my follies of that sort were done long ago—for the rest I haven't tried to do anything but live quietly by myself without fancy mysterious airs, and there is as decent stuff within me as in anyone. I have kept my head above this river of filth, some of the dirty rotten lies they have told about me have come back to me, but I have yet to find the person who uttered them to my face. I want you to know that I consider that my hands are clean and that I owe no one anything—save for the debt of friendship for a few people. I did not write the blurbs, the pieces in the paper, the foolish statements, nor did I tell lies: no one can take anything from me now that I value, they can have their cheap nauseous, seven-day notoriety back to give to other fools, but I am perfectly content to return to the obscurity in which I passed almost thirty years of my life without great difficulty. If anyone wants to know when I will have a new book out, I can answer without apology "when I have finished writing one and found some one who wants to publish it"—that is the only answer I owe to anyone (I don't mean you: you know the answer I have tried to make to you already)—and please, Max, if you can tactfully and gently, without wounding anyone, suggest to whoever is responsible for these newspaper squibs about my having written 500000 words, and more all the time,—that he please for God's Sake cut it out, I will be grateful. I am sure it was intended to help, but it does no good, I assure you I am not at all afraid or depressed at the thought of total obscurity again,—I welcome it, and I resent any effort to present me as a cheap and sensational person—in spite of my size, appetite, appearance, staying up all night, 500000 words, etc—I am not a cheap and sensational person: if there is going to be publicity why can't it tell the truth—that I work hard and live decently and quietly, that no one in the world had a higher or more serious feeling about writing, that I made no boasts or promises, that I do not know whether I will ever do the writing I want to do, or not, or whether I will be able to go on at all, that I am in doubt and distress about it, but that I work, ask nothing from anyone, and hope, for my own sake, that I have some talent and power in me—I say, I am not afraid of publicity like this, because it would be the truth, and it could not injure me save with fools.

I thank God I am in debt to no one: I have sent my family all I could, Mrs Boyd has had her full whack, the dentists are almost paid. Now, if they will all leave me alone, they can have the rest—if anything is left. I can't find out. I wish you'd find out for me and have Darrow send it to me. I've tried for a year to find out but I cant. I appreciate this paternal attitude, but it may be wasted on me, and I want to clear the board now. Above all, I don't want to owe you money. As thing stands, in my present frame of mind about my work, it is a blessing to me that I owe you no money and have no contract with you for a second book,—Max, won't you ask Darrow to send me whatever money is coming to me? As things stand now, it seems important to me that I should know where I stand financially and what I am going to have to do. I have earned my living teaching and in other ways before, and I believe I can earn my living again. As I told you the only thing that matters now would be to feel that the book has value and beauty for me, and that I have the power to do it—if I felt that I could do any work to support myself and feel good about it

Max, I have tried to tell you how I feel about all this, and now I want to sum it up this way:

Two years ago I was full of hope and confidence; I had compete within me the plans and ideas of at least a half dozen long books. Today I still have all this material, I have not the same hope and confidence; I have, on the contrary, a feeling of strong self-doubt and mistrust—which is not to say that I feel despair. I do not. Why this has happened I do not know—I think one reason is that I can not work in a glare, I was disturbed and lost self-confidence because of the notice I had, I think my success may have hurt me. Also, I had a personal trouble of which I told you something. I don't know whether this means I am unable to meet the troubles of life without caving in—this may be true, and in my doubt I think of some of the old books I read: "The Damnation of Someone or Another"[4]——"The Picture of Dorian Grey"[5]—in which spiritual decay, degeneration, and corruption destroys the person before he knows it—but I think that is literary night marishness—maybe these things happen, but I don't think they happened to me—I think I have kept my innocence, and that my feeling about living and working is better than it ever was. And I don't think I am unable to cope with the trial of life, but I think I may meet it clumsily and slowly, inexpertly, sweat blood and lose time. What I want to tell you is that I am in a state of <u>doubt</u> about all this.

Finally, the best life I can now dream of for myself, the highest hope I have is this: that I believe in my work and know it is good and that somehow, in my own way, secretly and obscurely, I have power in me to get the books inside me out of me. I dream of a quiet, modest life, but a life that is really high, secret, proud, and full of dignity for a writer in this country—I dream of a writer having work and power within him living this fine life untouched and uncoarsened by this filth and rabble of the gossip-booster sink—I dream of something permanent and fine, of the highest quality, and if the power is in me to produce, this is the life I want and shall have.

Thus, at great length, I have told you what is in my mind better than I could by talking to you, Max, do you understand that this letter is not bitter and truculent—save for these things and persons I despise. I want to tell you finally that I am not in <u>despair</u> over the book I have worked on—I am in <u>doubt</u> about it—and I am not sure about anything: I think I will finish it, I think it may be valuable and fine— or it may be worthless, I would like to tell you about it, and of some of the trouble I had with it. I can only suggest it: I felt if my life and strength kept up, if my vitality moved in every page, if I followed it through to the end it would be a wonderful book—but I doubted then that life was long enough, it seemed to me it would take ten books, that it would be the longest ever written, then, instead of paucity, I had abundance—such abundance that my hand was palsied, my brain weary, and in addition, as I go on, I want to write about everything and say all that can be said about each particular, the vast freightage of my years of hunger—my prodigies of reading, my infinite store of memories, my hundreds of books of notes return to devour me—sometimes I feel as if I shall compass and devour them, again, be devoured by them—I had an immense book and I wanted to say it all at once; it can't be done—now I am doing it part by part, and hope and believe the part I am doing will be a complete story, a unity, and part of the whole plan. This part itself has now become a big book: it is for the first time straight in my head to the smallest detail, and much of it is written—it is a part of my whole scheme of books as a smaller river flows into a big one.

As I understand it I am not bound now to Scribners or to any publisher by any sort of contract: none was ever offered me—neither have I taken money that is not my own. The only bond I am conscious of is one of friendship and loyalty to your house, and in this I have been faithful—it has been a real and serious thing with me.

I know that you want to see what I have done—to see if I had it in me to do more work after the first book, or whether everything burnt out in that one candle. Well, that is what I want to see, too, and my state of doubt and uneasiness is probably at least as great as your own. It seems to me that that is the best way to leave it now: the coast is clear between us, there are no debts or entanglements—if I ever write anything else that I think worth printing, or that your house might be interested in I will bring it to you, and you can read it, accept it or reject it with the same freedom as with the first book. I ask for no more from anyone. The life that I desire, and that I am going to try to win for myself, is going to exist in complete indifference and independence to such of the literary life as I have seen—I mean to all their threats either of glory or annihilation, to gin party criticism or newspaper blurbs and gossip, and to all their hysterical seven-day fames—if a man sets a high value on these things he richly deserves the payment he will get—as for me, I tell you honestly it is a piece of stinking fish to me—their rewards and punishments—I see what it did to writers in what they now call "the twenties"—how foolishly and trivially they worshipped this thing, and what nasty, ginny, drunken, jealous, fake-Bohemian little lives they had, and I see now how they have kicked those men out, after tainting and corrupting them and brought in another set which they call "the young writers"—among whom I have seen my own name mentioned. Well, I assure you I belong to neither group and I will not compete or produce in competition against any other person—no one will match me as you match a cock or a prize-fighter, no one will goad me to show smartness or brilliance against another's—the only standard I will compete against now is in me: if I cant reach it, I'll quit.

It is words, words—I weary of the staleness of the words, the seas of print, the idiot repetition of trivial enthusiasms—I am weary of my own words but I have spoken the truth here; is it possible that we are all tainted with cheapness and staleness, is this the taint that keeps us sterile, cheap, and stale in this country—when I talk to you as here and say what I know is in my heart am I just another Brown[6]—a cheap stale fellow who pollutes everything he talks about—justice, love, mercy—as he utters it. It isn't true—I am crammed to the lips with living, I am tired with what I've seen, I'm tired of their stale faces, the smell of concrete and [bent] steel, the thing that yellows, dries, or withers us—but did it mean nothing to you when I told you the beauty, exulting, joy, richness, and undying power that I had found in America—that I knew and believed to be the <u>real</u> truth, not the illusion?—the thing we had never found the pattern for, the style for, the true words to express—or was it only words to you; did you just think I was trying to be Whitman again. I know what I know, it crushes the lies and staleness like a rotten shell, but whether I can ever utter what I know, whether staleness + weariness has not done for me, I don't know—Christ, I am tired of everything but what I know to be the truth, and do not utter—I have it inside me, I even know the words for it, but staleness and dullness have got into me—I look at it with grey dullness and will not say it—it's not enough to see it: you've got to feel the thick snake-wriggle in each sentence—the heavy living tug of the fish at the line.

I'm out of the game—and it is a game, a racket: what I do now must be for myself,—I don't care who "gets ahead" of me—that game isn't worth a good god dam: I only care if I have disappointed you, but its very much my own funeral, too, I don't ask you to "give me a chance"—because I think you've given me one, but I don't want you to think this is a despairing letter, and that I've given up—I just say I don't know, I'm going to see: maybe it will come out right someday. By the way— I'm still working, I've been at it hard and will keep it up until I have to look for job: I may try to get work on Pacific coast. I'll come in to see you later, Max, please get Darrow to send me what money is coming to me.

When I was a kid we used to say of someone we thought the best and highest of—that he was "a high class gentleman." That's the way I feel about you. I don't think I am one—not the way you are—by birth, by gentleness, by natural and delicate kindness. But if I have understood some of the things you have said to me I believe you think the most living and beautiful thing on this earth is art, and that the finest and most valuable life is that of the artist. I think so, too; I don't know whether I have it in me to live that life, but if I have, then I think I would have something that would be worth your friendship. You know a good deal about me— the kind of people I came from (who seem to me, by the way, about as good as any people any where), and I think you know some of the things I have done, and that I was in love with a middle aged Jewish woman old enough to be my mother—I hope you understand I am ashamed of none of these things—my family, the Jewish woman, my life—but it would be a hard thing for me to face if I thought you were repelled by these things and did not know what I am like—I think my feeling about living and working and people is as good as you can find, and I want you to know how I feel: its so hard to know people and we think they feel inferior about things they really feel superior to, and the real thing that eats them we know nothing of.

I'm coming in to talk to you soon, but I can talk to you about some things better this way. Meanwhile, Max, good health and good luck and all my friendliest wishes.

Tom Wolfe

P.S.—I'm attaching a clipping a friend sent me from a Boston paper.[7] You see how quickly people can use an item like this injuriously—I think it has done harm, and I don't deserve it: please get them to cut it out

and leave me alone—

1. This letter signals the beginning of TW's suspicion that MP's responsibility to Scribners was in conflict with his loyalty to TW, as indicated by MP's pressure for a second novel. TW delivered "The October Fair" in 1933, which was partly used in *Of Time and the River* published in March 1935.

2. Probably Ernest Boyd

3. Possibly Louis Henry Cohn, a New York rare book dealer who wanted to publish a limited edition of TW's work in progress under the House of Books imprint.

4. *The Damnation of Theron Ware* (1896) by Harold Frederic (1856–1898).

5. *The Picture of Dorian Gray* (1891) by Oscar Wilde (1854–1900).

6. Probably John Mason Brown (1900–1969), theatre critic and lecturer.

7. Nowell quotes from this unlocated clipping: "Fiction is threatened with an epidemic of obesity. One of the latest symptoms in this country—the English situation is general and serious—is word from Thomas Wolfe who is working on a Maine coast island on a novel to be called *October Fair*. He confesses to a total of 500,000 words to date, and Charles Scribner's Sons are telegraphing their pleas for a process of selection, revision and condensation" (*Letters*, p. 310).

ALS, 1 p., PUL

c. January 1932

Dear Max: Part of this was written some time ago, and part very recently—and some of it quite rapidly.[1] I've simply tried to give you a man—as for plot, there's not any, but there's this idea which I believe is pretty plain—I've always wanted to say something about <u>old men</u> and <u>young men</u>, and that's what Ive tried to do here.

I hope the man seems real and living to you and that it has the unity of this feeling I spoke about. I could do a lot more to it, but I'd like you to see it. Please read all of it, Max—Tom Wolfe

1. "A Portrait of Bascom Hawke," *Scribner's Magazine*, April 1932; MP submitted the story without informing TW to the *Scribner's Magazine* short novel contest.

FROM: Alfred Dashiell   *CC, 1 p., PUL*

January 29, 1932

Dear Tom:

We have sent your manuscript to the press, and you will have a chance to make any necessary corrections in the galleys. We have placed $500, to your account. Is that the way you want it done?

I am writing you this note since I might miss you if you come in. I have to go down home due to the death of my sister-in-law. I shall be back the first of the week, probably Monday.

Sincerely yours,

Alfred Dashiell
Managing Editor

Mr. Thomas Wolfe.
111 Columbia Heights,
Brooklyn, N.Y.

ALS, 2 pp., Harvard
Harvard Club letterhead

1932

March 16ᵗʰ

Dear Tom:—Why didn't you come in. I'd hoped to get you for dinner since train doesn't go till ten.

Do have that 40,000 word piece done when I get back.—And if sooner give it to Dashiell[1]

Yours
Maxwell Perkins

1. Probably "A Portrait of Bascom Hawke," *Scribner's Magazine*, April 1932, or "The Web of Earth," *Scribner's Magazine*, July 1932.

FROM: *Alfred Dashiell*   *CC, 2 pp., PUL*

May 11, 1932

Dear Tom:

I am sending over the manuscript which I have. I thought it might be easier to work with this one. You will see that I have gone through it and corrected the obvious errors and fixed up the names.[1]

I have also tried to straighten out the punctuation, and have indicated some paragraphs. They may not be according to your ideas. I merely send them along for what they are worth.

I do think that a plethora of dashes makes reading harder. I have left them in where they seemed necessary, but cut them out otherwise.

Perkins still feels that the first page should not be used, or that some introductory paragraph should be placed before it. I am not so sure. I think perhaps you could use the first part of page two and run page 1 in after that.[2]

The chief thing to do is to cut 30 pages if possible. Then to change the name of Hugh Young, and also of Ambrose Featherstone if you think it necessary.

You may see some places that I have put in brackets. They were tentative suggestions for cuts. I do think in a number of places that you could make one paragraph do the work of two. The story would move much faster in the early part, which I think is desirable. I believe the story about Lydia and Ella Beals could be condensed. That seemed to me to spread out a little far. I think a part of the effect of the story is the speed with which the loom works, moving from one color to another.

I will talk with you some more about it the first chance you have. I am going away Friday afternoon, but will be back late Saturday night. Perhaps if your brother has to go back on Sunday you can come up afterwards.

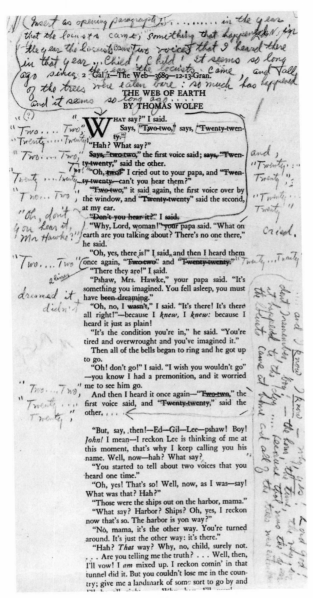

Wolfe's revised galley proof for "The Web of Earth" in *Scribner's Magazine* (July 1932). Wolfe changed the narrator's name from Delia Hawke to Eliza Gant when he collected the story in *From Death to Morning* (Houghton Library, Harvard University).

The story is all right. I do think it will be helped rather than hurt by cutting.
Sincerely yours,

Alfred Dashiell
Managing Editor

1. "The Web of Earth."
2. The story appeared with the headnote:

The rich story of a life, a tapestry of experiences and sensations woven from the fabric of a woman's memory, as she tells her son what begins as a simple episode and becomes in the telling a narrative covering seventy years. The author of "Look Homeward, Angel" has created a memorable character in Delia Hawke and through her has given reality to the events and people in her life. (*Scribner's Magazine* XI [July 1932], 11.)

TO: Scribner's Magazine
c. July 1932

TLS, 1 p., PUL

111 Columbia Heights
Brooklyn, N.Y.

The Editors,
Scribner's Magazine,
597 Fifth Avenue, New York.

Dear Sirs:

In view of the fact that the judges in the prize short novel contest have, after full consideration, eliminated all but two of the entrants, my story "A Portrait of Bascom Hawke" and one other, and in view of the fact that they have been unable to choose between the two for the first award and have recommended a division of the award, I hereby give my consent and full approval to such division of the award.[1]

Faithfully yours,
Thomas Wolfe

1. The three judges (Burton Rascoe, William Soskin, and Edmund Wilson) chose TW's story and John Herrmann's "The Big Short Trip."

FROM: John Hall Wheelock

CCS, 2 pp., PUL

July 19, 1932

Dear Tom:

Among the various fine things that I have heard from readers of "The Web of Earth," I thought you might be interested in the enclosed quotation from a letter just received from Mrs. Katherine Hayden Salter, the Wisconsin poet. I don't know Mrs. Salter at all well and I didn't even know that she was in the habit of reading <u>Scribner's</u>. You can see what enthusiasm your work has aroused her to, and she is a discerning person, not given to easy enthusiasms.

I'm sorry I got in so late yesterday afternoon, thereby perhaps missing a visit from you and a talk. I had just been down to the steamer to meet an old friend whom I had not seen for five years, on her return from Italy. I hope you'll be in again soon, dear Tom.

With all sorts of good wishes, as always,

Your friend,

J.H.W.

To
Mr. Thomas Wolfe
111 Columbia Heights
Brooklyn, New York

FROM: John Hall Wheelock   CCS, 2 pp., PUL

August 1, 1932

Dear Tom:

I don't want to bother a famous man with further tributes but I suppose you are so accustomed now to enthusiastic appreciation as to wear the edge off it a bit. However, I have a letter this morning from Robert Norwood,[1] the first I have had from him since his very serious illness, and it is so wholehearted and so spontaneous that I can't help quoting from it. He says: "I have been reading Tom Wolfe's amazing story, 'The Web of Earth.' Tom is a remarkable genius and this story shows that 'Look Homeward Angel' was not a flash in the pan. I have talked much to others about it—the most unusual thing of its kind I have ever read, marked with originality and with deep understanding of humanity."

All affectionate good wishes, dear Tom. I'm hoping to see you here soon.

As ever,

J.H.W.

To
Mr. Thomas Wolfe,
111 Columbia Heights.
Brooklyn, New York.

1. (1874–1932), religious poet and Scribners author.

FROM: *John Hall Wheelock*   *CCS, 2 pp., PUL*

August 31, 1932

Dear Tom:

It was awfully good to get your postal card[1] and I do appreciate all the good wishes for my vacation. I just got back to-day, after a very fine vacation, with only one cloudy day, so you see it looks as if your friendly wishes for me had prevailed upon the elements.

I hope you'll be coming in soon, Tom, and that we can have a good talk. During my stay in Easthampton I met quite a number of people who knew that I was with Scribners and talked to me about your book and also about your stories in the Magazine. You certainly have made an impression on your readers which in its intensity and enthusiasm is quite unique. I also had a visit from Van Wyck Brooks, and he told me of his lunch with you and Max, and how much he liked you.

Come in and see me, Tom.

As ever,
J.H.W.

To
Mr. Thomas Wolfe
111 Columbia Heights
Brooklyn, New York

1. Postcard unlocated.

CC, 1 p., PUL

Sept. 16, 1932

Dear Tom:

I am sending you the check you called up about. I hope you will very soon bring in some more manuscript.

Yours,
[Maxwell Perkins]

CC, 1 p., PUL

Sept. 23, 1932

Dear Tom:

I am enclosing herewith the check you called up about. Aren't you on speaking terms with me any more, or what?

Yours,
[Maxwell Perkins]

FROM: John Hall Wheelock

ALS, 2 pp., Harvard
Wheelock's personal letterhead

December 21,
1932

Dear Tom,

Where have you been keeping yourself? I have missed our talks in the office and the sight of your stalwart figure in my doorway.

I dare say you're out of town for the holidays or if not that you're "dated up" for Christmas. I tried to get you on the telephone to ask if you could take Christmas dinner with us on Sunday at 1.30, but learned that your telephone had been disconnected. It will be a very simple and unexciting occasion, just my mother, my uncle Bolton Hall, a little nine-year-old girl of his adoption, and myself. If you're in town and not otherwise engaged and care to come, just give me a ring. We'd love to have you and it would be a great pleasure for us all. I shall drop my professional rôle as publisher and promise you not to talk shop. If I don't hear from you, I'll know you can't manage it.

Max is out of town for a few days and the office seems bleak without his quiet but genial presence, though Whitney Darrow makes up, in volubility and general ebullience, for the absence of at least three men.

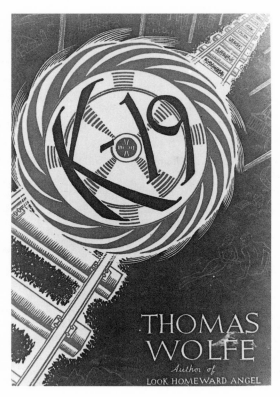

Salesman's dummy for Wolfe's withdrawn second novel. (University of North Carolina Library).

A NEW NOVEL *(title to be announced later)*

by **Thomas Wolfe**, author of *"Look Homeward, Angel"*

(Publication Date, Early November) Probably $2.50

This is an astonishingly eloquent and revealing book. K 19 is a Pullman car on a train that leaves New York on an afternoon and reaches Altamont in North Carolina the next morning. There are some nine or ten passengers in the car and as they are borne across the vast, still American country, so beautiful and so permanent, their hurried and chaotic lives are fully revealed: while the reader follows the threads of all these interwoven stories, he is conscious of the tragical drama of man's feverish transient life which is played against the profoundly beautiful permanence of nature.

© *Doris Ullman*

The sudden emergence of Thomas Wolfe was perhaps the most dramatic of American literary events in the last decade. His first novel was instantly acclaimed by the critics everywhere as an absolutely indigenous American work—and one full of beauty, humor, learning, and poetry. He shortly gathered about him a host of passionate admirers, whose number has increased ever since. They have waited eagerly for this new novel, and with the highest expectations. And these expectations will not be disappointed.

What leading critics said about Mr. Wolfe's first novel

LOOK HOMEWARD, ANGEL $2.50

"Worthy to be compared with the best of our literary productions."
—SINCLAIR LEWIS.

"It is a book of great drive and vigor, of profound originality, of rich and variant color . . . as interesting and powerful a book as has ever been made out of the circumstances of provincial American life. It is at once enormously sensuous, full of the joy and gusto of life, and shrinkingly sensitive, torn with revulsion and disgust. This is a book to be savored slowly and reread."
—MARGARET WALLACE in the *New York Times.*

"It is a rich, positive grappling with life, a remembrance of things past untinged by the shadow of regret, of one who has found his youthful experiences full of savor. No more sensuous novel has been written in the United States."
—JOHN CHAMBERLAIN in *The Bookman.*

"It comes through to you like fumes or like one supreme mood of courage that you can never forget, and with it is all the awe, the defilement and grandeur of actual life. . . . If I could create now one magic word that would make every one want to read the book I would write it down and be utterly satisfied."
—MARGERY LATIMER in the *New York Herald Tribune.*

[7]

A second novel by Wolfe was announced in the Scribners Fall 1932 catalogue, but Perkins canceled its publication.

Please forgive this hurried note, dear Tom, written amid the pre-Christmas confusion with all its rather futile little tasks. I'd have got in touch with you before, except for this telephone disconnection. Come if you can. In any case, I'll hope to see you before long.

With many good wishes, as ever

Your friend
Jack Wheelock

147 East 63 St.

TLS with holograph postscript, 2 pp., Harvard

Dec. 23, 1932

Dear Tom:

Forgive me for opening this. I guess you won't mind. I do not know where you are. I called you up and they told me "telephone disconnected." I suppose that means you have gone somewhere, but I hope you have left a forwarding address, and I hope you will write me.

I have just got back from Arkansas. Hemingway is coming on here soon. He is simply wild about your writing, and he wants to see you. He says the only thing he is afraid of is that you will quarrel with him.

Please let me know where you are. I was hoping to get you out for Christmas.- Maybe even now I can get you for New Years. Please write me,- and forgive me for opening this telegram. I only did it because I could not get you, and did not know exactly what to do with it.

Yours always,
Max

Had a fine time—Nearly froze to death. Want to tell you about it.—Just the way it was in Huckleberry Finn

MP

CC, 1 p., PUL

Jan. 13, 1933

Dear Tom:

Here is the $150 you asked for. I hope to see you soon,- and your story too.

Always yours,
[Maxwell Perkins]

ALS, 2 pp., PUL

c. February 1933

Dear Max: Here is the manuscript.[1] It is out of my book. Max, there are a dozen things I'd like to do this—I have a passage about Time that I want to put in, other things I want to take out—but I want you to read it now, I believe you can see what it is about. Max, it may be no good, or it may be good—I'm too tired to know at the moment—but of one thing I'm sure: it is made from the real stuff of life, it is made out of material I know to the bottom of my heart, and I have tried to put something of my vision of life in it. I ask you to remember that my book is about Time, I hope the Time theme is evident in this story.—Well here it is Max—its no good explaining any more—I hope it's good and you like it

Tom Wolfe.

I'm sending this by a friend.

Max, I haven't gone over this for errors in typing and punctuation—but I'll do that later

1. Probably "The Train and the City," *Scribner's Magazine,* May 1933.

TO: Alfred Dashiell, unlocated; from Letters, *p. 369.*
March or April, 1933

Dear Fritz:

I have done all that I can—and maybe more than I should. There is one short passage about Death which I have written in and which may be all right.[1]

The other <u>long</u> passage which I have inserted in the Fifth Avenue scene I want you to look at very carefully. I think the idea and purpose of it is all right, but don't let me do anything here to hurt the story—my head is not good enough today to know whether I have or not.

I think these proofs ought to be read again.

1. "Death, the Proud Brother," *Scribner's Magazine,* June 1933.

CC, 1 p., PUL

April 10, 1933

Dear Tom:

The enclosed income tax has to be filed by the 15th. You have to sign it and swear to it. And a check should accompany it. If you bring it back here before Saturday, you can swear to it, etc., before our notary, and we can send the check for you. I thought you would like to see it, and would be glad to see that it only calls for $7.14.

Always yours,

[Maxwell Perkins]

⌒

The following note presumably accompanied the work-in-progress that TW submitted to MP in April 1933.

TS, 6 pp., Harvard

NOTE

The concluding scenes of Anteus which are to follow will require one or two weeks work to include them in the manuscript. This whole manuscript is a first draft. There are still many things to be woven into it as it is and is intended to be a web of a man's memory of the past, but I hope its final purpose and relation to the Proteus section which follows may be evident from this first copy.

The plan for these remaining scenes that end this book and that lead directly into the book which follows which is called Proteus: The City, the opening scenes of which I am including with this manuscript, are as follows:

1 - There is a scene in which the narrator describes the life and movement on the road by day and some of the people that his brother meets along the road, and the life that flows around them in the towns they go to. There is a scene that describes the return home into the hills again by night.

2 - There are the final scenes at home, the night before departure, a family party in a restaurant, the streets of the town by night and then a scene similar to the scene about October at the beginning of the book.

The purpose of all these concluding scenes whether in the panorama of furious movement and human unrest over the earth or in the streets of passing towns or in the scenes after the return home is to emphasize and complete the ideas already described in this book. These ideas are:

1 - the frenzied dissonance and the tortured unrest in the lives of people from which the strong figure of the father has been removed and who no longer have any great image to which they can unite their power and energy or any central and direct unity to gather and control them and who are being driven like leaves across the earth in a fury of wild unrest and longing without a door to enter or any goal or summit to attain.

2 - The impulse drives the narrator to flight from home and wandering. When having returned home again and found his father dead he finds that now he can inhabit this life which he has known only as a phantom or as someone walking in a dream who sees, feels and remembers and experiences all things with a blazing vividness but who is unable to touch them, live in them or make them a part of him again.

The final scene begins at the moment of departure with the going of the train and concerns the journey of the train through the night and ends at morning as the train nears the city. This scene makes use of rhythms, memories and visions of time, the recurrent theme of wandering forever and the earth again, and the ideas concerning the eternity of the earth outside the train and the movement, unrest, and brevity of the lives of men who are being hurled across the earth in darkness which the movement of the train induces of which I already have the notes and to which I have already given the title - K-19.[1]

This scene and the end of this section ends at morning as the train begins to enter the tunnel to the city underneath the river, the first scene in Proteus: The City is about the river and the city and follows immediately upon this scene.

Finally, I want to give you the following information about the whole book. I have called this first section - Antaeus: Earth Again because Antaeus was a giant whose mother was the earth and who wrestled with Hercules. In my use of this fable I understand Hercules to be the million-visaged shape of time and memory, and it is with this figure that the narrator is contending in this whole section. According to the fable Hercules discovered when he threw Antaeus to the earth that his antagonist redoubled his strength each time he touched the earth and accordingly Hercules held him in his arms above the earth and conquered him that way. Accordingly, this part part of my book is about a man who is conquered by the million shapes of time and memory which came to life around him with every step he takes and every breath he draws, the life which was once his own, but which now he can no longer make his own no more than if he were a ghost.

In the beginning of the book the feeling is expressed that when a man's father dies the man must then discover a new earth for himself and make a life for himself other than the life his father gave to him or die himself. Therefore, the final words of Antaeus spoken just as the train which is taking him to the city nears the tunnel are these: "Antaeus, Antaeus, there are new lands. Child, Child, go find the earth again." That new land, new life and new earth is the city, and Proteus: The City follows immediately after, and just as Antaeus is revisiting and going back into the life of time and memory and just as I want, much more than I have ever in this first draught, to loot my life clean, if possible of every memory which a buried life and the thousand faces of forgotten time could awaken and to weave it into Antaeus like a great densely woven web, so has Proteus a forward going movement into time and is filled with all the thousand protean shapes of life in the city going on around him. I am giving you here the first part of Proteus which concerns the first year of a young man's vision of the city. The remainder of Proteus which you have not seen is written either in whole or in part.

[New page starts here—may not be continuation of the same memo]

The third[2] part of the book I have called for the present Faust and Helen, and of that third part you have already seen most of the concluding section, which deals with springtime in the city. The first part of Faust and Helen is only partly written; it begins on a ship and introduces the figure of the woman.

The fourth and concluding part of the book which will be called either Oktoberfest or October Fair will occur entirely upon the continent of Europe. For this part I have made notes but have written almost nothing. Its purpose is to conclude the fury of movement, unrest and wandering that drives men across the earth and to show that whether any final peace or assuagement can be given to people who have ever felt the Faustian hunger to drink and eat the earth, they cannot find the peace and certitude they sought by wandering or beneath a foreign sky.

Finally the last book deals with the impulse in men's lives to return, to find a dwelling place at home and a door that they can enter and it includes the general movement of the book which is stated in the words "of wandering forever and the earth again."

Therefore, of these four books you have now seen in the first draft almost all of Antaeus, part of Proteus and the concluding part of Faust and Helen. The fourth part of October Fair, as I say, is still, save for notes, drafts and scenes, unwritten.

It is now my desire to call the whole book Time And The River instead of October Fair as I think that Time And The River better describes the intention of the whole book. By the time you have read this new manuscript and this note you should be able, with what you have seen of the whole, to judge if the project is feasible or just a mad delusion on my part.

I myself believe it is feasible and believe now that after all the despair and suffering of the last three year that I have not been chasing a phantom or deluding myself with the fragments of a disordered intelligence. I believe, on the contrary, that it is possible for me to complete this book and have a coherent legend of the savage hunger and unrest that drives men back and forth upon this earth and the great antagonist of fixity of everlasting change, of wandering and returning, that make war in our souls. If this is incoherent it does not seem so to me now; that the book if completed would be one of the longest books ever written I have no doubt, but that so far as I am concerned, is no valid objection to its being done and if it is worth being done it seems to me that it is the publisher and the world of practical mechanics and salesmanship that must somehow adapt itself and not the world of the creator.

You know that I am so desperately anxious to get this great weight off my soul, that I will yield to you on any point that can be yielded, and solicit and be grateful for any help of editing and cutting that you can give me, but what I want you to do now, and what is desperately important to me is that you be able to get from the manuscript which I have given you some coherent idea of what I intend, and just tell me with naked frankness if what I intend is worth intending and worth doing and whether I shall continue.

I ask you to bear in mind that I am in a desperate frenzy to get something finally accomplished. I have written in less than three months time over 300,000 words and this present manuscript which I am giving you now has been done in the last five weeks and has I believe something like 150,000 words in it. As a man works with this frenzied haste he cannot give the best and the utmost that is in him; he is tortured by the constant memory of all the things he can and should do to improve it and all the power and richness that long and painstaking effort will sometimes give to a piece of writing. But I earnestly hope that if I have lost some of this I have gained something by the very frenzy with which I have gone ahead and that whatever has been lost enough has been left to show that the thing <u>could</u> be done if it is worth doing at all.

Now finally it is up to you to tell me whether you understand what I am trying to do. Whether it is worth doing and if I shall go ahead and for God's Sake do it without delay and with merciful even if brutal honesty.

Finally look at this outline once again:

Book 1– Antaeus: Earth Again (given to you here in rough draft with much left out that I want to put in, only the final three or four scenes lacking to make it a complete draft)

Book 2– Proteus: The City - given to you here in its first part and with most of the remainder written but still to be included in the manuscript.

Book 3– Faust and Helen - The final part of which you have read, of which you are printing two sections this spring in Scribner's Magazine;[3] the first part of which is mainly written either in full or in scenes and sections, still to be included.

Book 4– The October Fair - unwritten save for notes and rough drafts.

1. K-19 was the Pullman car on the New York–Asheville train. This section of the novel was broken up, but in 1932 Scribners expected to publish *K-19* as a separate novel. A facsimile of the publisher's dummy with the opening chapter has been published as K-19: *Salvaged Pieces*, ed. John L. Idol, Jr. (n.p.: Thomas Wolfe Society, 1983).

2. Typed as "first" but changed to "third" by an unidentified hand.

3. "Death, the Proud Brother," June 1933, and "No Door: A Story of Time and the Wanderer," July 1933.

Excerpt from MP's four-page report to Charles Scribner III, dated 18 April 1933 (PUL).

I do feel much encouraged about one thing though, although I can see unlimited work and struggle before it is fully accomplished;- that is Tom Wolfe's book. He brought me on Saturday something like 300,000 words of manuscript, considerable sections of which I had seen before. We already had here about 100, or 150,000 words. There is more to be done to fill in, but the book is really almost in existence now. There are many questions about it which will have to be argued out, and much revision and all that, just as was true of "The Angel."- But I really think that this book has half a dozen chapters in it that are beyond anything even in "The Angel"; and it may be a distinctly finer book than that. I had a sort of plan that after you come back, say in June or July, I might go off with Tom to the country, and spend a couple of weeks, and get the book into shape.

FROM: *John Hall Wheelock*   *CCS, 1 p., PUL*

April 20, 1933

Dear Tom:

Just a line to tell you that I had sent me from Switzerland the other day a review of the German edition of "Look Homeward Angel" which appeared in the principal Zurich newspaper, the Neuer Züricher Zeitung. It is quite long and exceedingly understanding and closes with the sentence: "This epic of the Gant family is the most powerful piece of writing that has come to us from present-day America." Sometime when you're in the office I'll translate the whole review for you, if you should care to hear it.

Best wishes to you, dear Tom.

As ever,

J.H.W.

To
Mr. Thomas Wolfe,
111 Columbia Heights,
Brooklyn, New York.

⌐⌐

TO: Alfred Dashiell, unlocated; from Letters, *p. 369*
c. May 1933

Dear Fritz:

I am leaving you the first seven galleys and will try to get the rest to you in the morning.[1] I have gone stale on this thing and my head won't work for me—but this is the best that I can do at present—and here is what I have done and the way I feel about it:

(1) I have rewritten about 80 lines in galleys *four* and *five* and estimate that I have saved about 350 words. Get the girl to type what I have written and then judge for yourself whether I have helped or harmed that section. You can cut the rewriting down all you can, but I feel the stuff on loneliness may set the mood for the scene that follows better than the present one.

(2) I think the prologue ought to stand as is.

(3) Of your minor cuts, I thought the most important one was the one about the drunken woman and the men who robbed her, and since I have already softened this I don't think it should be prettified any more and would like to see it included.

(4) Finally, if you can take my revision and cut it, if necessary, so that it would balance the needed cuts elsewhere, I would be grateful to you.

—And if my revision will balance up your suggested cuts in these 7 galleys, I will take my chance on the rest and try to cut so as to include the little scene I showed you.

I have taken your own galleys beyond galley 7 to work to-night.

1. According to Nowell, "The following note was clipped onto the first seven galleys of 'No Door' and left on Dashiell's desk after the office had closed for the day." "No Door" was published in *Scribner's Magazine*, July 1933.

TLS, 1 p., Harvard

June 10, 1933

Dear Tom:

I am enclosing a letter you are requested to write by the publishers addressed. You could simply mail this, though you have not actually seen the contract. It is here if you want to.

The next installment on your income tax is due on the 15th. If you will furnish the notice sent you by the government, we shall see that it is paid.

Everyone I know who has read "No Door" thinks it is even better than "Death the Proud Brother."

Always yours,
Max

FROM: John Hall Wheelock   *CCS, 2 pp., PUL*

June 13, 1933

Dear Tom:

The July issue of <u>Scribner's</u> came to my desk a few days ago and I have been reading your long story which now bears the title "No Door." I can't resist writing to tell you that a rereading of this story makes an even deeper impression on me than my first reading did—and that's saying a whole lot. I don't recall any other piece of writing like it; it is entirely your own and it is magnificent. Fine as your other stories in <u>Scribner's</u> have been, to me this is the finest of them all. If you had done nothing else in your whole life, this would justify you a thousand times over.

It is tremendously exciting to read a thing of this sort, so new and so real—and so completely on the side of life, on the side of everything that is vigorous and right. I know you get many letters, dear Tom, and this isn't written to bother you with one more, but simply as an outlet for the reverberations that your story has started up in me. The next time you are in the neighborhood, and in the mood, come in and we'll have another good talk.

As ever,
<u>J.H.W.</u>

To
Mr. Thomas Wolfe,
111 Columbia Heights,
Brooklyn, N.Y.

⌖

TO: John Hall Wheelock   *TLS, 1 p., PUL*

June 14, 1933

Dear Jack:

I want to thank you for your kind and generous letter about my story. It did me so much good to know you feel that way about it because I had worried considerably the last day or two about sections which had to come out on account of space and I was afraid so many cuts had been made that the completeness and substance of the story had been hurt by it. In that story I was really trying to say something which comes from a deep place in my life and which I think will color almost everything I do for years to come.

It makes me so happy that I succeeded with you and Max in saying what I wanted to say because there are no other two people in the world whose judgement and good opinion mean as much to me as yours. So thanks again for writing me as you did. I value these fine letters of yours and particularly this last one and your belief in what I do more than I can put down here in words.

As I have told you before, I have read some of your poems so often in the last two or three years and have been so deeply impressed by some of them that I am sure they have passed into my own work, and if you come upon evidences of that theft I want you to believe that it was done unconsciously and all I can hope is that it was sometimes done worthily.

I want to come in and talk to you the next time I go to the office. Meanwhile with all my thanks again and best wishes to you.

Your friend
Tom

⌖

FROM: John Hall Wheelock   *TLS, 2 pp., Harvard*

June 22, 1933

Dear Tom:

I have been reading your poem, "For Any Man Alive,"[1] and have been impressed by the terrific feeling pent up in it. It's a strange poem in that it is almost inarticulate and this very inarticulacy conveys, better than anything else could, what you are trying to say. I doubt if there is any word for this; it's a sort of onomatopoiea on a larger scale. The poem is so very much your own; of course it says in brief one of the things that you have developed along other lines and in greater detail in various parts of your writing. The poem sums up the predicament of every man living, as the title indicates, but it is a predicament which I think only the artist is aware of, except in occasional moments.

Thanks for letting me see the poem, Tom. I'm hoping we'll have another chat before long.

As ever,
Jack

To
Mr. Thomas Wolfe,
111 Columbia Heights
Brooklyn, New York

P.S. On all sides here I hear the same thing about "No Door." I haven't met a person here yet, who isn't enthusiastic about it.

J.

1. Unidentified.

⟜⟞

FROM: Alfred Dashiell   *ALS, 2 pp., Harvard*
c. June 1933

Dear Tom:

Here is a letter just received.[1] Please return it when you have read it.

This is the way people feel about you. It is the expression of thousands who don't write. Why then should there ever come to you moments of doubt? No author that I have known in my ten years here has ever aroused so much enthusiasm nor so many who look forward to new work of yours with such anticipation. No writer has ever stirred me as you have. No author has such a favorable critical audience awaiting him. Why do you disturb yourself with the mosquitoes? Or suspicions that people are likely to betray you? You are what you are. You can not be betrayed. Give your friends the same loyalty they [have] towards you.

Perhaps I should not write this but it tortures me to see you tortured. There is no necessity for it. You have a triumph awaiting you and you should not be kept from your reward by a perturbed spirit. Reason it out. Decide who are your friends—and don't let the rest bother you. Insulting letters are no novelty in this office. They used to worry me—and of course even now I don't welcome them but I have let them worry me no more [for] they usually come from people who have no comprehension of what I am trying to do. I know that I can not please

125,000,000 million people nor even a majority and so I place them in the category of those who are not my kind and entitled to their own opinions.

I'll talk to you about "Exile" when I see you. I think something can be made out of it.[2]

Yours,
Fritz

1. Letter from Donald V. Chacey, a naval aviator, praising TW's stories in *Scribner's Magazine*.
2. Unidentified.

♋

TO: *Alfred Dashiell*   *TLS, 2 pp., PUL*
                                                         June 28, 1933

Dear Fritz:

Thanks for your letter and for the enclosed letter from Chacey which I am returning to you. It is certainly a heartening and splendid thing to know that anyone feels this way about one's work

I won't say anything more about the letter now because I have just been talking to you over the telephone and said some of the things that I was going to write. Yes I think that it would be an excellent idea to ask him, when you answer his letter, if he has ever written anything about flying or his own experiences and why he does not send it in to you. If a flying man could really put down the sensation and experience of flying in such a way as to make the rest of us feel it I for one would be intensely interested in reading what he had to say. Of course we do not know whether he has the gift of putting such an experience into words but it is a hunch and it could do no harm to follow it.

I cannot tell you how much good it does me to know that such a person, whose interests are so remote from a literary life and who leads, as he says, a life of action, should think so well of what I do. While I have never felt that a man could do his best work for the huge public and that all good writing is in a way limited to a special and almost indefinable public, my feeling nevertheless is very strong that the best writing is not a precious thing and not limited to a little group of adepts and professional critics. In other words, I think there is scattered throughout the world the kind of public which this man represents, which is that limited yet hearteningly numerous group of people of fine feeling and intelligence and unprofessional appreciation. Somehow I really feel that the real mark of a writer's merit and the real measure of his success comes in the end far more from these people than from the professional literary critic and that it is really for the respect and belief of this unseen and unknown audience that a man instinctively does his work, and that is the reason I put such a high value on a letter like this one.

I do not know whether I can find the other two letters Chacey wrote me but I do happen to have a copy of the letter I wrote him and although it is pretty clumsily and badly written or dictated I am sending it to you because I thought you might like to see it as it will possibly make the whole situation clearer to you.[1]

Last of all Fritz, I want to thank you for your own letter which you sent along with Chacey's. I am not only deeply and sincerely grateful for what you say but I have also taken it to heart and recognize the truth of it. All I can say to you here is that the effort of writing or creating something seems to start up a strange and bewildering conflict in the man who does it and this conflict at times almost takes on physical proportions so that he feels he is struggling not only with his own work but also with the whole world around him, and he is so beset with demons, night-mares, delusions and bewilderments that he lashes out at everyone and everything, not only people he dislikes and mistrusts, but sorrowfully enough even against the people that he knows in his innermost heart are his true friends.

I cannot tell you how completely and deeply conscious I have been of this thing and how much bloody anguish I have sweat and suffered when I have exor-cised these monstrous phantoms and seen clearly into what kind of folly and mad-ness they have led me. But, I really think that even at the worst and craziest time of conflict and delusion we retain the saving grain of truth and judgment somewhere within us which keeps us from going completely out of our head. This is as near as I can come at present to telling you about it. But I live constantly in the hope, and I have never lost it, that a man can make his life better and cure himself of some of his grievous errors. In my good moments I do not believe any man on earth values the friendship and affection of his friends more than I and desires more earnestly to be worthy of their belief and is more cruelly tormented when he thinks he has mis-used them.

At the present time, however, I have given up cursing the iniquities of mankind and am venting my curses on the weather, and even feel a great surge of brotherly love and sympathy when I think of my eight million fellow atoms who are forced to sweat, melt, and swelter their miserable way thru the glutinous and interminable horror of a New York summer. If it would only turn cool again I think I could love everyone, even Mrs. Ella Boole.[2]

I will come in to talk to you about the story in a day or two.
Tom

P. S.   I have decided not to enclose the copy of my own letter to Chacey because I think he covers it pretty well in his own.

1. TW's letter to Chacey is published in *Letters*, pp. 363–64.
2. Ella Boole (1858–1952), head of the Women's Christian Temperance Union.

FROM: John Hall Wheelock   *TLS, 2 pp., Harvard*

July 17, 1933

Dear Tom:

Thank you so much for leaving the copy of Percy Mackaye's[1] letter, which I have read with the greatest happiness. It's a fine thing, Tom, to arouse such enthusiasm in a poet as critical as Percy Mackaye—and the letter is alive with a tremendous sincerity. I don't think Mackaye is much given to praising and his letter shows what a terrific impetus he received from your work.

The day after you called me up I had a line from Mackaye, which Max may have shown you. It begins with the sentence, "The work of Thomas Wolfe, which I have recently read in <u>Scribner's</u>, seems to me a colossal landmark in our poetic literature, for it is all quintessential poetry, both prodigious and delicate in power. It seems too good to be true that it should get published in a magazine." I think that is something that we can use in connection with our publicity.

I'm sorry I had to leave early on Friday, because otherwise I might have had the pleasure of one of our talks, dear Tom.

As ever,
Jack.

To
Mr. Thomas Wolfe,
111 Columbia Heights
Brooklyn, New York

1. (1875–1956), poet and verse dramatist.

TLS, 1 p., PUL
Brooklyn, New York

August 8, 1933

Dear Max:

In last Sunday's book section of The New York Times there was a favorable notice about the reception of "Look Homeward, Angel" in one of the Scandinavian countries—Sweden, I think.[1]

I think some sort of publicity also should be given to the fact that the book got fine reviews in Germany. Jack Wheelock read me the advertisements the German publishers sent me and the excerpts which they used from some of the leading papers of Germany, Austria and Switzerland, which are as good or better than anything I ever got in this country. Why should we conceal this fact? I notice that publishers of other writers use foreign reviews, which cannot touch these notices, and make full use of any favorable foreign publicity they get. The publicity I kicked about was that which seemed to me to be personal and gossipy and irrelevant and not substantiated by fact, but I see no reason at all to be ashamed of the fact that my book got fine reviews in Germany and Austria, and I do not see why that is not publicity which could be honorably and creditably used.

Therefore, since we both hope that I may again come through some day with a solid achievement and that you may profit from your investment in me why not make use now of what is honestly our own and what we might use to our advantage.

I am completing another section of my book which will be called The Hills Beyond Pentland, and which, I think, in some ways may be as good as anything I have done.[2]

I will come in to see you in a few days.

Tom Wolfe

1. Alma Luise Olson writing from Stockholm reported: "A translation of Thomas Wolfe's 'Look Homeward, Angel' has been favorably received by the critics as one of the significant novels coming out of America, a foretaste of all the pioneering vigor and originality that is still untapped in our native scene." "Scandinavia Considers Some New Regimes," *The New York Times Book Review*, 6 August 1933, p. 8.

2. Not incorporated in TW's published novel; parts of this section were published as stories and posthumously collected in *The Hills Beyond* (1941).

TLS, 1 p., Harvard

Aug. 9, 1933

Dear Tom:

We are sending out notes about the Scandinavian reception of "Look Homeward, Angel." Weber[1] had already seen the reference (<u>in</u> the <u>Tribune</u>, he said,) and was preparing to make use of it.

Why don't you give me the section on "The Hills Beyond Pentland" and let me read it, and so get familiar with that?- Because when we begin to get the book ready for the printer, you will probably want me also to understand it fully, all round. And it is a big book, and not easy to grasp. I wish you would give me that section and let me read it and say nothing about it.

Always yours,
<u>Max</u>

1. William Weber, head of the Scribners publicity department.

TLS with holograph postscript by Weber, 1 p., PUL

August 10, 1933

Dear Max:

Thanks for your letter. I will bring you the section called The Hills Beyond Pentland as soon as I can, although there is still a great deal more writing to be done on it.

Dashiell called me up yesterday and asked me if he could use "No Door" in an anthology which he is preparing and which he said would be published next spring.[1] I told hime he could if it was all right with you, but that I understood you were going to print a limited edition of it this fall.[2] I think he is going to speak to you about it.

I am also glad that notes are being sent out about the Scandinavian reception of Look Homeward Angel, but what interests me more and what I wrote you the letter about is the fine reviews the book got in Germany. Can't something be done about that?

I will bring you in the new section when I get it ready.

Tom Wolfe

Easy to combine the Scandinavian + German item in one note—make it more impressive.

W.

1. Dashiell included "The Web of Earth" rather than "No Door" in *Editor's Choice* (New York: Putnams, 1934).

2. This edition of "No Door" was not published.

TLS, 2 pp., Harvard

Aug. 23, 1933

Dear Tom:

Herewith is some royalty not, strictly speaking, due, but strictly speaking, earned. We are sending Mrs. Boyd a check for her commission.

I wish you had come down to lunch. It would have been vastly more fun, particularly as I know Kang was worried about whether he was going to get the boat, a little.[1] You must not blame us for not waiting longer than we did because it was evident that Kang was very much pushed for time,- going away for a year at least, and with a lot of errands to do,- and I could not rightly ask him to take any more of it for lunch than was necessary. I really think it was only his Oriental politeness that made him engage to go on that last day anyhow.

Yours,

Max

1. Scribner published Kang's *The Happy Grove* in 1933.

FROM: John Hall Wheelock   *CCS, 2 pp., Harvard*

September 12, 1933

Dear Tom:

I haven't seen you for a long time. I hope all goes well.

I had a letter this morning from Mrs. Katherine Hayden Salter, the wife of Professor Salter at the University of Wisconsin, and herself a poet of a good deal of quality. It seems that she has been reading "Look Homeward, Angel" and knowing that it was published by Scribners she wrote me about it. I'll quote just a few lines:

"I have just finished 'Look Homeward, Angel.' I've been going about in a semitrance for days because of it. The words 'Gargantuan,' or 'Rabelaisian' and the rest of the terms applied to it, all fit, but they leave so much—and to me, the most important part—unsaid. Never have I read any prose so prophetic, so richly concrete, yet so rhapsodic, so magnificently lyric as this. It takes one into the very heart of a stupendous vision. His genius seems to be a clairvoyance of intuition, a capacity for fusing tangible and intangible into a whole far more real than any bare realism could ever be. I could go on writing about it for hours, but naturally, I mustn't."

It is a pretty glorious thing, Tom, to have written a book about which so many people feel so strongly and which has given such tremendous happiness to people.

I'll hope to see you whenever you're in the neighborhood.

As ever,

J.H.W.

To
Mr. Thomas Wolfe
111 Columbia Heights
Brooklyn, New York

FROM: John Hall Wheelock   *TLS, 2 pp., Harvard*

November 18, 1933

Dear Tom:

I have made a few translations of excerpts from the most quotable German reviews, and given the original copy of these translations to Max. They seem to me almost the most wholeheartedly enthusiastic and affirmative reviews that I have ever read of any book in any language—and they also seem to me in many ways remarkably understanding. The German public has evidently taken your book to its heart.

I thought you might be interested in seeing these, and in case Max hasn't already sent them along I'm sending them herewith. I'll be only too happy to translate more of these reviews for you. Sometime when you're in, perhaps we can go over them together.

With best wishes, dear Tom,

As ever,
Jack.

To
Mr. Thomas Wolfe,
5 Montague Terrace,
Brooklyn, New York

TO: *John Hall Wheelock*   *TLS, 1 p., PUL*

5 Montague Terrace, Brooklyn,
New York, November 20, 1933

Dear Jack:

Thanks very much for your letter and for going to the trouble of making the translations of the German reviews. I do feel very proud of them and want to keep the copy you sent me, if I may. I hope Max got to see them too and most of all I hope they are just the beginning of something even better.

From the very beginning and of course even more now, I have had a feeling of great closeness and warmth for the Germans and for what I saw of Germany and their life. I wish I could go back again and I hope I may do something else they like and some day go back to see them.

Yesterday, which as you know, was a beautiful shining day, I took an eight mile walk right out through the enormous flat continent of Brooklyn to Coney Island. I had dinner in a very good place out there and wished you were with me. I hope we can get together sometime soon and meanwhile I send you my best wishes.

Thanks again for the letter and reviews.

Your friend,
Tom Wolfe

P.S. Jack, will you please keep the reviews, because the German publisher wants them sent back to him.

FROM: *John Hall Wheelock*   *TLS, 2 pp., Harvard*

November 21, 1933

Dear Tom:

We're keeping the reviews for you here and shall be glad to return them to the German publisher whenever you want us to. By all means keep the copy of the translation which I sent you. Any time you're in, Tom, I'll be glad to read out loud to you as many more as you care to hear. Every one of them is of interest and all of them show that the book is really understood in Germany. There is something in the German temperament, common to almost all Germans,—a vein of poetry which makes them eager for what the poet or creative writer has to offer and singularly intelligent about it. They really are a great people and when you think of what they have already given us in the way of poetry and music you begin to realize the strength and the depth of feeling they have.

Your walk sounds so nice, dear Tom, and I wish I had been along with you, for dinner also. I know how busy you are now, in the throes of this writing, but we'll have more time prehaps later on.

With many good wishes, as ever,

Your friend,
Jack

To
Mr. Thomas Wolfe
5 Montague Terrace,
Brooklyn, New York

CC, 1 p., PUL

Dec. 1, 1933

Dear Tom:

Robert Raynolds[1] suggested that you, he, and I have dinner on Friday, December 8th about seven. Could you manage it? I have had a nice letter from him, and must answer him, so let me know.

Always yours,
[Maxwell Perkins]

1 (1902–1964), novelist and friend of TW.

TLS, 2 pp., PUL

5 Montague Terrace, Brooklyn,
New York, December 15, 1933.

Dear Max:

I was pretty tired last night when I delivered that last batch of manuscript to you and could not say very much to you about it.[1] There is not much to say except that today I feel conscious of a good many errors, both of omission and commission and wish I had had more time to arrange and sort out the material, but think it is just as well that I have given it to you even in its present shape.

I don't envy you the job before you. I know what a tough thing it is going to be to tackle, but I do think that even in the form in which the material has been given to you, you ought to be able to make some kind of estimate of its value or lack of value and tell me about it. If you do feel that on the whole I can now go ahead and complete it, I think I can go much faster than you realize. Moreover, when all the scenes have been completed and the narrative change to a third person point of view, I think there will be a much greater sense of unity than now seems possible in spite of the mutilated, hacked-up form in which you have the manuscript, and I do feel decidedly hopeful, and hope your verdict will be for me to go ahead and complete the first draft as soon as I can, and in spite of all the rhythms, chants—what you call my dithyrambs—which are all through the manuscript, I think you will find when I get through that there is plenty of narrative—or should I say when you get through—because I must shame-facedly confess that I need your help now more than I ever did.

You have often said that if I ever gave you something that you could get your hands on and weigh in its entirety from beginning to end, you could pitch in and help me to get out of the woods. Well, now here is your chance. I think a very desperate piece of work is ahead for both of us, but if you think it is worth doing and tell me to go ahead, I think there is literally nothing that I cannot accomplish. But you must be honest and straightforward in your criticism when you talk about it, even though what you say may be hard for me to accept after all this work, because that is the only fair way and the only good way in the end.

I want to get back to work on it as soon as I can and will probably go on anyway writing in the missing scenes and getting a complete manuscript as soon as I can. I wanted to write you this mainly to tell you that I am in a state of great trepidation and great hope also. Buried in that great pile of manuscript is some of the best writing I have ever done. Let's see to it that it does not go to waste.

Yours always, Tom Wolfe

Max, I think the total length of the manuscript I gave you is around 500,000 words.

1. On 8 February 1934 TW reported to Henry Allen Moe, the secretary of the Guggenheim Foundation, on the work that resulted from a Guggenheim Fellowship. After describing the stories he had written for *Scribner's Magazine,* TW explained:

> There is one final thing about these pieces and their relation to the book. All of them, with the exception of The Four Lost Men, belong to the first book of a series, that is to the manuscript which Mr. Perkins now has, which will probably be called Time and the River, and which will be published this year. The Four Lost Men belongs to a second book of a series which will be called The Hills Beyond Pentland, of which I now have about 200,000 words in typed manuscript.
>
> The manuscript which Mr. Perkins now has for the first book is at present about 600,000 words long, but will be longer when I fin-

ish working on it, and, of course, shorter when we finish cutting it. Mr. Perkins suggests that the possible maximum in length, considering the publishing difficulty involved, the desirability of publishing each book in a singular volume, etc. is about 500,000 words. (PUL)

TLS, 1 p., Harvard

Dec. 16, 1933

Dear Tom:

Immediately after lunch I am going to begin on the ms., and expect greatly to enjoy it, for I have always enjoyed reading what you have done, and working in connection with it. It is a thing that does not happen to publishers often.- But I do hope you will go on writing those pieces which are missing, for that will hurry the whole work along.

Always yours,
Max

Undated memo to TW, presumably from MP for Of Time and the River

TL, 2 pp., PUL

THINGS TO BE DONE IMMEDIATELY IN FIRST REVISION:

1 - Make rich man in opening scene older and more middle-aged
2 - Cut out references to previous book and to success
3 - Write out fully and with all the dialogue the jail and arrest scene
4 - Use material from Man on the Wheel[1] and Abraham Jones for first year in the city and University scenes
5 - Tell the story of love affair from beginning to end describing meeting with woman, etc.
6 - Intersperse jealousy and madness scenes with more scenes of dialogue with woman
7 - Use description of the trip home and the boom town scenes out of the Man on the Wheel.
   You can possibly use the trip home and boom town scene to follow on to the station scene. Play up desire to go home and feelings of homesickness and unrest and then develop idea that home town has become unfamiliar and strange to him and he sees he can no longer live there.
8 - Possibly ending for book with return to the city, the man in the window scene and the passages, "Some things will never change"
9 - In the Night Scene which precedes the station scene, write out fully with all dialogue the episodes of night including the death in the subway scene
10 - Cut out references to daughter

OF TIME AND THE RIVER:
A Legend of Man's Hunger in His Youth
by **Thomas Wolfe,** author of *"Look Homeward, Angel."*

About 1,000 pages. Publication Date, April, Probably $3.00

The Author: *With the publication in 1929 of his first novel, "Look Homeward, Angel," Thomas Wolfe leaped into fame. Sinclair Lewis, in his Nobel Prize address in 1932, hailed it as one of the few books approaching greatness to come out of America. Since then, in the short stories that have come from his hand, Mr. Wolfe has given evidence of growing power, and the new work has slowly taken shape. Few books have been more eagerly awaited.*

The Book: "Of Time and the River" is an epic of the quest and pilgrimage of youth, more specifically of the American in his youth, but essentially of the young man in all lands and ages who has in him the hunger and urge of the creative artist. This pilgrimage begins in Altamont, N. C., the hero's birthplace, and takes him, through a great variety of experiences and adventures, to Boston and New York, thence to Oxford and finally to Paris, and into the countryside of France, from which he returns impelled by a growing homesickness for his own land. The book closes at Cherbourg, with a chapter describing the arrival of the ship which is to take him home.

It is difficult to convey the sweep and richness, physical and spiritual, of the huge panorama of this novel, the diversity of scene and background, the multiplicity and variety of sharply individualized characters, the force of its conviction, or the sheer beauty of the writing whereby all these are made to live. Prodigal and lavish as the American continent which is its underlying theme, the book is one of the few affirmative interpretations of America that we have had.

The Market: *Its immediate public will be those who have read or heard of "Look Homeward, Angel." Its potential public includes every reader capable of enjoying a work of fiction. With this in mind, it will have our backing to the utmost.*

[3]

The announcement for *Of Time and the River* in the Scribners catalogue was written before the novel was in type; the length and price were tentative.

11   Complete all scenes wherever possible with dialogue
12 - Fill in the memory of childhood scenes much more fully with additional sto-
      ries and dialogue

1. "The Man on the Wheel," part of the "Passengers" section of "K-19," was a fictional portrait of Henry David Stevens of Asheville.

⤸

TO: *Alfred Dashiell*   ALS, 2 pp., HRHRC
Late 1933

Dear Fritz: I'm sorry for the delay but here are the proofs of <u>The Four Lost Men</u>[1]—
all I've been able to do to it. I've worked all day on it, but I can't make my head
work well today—its' worn out and won't work for me—I feel as if I'm taking a big
chance with this and have never felt so uncertain about a mss. But I can't do any
more now; so will send it on.

I would appreciate it if you or Miss Buckles did this for me: on galley 2 towards
bottom where father says "The first vote I ever cast for President . . . . I cast in 1872
for . . . . . U.S. Grant"—will you please verify all these dates for me? I think I am
right about them, but I want the year and the Candidate to be right—in each case
the vote should be for the <u>Republican</u> candidate of that year.

Again, Max asked me to cut out references to whores and brothels in reference
to Our Presidents, etc. But I notice on galley seven a direct reference "—did they
not carry . . . . . Garfield, Arthur, Harrison and Hayes . . . . . the intolerable burden
of their savage hunger into the kept and carnal nakedness of whores"

If you want to keep this <u>as is</u>, its O.K. with me, but I think you will find that
I cut it out of mss. and wrote in a new phrase. If you want to use that, look at mss.
again. Please look over such corrections as I have made to see if you approve—if not
restore to original.[2] I'm awfully sorry to be so late and not to have done more—I'm
tired, but my head is too tired to work for me. <u>Be sure</u> to see that the <u>typewriten
insertion</u> goes in where indicated on Galley 4—Yours with thanks,

Tom Wolfe

1. Published in *Scribner's Magazine*, February 1934.
2. Dashiell maintained TW's revision.

⤸

TO: *Alfred Dashiell*   ALS, 4 pp., HRHRC
January 1934   *New York City*

Dear Fritz: Here's the story, with such corrections as I could now make. I think
I've succeeded in changing it to <u>past</u> tense everywhere—and will you please look at
the insertion which I have written in on page 9 to see if it is clear—and if I have

succeeded in doing what you suggested there—namely, to leave the knowledge of whether the dying man saw or did not see his wife meeting with her lover, in doubt. I've got to have another crack at this in proof, and know I can improve it.

As to the title, will you consider this one tentatively—<u>Dark</u> <u>In</u> <u>The</u> <u>Forest</u>, <u>Strange</u> <u>As</u> <u>Time</u> or <u>Dark</u> <u>In</u> <u>The</u> <u>Forest</u>, <u>Dark</u> <u>as</u> <u>Time</u> as a variant)—Don't ask me what the title means, I don't know, but think it may capture the feeling of the story which is what I want to do.1 This is all for the present—and please let me go over it again when you get proofs.

Yours,
Tom

P.S. I did not make the <u>cuts</u> on pages <u>5</u> and <u>6</u> as you suggested but rather omitted the reference to Uncle Walters drawers to avoid [arousing] the natural repugnance of your readers, etc. If you think there's too much of this [dialogue], go ahead and cut it out, but I wish you'd look it over again to make sure.

Tom.

1. Published as "Dark in the Forest, Strange as Time," *Scribner's Magazine*, November 1934.

TLS, 1 p., Harvard

May 11, 1934

Dear Tom:

I am sending you herewith a check for your balance. Most banks require a balance of $500. I don't know whether in Brooklyn you can start an account on this amount. When we get the Heinemann payment you will have a balance of $500, but you are not allowed to draw below that amount without paying something for service to the bank.

I am enclosing herewith our check for the balance here of $73.17. I hope I shall see you soon.

Always yours,
Maxwell Perkins

<table>
<tr><td>TO: John Hall Wheelock</td><td align="right">ALS, 2 pp., PUL</td></tr>
<tr><td>August 1934</td><td align="right">Brooklyn, New York</td></tr>
</table>

Dear Jack: I am leaving you five more galleys up through galley 11.[1] I would have had more but had to correct proofs of the stories in addition. I found little to do here although I am not wholly satisfied with the way it <u>flows</u>—I put some question marks in margins of galleys 10 and 11 for this reason: the tense changes from past to present—present when describing the look of the little town from the train window. Do you find this change of tense jumpy and confusing—and if you do will you change it all to past tense? I hope to give you some more galleys tomorrow and to get on now more rapidly

Tom

1. MP had taken *Of Time and the River* away from TW and set it in type.

TLS, 1 p., Harvard

Aug. 24, 1934

Dear Tom:

I am enclosing the royalty report so that it will be in your hands. I have inquired about the Czechoslovakian payment of $135, and the Modern Library payment of $500,[1] and find that they were both reported on the previous report, having been received before the date of this one. If you have your copy of the previous report, you will find them accounted for.

Always yours,
Maxwell Perkins

1. *Look Homeward, Angel* was reprinted in 1934 as a Modern Library Giant priced at $1.25.

FROM: Louise Perkins   *LP's personal letterhead, ALS, 2 pp., Harvard*
Postmarked 28 August 1934

Listen Tom, if any one else were as mean to Max as you were to night you would fight him![1]

You know that he is your friend - really your friend - and that he is honorable. Isn't that enough?

Please dont behave that way. It is partly because I have been so horrible and disappointed him so much that I beg you not to do it.

Louise -

1. During the summer of 1934 TW, MP, and Louise Perkins often ate dinner together at the Chatham Hotel. In a 27 July 1934 letter to Elizabeth Lemmon, TW wrote, "Louise and Max and I get together and pound the table and shake our fists and argue about Communism" (*Letters*, p. 420).

FROM: John Hall Wheelock   CCS, *2 pp., PUL*

September 17, 1934

Dear Tom:

I went over the French passages with our Mr. Hondot and he confirmed my corrections and said that everything is now in order.

When are you going to let me have back the first 38 galleys which you and I went over together and which are, as I recall it, now ready for the printer?[1] Max and I both feel that you ought to cut out of that part of the book the Harrison and Hayes passage in the boy's memory of his father on the porch. It isn't needed in the book and if it were used there it would spoil it for a story which should go into the book of stories.[2]

I enjoyed our dinner together so much, dear Tom. We must do it again soon. With all sorts of good wishes.

As ever,
J.H.W.

To
Mr. Thomas Wolfe
5 Montague Terrace,
Brooklyn, New York.

1. On 5 September 1934 MP reported to Frere-Reeves of Heinemann: "The struggle with Tom goes on. The present stage is that one hundred galleys of the book have been set up, about half. Tom has had them for quite a long time, and I cannot get him to give them up, but expect to in the end, which should not be far distant. There are still gaps in the book which should be filled in with about 5,000 words each, but for one of them Tom has supplied copy to the extent of 70,000 words. You can guess how it all goes on. We quarrel furiously, but the after-effects of the quarrels on Tom are generally good" (PUL).

2. "The Four Lost Men," *Scribner's Magazine*, February 1934, later included in *From Death to Morning*.

FROM: John Hall Wheelock   CCS, *2 pp., PUL*

January 12, 1935

Dear Tom:

I found your note this morning and I am leaving the manuscript of the additional material for you, as requested. You will see that it has been copy-edited for the printer, and I have indicated to him that it is to stand just before the last paragraph of the book. I spent quite a little time studying the spacing and came to the conclusion that the final quotation from the Song of Solomon should not stand entirely by itself. It is much stronger to have it connected with what precedes it. It will then be followed by a space and the final paragraph will stand by itself.[1]

Dear Tom, time is pressing and we are behind our schedule already. I hope you won't find much to change in this copy. I feel sure of it as it stands.

As ever,

J.H.W.

1. TW followed Wheelock's suggestion.

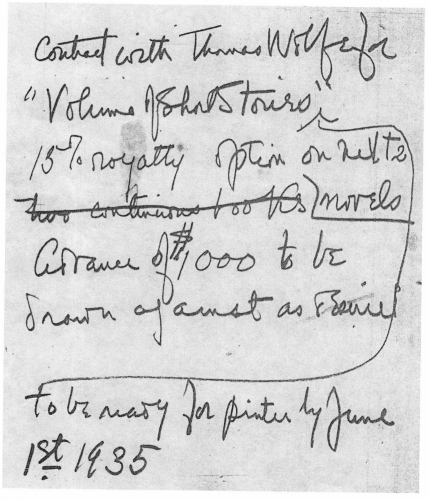

Perkins's contract memo for the collection of Thomas Wolfe's short stories that became *From Death to Morning*. The option on Wolfe's next two novels was struck out in the final document (Princeton University Library).

ALS, 6 pp., Harvard

Jany 21ˢᵗ, 1935

Dear Tom:—I'm committed to Key West now, however impossible it seems, to go, + since, when I return, Of Time + the River will be a book, I'm taking this last moment to say what I've long been on the point of saying:—[1]

Nothing could give me greater pleasure or greater pride as an editor than that the book of the writer whom I have most greatly admired should be dedicated to me if it were sincerely done. But you can not, + should not try to, change your conviction that I have deformed your book, or at least prevented it from coming to perfection. It is therefore impossible for you sincerely to dedicate it to me + it ought not to be done. I know we are truly friends + have gone through much in company + this matter, for my part, can have nothing to do with that, or ever shall. But this is another matter. I would have said this sooner but for some fear that you would misinterpret me. But the plain truth is that working on your writings, however it has turned out, for good or bad, has been the greatest pleasure, for all its pain, + the most interesting episode of my editorial life. The way in which we are presenting this book must prove our (+ my) belief in it. But what I have done has destroyed your belief in it + you must not act inconsistently with that fact. As for your preface there is this obstacle to it at the start: a reader is meant to enter into a novel as if it were reality + so to feel it, + a preface tends to break down that illusion, + to make him look at it in a literary way. But perhaps that is in some degree a literary objection to a preface + when your's began so finely I thought you might be right to have it. But when I read more of it today it seemed to me you did the very things you meant to avoid doing in the novel: you made the book seem personal + autobiographical, + by showing resentment against those who objected to the apparent reality (as the preface implied) of the characters in the Angel you opened yourself to the same charge against this book + notified the whole public that it might rightly be brought.—And of the whole public not a handful can understand the artist's point of view or the <u>writer's</u> conscience. In these + other ways, I thought, you bared yourself to all the enemies you have + I told you so because I am your friend—

Max

P.S. I thought that woman looked dangerous![2]
<u>MP</u>.

1. MP went to Key West to work with Hemingway on *Green Hills of Africa* (1935).
2. Possibly drunk woman in bar.

ALS, 3 pp., Harvard
MP's personal letterhead

Friday Feby 8ᵗʰ

Dear Tom:—I have seen the dedication in your book +, whatever the degree of justice in what it implies, I can think of nothing that could have made me more happy.¹ I won't go further into what I feel about it: I'm a Yankee + cannot speak what I feel most strongly, well. But I do wish to say that I think it a most generous + noble utterance. Certainly for one who could say that of me I ought to have done all that it says I did do.

I am glad the book is done because now it will be published.—But, although I had moments of despair + many hours of discouragement over it, I look back upon our struggles with regret that they are over. And, I swear, I believe that in truth the whole episode was a most happy one for me. I like to think we may go through another such war together.

Always Yours
<u>Max</u>

1. One draft of TW's dedication read:

TO

MAXWELL EVARTS PERKINS

A great editor, and a brave and honest man, who stuck to the writer of this book through times of utter hopelessness and doubt and would not let him give in to his own despair, the dedication of a work to be known as *Of Time and the River* is offered with the hope that it may be in some part worthy of the devotion, skill, the loyal and unshaken friendship that was given to it, and without which it could never have been written, with the hope that all of it may be in some part worthy of the loyal faith, the skill, the patience and devotion, without which none of it could ever have been written, and which were given to it always by a great editor and a brave and honest man. (*Notebooks*, p. 666. See illustration on p. 130.)

FROM: John Hall Wheelock   *TLS, 3 pp., Harvard*

March 1, 1935

Dear Tom:

This is a short line, on stationery from an office by this time quite familiar to you, to wish you every good thing one friend can wish another. I hope that you're going to have a glorious time and that you may combine with it some of the rest that you surely deserve. I think you ought to give yourself such a rest before you tackle any new work—though I know it will be hard for you to keep away from writing that long.

To

MAXWELL EVARTS PERKINS

A GREAT EDITOR AND A BRAVE AND HONEST MAN, WHO STUCK TO
THE WRITER OF THIS BOOK THROUGH TIMES OF BITTER HOPELESS-
NESS AND DOUBT AND WOULD NOT LET HIM GIVE IN TO HIS OWN
DESPAIR, A WORK TO BE KNOWN AS "OF TIME AND THE RIVER" IS
DEDICATED WITH THE HOPE THAT ALL OF IT MAY BE IN SOME WAY
WORTHY OF THE LOYAL DEVOTION AND THE PATIENT CARE WHICH
A DAUNTLESS AND UNSHAKEN FRIEND HAS GIVEN TO EACH PART OF
IT, AND WITHOUT WHICH NONE OF IT COULD HAVE BEEN WRITTEN

The dedication printed in *Of Time and the River,* reduced from Wolfe's original statement (Princeton University Library).

We're all looking forward with confidence and excitement to Friday, March 8. As you know, I feel and have felt all along that this book is going to have a material success as well as every other kind. To my mind it is one of the few really great books to come out of America, and I think it has qualities which are so overwhelmingly good, so full of life and so genuine in their force and conviction that no reader of any feelings at all will be able to resist it. I think you ought to feel very proud and happy to have written such a book.

We are going to miss you, dear Tom, and the office will seem very lonely. I shall think of you and look forward to your return. It has been the greatest happiness to have any part, however small, in getting "Of Time and the River" ready for publication.

My mother joins with me in sending you affectionate greetings and best wishes.

As ever your friend,
Jack

To
Mr. Thomas Wolfe
Ile de France
French Line,
New York City.

ALS, 1 p., PUL

New York City,
March 1, 1935

Dear Mr Perkins:

I am giving you the manuscript of <u>Of</u> <u>Time</u> <u>And</u> <u>The</u> <u>River</u> and of course you are free to dispose of it in whatever way you like.[1]

Sincerely,
Thomas Wolfe

1. MP declined the gift because he regarded it as improper for an editor to accept an author's manuscript.

Cable draft, 1 p., PUL

March 8, 1935

Thomas Wolfe
American Express Co.
Paris (France)

Magnificent reviews somewhat critical in ways expected full of greatest praise
Max

Cable, PUL
Paris

DEAR MAX TODAY IF I MISTAKE NOT IS WEDNESDAY MARCH THIR-
TEENTH I CAN REMEMBER ALMOST NOTHING OF LAST SIX DAYS
YOU ARE THE BEST FRIEND I HAVE I CAN FACE BLUNT FACT BET-
TER THAN DAMNABLE INCERTITUDE GIVE ME THE STRAIGHT
PLAIN TRUTH.[1]
TOM.

1. In his draft for this cable TW called MP "the best and truest friend I have" (*Note-books*, p. 675).

The dust jacket for Wolfe's second novel, his best-selling book (Thomas Cooper Library, University of South Carolina).

Cable, Harvard

Sent 14 March 1935

GRAND EXCITED RECEPTION IN REVIEWS STOP TALKED OF EVERY-
WHERE AS TRULY GREAT BOOK STOP ALL COMPARISONS WITH
GREATEST WRITERS STOP ENJOY YOURSELF WITH LIGHT HEART
STOP WRITING
    MAX

CC, 3 pp., PUL

March 14, 1935

Dear Tom:
    Everybody outside of this house, outside the business, was amazed by the
reception of "Of Time and the River." In the business it was expected, but even
there, the excitement of the reviewers and their enthusiasm, was beyond the degree
of expectation. You told me not to send you the reviews (I did send you a cable on
the 8th which you must have got) but I am sending you herewith the first thing I
can lay hands on that gives any kind of summary,- excerpts from some of the
reviews. The reviews on the whole I think are much better than these excerpts could
indicate. They all make parallels with the great writers, except in a few instances
where no parallels are made. About the only one that mentions a contemporary is
the one by Chamberlain[1] which mentions Lewis. Honestly, unless you expected no
degree of adverse criticism at all, because of course there was that about too great
length and the sort of things we all talked of, I cannot imagine why you should have
any restraint upon your happiness in this vacation. If any man could rest on laurels
for a bit, the man is you. As for the sale, we cannot tell yet how it will go on because
a large number of copies—some fifteen, seventeen thousand—were distributed to
the stores, and it will take a little while for them to sell out. But we are getting some
reorders now, and we have printed five editions,- 30,000 copies. The Times, Tribune, and Saturday Review gave you full front pages, and your picture was everywhere. People who went out on Sunday afternoon to teas, etc., as Louise did, and
Wheelock, where they were not publishing people, but just regular people, the book
was excitedly talked about. We have a splendid window of which I have a copy to
show you.[1] None of the things you feared about the book were even hinted at, and
your position is enormously enhanced in every kind of way. So, for Heaven's sake,
forget anxiety, which you haven't the slightest ground for but every ground for the
greatest happiness and confidence, and enjoy yourself.
                    Always yours,
                    [Maxwell Perkins]

P.S. A lot of letters have accumulated for you, but I am holding them as you directed. I am just writing this line the moment I got to the office and mailing it immediately so as to get it to you as soon as can be done.

    1. John Chamberlain previewed *Of Time and the River* in "Books of the Times," *The New York Times*, 8 March 1935: "It is undoubtedly the richest American fiction since 'Arrowsmith' and 'An American Tragedy'" (p.19). Chamberlain formally reviewed the novel on 12 March: "As one makes the acquaintance of person after person, one feels like rising to exclaim, 'Is there any living being whom Wolfe can't put before you in a novel?' Even his Rotarian-minded business men have detail, an edge, a bite to their characterization that might move Sinclair Lewis to homicidal envy" (p.19).

    2. Scribners Bookstore window display.

FROM: John Hall Wheelock   *TLS, 2 pp., Harvard*

March 27, 1935

Dear Tom:

    I haven't wanted to disturb you with a voice from the world whose cares and excitements you have extricated yourself from for a short time, but I can't resist sending you this letter from the young girl whom you have heard me speak of, Ruth Colburn Bowler—the one who had such a serious case of infantile paralysis. The letter is significant because it reveals the excitement and enthusiasms which your book arouses not only in literary people but in people of all sorts, old and young. It is these letters which make me believe that if we can only find a way of getting it to their attention, this book ought to sell to almost every reader of fiction in the country.

    I hope you are having a fine rest and a grand time. You certainly have earned them. The splendid reception the book had is by this time, I don't doubt, old stuff to you. Personally, I do not recall any book during my quarter of a century with the House which has been greeted with such overwhelming admiration, enthusiasm and excitement. The reviews have borne out what I have long known, that you are one of the few really great writers, the creator of a world all your own.

    We miss you, dear Tom, and the office seems lonely without you. I send you all sorts of affectionate greetings, in which my mother joins.

                         As ever,

                         Jack

To
Mr. Thomas Wolfe
Paris, France.

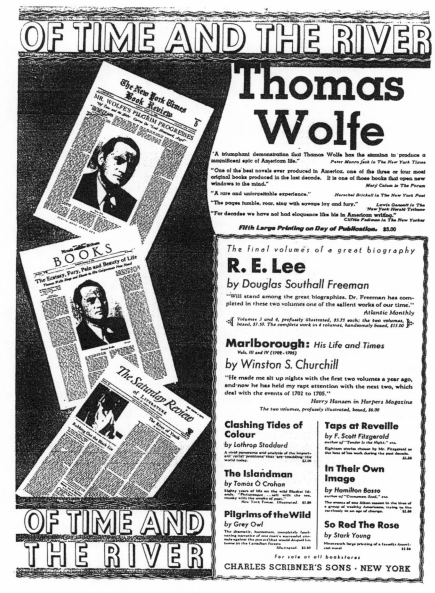

This full-page advertisement appeared in *The New York Times Book Review* on 24 March 1935, two weeks after the publication of Wolfe's second novel.

ALS, 132 pp., PUL
St. George's Court letterhead, London

*This is Section one—<u>Am sending letter in sections</u>
Sunday March 31,
1935

Dear Max: I know I should have written you before this, but until the last two or three days I have written no one at all—save for one or two, letters written on the ship—and of course have saved your letter to the last, because it was probably the one which should have been written first.

—Thursday—April 4th—I am picking this letter up again after three or four days intermission—I seem to have a hell of a time getting on with it, which is strange, as it is the one I most especially want to write—Charley Scribner is in town and called me up day before yesterday and I had lunch with him and his wife at their hotel yesterday and am meeting them again for dinner tomorrow night—It was good to see him, and in spite of Mrs Scribners instructions that we should not talk shop, I'm afraid we did talk shop—I have stuck to my resolution not to read reviews in the American papers, but I confess that I was unable to resist the temptation to buy N.Y. papers of recent dates to see what your advertising was like, and if any mention of the book in sales-lists was made—I saw a fine big page advertisement in the Times for Sunday March 24th—and also ads in other papers—Charley had several clippings that showed the book on best seller lists, and the latest one I saw—the N.Y. Times for Monday March 25 showed it leading in New York, Philadelphia, Washington and San Francisco—my own South apparently has left me flat—of course, Max, this is good and cheering news and I hope it will continue and mean that you will sell the book—the copies that you have printed—not only in order to pay off my money-debt to Scribners, but so that both Scribners and myself may get a little profit—for me, also, a little feeling of security—How unreasonable and contradictory our natures are! It would be fantastic and comical to know that I had written a "best seller," it would be wonderful to get the money that would come from it, and yet I would be troubled by it too—to know I had written a best seller, was a best-seller kind of writer: I would worry then to know what was wrong with my book, whether you and I had done something to cheapen it and make it popular—I was in a very bad state when I got over here—but think I am much better since coming to England a week or so ago—People have been very kind to me here—Frere Reeves, his wife, Hugh Walpole, some people I know in Hampstead and in Bloomsbury, etc—and the English have a way of putting you into an ordered and regular way of life, which I certainly needed badly—I am living in what is called a service flat in an old square right in the heart of fashionable London, Mayfair—it is much too grand for me and much too expensive—5 guineas ($25) a week—but it is so damned comfortable and well run that I hate to leave it—There is a valet like Ruggles of Red Gap,[1] and neat maids, and in the living room a nice coal fire—They bring up breakfast and set a morning table every morning—come in and tell me it is ready and I come out and read the morning Times and eat ham and eggs, kippers, sausages, marmalade and tea.—Frere Reeves was waiting for me at Folkestone when I crossed the channel, I was in a sorry shape, but it was good to see him, and the familiar look of England again, which makes me feel at home, and as if I've always known it—He drove me up to his week-end house which was only fifteen or twenty miles from Folkestone overlooking a beautiful tract of green country known as The Romney Marshes—His wife was waiting for us, we had tea, and went for a walk across the fields and through a wood, and I began to feel better—We came back and had a fine dinner of English roast beef, tart, cheese, wine etc—and started to drive up to London about ten o'clock that night—I was dozing off to sleep whole way up, went to a hotel for the night and got my first good nights sleep in weeks—In Paris I couldn't sleep at all—I walked the streets from night to morning and was in the worst shape I have ever been in in my life—all the pent-up strain and tension of the last few months seemed to explode and I will confess to <u>you</u> that there were times there when I really was horribly afraid I was going mad—all the unity and control of personality seemed to have escaped from me—it was as if I were on the back of some immense rocketing engine which was running wild and over which I had no more control than a fly—I came home to my hotel one night—or rather at daybreak one morning—tried to get off to sleep—and had the horrible experience of seeming to disintegrate into at least six people—I was in bed and suddenly it seemed these other shapes of myself were moving <u>out</u> of me—all around me—one of them touched me by the arm—another was talking in my ear—others walking around the room—and suddenly I would come to with a terrific jerk and all of them would rush back into me again—I can swear to you I was not asleep—it was one of the strangest and most horrible experiences I've ever had—There were about three days of which I could give no clear accounting—and loss of memory of that sort is to me one of the worse things that can happen—That was the reason I sent you that frenzied telegram—I had found your first cable when I got to Paris, but I wanted to know the worst—Your second cable cheered me up tremendously and at last when your letter with the excerpts from the reviews came I felt enormously relieved—I hope to God it all really is true as you said—that we have had a genuine and great success and then when I come back I will find my position enormously enhanced—If that is true I feel I can come back and accomplish almost anything—If that is true—if it is true that we have successfully surmounted the terrible, soul-shaking, heart-rending barrier of the accursed "second book"—I believe I can come back to work with the calm, the concentration, the collected force of my full power which I was unable to achieve in these frenzied, tormented, and soul-doubting last five years.—More than ever before, I have come to realize during this past month when I have had time to look back on that period and take stock of it—More than ever before, I have come to realize how much the making of a book, becomes an affair of honor to its maker. The honor of the artist—his whole life, all his character and personal integrity, all that he hopes and wants and dreams of, everything that gives his life any value to him—is at stake each time he produces any work—and that is really what the whole business of creation amounts to in the end—I hope to God that you and I have come through this ordeal honorably—I hope that we have won a true and worthy victory. You, I think, have done so in your great labors with me as an editor and a man—As for myself, the victory, if I have really won it, while a precious one, is not entire and whole as I would make it—If I have made my stamp come through, if through the ordeal and the agony of that book, the main outline of my full intention is revealed—that is a victory. But I can not ease my heart with the thought that I came through unshaken—I was badly shaken, time and again I was driven to the verge of utter self-doubt and despair by the sense of pressure all around me—the questions asked, the doubts expressed about my ability to write another book, the criticisms of my style, my adjectives, verbs, nouns, pronouns, etc, my length and fullness, my lack of Marxian politics and my failure to expound a set position in my writings—by all this, and countless other evidences of this pressure, I allowed myself so seriously to be disturbed and shaken that once or twice I [may] have been upon the very brink of total failure and submission. And now although, thanks to your great and patient efforts I may have won through to a victory—and pray to God this may be so!—that victory, as I say, is but a partial one, the full sum and import of my purpose has not been revealed.—I feel I have by no means begun to make a full and most effective use of my talent, and I hope this book will give me a position of some security, and freedom at last

This is Section <u>Two</u>

from the kind of perturbations that have tormented me these past five years, so that I may be able to achieve the concentration and totality I desire—

Sunday April 7—Well, here I go again—and I'm <u>bound</u> to finish this time— because it's an English Sunday and as I look out on Hanover Square there is nothing except the fronts of houses—not a person in sight, not a sound except a bird in the park—just an enormous slab of petrified time—thats' England on Sunday—I saw Charley and his wife again on Friday night—wedging into a dress suit I haven't worn for years—it is horrible how fat and heavy I've become—I've got to remedy it somehow—I told Mrs Scribner to have a barrel ready when I got there, for I didn't know what would happen if I drew a deep breath. We had dinner together and spent the rest of the evening talking in their rooms—most of the talk being about home again—Scribners in particular, why you wore your hat in the office—Mrs S. was particularly anxious to know about that and I volunteered my own explanation—whether Jack has had a great mysterious love—she was sure he could not have written some of his poetry if he hadn't—and the various manifestations of Whitney in all his forms—I have had several long talks with Charley and got to know him better than I ever did before—I think he is a very fine, a very generous and sensitive man, with an almost anguished sense of his responsibility, the most earnest desire to be fair and just and generous to all his people. He told me that he felt that Scribner's now constituted a tradition and that he felt it was somehow his duty to preserve it and pass it on—I told him that I thought he was right in feeling this way, and speaking as an "outsider" who had had some experience with the house and a chance to observe and know its people for the past five years, I was certain that dozens of people there—even people in subordinate positions—felt the same way about the place as he did; and that I had never seen another place where the spirit and feeling of the people was on the whole as good.—Charley seemed particularly anxious to do something for Scribner's while he is here in England—he told me that since Galsworthy's death there has been no one to fill his place on the list. He thought Hugh Walpole might do this, and told me that Walpole is dissatisfied with Doubleday and had approached Scribner's indirectly through an agent. At any rate, I took Charley at once up to see Frere Reeves who, although not Walpole's English publisher, is very intimate with him, and of course had former connections with Doubleday. Charley put the matter to him, and told him that he had heard Walpole was dissatisfied with Doubleday and would like to come to Scribners—Reeves said he thought these facts were correct and agreed it would be proper to write or speak to him—Charley wrote a letter, but Walpole has gone away on a three weeks cruise to Greece—That is the way the matter stands: I offered to help in any way I can—if anything I can do <u>will</u> help—and since there seems to be nothing at all improper in the circumstances. But, although I did not tell Charley so—and have myself no knowledge of publishing, I thought he had too high an idea of Walpole's value and of his ability to take Galsworthy's place. I have not read many of his books, in recent years, of course, his reputation has been in the decline, and he has been the subject of much criticism, including a cruel portrait by Somerset Maugham in one of his books[2]—which by the way in many respects was amazingly accurate—Walpole for example has a little book filled with names and engagements and when asking you to lunch will consult it, etc—But Charley told Frere Reeves jokingly that Walpole was "a good selling plater"[3]—in contrast to a fellow like me, for instance, who was a horse who might run like hell, and put up a performance that Walpole couldn't touch, but on the other hand might fall down completely—Walpole, you see, being the kind of animal who might not touch the heights, but would always perform creditably and "never do anything bad."—Now, this certainly doesn't hurt my feelings—in fact, I think human vanity is such that we are inclined to be pleased at being considered the "eccentric genius"—but in the end I think such reasoning is wrong—i.e. if it were true—just for the sake of illustration—that I am a man of great talent and Walpole a mediocre one, I think it would be much more likely that my own performance would be consistently better than his—and that the house would profit by me—This has nothing at all to do with me but simply with that rubber-stamp judgment of people that seems to me so profoundly wrong—I am going to talk to you about it in a moment in connection with these excerpts from reviews you sent me, for I think we may do something about them that is important and needs to be done—As to Walpole again, I think it very likely that you can have him if you want him—My impression of the man is this: a very amiable, genial, robust-appearing kind of man, with much real friendliness and generous feeling in him towards other people, particularly young writers starting out. But also a man completely sold out to success, comfort, "getting on"—so much so now that, no matter what the purpose and ideal (if any) of his youth may have been he no longer could make the sacrifice, the effort, and the risk of attempting an important work. He was apparently a little ruffled at the criticisms made of his books in recent years, and he told me never to accept the opinion of unsuccessful people about anything—this seems to have some truth in it until you reflect that it is often dangerous to accept the opinion of successful people, too.—Walpole, I think, is a man for whom the work of writing has become a necessary but rather tedious adjunct to the more pleasant occupation of being a successful popular novelist—He has a magnificent apartment overlooking the Green Park, 3 flunkies to wait on him, and an immense treasure in original mss, autographed first editions, paintings, sculptures, jade and amber ornament etc—For three hours every morning—from 10–1—his servants have orders that he "is not to be disturbed" by anyone—it is during this time, I suppose, that he writes his novels—one a year, he told me, for the last 25 years—The rest of the days is all mapped out in the little black book—lunch with so-and-so, the young first-novelist at one, address Golder's Green Woman's Club at three, tea at Atheneum with Sir So-and-So at five, dinner with Lord and Lady this and that at seven, theatre with somebody later, read the new books and write column for Herald-Tribune book review before going to bed.—There's your "selling plater" and of course I hope you get him and that his books are profitable for the house—he has diabetes, by the way, and takes a heavy injection of insulin twice a day—almost died of arthritis Christmas, but looks the picture of ruddy, robust, English-country squire-hood.

—Another bit of news that may interest you: Frere Reeves called up the other day and told me that the Book Society (?—leading English book club, anyway) of which Walpole is a member are apparently interested in Of Time And the River, and had indicated they might choose it, if he deferred his proposed publishing plans—I think he intended to publish in June—He said it was not a definite promise but that it looked fairly sure, and of course I agreed that it would be right to defer publication to fit in with their plans if they agree to take it—it would help the sale enormously, Frere said.—As for my other plans, it looks now as if I'm going to Berlin the end of this week or beginning of next, from there to Copenhagen, and then on to Russia in time for the May Day celebrations—This because I am now planning a monumental work in three volumes on The Success of Russian Communism, and following the example of some of my American colleagues, I figure I shall need at least a week in Russia to gather the necessary material.

—It looks as if I've got to go to Germany—it is apparently the only way of getting any money—if there is any—I understand it can not be taken out of the country, so I might as well go there and spend it. I wired the German publisher a week ago and asked him if he wanted the new book and what his intentions were, and said I was coming to Berlin. He wired back emphatically that he did want it, was "enchanted" to welcome me to Berlin, and when would I arrive.—To which I wired back, on Frere Reeves [   ] business advice, that I was delighted, but was also hard up, and what sort of offer would he make.—To which he answered that he was "certain" I would be satisfied with his offer, and offered to pay the expenses of my trip—That's how the matter now stands, so I suppose I'm going.

—My money has melted away like snow—Europe, particularly France, is now horribly expensive for the impoverished and devaluated Americans—of course, I bought round trip steamship's passage which was around $250 before leaving—at any rate I've got my ticket home, although its by the French line, and if I go to Germany, there's no way of using it unless I can turn it in (as they said I could) and exchange it for passage on a German or Swedish boat—In addition to that there have been railway fares, visas, etc—I am buying clothes—an overcoat, a hat, having shirts made, and a suit of clothes by Prince of Wales trousers maker, and will be the damndest dude in American literature when I come back—but still owe about $65 on clothes, etc, and counting up this morning found I had only $250 left—I hope to God you really <u>are</u> selling that book. Thank heaven, I don't have to see the look on Cross's[4] face when he hears the bitter news—Having been bitten by the bug of foppishness I would now go the whole hog and get another suit of clothes—they make 'em so good here—but perhaps had better not until I know more about the extent of my prosperity—

Max, I have done no writing—i.e. no formal work—since coming here—but I have kept a sort of note-book, or diary, in an enormous book I carry around in my pocket—The Paris parts, because of my state at that time, is somewhat distracted, incomplete, but the whole will be fairly complete by time I finish—and in spite of my state of mind over book, etc, I have seen and noted some very amusing and interesting things, persons, events—one, for example, in Paris late one night that tells more about the French and their character than whole volumes of speculation—It was in a <u>bistro</u>—i.e. a cheap bar with a few tables, a semi-circular bar of zinc, man behind bar, avaricious dark-visaged madame at cashier's desk counting up coins with holes in them, a couple of waiters, two young, apathetic, unsuccessful looking prostitutes at tables with a beer before them—two-o'clock in the morning, Place St Michel: at the bar only two customers, one a dingy looking little man, harmless, but very drunk, pounding on zinc bar, arguing in hoarse loud voice with bar man and other customer—Bar man young, hawk-visaged Frenchman, alert and able looking, blue apron, sleeves rolled up, keeping sharp eye on situation as barmen do the world over, finally calls on drunk to pay up and get out. Little dingy drunk refuses to pay—he owes <u>three</u> francs—gets very hoarse and obstreperous, pounds on bar, and finally offers to fight—"Very well! Good!" says bar man coolly—"But if you are going to fight, why don't you take off your coat?" The little drunk considers this with drunken solemnity for a moment, then wagging his head in drunken agreement says: "Good! All right! I <u>will</u> take off my coat!"—and considers the idea such a good one that he not only takes off his overcoat, which he hands to one of the waiters, but peels off his <u>other</u> coat as well, and hands it to other waiter—at which dark-visaged "madame—who has been murmuring tender cajoleries to a little dog and feeding him sugar which she cleverly conceals in her hand under her [   ] and various other places, making him hunt for it— "Say! Ah —

This is Section <u>Three</u>

you are wicked, you! . . . You're the naughty one!" <u>etc</u> One of the grotesque things in them is this sentimentality towards animals and their hard-boiled treatment of each other—Anyway she now turns from this tender dog-baby-talk and begins to screech out brusk instructions to the waiters who have both of the poor little drunk man's coats, the bar man speaks a few curt words of instructions to them, and the waiters grinning from ear to ear with delight rush off triumphantly towards the back of the place bearing the little man's two coats as security for his unpaid three francs—At this, of course, he is wildly indignant, bellows with rage, and takes a drunken swing at the barman. This is just what the barman has been waiting for— he vaults over the zinc bar like a flash, the waiters rush up, and they bounce the poor little man, minus both his coats, and in his shirtsleeves, right out on his ear—on the cold and frosty pavements of the Place St. Michel—Now I submit that this is a French story: the little man would very probably have been bounced out on his ear in England or America, but I think it is highly improbable that we would have thought of getting his two coats away from him first.—Anyway, I have kept this sort of diary, people, events, conversations of all sorts—the great boat race between Oxford and Cambridge Saturday—which I saw—a wonderful spectacle and the look and talk of the English poor all around me, lining the banks of the Thames as the crews came by—What it is like being back in Europe for an American after the last four years in America—how Europe seems to me now after the first abashment and bewilderment of my first visits in the twenties has worn off—why I know I could not live here—my other trips—I intend to make the same sort of notes for Germany and Russia if I go there—just what I see and feel and hear—and it occurred to me that the whole thing—starting the moment I left New York on ship until I return—very much pruned and condensed, of course—might make inter- esting and entertaining reading under some such title as "The Busman's Holiday"— What do you think?

—Now, as to those excerpts from the reviews you sent me—They were splen- did, wonderfully [   ], and I hope they were not too hand-picked—i.e. I hope that, as you said, they were taken more or less at random and if the reviews, on the whole were, as you say, better than these excerpts would indicate that would be wonder- ful—But even from these excerpts, good as they are, and from one or two indica- tions in advance notices before I left New York I think I can spot the trend of some of the [   ]—Max, Max, perhaps you think I hate all forms of criticism, but the sad truth is, how much more critical am I, who am generally supposed to be utterly lacking in the critical faculty, than most of these critics are. God knows, I could profit by a wise and penetrating criticism as much as any man alive, but as I grow older I am beginning to see how rare—how much rarer even than Lear, Hamlet, the greatest productions of art—such criticism is—and how wrong-headed, false, and useless almost everything that passes as criticism is—I know for example that the great length of the book will be criticized—but the real, the tragic truth is that the book is not too long, but too short—I am not talking of page-length, word-length, or anything like that—as I told you many times, I did not care whether the final length of the book was 300, 500, or a 1000 pages so long as I had realized com- pletely and finally my full intention—and that was not realized—I still sweat with anguish—with a sense of irremediable loss—at the thought of what another six months would have done to that book—how much more whole and perfect it would have been—Then there would have been no criticism of its episodic charac- ter—for, by God, in purpose and in spirit, that book was not episodic but a living whole and I could have made it so—the whole enwrought, inweaving sense of time and of man's past conjoined forever to each living [   ] moment of his life could have been made manifest—the thing that I <u>must</u> and <u>will</u> get into the whole thing somehow—Again, people will talk of the book having taken five years to write, but the real truth of the matter was that it was written practically in the whole in a year—it was written too fast, with frenzied maddened haste, under a terrible sense of pressure after I had written two other antecedent books and found I had not got back to a true beginning.—It is the work of frenzied, desperate, volcanic haste after too much time had slipped away, and no one will know that—Even now, I not read the book, save for a page or two at a time—at every point the deficiency of my performance compared with the whole of my intent stares me in the face—the countless errors in wording and proof-reading—for which <u>I</u> alone am utterly to blame—but which in my frenzied state of mind I let pass by stab me to the heart—I was not ready to read proof, I was not through <u>writing</u>—the fault is my own. I fell down on that final job, the book was written and typed and rushed in to you in such frantic haste day after day that I did not even catch the errors in wording the typist made in an effort to decipher my handwriting—there are <u>thousands</u> of them—I don't know where to begin, but for God's sake, if it should be vouchsafed us that <u>more</u> editions will be printed, try to catch these:⁵

page 506 "The Hudson River drinks from out <u>of</u> the inland slowly"—
Cut out <u>of</u>
page 509 "our <u>craving</u> flesh"—for "craving" print "waning"
p 510 "mining against the sides of ships"—for "mining" print "moving"
page 665 "The <u>minute-whirring</u> flies buzz home to death"—for "minute-whirring"—put "minute-winning"
page 663—"Battersea <u>Lodge</u>"—put "Battersea Bridge"
page 678—"I can <u>list</u> to nothing else"—put "listen"
page 678—"right across the character of my brain"—for "character" put "diameter"
page 678—"Hummel Vee"—put "Hummel Bee"
page 680—"I am as naked now as <u>sorry</u>"—put "sorrow."
page 517—"at this <u>gigantic</u> moment" substitute "<u>propitious</u>" for "<u>gigantic</u>"
page 519—"<u>ah</u> petty"—"so petty."
page 545 "<u>envy</u> and departure"—"error and departure"
page 545 "race of African <u>beings</u>"—"African <u>kings</u>"
page 545—"leonic"—"leonine"
<u>page 545</u> "the <u>bad</u> and almost brutal <u>volume</u>"—"the <u>hard</u> and almost brutal <u>violence</u>"
page 545—"<u>marked</u> his pain"—"<u>masked</u> his pain"
page 546—"shaking his <u>beard</u>"—"shaking his <u>head</u>"
page 549—"And nothing finally but night and dullness"—"night and darkness"
* page 576 (a horrible error) a hiatus between sentences, utterly meaningless—" . . . smiling his radiantly gentle and good-natured smile," I don't agree with you spoke with a crisp—etc
Change to
❡ "I don't agree with you"

¶ She spoke with a crisp but obstinate conviction, "Joel, I <u>know</u> I'm right!"

¶ "All right," he said quietly, "Perhaps you are—about the goal—but about the pavilion—I'd like to argue with you about that"

(Or better still, Max, since I cant remember, why not look up the manuscript and find out what I really did say!)[6]

page 588—"<u>ever-long</u> immortality"—put "ever-<u>living immortality</u>"

page 596—"dyed hair of straw-<u>blade</u> falseness"[7]—"straw-blonde falseness"

page 662—"ate cinq cent mille"—"et cinq cent"—

page 662—"a fond d'artichaut <u>moray</u>"—"a fond d'artichaut mornay"

page 669—"the man who wrote <u>Batouale</u>"—"<u>Batouala</u>"

page 671 "the great mirrors reflecting <u>these</u>"—"reflecting <u>them</u>"

page 672—"the veteran of a million <u>lives</u>"—"a million <u>loves</u>"

page 673—"the flat heavy <u>mark</u>"—"the flat heavy <u>smack</u>"

page 673—"<u>Light</u> up your heart"—"<u>Lift</u> up your heart"

page 676—"with mean and <u>senile</u> regret"—"the mean and <u>servile</u> regret"[8]

—Max, Max, I cannot go on, but I am sick at heart—we should have waited six months longer—the book, like Caesar, was from its mother's womb untimely ripped—like King Richard, brought into the world "scarce half made up"—

Before I went away, you wrote me, in reference to the introduction I wanted to write, that you were trying to "save me from my enemies"—Max, my enemies are so much more numerous than you expect—they include, in addition to the Henry Harts, Wassons, and others of that sort, the Benets, the I.M.P's, the F.P.A's, the Morleys, the Nathans, the Mark Van Dorens, the Mike Golds, and others of that sort—they include also the Lee Simonsons, the Theatre Guilders, the Neighborhood Playhousers, the Hound and Horners, the Kirstins, Galantieres[9]—and all that crowd with all its power and wealth—and I fear we have played directly into their hands by our carelessness and by our frenzied haste—our failure to <u>complete</u> just when completion was in our grasp—I gravely fear that by the time this reaches you the reaction will have set in—the enemy will have gathered itself together and the attack begun—I can't go through five more years like this last five—my health is gone—my youth is gone—my energy is gone—my hair is going, I have grown fat and old—and for all my agony and anguish—the loss of my youth and health—what have I got?—I've got to have some security and repose—I've got to be allowed to finish what I've begun—I am no longer young enough, I have not energy or strength enough to go through it again—

—For God's sake: try to kill false rumors

This is <u>Fourth</u> and
Last Section

when you hear them—before I left I saw that they were beginning to make another rubber stamp under the name of "criticism"—apparently they had discovered that I was six and a half feet tall, and very large—therefore it follows that all my characters are seven feet tall—bellow and roar when they talk—that I can create nothing but a race of gigantic monsters—Max, for Christ's sake, I beg and plead with you, don't let this horrible god-damned lie go unanswered—I have never created a monster in my life, none of my people are seven feet tall—the <u>fault</u> the <u>fault</u> always—as <u>you</u> should know—is not that we exceed the vital energy of life but that we fall short of it—and that a horrible misbegotten race of [ ] critics whose lies have grown underneath a barrel call out "monster" and "exaggeration" at you the moment you begin to approach the energy of life—You yourself told me you took one of your daughters through the Grand Central Station and showed her twenty people who might have stepped out of the pages of Dickens—and not a day of my life passes—a day spent in the <u>anguish of intense and constant speculation</u> and not at <u>literary cocktail parties</u> that I do not see a hundred—no, a thousand—who, if you put them in a book, would immediately bring down upon your head the sneers of the Patersons, the Benets, the Van Dorens, and all their ilk of "monsters," "seven feet tall," "untrue to life"—etc.

—In Christ's name, Max, what is wrong with us in America? The whole world—not myself alone—wants to know. The English ask me, + the French ask me, everyone asks me, Why do we cry out that what we want is life, and then try to destroy and kill the best people that we have? Why do our best writers, poets, men of talent turn into drunkards, dipsomaniacs, charlatans, cocktail-cliquers, creators of Pop-eye horrors,[10] pederasts, macabre distortions etc—I tell you, it is not I alone who ask the question, but everyone here—all of Europe knows it. Why is it that we are burnt out to an empty shell by the time we are forty, that instead of growing in strength and power we are done for—empty burnt out wrecks at an age when men in other countries are just coming to their full maturity.—Is it because the seeds of destruction are <u>wholly</u> in ourselves—that there is something in the American air, the weather of the American life that burns the lives of men to rust as quickly as it rusts iron and steel—Or is it perhaps that there is in us a sterile, perverse, and accursed love and lust for death that wishes to destroy the very people that we set up—the people who have something to give that may be of value and honor to our life. Is it because we take a young man of talent—a young man proud of spirit, and athirst for glory, and full with the urge to create and make his life prevail—praise him up to the skies at first, and then press in upon him from all sides with cynics eyes and scornful [faces], asking him if he can *ever do it again* or is done for, finished, no good, through forever. Is it because we deal this [hand] of death to young proud people—telling them they are the lords of the earth one year, and the glory of their native's country—and the next year sneering, jeering, laughing, reviling, scorning and mocking them with the very tongues that sang their praises—just a year before. Is this the reason why we "fail."—the reason that our finest artists are destroyed?—Tell me, is this the reason—men in England also ask me; they all want to know—and then how easy for them all, when we <u>are</u> done for—when we have been driven mad, when we are drunkards, dipsomaniacs, perverts, charlatans, burnt out shell—how easy it is for the whole pack to pull the face of pious regret—to sigh mournfully—to say—"What a pity!—We had hoped once—He looked so promising at one time!—What a shame he had to go and waste it all!"—

I know your answer to these questions—that the strong man is as Gibraltar—that all these assaults will fall harmlessly against his iron front, the impregnable granite of his invincible soul—but, alas, no man is strong as that—it is a pleasant fable—his great strength is needed, to be concentrated on the work he does—and while his [ ] and every sinew of his life is is bent to the great labor of creation, what shall protect him from these coward-hordes who come to destroy his life from every side—Why should the artist—who is life's strongest man, earths greatest hero—have to endure this in America of all the countries of the earth—when his task alone is so cruel hard there—the need for a new language, the creation of a new form so stern and formidable—why should he have to do this great work and at the same time withstand the murderous attack of death-in-life when in every country in Europe the artist is honored, revered, and cherished as the proudest possession that a nation has?—

Take this for what it is worth—If you think it extravagant, then take it so, but see the core of truth in this as well—I have given my life to try to be an artist, an honor to my country, to create beauty, and to win fame and glory, and the honor of my people, for myself. What has it got me. At the age of 34 I am weary, tired, dispirited, and worn out. I was a decent looking boy six years ago—now I am a bald, gross, heavy, weary looking man.—I wanted fame—and I have had for the most part shame and agony—they continue to speak of me as a "writer of promise"—and if I only do 197 impossible things—which they doubt that I can do—something may come of my work in the end. The Paterson woman says my people are all seven feet tall and talk in bellowing voices—she says take away his adjectives, nouns, verbs, pronouns, words of violence, height, altitude, colour, size, immensity—and where would he be—the Mark Van Dorens say take away his own experience, the events of his own life, forbid him to write about what he has seen, known, felt, experienced—and where would he be? The Fadimans[11] say take away his apostrophes, declamations, lyrics, dreams, incantations—and where would he be?—The Rascoes say he has no sense of humour—this to the man who created old Gant, wrote the lunch room scenes in the Angel, Bascom Hawke in the River, The Web of Earth, Oswald Ten Eyck, the Countess, the Englishmen at the [   ] and all the others[12]—the Communists say he is a romantic sentimentalist of the old worn-out romantic school with no Marxian code and the Saturday Reviewers a depicter of the sordid, grim, horribly unpleasant and [   ] school—and so it goes—in Christ's name what do these people want? Apparently, I would be a good writer if I would only correct 3,264 fundamental faults, which are absolutely, profoundly, and utterly incurable and uncorrectable—so what in Christ's name am I to do?—In God's name how am I to live?—What's before me?—I tell you, Max, I cannot put in another five years like the last—I must have some peace, security, and good hope—I must be left alone to do my work as I have planned and conceived it—or the game is up—I am tired and ill and desperate, I can't go on like this, forever—I got hurt somehow in Paris—how I dont know—during one of those three days I cant remember—I don't know whether I'm ruptured or not—I haven't the faintest idea, memory, or recollection of what happened—whether I got slugged in some joint or ran into something—but I woke up with a bruise above my groin the size of a saucer, and ever since it felt as if something has been torn loose inside me— Forgive these wild and whirling words—you are the friend I honor and respect more than anyone else—I hope and pray to God you may have some use and credit from my life—in return for all you have done for it—just as I hope that I can make it prevail—as by God's will, I hope and trust I yet may do—

This is all for the present—if there is any great good news for God's sake send it to me—at any rate stay with me, be my friend, and all may yet be well,—Take this letter—or rather this Chronicle, this history, for what it is worth—weed the good from the bad—and consider what truth is in—I'm sending it to you in three or four instalments because I cant get it in one letter—Goodbye, good luck and good health and love to all the family—Tom

1. The English butler in *Ruggles of Red Gap*, the popular 1915 novel by Harry Leon Wilson (1867–1939).

2. *Cakes and Ale: Or the Skeleton in the Cupboard* (1930).

3. A horse who is entered mainly in selling races, i.e., a dependable but not outstanding horse.

4. Robert Cross, Scribners accounting department head.

5. The many errors in *Of Time and the River* attracted reviewer attention. See appendix 5, for lists of additional errors.

6. The emended text reads: "*I don't* agree with you about the background, Madge. . . . I think you're wrong: I'd like to argue with you about that."

7. The emended text reads: "straw-pale."

8. Scribner made all of TW's emendations except in the two cases noted.

9. Henry Hart (1903–1990), author and editor at several New York publishing houses including Scribner.

Ben Wasson (1899?–1982), author and literary agent.

Isabel M. Paterson (I.M.P) (1885–1961), literary columnist for the *New York Herald Tribune*. In her 24 February 1935 review of *Of Time and the River* Paterson wrote that "it might be an interesting experiment to take one of his chapters and eliminate all the superlatives, the adjectives, indicating altitude, volume, and violence. . . . Step it down again to life size, and see what would remain. . . . Let the characters say what they have to say, instead of roaring, whining, stuttering or gasping. . . . The remainder we feel sure, would still be interesting, but would it impress the genteel critics so much?" (p. 18; the ellipses are in the original).

Franklin Pierce Adams (F.P.A.) (1881–1960), writer of "The Conning Tower" column for the *New York Herald Tribune*.

Christopher Morley (1890–1957), poet, novelist, and editor for the *Saturday Review of Literature*.

Robert Nathan (1894–1985), poet and novelist.

Mark Van Doren (1894–1972), poet, critic, and editor for the *Nation*. In his essay "The Art of American Fiction" (*Nation*, 25 April 1934), Van Doren criticized *Look Homeward, Angel*: "Old Gant was the masterpiece of that work, and as such was testimony to Mr. Wolfe's undeniably huge talent in characterization. But Gant had a son, and the son so weakens the book with his self-pity that the public is justified in asking Mr. Wolfe whether he can keep himself out of the picture in books to come" (p. 473).

Michael Gold (Irving Granich) (1894–1967), novelist and editor of *The New Masses*.

Lee Simonson (1888–1967), scenic designer for the Theatre Guild.

Theatre Guild, theater company devoted in the 1920s and early 1930s to presenting artistic, noncommercial plays. In 1923 the Guild rejected TW's play *Welcome to Our City*.

Neighborhood Playhouse, small New York theater company similar to the Guild. Aline Bernstein designed sets and costumes for many of their production.

Hound & Horn, literary magazine founded by Lincoln Kirstein (1907–1996), writer and ballet patron.

Lewis Galantière (1895–1977), playwright, critic, and translator.

10. Reference to William Faulkner's *Sanctuary* (1931).

11. Clifton Fadiman (1904–1999), book reviewer for the *The New Yorker* and Book-of-the-Month Club judge. In his 9 March 1935 review of *Of Time and the River* Fadiman criticized TW's excessive language: "There are thousands of these prose Swinburne passages, all marvellous until you ask what they mean. Thus it is impossible to say any one thing of Mr. Wolfe's style. At its best it is wondrous, Elizabethan. At its worst it is hyperthyroid and afflicted with elephantiasis. As Stevenson and Pater well knew, it is the blue pencil that creates the purple patch; but I suppose if Thomas Wolfe could use a blue pencil he would not be Thomas Wolfe. Still, he might be somebody even better" (p. 69).

12. (Arthur) Burton Rascoe (1892–1957), literary critic. Rascoe wrote at the end of an otherwise positive review of *Of Time and the River* that TW "has no evident sense of humor; nor any true sense of comedy" (*New York Herald Tribune*, 10 March 1935).

TO: *John Hall Wheelock*   *ALS, 18 pp., PUL*
                            St. George's Court letterhead, London

Tuesday, April 9, 1935

Dear Jack: I have certainly treated you badly in the matter of writing you—but I know you will excuse this long delay when I tell you that I was completely worn out when I got over here and in a state of nervous frenzy that made writing almost impossible. Since coming to England a couple of weeks ago I have been much better—people have been very kind and friendly to me here and the English put you somehow into an ordered way of living—I have begun to eat and sleep with some regularity, and I think I am now beginning to come back and will be all right. I began to answer a few letters a week ago, and wrote your mother thanking her for her fine and heart-warming steamer letter. I hope she has my reply by this time and is able to decipher my hen-tracks. I want to thank you also for your fine and generous letter which came to the steamer, and also to thank you for your other letter containing the letter Miss Bowles[1] sent you—will you please tell her for me how deeply I appreciate—how much I am cheered by—her letter? I dare not expect such generous enthusiasm from every reader but if I got only a portion of it, then I would never doubt of my book's success.

I have had no mail since leaving home except your letter, and two cables and a letter from Max containing excerpts from the reviews, and as I have resolutely refrained from reading the American papers, all I know about the book's reception is what you and Max have told me. I know you and Max are naturally eager to give me all the good news there is, but I know also that neither of you would invent good news just to make me feel better—and since you both say the news is good I rejoice with all my heart, and I hope success continues and grows and prospers and that neither you nor Max will have any disappointment in your hearts over the reception of the book, in view of the great labor you both put into it.—I finally completed a letter—call it rather another volume—to Max yesterday and sent it off to him in four different envelopes—since one would not hold it. I hope all four get to him safely and at the same time and that he manages to get them in their proper order and to decipher them—it was written over a week's time and in it, I am afraid, I run the gamut of emotions from Revelations to Lamentations—But I suppose he knows me well enough by this time to make allowances. In the letter, by the way, there was a list of additional corrections with the page and word, and if the book should go into another edition after he gets my letter I hope it will be possible to have these corrections made—Jack, here are a few more corrections, some of which may have been made, but I doubt it—will you make a note of these:

page 853: "Do not make echoes of forgotten tune"—for "tune" read "time"

page 855—"the Devil on Sunday"—should be the Devil in Society"

page 861—"the rails are laid across light bunched miles of golden wheat" should be "the rails are laid across eight hundred miles of golden wheat"—

page 863 "the Lindquist girl"—put "the Lundquist girl"

page 868 "the alluvial gluts, the chains of the continent"—put "the drains of the continent"

page 870 "we are the sons of our father, whose life like ours was loved"—the whole phrase should read "we are the sons of our fathers whose life like ours was lived in solitude and in the wilderness" (please change "loved" to "lived" but use your own judgment about changing the whole phrase as I have written it.)[2]

page 912 (This is just a suggestion for your consideration—Do what you think best about it)—"Proud, potent faces of rich Jews, alive with wealth and luxury, glow in the rich lighted cabins of the night; the doors are closed, and the ship is given to the darkness and the sea."—This is identical with the present version save for the addition of the words "of the night"—if you think they add to the rhythm and effectiveness of the sentence put them in—otherwise, leave them out.[3]

—Well, Jack, I hate to annoy you now with these fresh troubles, but I hope earnestly that now I will go on, after the frenzy and labor of the last five years, to work with greater security, calm, and certitude, and that you will not again have to go through such labor with me. This is all for the present: thank you again, dear Jack, for all you have done for me, and most of all for your belief and friendship— I'm going to Berlin from here to see my German publisher and may go on from there to Russia and Scandinavia—Anyway, I hope to see you sometime in May— Meanwhile, with all good wishes

Your friend—Tom

1. Unidentified reader.
2. The only change made was the emendation of "loved" to "lived."
3. Insertion of "of the night" not made in final sentence of the novel. All other emendations made except where noted.

Postcard of Hogarth's Servants *(c. 1750s)*
by William Hogarth (c.1695–1764), PUL
London

Postmarked 10 April 1935

Dear Max: This is the way people ought to look—and the way they always have looked—I see them around me every day—This is the only thing that <u>beats</u> time—if I could ever do it in a book I'd die happy *[Recto, beneath painting]*

    You didn't know I knew a lot about pictures, did you? Well, I do—about this kind—the "Old Masters"—Titian, Veronese—etc mean nothing to me—Only these men like Hogarth who had the sense of life that could speak to me in a language I know—<u>This</u> is one of the most wonderful pictures I ever saw. *[Verso]*

❱❱

TO: Maxwell Perkins

Postcard of The Usurers
by Marinus van Reymerswaele (1509?-1567?), PUL
London

Postmarked 10 April 1935

[Recto, beneath painting]
And maybe this is the way they always <u>have</u> looked too—the real title of this picture is Two Bankers <u>or</u> The Usurers—Does it look like anyone you ever saw?[1]

    1. Probably a reference to Robert Cross and Whitney Darrow.

❱❱

TO: Louise Perkins

Typed copy of ALS , 5 pp., UNC
London

Thursday, April 18, 1935

Dear Louise: I was surprised and delighted to get your cable and the news that you and Elizabeth and Peggy are coming over here in June, and if my answer to you was at all delayed the reason was that your cable was sent to Paris and then sent on here by mail. Nothing would give me more pleasure than to meet you and the children and if anything I knew or could show you would be of interest to you, the occasion would give me the greatest happiness—

    But as I told you in my cable I may not be in Europe when you arrive in June: my plan was to return to America sometime in May—I don't know what publishing plans Max may now have in mind concerning me, but he originally intended to publish a volume of my stories in the Fall, and if he does that, I want to come back and try to make the book as good as I can before it is published.—I wish you could persuade Max to take a short vacation now—in May—bring Elizabeth with you, if she can come, and have Peggy meet you in June when school is out. If Max felt he could not stay away for long, you could get a fast boat and he could spend three or

HOGARTH.   HOGARTH'S SERVANTS 1374

Dear Max, this is the very people ought to look — all the way they always have looked — I see them around me every day, this is the only thing that beats time — if I could ever do it in a book I'd die happy

MARINUS   THE USURERS (944)

But maybe this is the way they always have looked too — the real title of this picture is Two Bankers — Does it look the same

Two postcards mailed by Wolfe to Perkins from London on 10 April 1935 (Houghton Library, Harvard University).

four weeks over here and have a vacation—which he sorely needs—He could still get home by June, in ample time to make his preparations for the Fall season—I mention this, not only because the weather and the country is now getting lovely and would be beautiful in May, but also because, as I understand it, the Spring publishing season slackens up at about this time, and it seems to me, from Max's point of view, there could not be a better time to take such a vacation—particularly since I shall want his help so much a little later—I don't think there is anyone in the world—particularly at Scribners—who would not enthusiastically approve of a holiday for Max—so I wish you'd all do it—If Elizabeth couldn't come now, or if you'd rather have her come with Peggy, you and Max could come, and the girls could meet you later—Personally, I see no reason why two grown-up girls are not perfectly capable of making a five day journey by themselves in a trans-atlantic liner—and that's all it would amount to—You could meet them in Paris, London, or Berlin— or at the boat—there's no trouble at all about it—I am urging this plan—not because I have much hope that it will happen, because frankly I do not believe Max will agree to it—but because, by one of those sudden and blinding flashes of intuition which (whether it sounds boastful or not) <u>have rarely played</u> me <u>false</u>, I feel profoundly that he <u>ought</u> to agree to it, that a <u>wise instinct</u> on his part would make him agree to it, that if he came now, this trip would have a good and fortunate result, which he would never regret. The one thing I have observed in Max in the last few years which worried me and which seemed wrong was a growing tenacity in the way he stuck to business—what seemed to me sometimes an unreasonable solicitude and preoccupation with affairs which might be handled by proxy or in less exhausting ways. It is surely a sort of vanity, even in so modest a man as Max, to feel that a business cannot run itself if he is absent from it for a few weeks.- No one on earth—and I, as you know, have reason to know this better than anyone— no one on earth can do the kind of work Max does, no one could take his place in doing that—and if it were a question of some valuable work that <u>had</u> to be done now, there would be nothing for him to do but stay and do it—but my guess is that at just this moment—this season—there really is no such work—and that such a journey as I have proposed, brief as it is, would give him a spiritual and physical refreshment that in the end could work nothing but <u>the greatest good</u>. Max is now at the summit of his powers—the best work is still before him: it would be a tragedy if he in any way blunted or impaired his great faculties at this time simply because he failed to take advantage of a chance to recuperate and replenish his energies. Another reason I wish you could come now is this:—I think, from certain things I have seen, that this is not only a critical and immensely interesting period in the life of Europe, but also this particular time—the month of May—has several events of extraordinary interest—Here in England, for example, they are making preparations for the King's Jubilee—if you could possibly get to London by May 6th you would be able to see a kind of stupendous pageantry that the world may never see again, and that certainly none of us are likely to see in our lifetime—It should be an immensely interesting thing—I shall not be here myself to see it unless you and Max decided to come—because I have got to go to Berlin in a day or two and from there propose to go to Russia (in time for May Day if possible) and back to Copenhagen, and so home—but if you and Max could come, I could meet you anywhere you like—The best address I can give you at present is The American Express Co., Berlin, if you could come and would cable me there before I go to Russia. I would change my plans and meet you anywhere.

Of course, in all of this, outside of my earnest conviction that such a trip could do Max nothing but good, there is also some special pleading for myself. Nothing could possibly give me greater happiness than to meet you and Max and spend some time, however brief, with you over here—the blunt truth of the matter is that none of us are chickens any more—Max is getting on to 50 and I am almost 35, and this thing I have often dreamed of—of looking at some of these old societies and civilizations with him, and seeing together some of what they have to offer—this pleasant dream, I say, will probably remain forever just a dream unless it is now realized.

This is all I can say, and of course I fear my arguments are useless. At any rate, I think it's grand that you and the girls are coming—if I am here I should be delighted to see you—and if I miss you, I wish you the happiest and most interesting kind of journey—If you want to reach me within next ten days, try American Express Co., Berlin—Meanwhile, with best wishes and love to all,

Sincerely,
Tom Wolfe

FROM: John Hall Wheelock   *TLS, 5 pp., UNC*

April 18, 1935

Dear Tom:

I was delighted to get your fine letter of April 9, and my mother was made very happy by your earlier letter to her, which she has read many times and treasures.[1] She is tremendously enthusiastic about the book and incidentally has got a lot of people to read it—out of her enthusiasm. Many is the discussion that has gone on in our house about it, and I have yet to meet the person who has read the book and hasn't been fairly swept off his feet by its force and beauty.

I don't wonder that you were exhausted when you reached Paris. I'm glad you're getting rested and into a regular way of life again. If you can manage not to do any thing for a while, I think it would be a wise thing. Give yourself a chance to catch up.

"Of Time and the River" continues to hold the center of the stage here in the book world. I've never seen a book arouse more wide-spread or more whole-hearted praise and enthusiasm. You have taken your place as one of the great writers. As Max has written you, the only criticism has been along the lines which you will remember I predicted and has reference for the most part to a certain over-profusion and extension in the writing itself, faults which are almost inevitable ones of any great writer who gives himself in a generous and lavish outpouring and who, unlike so many, has too much rather than too little to say. I enclose a random page taken from one of our bulletins, which gives you in a brief compass excerpts from some of the important reviews.²

At the moment the book business is slower than it has almost ever been, and we get the same report from other publishers—but in spite of this, "Of Time and the River" continues to move along steadily.

Max gave me your letter to him, in four volumes, to read, and I knocked off work for the day and enjoyed it. Fully fifty per cent of all the corrections which you listed in your letter to him and in your letter to me were made some time ago and are registered in the last edition. The remaining fifty per cent I have now instructed the Press to make, and they will register in the next edition, whenever that is. All these corrections have been transmitted to Heinemann, and also to your German publishers. I feel most emphatically that the addition to the last paragraph of the phrase, "of the night" adds nothing, and to my ear spoils rather than improves the cadence. So that, since you have left it to me, I will not make this change.

Well, dear Tom, here's wishing you every fine and happy thing. You'll have some interesting times in Russia and Germany. It will be good to see you again when you get back, for we miss you here.

As ever, dear Tom,

> Your friend,
> Jack

To
Mr. Thomas Wolfe,
c/o Mr. Frere-Reeves.

P.S. A splendid review appears to-day in <u>Vanity Fair</u>, and also a large picture of you on the page which they occasionally run, entitled "We nominate for the Hall of Fame."³

1. Letter unlocated.
2. Bulletin unlocated.
3. In a review titled "Praise and Prejudice: The Greatest Novel of the Year" George Dangerfield wrote that *Of Time and the River* "is the most remarkable American novel since *Moby Dick*" (May 1935), 56.

CC, 3 pp., PUL

April 20th, 1935.

Dear Tom,

I've read your letter with the greatest pleasure up to the part where you began to get going against the tribe of critics.- I sympathize with all that too, but am concerned by feeling that you have got a wrong idea of the reviews in spite of what I have said. The reviews really were splendid, Tom, and what strange chance was it that led you to see the very worst thing said by anybody,- Burton Rascoe's statement

FALL PUBLICATIONS

STORIES
by Thomas Wolfe,
author of "Look Homeward, Angel," and "Of Time and the River"
Publication Date, October $2.50

The Author: *Mr. Wolfe has been called a man of authentic genius by leading critics. This book will support their judgment.*

The Book: Two of the stories are short novels—completely objective studies of women. One, "The Web of Earth," runs to 30,000 words, and "A Woman's Life" to 25,000 words. In these two stories the complete beings of one old woman and a young woman are completely unfolded with consummate skill.

Among the other stories are "The Men of Old Catawba" (full of earthy humor, a genuine American piece), "One of the Girls in Our Party" (an affectionate satire on the Middle Western school teacher), "The Four Lost Men" (which is based on a memory), "Circus at Dawn," "Dark in the Forest, Strange as Time," "Gulliver" (which shows how the world looks to a man of six feet six), and a number of others.

One would not think that after two vast novels new aspects of Wolfe's talent could be revealed—but they truly are. His humor, in particular, comes into full and brilliant play.

The Market: *Readers of "Of Time and the River," and every one interested in good fiction.*

The Scribners Fall 1935 catalogue entry for the still-untitled *From Death to Morning*. In response to the critic Burton Rascoe's assertion that Wolfe's fiction was humorless, the text emphasized the stories' comic elements.

that you had no sense of humor. That enraged me too, since even in the most tragic parts of the book there is humor. I think maybe Rascoe meant that Eugene had no sense of humor, which would at least be a more reasonable statement; for he does not exhibit it excepting occasionally and certainly to nothing like the degree the author does. But Rascoe's review was highly enthusiastic and excited, and I suppose the answer is that Rascoe has no sense of humor, which I think is the case.

The actual royalty sale to date is almost exactly 20,000 copies. The book has been second and third on every best seller list right along and even when third has been given twice as many book stores as the book below it. In fact "Of Time and the River" is one of the only three novels that is selling at all. The last six or seven weeks have been very bad,- but there are now signs of recovery, (along with the stock market,) and we can hope this will be one of those brief blights that have fallen upon business at intervals during the last four years. "Of Time and the River," cannot be stopped even by bad business. Everybody knows of it and everybody who hasn't read it seems to be going to. Even my mother read until she came to the scene between Dr. Maguire and the nurse. Mamma was all for the Doctor but the nurse was simply "too horrid." But Louise was reading her selections yesterday afternoon, particularly the one about Miss Telfair which she delighted in. She wants me to bring you to Windsor next summer, and I will too, if you will come.- And I'll show you some beautiful places there.- But I told her she might see herself portrayed in a novel along with the rest of the tribe,—which didn't alarm her.

If you think of a title for the stories, cable it. We are making up a dummy without a title and as I didn't want to worry you I haven't asked you before, but you might have found one.

Miss Nowell has sold enough stories (Gulliver to us)[1] to net you close to $1,000. or more, and as a sale of 20,000 copies even, will bring you $9,000. royalty, you ought to have the security you want for at least two years. As for the book of stories, I am very anxious to get this done rapidly, and we must tackle it as soon as you get back. These stories refute some of the criticism of you as being a too subjective writer. The woman's story[2] and "Web of Earth" are entirely objective. And that is true of several of the other stories. You have completely imagined whole natures of people totally unlike yourself. I think these stories will show them a few things more you can do and will give them another surprise. This is the way to answer critics. I showed your letter to Jack, partly for his own sake and partly on account of the corrections which had mostly been made a long time ago, and partly on account of your wanting the critics answered. He agreed with me about that. There is no need to answer them. Even if we couldn't answer them with what you wrote, it would be a mistake to get into a controversy and argument. The publisher is not supposed to be an impartial judge and I never knew any good to come from getting into a dispute.- Anyhow nobody could complain of the press you got. The praise utterly overwhelmed the few unfavorable comments. Yesterday Vanity Fair gave almost a whole page to an extremely enthusiastic review and also placed you in the Hall of Fame. I am enclosing the picture. You have unquestionably gained enormously in prestige by this book and in great repute in every sense on account of its publication. I've got lots more to say to you, but I'll say it next week when Miss

Wyckoff[3] is here,- she's gone off to Bermuda, leaving the old grey mule to keep the tread mill running. Have a grand time, but come back soon.

Tom, go see a doctor about the bruise. It might mean a hernia and then should be fixed.

Thanks for the post cards.- I have told many people you know a hell of a lot about pictures.- Just saw Henry James Forman,[4] an old boy.- Crazy about your book. "genuine work of genius."

Always your friend,
[Maxwell Perkins]\

1. "Gulliver, the Story of a Tall Man" *Scribner's Magazine*, June 1935
2. "In the Park" was published in *From Death to Morning* (1935), TW's short-story collection.
3. Irma Wyckoff, MP's secretary.
4. Henry James Forman (1879–1966), lecturer and travel writer.

TO: Irma Wyckoff, unlocated, from Letters, *p. 458.*

University Arms Hotel, Cambridge, England

Wednesday, April 24, 1935

Dear Miss Wyckoff:

I've wanted to write you for a long time to say hello, and tell you again how much I appreciate all your services to me, so generously and cheerfully given when you had other work to do, and to hope that all goes well with you and the others at Scribners. Imagine you have quite a parcel of mail for me—hope it hasn't been too great a bother—and if not too much extra trouble will you kind of keep it in chronological order? Also, if any beautiful women come in and ask for me, get their name, address, and telephone number and tell them I'll be back very soon and will get in touch with them immediately; but if they look and talk mean, ugly and vicious, tell them you don't know where I am, but that last you heard I sailed for Skaggeraks of Norway on a very slow sailing vessel for a polar expedition and that you expect me back in about five years. Good-bye and good luck and best wishes to all.

FROM: Irma Wyckoff

TLS, 2 pp., Harvard

May 4, 1935

Dear Mr. Wolfe:

That is the very nicest letter I have ever had from an author,- but of course it comes from the very nicest author we have ever had.

The only difficulty about your instructions for the women who come in is that

I am afraid it might be as it seems to be with Mr. Perkins. The ones he thinks attractive (and I guess that is most of them) I think ugly and vicious, and I should hate to send some fond lady away for five long years. There are several, all with the same telephone number, not all of them beautiful, but none of them vicious, who are looking forward impatiently to your return. Perhaps the number will sound familiar,- Volunteer 5–0650.

It's been fun watching your package of mail grow bigger and bigger each day, and I'll see what can be done about the chronological order.

Mr. Perkins is at the moment away on one of his "business" trips, and the mill just creaks along.

Sincerely yours,
Irma Wyckoff

TO: *John Hall Wheelock*   *Postcard of Grimburgwal, PUL*
Early May 1935   *Amsterdam*

Dear Jack: I have been here in Holland several days and am going on tomorrow to Germany. Will be sorry to leave here—it is a nice country—I hope all goes well with book Best wishes and love to all—T.W.

Cable, Harvard
17 May 1935

WILL YOU BE VISITING NOVELIST COLORADO WRITERS CONFERENCE HELD JULY TWENTY TWO AUGUST NINE PAY TWO HUNDRED FIFTY FOR TEN DAYS ONE LECTURE BY YOU ROUND TABLE CONFERENCES ON NOVEL CONFERENCES WITH STUDENT AUTHORS CABLE REPLY AND PROBABLE DATE OF YOUR RETURN MAX

Cable, PUL
20 May 1935   *Berlin*

ACCEPT COLORADO OFFER RETURN EARLY JUNE NO TITLE STORIES YET DEATH PROUD BROTHER SHOULD BE INCLUDED WAIT FOR ME.
TOM.

TO: *John Hall Wheelock*   *Postcard of Brandenburger Tor mit*
                                                         Reichstagsgebäude, PUL
Mid-May 1935   *Berlin*

They think I'm hell here—Americans best writers in world etc—so they say—
Ambassador's beautiful daughter[1]—all meals in embassy—parties—pieces in
paper—never got this at home and dont want to but its <u>unbelievable</u>

    1. Martha Dodd (1908–1990).

♿

TO: *Maxwell Perkins*   *Postcard of Brandenburger Tor, PUL*
Mid-May 1935   *Berlin*

Understand "Byron woke one morning to find himself famous"—Have been in
country—[   ]—Holland—several weeks—Got here and immediately—like dyna-
mite—ambassador's beautiful daughter—all the other ambassador's beautiful
daughters—newspapers—beautiful women—suppressed [   ] etc—Why should I
not like these people as [Whitney] told you—they think—they really think we're
the best writers today

♿

                                                  Postcard the Weimar marketplace, PUL
Postmarked 23 May 1935   *Weimar, Germany*

Dear Max: I am down here on a trip with Miss Martha Dodd who is the daughter
of the American ambassador in Berlin—they have all been wonderfully kind to
me—I am almost exhausted with Berlin hospitality—I have seen and heard some
wonderful things here and will tell you of them—Miss Dodd sends her greetings to
you—Tom

♿

                                  TLS with holograph second postscript, 10 pp., PUL

                                                      May 23, 1935
                                                      The Wartburg
                                                      Germany

Dear Max:
    I meant to write you before but for the last two or three weeks at any rate writ-
ing anything has been impossible. I don't know what my status quo may be in New
York but in Germany I have been the white-haired boy. I don't think I could stand
another two weeks of it but the last two weeks have been an extraordinary and won-

derful, and even enchanted period of my life because I have never known such a time before. I am so glad to have known it, so grateful, I shall never forget it. I have heard it said that Lord Byron awoke one morning at twenty-four to find himself famous. Well, I arrived in Berlin one night, when I was thirty-four, and got up the next morning and went to the American Express and for the last two weeks at least I have been famous in Berlin. I found letters, telephone messages, telegrams etc., from all kinds of people, including Rowohlt, my publisher here and the daughter of the American Ambassador, Martha Dodd, who is typing this letter for me. For two weeks I have done nothing but meet people of all sorts, go to parties, have interviews, get photographed by the Associated Press- and I have literally lived at the Ambassador's house. I have taken most of my meals there and if I didn't have my room there it did not matter much because I have had no time for sleeping, and since daylight now comes at three o'clock in the morning anyway in Berlin and Miss Dodd, her brother and I have sat up most of the night talking I have almost forgotten how to sleep. It did finally get a little too much for us so yesterday Miss Dodd and I left Berlin in her car and all through a wonderful sunlit day drove down south west through this magnificent, beautiful and enchanted country. We spent the night in the old town of Weimar and today we went about the town and saw first, Goethe's Gartenhaus in a wonderful green park and the rooms where he lived and worked and the saddle he sat on when he wrote, his high old writing desk and many other things that he used and lived with, and made his life and work seem real and near to us. Then we went to the fine old house in Weimar where he lived later on and where all the evidences of his great and illimitably curious intelligence-his laboratories, his work-shops, his great library, his rooms for his experiments in physics, chemistry, electricity and optics, have been exactly and truly preserved. Then we went about the town some more and visited the crypt where Goethe and Schiller are buried side by side and finally with regret we left that wonderful and lovely old town that seems to me at least to hold in it so much of the spirit of the great Germany and the great and noble spirit of freedom, reverence and the high things of the spirit which all of us have loved. Then we came here through one of the most indescribably lovely and magical landscapes I have ever seen. And tonight we are staying here in the Wartburg, a great legendary kind of hill from which came the legend that inspired Richard Wagner to write Tannhauser. We are going back to Berlin tomorrow through the wonderful Harz Mountains and I have not space or power enough here to tell you how beautiful and fine and magical this trip has been. I am telling you all this because you and I have often talked about Germany and the German people whom you do not like as much as I do and about what has happened here in recent years. But I want to tell you that I do not see how anyone who comes here as I have come could possibly fail to love the country, its noble Gothic beauty and its lyrical loveliness, or to like the German people who are I think the cleanest, the kindest, the warmest-hearted, and the most honorable people I have met in Europe. I tell you this because I think a full and generous recognition must be made of all these facts and because I have been told and felt things here which you and I can never live or stand for and which if they are true, as by every reason of intuition and faith and belief in the people with whom I have talked I must believe, are damnable.

Now I so much want to see you and tell you what I have seen and heard, all that has been wonderful and beautiful and exciting, and about those things that are so hard to explain because one feels they are so evil and yet cannot say so justly in so many words as a hostile press and propaganda would, because this evil is so curiously and inextricably woven into a kind of wonderful hope which flourishes and inspires millions of people who are themselves, as I have told you certainly not evil, but one of the most child-like kindly and susceptible people in the world. I shall certainly tell you about it- someday I should like to write something about it, but if I now wrote even what I have heard and felt in two weeks, it might bring the greatest unhappiness and suffering upon people I have known here and who have shown me the most affectionate hospitality. But more and more I feel that we are all of us bound up and tainted by whatever guilt and evil there may be in this whole world and that we cannot accuse and condemn others without in the end coming back to an accusal of ourselves. We are all damned together, we are all tarred by the same stick and for what has happened here we are all in some degree responsible. This nation today is beyond the shadow of a vestige of a doubt full of uniforms and a stamp of marching men- I saw it with my own eyes yesterday in one hundred towns and villages across two hundred miles of the most peaceful, lovely and friendly looking country I have ever seen. A thousand groups, uncountable divisions of the people from children eight years old to men of fifty, all filled beyond a doubt with hope, enthusiasm and inspired belief in a fatal and destructive thing- and the sun was shining all day long and the fields the greenest, the woods the loveliest, the little towns the cleanest and the faces and the voices of the people the most friendly of any I have ever seen or heard, so what is there to say?

I have felt a renewed pride and faith in America and a belief that somehow our great future still remains since I came here to Berlin and met some of the Americans here, particularly the father of the young lady who is writing this letter. He is a historian, a man who was born on a farm in my own state of North Carolina and who had spent his whole life before he came here in teaching and in the contemplation of history. He is I believe what is known as a Jeffersonian Democrat and believes in the society of free men and the idea of democracy which he thinks has never been given a fair and practical experiment anywhere on earth. I don't know whether he is right or wrong in this, his daughter I think is leaning toward the Communistic side because of some of the things she has seen and known here. But their home in Berlin has been a free and fearless harbor for people of all opinions, and people who live and walk in terror have been able to draw their breath there without fear, and to speak their minds. This I know to be true and further, the dry plain, homely unconcern with which the Ambassador observes all the pomp and glitter and decorations and the tramp of marching men would do your heart good to see. I wish you could have been there the other night in his house when he came back from attending Hitler's two hour and forty minute speech which was delivered to that group of automatic dummies that now bears the ironical title of the "Reichstag" and which was broadcast all over Germany. It was wonderful to hear him tell his wife "the way the Jap looked and the way the Englishman looked and how the Frenchman looked pretty hot about it and how he himself shook hands with the Dutchman on the way out and said 'very interesting but not entirely historical' and how the Dutchman grinned and agreed." It was Emerson who said that if you heard the pop of a popgun not to believe it was anything else but a pop of a popgun, even if all the captains and kings of the earth told you it was the roar of a cannon- he said it better than this but that was the substance and I always felt it was an American thing to say and was glad that an American said it. I think the Ambassador here is a man like this. I cannot tell you anymore now but I will tell you all I can when I come back. This has been in many ways an extraordinary and wonderful trip. I have remembered so many vivid and exciting things about it, I have seen so many different kinds of life and people I feel myself welling up with energy and life again and if it is really true that I have had some luck and success at home I know I can come back now and beat all hollow anything I have ever done before and certainly I know I can surprise the critics and the public who may think they have taken my measure by this time- and I think I may even have a surprise or two in store for you. If this sounds like bragging let me feel this way until I try to put it to the proof- in any case it can do no harm. After leaving London I went up to the county of Norfolk in England, a somewhat remote and out of the way place but a real blunt and good England I had never seen before. I lived around the little towns in the countryside for a week or two and saw some wonderful things and people and then I went to Holland for a week and then came on to Germany and Berlin and am writing you to-night from the Thuringian forest. I am going on to Scandinavia next week, will stay a short time in Denmark and think I will come home from there. Anyway I hope to see you the first part of June. Please don't go too far with the stories before I get there. There are things I can do that will make them much better and if you will only wait on me I will do them and we will have a fine book of stories and unlike any I know of. I think The October Fair[1] is going to be a grand book and we will try to meet the criticism of the critics and to show them I am improving and learning my business all the time. The book I am living for, however, is the Pentland book- it is swelling and gathering in me like a thunderstorm and I feel if there is any chance of my doing anything good before I am forty it will be this book. I feel such a swelling and exultant sense of certitude and such a feeling of gathering power and fulfillment that I tremble when I think about it and I hope to God that nothing happens to me or to my life, that I do not ruin myself with alcohol or some other craziness that can be avoided, before I get to it. Of this I am resolved: that if there has been any stir and public interest in this book I shall become more private and withdrawn in my life than ever before when I get back home and will allow myself in no way to be drawn out of it- I will go down deeper in myself than I ever have before and you must try to help me in every way to do this. It has been a great thing for me today to go to Goethe's house in Weimar and to see the way he lived and worked. I may never be able to be a great man like this- the life of a great man always fills me with hope and strength and gives me a renewed faith and makes me despise all the cheap and low little lives and base aspirations that you see about you in the lives of so many men today. Goodbye for the present, Max. This letter like its author is too long. It is now two o'clock in the morning and I have almost exhausted the girl who is typing it. I hope the letter will not exhaust you as the last one must have- also I hope that you and all are well and happy- that you will give my love to all the family. It will be good to see you again. I am looking forward to seeing you all. Meanwhile with all my best wishes,

Sincerely,

Tom

P.S. I hope you got my cable all right saying I would be glad to take the Colorado offer to go out there in July. The girl who is writing this letter, Miss Dodd, has written a story about Germany which for obvious reasons is written under an assumed name, which you might be interested to read. I hope she will let me show it to you. P.S. Saturday, May 26—Dear Max—I got back to Berlin last night at midnight after a magnificent and beautiful trip—Today I went to the American Express Co, and found there a letter from one Harry Weinberger, "counsellor at law" etc of 70 West 40th St New York, who says he represents Mrs Madeleine Boyd in reference to her "claim for agents commissions on royalties on your books published by Scribner's— He threatens suit, and wants to know when I will return, etc. This was the thing you said could not "happen"; the thing "she would not dare to do because she knew she was ruined by her dishonesty" etc. Well, she has done it, as I told you she would, because we were foolish, benevolent, soft-hearted, weak enough—call it what you like—to make the thief sign the confession of her theft when she was weeping, sobbing, crying in abject fear at the discovery and possible consequences of her crime— I have said things to you about Germany in this letter, but I want to tell you this—that if America has really at last become a place (as many people believe it has, where the thief, the criminal, the shyster can batten on blackmail, lies, and filth, and steal the earnings and the life of the good and decent man and the artist—if this has come to pass, I say, then by God, I no longer want to be an American, I will renounce and leave a place that has become so damnably rotten and accursed—by God, I will come here to Germany and become a citizen, because by comparison it is a haven of freedom, honor, honesty, and salvation for the artist and the decent honest man—Tom

1. Originally *The October Fair* was TW's working title for his second novel. The first half of this story developed into *Of Time and the River*. TW rewrote the second half, which Edward C. Aswell adapted for *The Web and the Rock* (1939).

Postcard of Goethe's bedroom in Goethe-Nationalmuseum, PUL
Postmarked 24 May 1935   *Weimar, Germany*

Dear Max:—Goethe died in this little room while sitting in the chair beside the bed—His study, laboratories, work rooms and library are just outside He made his wife and children live upstairs—out of the way

↜

TO: John Hall Wheelock   *Postcard of Goethe's garden house, Weimar, PUL*
Postmarked 24 May 1935   *Eisenach, Germany*

Dear Jack: They have overwhelmed me with kindness, hospitality, and good wishes here in Germany—and the country is a magic, beautiful, and lovely place—But there are other things I want to tell you when I come back—Tom

↜

Postcard of Goethe's portrait, PUL
Late May 1935   *Eisenach, Germany*

Dear Max: Here is a man you do not like from a nation you don't like so well—I like both the man and the nation but I have some very interesting and perhaps disturbing things to tell you when I get back—Tom

↜

Picture postcard of a wood carving of an Egyptian Girl, unlocated; from Letters, *p. 466.*

Berlin
Tuesday, May 28, 1935
Dear Max: I'm just about 2500 years too late to have known this girl but she's pretty grand, isn't she? I must leave here in a few days although everyone is urging me to stay. I have never known such friendship, warmth, good will and affection as these people have shown me—hate to leave.

AL, 3 pp., PUL
Hotel Am Zoo letterhead, Berlin

Sat
June 8
1935

Dear Max: These photographs were made by "Die Dame"—a German magazine that corresponds to Vanity Fair.[1] I have written a piece for them and they are
using one of these pictures—the one with the fist—when they publish the piece—
I thought the photos pretty good and am sending you one of each—Am leaving
here for Denmark in day or two and expect to sail for N.Y. about June 20—Sent
you a cable yesterday[2] concerning Rowohlt acting as Dutch agent and agent for all
Continental Europe and hope to find an answer at Amex co this morning—The
gay social whirl continues—I am now <u>sleeping</u> as well as <u>eating</u> at the American
embassy—why the hell I am keeping the hotel room I dont know—I come back
here to get mail and telephone calls—When I do I find my room filled with magnificent flowers which beautiful women have brought here in my absence—It has
been wonderful, thrilling—and very comical. There have been all sorts of stories in
the papers—my name has been mentioned in connection with Sinclair Lewis and
for that reason, I think, they think I'm very rich Last week one of the papers came
out with a photograph of a magnificent sailing yacht upon the Wannsee—a fashionable lake resort a few miles from town—It said the yacht belonged to "the
famous American novelist Thomas Wolfe" and that I was lavishly entertaining a
party of beautiful moving picture actresses aboard her—of course I had never seen
the damned yacht and someone told me I had met one beautiful moving picture
actress at a night club, but I didn't know who she was—The funniest part of all is
that the yacht really <u>does</u> belong to a young English artist that I met at the Greek
embassy—he has been saving up his money for

[*The rest of the letter is missing*]

1. Photos lost.
2. Cable unlocated.

～

Cable, Harvard

Received 8 June 1935

LONDON REGISTRATION PRECEDES AMERICAN PUBLICATION
THEREFORE THINK DUTCH RIGHTS PROTECTED BOOK NOW
UNDER OFFER HOLLAND ALSO MOST OTHER CONTINENTAL
COUNTRIES SEVERAL ALREADY SOLD CONSIDER INADVISABLE DIS-
TURB PRESENT ARRANGEMENTS DO COME HOME MAX

Postcard of Die Niederlandischen Sprichworter [The Netherlandish Proverbs]
(1559) by Pieter Breughel (1525–1569), PUL

Berlin

June 12—1935

Dear Max: I don't know if the U.S.A. postal authorities will let me send this card to
you[1]—but if you get it—please keep it for me—this is the painter I like best Tom

    1. TW may be concerned because the painting depicts several nude figures.

∽

Postcard of Frederiksborg Slot Castle, PUL
Denmark

Postmarked 8 June 1935

I found the girl all right, Max—not here, but in Berlin—I miss her so much it
hurts, and I am horribly worried, too,—I've got to come back home and work. For
God's sake keep people away from me if there are any—Tom

∽

Postcard of Copenhagen cityscape, PUL
Copenhagen

Sunday, June
16

Dear Max: I plan to sail for home on the Europa next Friday, if I can persuade the
G.D. French to transfer my return ticket to the German line. I have been here just
a day or two—a beautiful city and nice people but I am horribly worried and distressed at present moment and hope all is well with me—Tom

∽

Postcard of TW on steps of large building, PUL
Copenhagen

Postmarked 21 June 1935

Dear Max: I have a letter from a New York publisher with quoted excerpts which
informs me that Scribners last month carried 3 printed attacks on me one from
Miss Evelyn Scott, one from Mr. Ernest Hemingway—the Big Big He Man and
Fighter With Words Who Can't Take It—and one from Professor Wm Lyon
Phelps.[1] He wants to know why I should still consider Scribners my friends—Can
you think of an answer? This is a good picture, isn't it?

    1. The June 1935 issue of *Scribner's Magazine* published TW's short story "Gulliver,
the Story of a Tall Man," and included three references to TW.

In her book review of *Of Time and the River* Scott wrote: "Reflective without the mental discipline for illuminating his own moments of blindness, he mingles platitude with poetry in a quantitative effect which makes of this book a colossal fragment; sometimes gorgeously, sometimes childishly, commemorating a phase of young culture lost to Europe" (4).

In the second installment of *The Green Hills of Africa,* Hemingway wrote: "Writers are forged in injustice as a sword is forged. I wonder if it would make a writer of him, give him the necessary shock to cut the over-flow of words and give him a sense of proportion, if they sent Tom Wolfe to Siberia or to the Dry Tortugas. Maybe it would and maybe it wouldn't. He seemed sad, really, like Carnera" (340).

In his monthly column "As I Like It," Yale professor Phelps recommended one hundred new books for 1934. For the entry on *Of Time and the River* Phelps wrote, "This is the only book I include without a distinct personal recommendation. I include it because of its universally enthusiastic reception. I have not had time to read so long a book. I hope it is all 'they say' it is" (380).

⤳

TO: *Maxwell Perkins*

postcard of TW on balcony of
large municipal building, PUL

Postmarked 23 June 1935

Copenhagen

"Although both [Wolfe and the late D. H. Lawrence) were sprung from the socially obscure, neither shows any feeling of <u>class</u> resentment"—from a review.[1]

1. TW quotes Evelyn Scott's review, which reads: "Both were sprung from the socially obscure; but the work of neither is tinctured by *class* resentment" (4).

⤳

TO: *Alfred Dashiell*

Postcard of Hamburg,
Steckelhörnflet und Nikolaikirche, PUL

Postmarked 29 June 1935

Bremen, Germany

I'm crammed to the gills with kultur, kuche, and antiquity so I'm coming home again

⤳

TO: *Maxwell Perkins*

Postcard of Alt-Hamburg,
Sonniger Winkel im Kornträgergang, PUL

Postmarked 29 June 1935

Bremen, Germany

This is a good one isn't it?

FROM: John Hall Wheelock   *Wire, Harvard*
4 July 1935

THOMAS WOLFE
    SS BREMEN DOCKS 330 PM WEST 46 ST
AFFECTIONATE GREETINGS AND HEARTY WELCOME DEAR TOM
YOU RETURN A CONQUEROR
                                    JACK.

∽

Postcard of Rocky Mountain National Park, Colorado, PUL
Postmarked 30 July 1935   *Greeley, Colorado*

Dear Max: I've seen no mountains yet but the West is wonderful—blazing hot, but crystal air, blue skies—The journey across the country was overwhelming—I've never begun to say what I ought to say about it—Tom

∽

TLS, 2 pp., Harvard

Aug. 2, 1935

Dear Tom:
    When I got back from Virginia I learned that you had performed the miracle of finding that correspondence.[1]- And Mitchell[2] told me that he did not really think there was any case at all. He wanted the name and address of the Czecho-Slovakian publisher, and I sent it to him.
    I am sorry about the mountains not being visible when you are in them, but I used to know a man who could prove that there were no such things as the Rocky Mountains at all. But there are the Blue Ridge mountains, and Elizabeth[3] and I drove along the summits of them on a new road they have put down. You could see them all right, stretching all around at times, very blue.
    Mrs. Jelliffe[4] came in yesterday.- She had heard about your searching for your letters from her housekeeper, and I told her you had found what you wanted. She was going right back to Lake George.
    Louise and the children wrote that they had made great use of the information you gave about London. Louise called me up the other night from Paris, and scared me to death while I was waiting, knowing that there was a call from "overseas."- But apparently it was just to say Hello.- at $25 a minute! Bring on your Revolution.
    Don't go and stretch your travels out too long.
    I am enclosing a note that just came.
    Yours,
    Max

1. MP refers to the correspondence between TW and his agent, Madeleine Boyd, who had filed a lawsuit against the author.

2. Cornelius Mitchell, lawyer retained by Scribners to represent TW in the Boyd case.

3. Elizabeth Lemmon, MP's cousin.

4. TW befriended Belinda Jelliffe, wife of psychiatrist Smith Ely Jelliffe, after she wrote him a fan letter. He promoted her writing career by introducing her to MP. In 1936 Scribners published her autobiographical novel *For Dear Life*. See *Wolfe and Belinda Jelliffe*, ed. Aldo P. Magi and Richard Wilson. (n.p.: Thomas Wolfe Society, 1987).

TLS with holograph postscript, 5 pp., PUL
University of Colorado letterhead, Boulder[1]

August 12, 1935

Dear Max:

Thanks for your letter of August second. This is the first letter I have written since I came out here and the first chance I have had to write you. The Writers' Conference is over, and I am leaving here today for Denver and expect to be on my way for Santa Fe and the Southwest in another day or two. This has been, and is going to be, an extraordinary trip. The West is like something that I always knew about. I feel good and have been immensely happy ever since I came here. The country is magnificent. I took a long trip yesterday up into the Rocky Mountain National Park and saw some of the most glorious scenery from a height of thirteen thousand feet that I have ever seen. The people here have been wonderfully kind and hospitable, and between the Writers' Conference lectures, talks, reading manuscripts, conferences, and being taken around to parties, I am pretty well tired out today. We're almost a mile high here. I have been constantly exhilarated and ravenously hungry ever since I came here.

Some remarkably interesting things happened out here at this Writers' Conference. It is the first one I ever attended and perhaps the last, but I have been astonished at the quality of the talks that have been made and the instruction that has been given, and I think something very interesting and important may come from here. A number of the people who attended gave me their manuscripts to read and I have taken the liberty of suggesting to three people that they send their manuscripts to you immediately for a reading. I don't know if anything will come of it or not because of the pressure of time and the great amount of manuscripts to be read I was unable to judge just what possibilities the manuscripts had, but it seemed to me that these three at any rate were interesting enough to justify a reading. Two of them, which are manuscripts of novels, are in an incomplete, unfinished state, but I advised the authors to send them to you anyway, with a note saying that I had suggested it. The other manuscript is a book written by a woman named Spence about her mother, who was the wife of a Methodist preacher and a pioneer in Idaho only forty years ago. I was able to read only four or five chapters picked at random from different sections of the book, but I was tremendously interested because of what seemed to me the immense value of the story as a human document. She has written it in the form of an autobiography—that is, the mother herself is telling the story all the time—and it seems to me she has been very successful in creating the illusion of a person talking. It is very plainly written in an immensely sensible style which does not pass judgement on or enter into controversy about religious or social matters and which, on that account, is very convincing. It seemed to me that there was a very deep and quiet emotion all through the book, although there was nothing that had the fire of a hot and sudden passion, and it may be that the book is a little too pedestrian on that account. I have just suggested that she send the manuscript to you because the subject matter, the history of this family, the story of their absolutely pioneer life in Idaho and other parts of the west at the incredibly short period of only thirty-five or forty years ago was intensely interesting to me, and I think you may find something very valuable in it and be able to make suggestions to the author that will help her.

The other two books are written by a young man named Thompson from Texas and a man named Moses from California. I think something may come from this Thompson man. He is still very young, extremely shy and sensitive, but his manuscript, of which I was able to read only fifty or sixty pages, not only showed a greater maturity and writing skill than any other that I looked at, but it also had a genuine originality. It seemed to me that he had the power to create character. There are three cowboys in the book, a grotesque trio, who were very convincing and very vividly drawn, and other characters who promised well, and furthermore, the man's idea for the book, as he explained it me, is one of the most interesting and subtle I have heard in a long time. The manuscript is unfinished, perhaps nothing can be done about it, but I thought it was worth your looking at.

The third man, Moses, has written one of the most extraordinarily freakish kind of manuscripts I have ever read. I really doubt whether anything can be done about it because I can't make out from talking to him whether he knows what he has done or is just as freakish and capricious in his understanding of his own work as the work itself. He is a lawyer in Los Angeles, and the book starts with a divorce suit in a Los Angeles court between a young woman and her husband, who turn out to be two of the principal characters in the story, and from then on the action goes at a nightmare pace. It is a curious mixture, unlike anything I have ever seen before. It begins with this young man and his wife and their friends, who have the ordinary names that people do have, and in with these characters are mixed others with such names as "Attorney Lockjaw," "Senator Bull," "Detective Ferret," and so on. The book is a kind of curious melange of straight fiction, Pilgrim's Progress, Evelyn Waugh, and sensational Hollywood melodrama. Although the manuscript is not very long, there are almost 150 chapters, some of them not over a page or two in length. I talked with the author in an effort to find out if he knew where he was going, and I tried to point out to him that although all these elements of allegory, melodrama, fantasy, and fiction might be mixed together in a book, the author himself ought to have and to show that he has, some coherent controlling attitude of his own. His answer to this was that American life really did have in it all these grotesque and conflicting elements and that he was merely putting down what he had seen and known himself. So there it is. As I say, I don't know where any thing can be done with it or what value it has, but because I had never seen anything like it, I suggested that he send it to you. I have told all these people that I would write to you and let you know that I had suggested that they send their manuscripts in for a reading, and that is the main reason for this letter.[2]

Now, as briefly as possible, a few words about other things. I note what you say about the Boyd matter, and I hope you are right in believing her case has been destroyed and that we shall hear no more from her.[3] Nevertheless, Mr. Mitchell has written me by air mail and has very urgently requested me to try to find the letter she wrote in answer to my own letter dismissing her as my agent, and is further asking me to get in touch with the Czecho-Slovakian publishers of Of Time and the River to cable them if necessary in an effort to get a copy of their correspondence with Mrs. Boyd establishing from their side as well the fact that she wrote them saying she was no longer my agent. It is also said that Mrs. Boyd's attorney speaks of some mysterious third person who was "a mutual friend" of both of us and who is willing to testify that, at a time subsequent to the time I wrote the letter dismissing Mrs. Boyd as my agent, he had a conversation with me in which I agreed to a reconciliation and to retain her services as my agent for future work. As you know, this is an absolute and utter falsehood, and not only have I never seen nor written to Mrs. Boyd since I wrote the letter of dismissal, but I have never had any word of communication with her through any other person in any way whatever, and of course I have no idea who this mysterious third person may be. Upon the basis of all these things, Mr. Mitchell informs me that he has entered a notice of appearance, whatever that may be. Whatever it is, I fear it means the long, involved, and costly operation of the courts of law and of lawyers, and although I feel confident that we can eventually defeat this woman's outrageous claims, I am bitterly indignant over the fact that my own honesty and pity for her wretched behavior, my failure to secure an absolute release at the time of her cowering and abject confession have now put me in a position where these people can threaten me with suit and try to take from me a portion of my earnings. It is an ugly and intolerable situation, and what is most shameful about it now is the fact that even if I defeat her claims, I can do so only at the cost of a large sum of money for legal services and of an utterly shameful waste of my time, my energy, my temper, and what is most important, of human faith in other people and in the integrity of their intentions. This business of pawing through stacks and bales of old letters trying to find every little scrap of writing which a person once wrote to you is a disgusting one. I worked for three days going through great stacks of letters in an effort to find everything the woman had ever written to me and everything which seemed to me to bear on the case, till finally I had succeeded in collecting a great mass of evidence, including my letter of dismissal, everything in fact which Mr. Mitchell said he wanted. Now he wants this letter which she wrote to me, and of course I have no idea where it is and will have no opportunity to look for it until I get back to New York and have to go through the whole accumulation of years of letters again. I am not going to let my life be eaten up and consumed by harpies. I have my work to do, and as my friend and publisher, I ask you in the future to try to help me in every way possible to keep me from this kind of shameful and ruinous invasion. Finally, you must not put the manuscript of a book of stories in final form until after my return to New York. If that means the book of stories will have to be deferred till next spring, then they will have to be deferred, but I will not consent this time to allow the book to be taken away from me and printed and published until I myself have had time to look at the proofs, and at any rate to talk to you about certain revisions, changes, excisions, or additions that ought to be made. I really mean this, Max. I have money enough to live on for a while now. I do not propose to trade upon the success of Of Time and the River. I propose rather to prepare my work in every way possible to meet and refute, if I can, some of the very grave and serious criticisms that were made about the last book, and as my friend and the person whose judgment I trust most, you must help me to do this. I am coming back to New York in September. My mind is swarming with new material and the desire to get back and finish up The October Fair as soon as possible, but before we do that we must first do a thorough, honest and satisfactory job upon the book of stories, From Death to Morning, we must get the Boyd matter settled, we must get the deck cleared for action, otherwise another shameful and revolting waste of talent right at the time of its greatest fertility and strength is likely to occur. And if this happens, I am ready to go to Siam, Russia, Timbuctoo, or take out citizenship under the benign and democratic governance of Adolph Hitler, where, by comparison, the rights of men and of freedom and integrity individual are respected. This is all for the present.

I will be in the Southwest next week and then on to California, the Northwest, back through Idaho, Wyoming, and St. Louis and so back east again. And if they don't kill me out here with hospitality, or in New York with blackmailing lawsuits and so forth, I'll have some good stories to tell you and a lot of work to do in the winter. I am so glad you saw Elizabeth and enjoyed the trip to Virginia. Please remember me to everyone in the office.

Tom

P.S.—Max, forgive my ill temper—I am exasperated beyond measure by this Boyd thing—and I must work now—please help me in every way!

P.S—Denver, Tuesday 13—I have just written a long letter to Mr Mitchell, my lawyer, and told him I would telegraph my address to you and that he could get in touch with me [through you]

1. TW was attending the Writers' Conference at the University's Extension Division.

2. Scribners did not publish any of the three writers TW recommended.

3. On 5 August 1935 Boyd informed MP that her lawyer Weinberger had advised her that she had a claim against TW for agent's commissions. On the same day MP wrote to Aline Bernstein asking her to talk to TW's lawyer Mitchell about this matter: "If you would, I should be glad to tell him so, and I think it would be altogether in Tom's interests. I do not think anybody ought to yield to the pressure of a lawsuit when there is no justifiable legal claim" (PUL).

ALS, 3 pp., PUL
Brown Palace Hotel letterhead, Denver

Aug 13, 1935

Dear Max: I am giving this letter to Mr Dixon Wecter,[1] who is on the faculty of the University of Colorado. I understand he is a very gifted writer, his articles have been appearing recently in the magazines, and since he may have a book ready for publication some day, I have suggested that he come in to talk to you.

I am on my way to Santa Fe, Mabel Dodge Luhan,[2] et al, in a day or two, Western hospitality is wonderful but exhausting.

Tom.

1. (1906–1950) Mark Twain scholar, historian, and Scribners author.
2. Mabel Dodge Luhan (1879–1962), literary patron of D. H. Lawrence.

Wire, 1 p., PUL

15 August 1935

MAXWELL PERKINS, CHARLES SCRIBERS SONS
SEND MAIL LAFONDA HOTEL SANTAFE NEWMEXICO UNTIL FURTHER NOTICE

TOM WOLFE.

CC, 4 pp., PUL

Aug. 20, 1935

Dear Tom:

I hope this letter will catch you at Sante Fe, but I feel nervous about your being there in the vicinity of Mabel Dodge Luhan. Besides, you ought to be heading back here. I had quite a long letter from Fred, and I told him what you were doing, and said that by the time you got back you would have had a seven months' vacation which was more than he and I put together had had in our whole lives. Besides, a large part of the proof of the stories is here. How you can think badly of them I cannot imagine, but they are waiting for you anyhow.

Miss Nowell's office has sold "The Bums at Sunset" to Vanity Fair for $175,[1] and we have received payment on a second printing of 10,000 from the Modern Library. We are getting orders every day for "Of Time and the River" though things are slow at the moment. But it pushes along.

I can guess at what Mrs. Boyd is driving: the mysterious person referred to I believe is Mrs. Bernstein, but she will do them no good; and the agreement you made to pay her 10% on "Of Time and the River" refers to that time when you and

I and she had lunch at the Chatham, when you did verbally agree to that.- But that was previous to the German incident when you broke off your contract. Mrs. Bernstein came in here and talked to Mitchell, and I think he was satisfied with what she said. Afterward I had lunch with her at the Chatham, very pleasantly, and at the moment she seems to be quite contented and in good spirits. Apparently she has been ill with pleurisy and implied that all the trouble was mostly caused by the state of her health. Anyhow she won't say anything damaging to you, I feel sure, in the Boyd matter. I know it is troublesome, but everybody has those kinds of trouble,- they are part of life. Like fleas to a dog, as the fellow said, they are probably good for us.

One of the manuscripts you recommended has come, but I have not yet had a chance to read it. Jack's on his vacation, which makes things more difficult for the time being.

A lady from the Brooklyn Institute called up to get you to do the opening one of a series of literary lectures. I told her that we would forward anything she wrote, but that I did not think you would be able to undertake what she wanted to because you had large plans for work which could not be delayed.

Always yours,

[Maxwell Perkins]

P.S. I forgot to say that the letters about the Boyd matter have come from the German publisher, and I sent them on to Mitchell by registered mail.- And Miss Nowell's office is also proceeding in some discreet way, to get other letters you spoke of from abroad. Miss Nowell has had her operation and everything turned out very favorably. I have had a letter from her telling me that.

1. Published in October 1935.

⤳

Postcard of Prehistoric Cliff Dwellings,
Pueblo of Puye, near Santa Fe, New Mexico, PUL

Postmarked 26 August 1935

Dear Max: This is the most magnificent country—wild, arid, friendly, magnificent—just the way I always knew it would be—I had a fight with Mabel Luhan the moment I walked into her house and left immediately but everyone else seems to like me—Tom

Wire, 1 p., PUL

27 August 1935

FORWARD MAIL GENERAL DELIVERY SANFRANCISCO:
TOM

❧

Postcard of Grand Canyon
taken from painting by Gunnar Widfross, PUL
Grand Canyon

28 August 1935

Dear Max: You can get no idea of this from a post card but, it is stirring and incredible—I begin to see how inadequate all I have said and written about this country really is

❧

CC, 3 pp., PUL

Aug. 30, 1935

Dear Tom:

I am sending you the very first English review, and you ought to like it.- From the Times which is probably the most influential paper,- or at least I always thought so, though probably you know more about that than I do.[1] I think it is a good indication of what may come, especially as the English always speak with much greater restraint in praise than we do.

If you can manage to answer any letter, answer that Brooklyn outfit's invitation to speak. They keep calling me up and I tell them you are way behind in your work and will want to settle right down to it when you get back, but they are very keen to get you and say that they will put your lecture later on if you will give it. I would like to see you give it, except that I do think you ought to give all you have to work.

I have been through the stories, and I think they are very fine stories.- They show how objective you can be, and how varied you can be, and I was looking at the book from that point of view considerably. It would be an answer to what you have had in adverse criticism. It is a fine book.- But I'll wait and argue with you when you come back, over a glass of coca cola.

I hope you won't quarrel with anyone else, but if you had to quarrel, I would suppose that Mabel Dodge Luhan was the right person to quarrel with. I myself never quarrel except with you, but I think I could always do it with her,- and perhaps with Gertrude Stein if I had the courage.

Everything goes along all right. I had another letter from Fred, and enlarged on my suggestion that he should keep an inn.

Yours,

[Maxwell Perkins]

1. *Times Literary Supplement*, 22 August 1935. The unsigned review concludes that TW "may have many faults—he can be both verbose and repetitive—but they must be, for those who can stay the course to the end, burnt up in the full and steady flame of his positive achievement" (p. 22).

ALS, 14 pp., PUL

1935

Send mail to General Delivery, San Francisco.

Sunday Sept 1,

Dear Max: I am sending you with this letter the proposed dedication for the book of stories. Will you and Jack please read and consider it carefully and decide whether you think it should be used? I had originally intended to dedicate <u>The Hills Beyond Pentland</u> to my brother, Ben, but because of the nature of the book of stories, and the subject matter involved, it has occurred to me that the present book might be a more fitting subject for the dedication. What do you think? At any rate, here's the dedication—I will abide by your judgement. Finally, please let me urge on you again the desirability of getting a good order in the arrangement of the stories—I mean, so far as possible, the arrangement really should, so far as we make it do so, illustrate the title, <u>From Death to Morning</u>—that is, they should progress in a general way beginning, say, with <u>Death The Proud Brother</u>, and ending perhaps, with such a piece as <u>The Web of Earth</u>   Max, I think you might be surprised to know of the interest people out here have taken in the stories. I met Miss Edna Ferber,[1] the novelist, in Santa Fe, the other day, and had lunch with her—She spoke most generously of everything I had done, but said she thought the stories were the finest things I had yet written—In the same way, a number of these moving picture people here in Hollywood—directors and other executives—know all about my work and are collecting it—I have met several who have a copy of every story I ever wrote, including the college stuff of Chapel Hill days-furthermore, they've read it—I met one director yesterday who began to rave about The Web of Earth—others about Death The Proud Brother—As for myself, I feel there is as good writing as I've done in some of the stories—it represents important work to me, and I think we should spare no pains to present it in as important and impressive a way as possible—I think you may be a little inclined to underestimate the importance of arrangement and presentation, and may feel that the stories can go in any way, and that the order doesn't matter much—Perhaps you are right—my own feeling, however, is that in a general way the stories do have a kind of unity—and should be presented with an eye to cumulative effect—as the title <u>From</u> <u>Death</u> <u>to</u> <u>Morning</u> indicates—There is so much more that I want to say to you—so much more I want to do, include, write—and I know I have done little. There are at least half a dozen big stories I should have written and that should be included—and all kinds of minor things—the scene in the railway station, some of the night scenes; so many things bearing upon death and night and morning that could be put in to weave the whole thing together—in particular a scene where old Bascom (in The Hills Beyond Pentland) looks down from the mountain in the town of Altamont and tells his 12 year old nephew about the Pentlands—this could be used wonderfully to lead right into <u>The Web Of Earth</u> and by doing a few things like this I know <u>the whole book</u> could be woven together and given a tremendous feeling of unity and cumulative effect that you almost never find in a book of stories—But please consider them carefully, Max—I could say much more, but you know what I mean—and as the drunken top-sergeant in <u>What Price Glory</u> yelled after his commanding officer—"Wait on me, Captain—Baby's coming"![2]

Yes, I agree with you, I've had 6 months vacation, and that ought to be enough for any man—And it is, I feel guilty as hell, and eager to get to work again—But Max, it has been a thrilling wonderful experience—these last six months—I am filled to bursting with the richness and variety of it—and as for this trip to the West, I have no words here to tell you of the beauty, power and magnificence of this country—Thank God, I have seen it at last!—and I know that I did not lie about it, I know I have not yet begun to put it down on paper, my store of wonderful subject matter has been enormously enriched—I have some amazing and fantastic stories to tell you—this moving picture world, as well—I have met the famous stars, directors, producers, writers etc, have seen them at work—this is simply incredible, and in the midst of all the false and unreal world, the technical, building, working world is simply amazing in its skill and knowledge—Good God! I could write a magnificent book even about this place if I lived here a year—they want me to stay, have offered me a job, and mentioned huge sums, but perhaps I shall resist—Everyone has been wonderfully kind all through the West—lavish generous hospitality, I am almost worn out by it—here as well: Dorothy Parker seems to like me, swears she does, and last night told a room of people that I was built on a heroic scale and that there was no one like me—Maybe the old girl is laughing at me behind my back and making wicked jokes about me but I think she meant what she said—she and her young husband are living in a magnificent imitation Colonial house and just bought a new Packard the other day[3]—and the liquor and hospitality flows like the Mississippi—I am going there again this afternoon—Yes, I know I have stayed too long, but Max, Max, you <u>must</u> wait on me—I've <u>got</u> to see San Francisco—above all I must see that wonderful town—in the end, we shall not lose by it—Then, if you like, I'll cut it short and come straight home, only I'd hoped to see a little of Oregon, Salt Lake City, and stop off a day in St Louis to see where Grover died on way back[4]—I'll be home in two weeks—Now, Max, please wait on me—don't take the book away before[5]

[Accompanying the letter are 2 pp. of dedication material for From Death to Morning.*]*

To

The Honorable Memory Of His Brother

Benjamin Harrison Wolfe

(Oct—1893—Oct—1918)

And to the proud and bitter briefness of his days, the brave integrity of an obscure life to which life itself could have added nothing but fulfilment, and from which even death could take nothing but the noble, scornful and generous radiance of his lonely and inviolate spirit, the writer dedicates this book, believing that of all his work which has been published, the present volume may offer both to death and life, the matter worthiest of such commemoration.

Note: To Be set apart and italicized

Up on the mountain, down in the valley, long, long in the hill, Ben, cold, cold, cold.

1. (1887–1968)

2. The play *What Price Glory?* (1924), by Maxwell Anderson and Laurence Stallings, ends with Sergeant Quirt calling after his Captain, "Hey, Flagg, wait for Baby!"

3. Dorothy Parker (1893–1967) and her husband, Alan Campbell (1904–1963), worked as a screenwriting team during the 1930s and 1940s.

4. TW's brother, Grover, died in 1904 while Julia Wolfe was operating a boarding house at the St. Louis World's Fair. TW responded to his brother's death in "The Lost Boy," *Redbook*, November 1937.

5. The rest of this letter is missing. *The Letters of Thomas Wolfe* continues: "I get back. I've some wonderful things to tell you. Are Louise and the girls home yet?" (p. 488).

Postmarked 11 September 1935

Postcard of Oakland Bay Bridge, PUL
San Francisco

Dear Max: This is a fascinating and wonderful city—we can be proud of it— They are trying to get me to stay but I am leaving today and will see you in a few days—Feel fine, but do you think I will be able to work again?

Postcard of Reno Street, PUL
Reno, Nevada

Thursday
Sept 12, 1935

Dear Max: You wouldn't think it from this picture but you're looking at more red-hot wide-open gambling hells to the front foot here than you ever saw before in a similar space—It is now 8 o'clock at night and the place called <u>The Bank Club</u> in the picture is packed and jammed with men in overalls, shirt sleeves, sombreros and tables loaded with silver dollars

&

TO: *John Hall Wheelock*   *Postcard of gambling tables in the Bank Club, PUL*
Reno, Nevada

Sept 12, 1935

Dear Jack: This is no exaggeration—there are dozens of these places—wide open and going full blast all night long—The West is glorious
                    Tom

&

ALS, 11 pp., PUL
The Riverside Hotel letterhead, Reno, Nevada

Reno,
Thurs, Sept 12,
1935

Dear Max: I am a little worried about something—and if you see fit, won't you take steps about it right away? It is this—at various times during the last month—at Boulder and elsewhere—I have discoursed very eloquently and persuasively about my book of the night which is beginning to interest me more and more all the time. I have told how much of my life has been lived by night, about the chemistry of darkness, the strange and magic thing it does to our lives, about America at night—the rivers, plains, mountains, rivers in the moon or darkness (last night by the way coming up here through the Sierra Nevadas there was blazing moonlight, the effect was incredibly beautiful)—and how the Americans are a night-time people, which I have found out everywhere is absolutely true—Now, I'm afraid I've talked too much—please don't think I'm fool enough to think anyone is going to, or can, "steal my ideas"—but people have been been immensely and instantly absorbed when I told about my book—and have at once agreed to the utter truth of it.—I have got hold of an immense, rich, and absolutely true thing about ourselves—at once very simple, profound, and various—and I know a great and original book—unlike any other, can be written in it—and I dont want some fool to get hold of it and write some cheap and worthless thing—the idea is so beautiful and simple that some bungler could easily mutilate it.

It will be years before I do it—but it keeps gathering in me all the time—I don't know yet exactly what form it will take—or whether it can be called a "novel" or not—I don't care—but I think it will be a great tone-symphony of night—railway yards, engines, freights, dynamos, bridges, men and women, the wilderness, plains, rivers, deserts, a clopping hoof, etc—seen <u>not</u> <u>by</u> <u>a</u> <u>definite</u> <u>personality</u>—but haunted throughout by a consciousness of personality—In other words, I want to assert my divine right once and for all to be the <u>God</u> <u>Almighty</u> of a book—to be at once the spirit to move it, the spirit behind it, never to appear, to blast forever the charge of "autobiography" while being triumphantly and impersonally autobio-graphical—Can't you do this, if you think best, and something tells me that it may be best?:—Make an announcement to this effect—that I have for years been inter-ested in the life of night (<u>not</u> nightclubs) and have been slowly acquiring an immense amount of material about it, that the book is slowly taking form, but will not be ready for years when these other books are out of the way, and that it is at present called <u>The</u> <u>Book</u> <u>Of</u> <u>The</u> <u>Night</u>[1]—You might put in something about <u>Sat-urday</u> <u>Night</u> <u>in</u> <u>America</u> (when I get back I'll tell you about Longmont, Colorado on Saturday night—I've told you before what Saturday night does to us here in America and one part of the book has to do with this)—at any rate, Max, I've talked to other people about it, and since this is one of the most precious and valuable ideas I've ever had—do what you can to protect it for me now—Why can't we do this—you could even say that I am so interested in the book that I am now at work on it, and that it <u>may</u> appear before the other books of the <u>Of</u> <u>Time</u> <u>and</u> <u>the</u> <u>River</u> series come out—this would do no harm, would arouse interest and discussion, and might serve the purpose of throwing some of my various Mrs B's off the track for the present—

As for the Brooklyn lecture thing—answer for me, as you think best. I could certainly do it, I could probably do it well, the talk at Boulder went over beauti-fully—but let us first consider this: Do you think it is well for me to get into the lecture habit—I am getting offers now all the time—and do you think it is good for my <u>special</u> writing reputation to become known as a public lecturer? Also, what are we to work on next—<u>The</u> <u>October</u> <u>Fair</u>, the Pentland book, the Book of the Night, short stories—or what?—when do you want to publish next, and when do we begin to work again?—I am just mentioning these things for your consideration—I could probably do the lecture without great difficulty—and if law suits and crazy women are going to destroy my work, and take up my time arguing, I might as well pick up what extra money I can. But you be judge and answer the Br'klyn people as you see fit. Whatever you say will be all right with me.

Other matters rest until I see you in few days. I've stopped off the day to see this town—incredible little 15000 one street place with gambling hells and bars and dance halls open all day and all night, gray faced faro and roulette men, silver dol-lars stacked up by the tons—catching Overland Limited at 5 o'clock in morning in order to see Nevada and Utah deserts by day—then in Salt Lake for day—then St Louis for few hours—then back home—Tom

1. TW later retitled this material *The Hound of Darkness*, but never completed it. He published a section, "A Prologue to America," in *Vogue*, February 1938. Pieces were later incorporated by Aswell in *The Web and the Rock* and *You Can't Go Home Again*. See *The Hound of Darkness*, ed. John L. Idol, Jr. (n.p.: Thomas Wolfe Society, 1986).

TO: *John Hall Wheelock*
Late September 1935

ALS, 15 pp., PUL
New York City

Dear Jack: Here are the remainder of the proofs for <u>Death</u> the <u>Proud Brother</u>, which I have now read and corrected

Now, about what is probably the most important matter first—your comment on Galley 22 that my story really ends there and that what follows is another thing: I see your point and feel a break myself, but wonder if the inclusion of a phrase at the very beginning of this passage which would refer it to the death scene that has gone before—would not help?—What do you think?—A much more serious question however, is this: the passage that follows to the end of the story is really one of my most ambitious apostrophes—to Loneliness, and Death and Sleep—It is the kind of thing that some of the critics have gone gunning after me for—but it is also the kind of thing that many people have liked in my writing, and that some say they hope I never lose—This passage in particular—about Sleep and Death, etc—has made [friends]—Now, what do you think—It's a pretty serious matter to me, because if it really is better that I cut out this <u>kind</u> of writing entirely, it is a fundamental thing and I must seriously change my whole method and style everywhere— But <u>I</u> want <u>you</u> to <u>say</u> what <u>you</u> think![1]

—About other things: Please note the changes I have made in Galley 12—taking out the word "Esther" and substituting "the woman"—Do you think it is now clear, and also a change for the better?[2]

I note your red marks on Galley 14—the remarks about the mistress—This passage now refers to "the woman" rather than to Esther—Do you want it cut? I have indicated several ¶s on Galley 20 with a line and question mark—I feel something a little stiff and inept here—it is part of a much longer part that was cut out— will you read it, and tell me if you can find the trouble, if any?

* <u>Galley 23</u>: You marked several phrases and sentences as having been duplicated in <u>Of Time</u> and <u>the River</u>—that's true, they are.—This was written first—do you think their inclusion here would be a serious error?—The trouble is, I have trouble thinking of an adequate substitute for the passage

"They come! Ships Call!—etc"[3]

* Finally, in apostrophe to Sleep I have capitalized <u>Sleep</u> throughout save in the concluding phrase "—Sleep, sleep, sleep"—I did this to avoid confusion—but do you think in the phrase "In <u>Sleep</u> we lie all naked and alone—" would arouse obscene comment—[4]

As to shorter phrases—which I had repeated in other stories I have either modified them here, or let them stay, preferring them to go in here rather than in the other stories

Tom

Ill try to get in before closing time to see you

[Accompanying sheet, probably in John Hall Wheelock's hand.]

    No Door

1   Death the Proud Brother

    Gulliver

1   Face of the War

    Only the Dead

    Dark in the Forest

1   Four Lost Men

    Bums at Sunset

    One of the Girls

1   In the Park

    Cottage by the Tracks

    Men of Old Catawba

    Circus at Dawn

1   Web of Earth[5]

1. The majority of the story's apostrophe was retained for book publication. TW cut the first paragraph:

> As from dark winds and waters of our sleep on which a few stars sparely look, we grope our feelers in the sea's dark bed. Whether to polyped spore, blind sucks or crawls or seavalves of the brain, we call through slopes and glades of night's dark waters on great fish. Call to the strange dark fish, or to the dart and hoary flaking of electric fins, or to the sea-worms of the brain that lash great fish to bloody froth upon the sea-floor's coral stipes. Or, in vast thickets of our sleep call to blue gulphs and deep immensities of night, call the cat's bright blazing glare and ceaseless prowl; call to all things that swim or crawl or fly, all subtlest unseen stirs, all half-heard, half-articulated whisperings, O forested and far!—call to the hooves of sleep through all the waste and lone immensity of night: "Return! Return!" (*Scribner's Magazine* 93 [June 1933]: 388).

2. TW changed "Esther's sister," in *Scribner's Magazine*, June 1933, to "the sister of a woman that I loved" for *From Death to Morning*.

3. The passage was retained.

4. The passage was retained.

5. TW included this list with his undated letter to Wheelock. It gives the final order of the stories, except for "Gulliver" and "In the Park." "Cottage by the Tracks" was renamed "The Far and the Near." The lowercase "l" in the margin designates a long story.

TO: *John Hall Wheelock*
Late September 1935

ALS, 1 p., PUL
New York

Dear Jack: Here are the Galley Proofs of <u>The Face Of The War</u>, which I have now read and corrected—Will you please observe Galley 26—and the words <u>screw</u> and <u>puss</u> which I have written in, and tell me if we can use them—Tom[1]

1. Scribners allowed TW to use "puss" but not "screw." *From Death to Morning:* "I'll come back here and smack yuh right in duh puss" (80). *Modern Monthly* had substituted a dash for "puss" in the story's magazine appearance (June 1935).

❧

TO: *John Hall Wheelock*
Late September 1935

ALS, 1 p., PUL
New York

Dear Jack: Here is the Gulliver story, which I have read and corrected—The story doesn't satisfy me, however, particularly at the end, which does not <u>end</u> so much, I feel, as just break off—it is really a fragment and I may talk to you about it Monday
Tom

❧

TO: *John Hall Wheelock*
Late September 1935

ALS, 1 p., PUL
New York

Dear Jack: Will you please note the paragraph transposed from Galley 43 to 44 and the slight changes I have made and see if you do not think they are for the better. If not, please restore them to their original form.—Also is the revision in The Four Lost Men (Gal. 44) O.K.?
Tom

❧

TO: *John Hall Wheelock*
Late September 1935

ALS, 1 p., PUL
New York

Dear Jack: Here is the proof of the only story left (except <u>The Web</u>)—Note that I have changed the title to <u>The Far And The Near</u>.[1]—Also observe changes on Galley 82 which have been done with a view to changing the attitude of the two women to a <u>timid</u> and <u>uneasy</u> <u>unfriendliness</u> rather than surly hostility—Also last sentence.—if you think changes good let them stand—if not, erase them—Tom[2]

1. The story was originally published as "Cottage by the Tracks" in *Cosmopolitan*, July 1935.

2. TW added the final sentence for book publication: "And he knew that all the magic of that bright lost way, the vista of that shining line, the imagined corner of that small good universe of hope's desire, was gone forever, could never be got back again" (p. 168).

FROM: John Hall Wheelock   *CCS, 2 pp., PUL*

October 18, 1935

Dear Tom:

All the proofs of "From Death to Morning" are in the printer's hands, and publication is scheduled for November 15. This means that there can be no delay anywhere along the line. In the case of the final story, "Web of Earth," I have sent the printer duplicate galleys from our files, and if there are any corrections you wish to make, they can be made in page proof, which I hope to have to-morrow.

There were a few typographical corrections in the galleys of "Web of Earth" which you have. I want to transfer these few corrections to the page proof. Would you therefore let me have these galleys back at once, for a little while?

We have all the material for the front matter, including copy for the dedication which you had previously shown me. Your wishes will, of course, rule, but dear Tom, don't you think the purpose of the dedication would be equally well served if it simply read,

To
The Memory of My Brother
Benjamin Harrison Wolfe
(October 1895 - October 1918)

Up on the mountain,
down in the valley,
long, long in the hill,
Ben, cold, cold, cold.[1]

Max feels as I do about this.

As ever, dear Tom,
J.H.W.

To
Mr. Thomas Wolfe,
865 First Avenue,
New York City.

The dust jacket for the only short-story collection Wolfe published in his lifetime.

1. The published dedication reads:

TO
THE MEMORY OF HIS BROTHER
BENJAMIN HARRISON WOLFE
AND TO THE PROUD AND BITTER BRIEFNESS OF
HIS DAYS
OCTOBER 27, 1892—OCTOBER 20, 1918

Up on the mountain, down in the
valley, deep, deep, in the hill,
Ben, cold, cold, cold.

❧

FROM: Charles Scribner's Sons   *CC, 1 p., PUL*

January 6, 1936

Dear Mr. Wolfe:

We are obliged to report to the Treasury Department all payments for salaries, royalties, etc., when such payments amount to $1,000. to a single person or $2,500. if married.

We are, accordingly, reporting amount paid to you during 1935 as $6,332.89. We trust you will find this in agreement with your records.

Yours very truly,
CHARLES SCRIBNER'S SONS.

❧

TLS, 1 p. Harvard

Spring 1936

Memo for Tom Wolfe

George Schrieber, 145 West 14th Street, an artist, asks you to pose for fifteen minutes so that he can draw you for a book to be published by Houghton Mifflin on famous contemporary authors.[1] He seems to have everybody in it including Sinclair Lewis, Christopher Morley, etc. This is all right so far, but he also wants you to furnish a 250-word autobiography. If this is to be done, it must be done before May first.

Max

1. TW's portrait and his autobiographical sketch were included in *Portraits and Self-Portraits* (Boston: Houghton Mifflin, 1936).

the
story of a
NOVEL

by
THOMAS WOLFE

author of "Of Time and the River"

How does a great novel come into being? What is its genesis? How does it develop? What are the sensations of a literary artist as characters take form beneath his pen? These and similar questions often come to the mind of every reader of fiction — and they have never been answered with such frankness, honesty, and conviction as in this brief "credo" of an outstanding American novelist. Here is the soul of an artist laid bare, with all his hopes, fears, doubts, and aspirations. But it is not only about Mr. Wolfe's own books — it is about all writing and about American writing especially — a book that every one must read, and that every one of the many thousands who enjoyed Mr. Wolfe's novels will find permeated by the same "insatiable and enormous eagerness in life and living" that placed the stamp of genius on his novels.

The subject matter of this book created a literary sensation when it appeared in *The Saturday Review of Literature*. It inspired an editorial on Mr. Wolfe and his writing in *The New York Times*, John Chamberlain devoted his column to it, and it attracted favorable comment from critics all over the country.

(center, handwritten) The Story Of A Novel — Thomas Wolfe

the story of a NOVEL = Wolfe = Scribners

"In these days when some of our best writers are tired or short of breath it is thrilling to contemplate and to read the teeming novels of Thomas Wolfe."
BURTON RASCOE in *The New York Herald Tribune*

OF TIME AND THE RIVER

"He gives you an experience you can't just file away under Miscellaneous. ... For decades we have not had eloquence like his in American writing. ... At his best he is incomparable. ... *Of Time and the River* is a wonderful, flashing, gleaming riot of characters, caricatures, metaphors, apostrophes, declamations, tropes, dreams."
CLIFTON FADIMAN in *The New Yorker*

LOOK HOMEWARD, ANGEL

"As interesting and powerful a book as has ever been made out of the circumstances of provincial American life. It is at once enormously sensuous, full of the joy and gusto of life, and shrinkingly sensitive, torn with revulsion and disgust."
MARGARET WALLACE in *The New York Times*

by Thomas Wolfe

Published by CHARLES SCRIBNER'S SONS

From Death
to Morning
Fourteen Stories by
THOMAS WOLFE

"These stories are Mr. Wolfe's peculiar property; they belong to him with the certainty of style and introspection — no other can match them; and they show the most striking literary personality of our day."
PETER MONRO JACK in *The New York Times*

"What stories they are! ... They are cumulative evidence of his right to be classed as one of the great American novelists, if not the greatest."
Philadelphia Ledger

"Reading the work of this genius is like listening to Wagner or watching the aurora borealis. It is an experience beside which the mill run of most fiction seems trivial and insignificant."
The Chicago Tribune

The dust jacket for Wolfe's account of writing *Of Time and the River*, which resulted in Bernard De Voto's charge that Wolfe could not write without Perkins's assistance (Thomas Cooper Library, University of South Carolina).

Wire, 1 p., PUL
Boston

17 March 1936

TELL CALVERTON[1] OUT OF TOWN WROTE BOOK BEGINNING GOES
WONDERFULLY FULL OF HOPE
    TOM.

    1. V. F. (Victor Francis) Calverton (1900–1940), editor of the leftist magazine *Modern Monthly.*

FROM: John Hall Wheelock

TLS, 2 pp., Harvard
April 16, 1936

Dear Tom:

    I know that you're at work and that I oughtn't to disturb you, at this time, even with a letter, but I have just been rereading, in its book form, your magnificent "The Story of a Novel,"[1] and I feel that I really must tell you how deeply it affected and impressed even a hard-boiled editor, upon rereading. The book is unique. I can think of no other instance where a great writer has shared so generously with others his own experience in becoming a writer, his own torment and exaltation in the process of creation. And you've done it so superbly. The book is really profound—what it has to say is of such tremendous significance to every writer. This "Story of a Novel" is one of the finest introductions to and interpretations of your work that the general reader could have. I'm sure that it's going to bring you new readers and that it will become a classic of its kind. There certainly has never been a book like it.

    You see I have to let you know my very strong feelings after a critical rereading, but this letter is sent with the strict understanding that it is not to be answered. We'll probably be seeing each other before long.

    With many good wishes, dear Tom,

As ever,
Jack

To
Mr. Thomas Wolfe,
865 First Avenue,
New York City.

    1. TW's book-length essay published by Scribners in 1936.

CHARLES SCRIBNER'S SONS
PUBLISHERS, IMPORTERS AND BOOKSELLERS
597 Fifth Avenue
NEW YORK

YOUR ORDER No.

No.

DATE September 25, 1935.

CLAIMS FOR DAMAGES OR SHORT-
AGES MUST BE MADE IMMEDIATELY
ON RECEIPT OF GOODS.

TERMS: NET CASH
PAYABLE WITH EXCHANGE ON
NEW YORK

Sold To   Mr. Thomas Wolfe

No.

Sent Per

QUANTITY	DESCRIPTION	EDUCATIONAL	TRADE	TOTAL
	To excess cost of author's alterations on:			
	OF TIME AND THE RIVER			
	Cost of composition and electrotyping	2479.06		
	Cost of corrections		1676.41	
	Allowance according to agreement - 20% of $2479.06		495.81	$1180.60

The bill for the cost of excess alterations in the proofs for *Of Time and the River.*
Wolfe protested this charge, arguing that Perkins had rushed the book into production before Wolfe had been permitted to revise it, so that his proof changes
were editorial expenses—not authorial (Princeton University Library).

TLS, 6 pp., PUL
TW's personal letterhead, 865 First Avenue, New York City

April 21st, 1936

Dear Max:

I want to tell you that I am sorry I got angry last night and spoke as I did. The
language that I used was unjustifiable and I want to tell you that I know it was, and
ask you to forget it.

About the matter I was talking to you about however, I feel just as strongly
today as I did last night. I don't want to re-hash the whole thing again. We have
talked and argued about it too much already, but I do want to tell you honestly and
sincerely that I am not arguing about the two or three hundred dollars which would
be involved if I were given my old royalty of 15%, instead of the reduced one of
10%. I admit that there can be no doubt that I agreed to this reduction of my roy-

alty before the publication of the book and at the time when estimates of cost of publication were being prepared, I told you that I hoped the book could be published at a very moderate price of 75¢ or a dollar. Not only because I thought it might be better for the success of the book itself, but also because I am not willing to make use of any past success I may have had, or take advantage of any present reputation I may have in the eyes of the public to publish so short and small a book at a high price. Now I don't want you to think that I am trying to dictate to my publishers the price for which I think my book ought to be printed. You told me an author had no right to dictate such prices and that in fact, the price the publisher put on his books was none of his business and although I think the subject is open to debate, I am on the whole, inclined to agree with you and was really not trying to dictate any prices, except what I told you when the publication of the book was discussed and I hoped personally, it would be brought out at a low price of 75¢ or a dollar.

You told me that it would be impossible to bring it out for as low a price as 75¢, but we all had hoped, I believe that it might be brought out for a dollar. Later, when estimates on the cost of publication came in, it was agreed that the price would have to be $1.25 and either then at that time, or previously I had agreed to a reduction of my customary royalty from 15% to 10% and I believe the 10% was to cover the first three thousand copies and that if the book sold more than that, I would get an increased royalty. The reason that I agreed to this reduction was because I knew the publisher was not likely to profit very much by the publication of so small a book and because I agreed with you the publication of the book was nevertheless, probably a good thing, and finally because you told me that even at the $1.25 price, the margin was very small and you thought I ought to accept the royalty of 10%, which I agreed to do.

Now the book has been published and the other day when I got my own advance copy, I saw that the price had been still further raised from $1.25 to $1.50. This was the first knowledge that I had that the price had been raised. I agree with you that I probably have no right to argue with you about the price of a book or to have a say as to the price it ought to sell for. I also agree that if the book is successful and sells, I stand to profit in my share of the royalties at the increased price as well as does the publisher; but I don't think that either of these facts is the core of the matter, and they are certainly not what I am arguing about.

What I am arguing about is this, - that I agreed to accept a reduced royalty upon the basis of a dollar or dollar and a quarter book - and the reason that I agreed to accept the reduction was because it was presented to me that the cost of making the book was such that it would be difficult for the publisher to give a higher royalty and have him come out clear. Then after agreeing to this reduced royalty, upon my understanding that the book would be published at a dollar and a quarter, and having signed a contract accepting the reduced royalty, I find that the price of the book, without my knowledge, has been raised to $1.50, and is being published at that price. When I discussed that fact about a week ago, when I got my own advance copy, I told you that in view of the increase in price, I thought you ought to restore my former royalty of 15%. I still think that you ought to do so and have told you so repeatedly, and you feel you ought not to do so, and have refused to do so.

You have been my friend for seven years now and one of the best friends that I ever had, I don't think anyone in the world is more conscious than I am of what you have done for me, of how you stuck to me for years when I was trying to get another book completed and when so much time elapsed that people had begun to say I might never be able to write again. I think you stuck to me not only with material aid and support that Scribners gave me, during a large part of the time, when I had no funds of my own, but you stuck to me also with your own friendship and belief and spiritual support, and you not only gave me these priceless things, but you also gave me unstintedly, the benefits of your enormous skill and talent as an editor and a critic. I do not think a debt such as I owe you can ever sufficiently be repaid, but I have tried to do what I could through work, which I know you do value and through public acknowledgment which I know you do not want and on which you don't put the same value as you do upon the more important fact of work. So having said all this, and feeling this way toward you, and about what you and Scribners have done, I want to repeat again that I do not think it is right or proper for you to with hold from me my full and customary royalty of 15%, the circumstances being what they are.

I do not question your legal and contractual right to do this. I agreed to the reduction at the time and for the reason I have mentioned. I signed the contract and I am, of course compelled to abide by it. But I think it is up to you now in view of the facts I have mentioned, and since the reason of the reduction of the royalty - namely, the low price of the book is no longer true, - I think it is up to you and Scribners of your own accord to give me my 15%. It will not amount to much, even if you sell the entire three thousand copies, which the 10% royalty covers, - I don't think it will amount to more than two or three hundred dollars and I am not arguing with you about that. But just because you have been generous and devoted friends, and because my feeling toward you has been one of devotion and loyalty, I do not want to see you do this thing now which may be legally and technically all right, but is to my mind, a sharp business practice. I know that you yourself, personally, do not stand to profit one penny whether I get 10% or 15%. I know that you yourself, probably did not suggest the reduction in royalty or fix the price of the book, but I also know the way I expect and want you to act now as my friend. It seems to me that it is imperative that you do this just exactly for the reason that I consider you all my friends and have always lived and felt and thought about you in that way and not as people with whom I had business dealings and who were going to use whatever business advantage they considered legitimate in their dealings with me.

You know very well that I am not a business man and have no capacity for business and that in matters of this sort, I am not able to cope with people who are skilled at it, but where it concerned you and Scribners, I have never thought for one moment, that I would have to cope with it. The thing I really feel and beleive is that at the bottom of your heart, you agree with me and my position in this matter and know that I am right as I know you agreed with me in the matter of almost $1.200, which I was charged for corrections in the proof of "Of time and the River." I'll admit that there too, I am legally responsible and signed the contract which had a clause in it stipulating the cost to the author if the changes and corrections in the proof exceed a certain amount. But the truth of the matter is as you know, and as you said at the time when the bill was first shown to me, that a great many of these corrections came as the result of the work we were both doing on the manuscript, and as a result of the editorial help and advice and the suggestions you made which were so generous and so invaluable. For this very reason perhaps, I ought not to harp upon the subject or complain about having to pay almost $1.200 for corrections that helped the book, but you said at the time the bill was shown to me that in view of the circumstances and the way the corrections were made and done, you didn't think I ought to have to pay as much money as that, and I understood you even to say that if I felt too strongly that I ought not to pay and that the bill was unfair, I would not have to pay it. Well, I don't feel that strongly about it, I think I made a lot of corrections on the proof on my own hook and I think that if these corrections were excessive, I ought to pay for them like anyone else. But I do feel that the bill of almost $1.200 is excessive and that I am being made to pay too much for corrections which I'll admit helped me and the book, but which were partly done with your collaboration.

I didn't mean to bring this into the letter at all. One of the main reasons for my whole feeling about this thing and about the reduced royalty is that, as you know, during the last year, I have been made the victim of almost every kind of unfair and dishonest procedure from people who have taken my money in the past, bringing suit against me, in an effort to get more money, to people walking off with my manuscript, making use of my name for public gatherings when I have not given my consent, appointing me judge to contests I know nothing about, selling my autograph and every other form of parasitism and skin game imaginable. The time has come when it has got to stop, I am not going to submit to it any longer if I can help it. And certainly I don't expect to see the people that I have considered the best friends I have, make use of any of the unfair advantages, however legal they may be, that some other people have made use of.

I want to ask you this; if your refusal in this matter is final and you insist on holding me to the terms of the contract I signed for The Story of a Novel, don't you think that I, or anyone else on earth for that matter, would be justified henceforth and hereafter, considering my relations with you and Scribners were primarily of a business and commercial nature, and if you make use of a business advantage in this way, don't you think I would be justified in making use of a business advantage too if one came my way? Or do you think it works only one way? I don't think it does and I don't think any other fairminded person in the world would think so either. As you know, I never gave a moment's serious consideration to any offers or persuasions that were made to me by other people and I think that you know very well that such offers were made. And that in one case at least, a very large sum of money was mentioned at a time when I, myself, had nothing. You not only knew of the occasion, but I telephoned you of it just as soon as the person telephoned and asked if he could talk to me. I informed you of the telephone call at once and told you I didn't know what it meant and you told me what it did mean, and furthermore told me I had a right to meet the man and listen to what he had to say and even consider what he had to offer. Well, I suppose that's business practice and everyone agrees that it is fully justified and that a man has a right not only to listen, but to take the best and most profitable offer. That's business practice, maybe, but it has not been my practice. I did meet the man, I did listen to what he had to say and I paid no attention at all to his offer. What do you think about this any way? If people are going to get hard-boiled and business-like, should it all be on one side, or doesn't the other fellow have a right to get hard-boiled and business-like too?

I understand perfectly well that even publishers are not in business for their health, even though you have said that none of them make any great amount of money out of it. And I don't expect my relations with my publisher to be a perpetual love feast, into which the vile question of money never enters, but I do say, that you cannot command the loyalty and devotion of a man on the one hand and then take a business advantage on the other. I am sorry to have to say all this. I want to repeat how much I regret my language of last evening, but I also want to say that about this matter of the royalties, I feel as strongly and deeply now as I did then. I am writing this letter to you as a final appeal. You may think I am kicking up a hell of a row over nothing but I do think it is something, a great deal, not in a money way but in the matter of fair dealing, and I am writing to tell you so.

Sincerely,
Tom Wolfe

TLS, 3 pp., Harvard

April 22, 1936

Dear Tom:

I am giving directions to reckon your royalties on "The Story of a Novel" at 15% from the start. The difference in what you will receive if 3,000 copies are sold, between the ten and fifteen percent royalty, will be $225.00. We certainly do not think that we should withhold that sum of money if it is going to cause so much resentment, and so much loss of time and disquiet for all of us.

I would rather, simply agree to do this and say nothing further, but I should not have the right to do it without telling you that the terms as proposed on the $1.50 price are just, and that if the matter were to be looked upon merely as business, we should not be justified as business men in making this concession. You are under a misapprehension if you think that when we suggested a reduction of royalty—such as in similar cases have been freely made by writers of the highest rank, at least in sales—we were basing the suggestion on the question of price. I do remember that the price of $1.25 was mentioned as a desirable one, or a probable one, but the idea of the royalty was not dependent upon that. We could not at that time know what the price would have to be. We found that the price had to be higher because of the question of basic costs which come into every phase of the handling, advertising, promoting, and making of a book. Many of these basic costs do not vary at all because of the size of the book. We do not want to put our prices any higher than we are compelled to, and in fact more than most publishers, have tried to keep them low. We put them up only because we have to. The terms we proposed were therefore in my opinion just.

You return to the question of the excess corrections which were, I believe, $1100.00. If I gave you the impression that I thought this was unfair, it came from my dread of the resentment I knew you would feel to have them deducted from your royalties even though they have always been taken into account in every publisher's contract, and generally at only half the percentage that we allow for them. I once said to you in Charles Scribner's presence that you had a good technical argument for not paying these corrections because you did not make them, and therefore could say that they were not author's corrections, but publishers' corrections. This would be true, since you did not read your proof, but if you had done so, is there any doubt but what these corrections would have been much larger? They were almost wholly unavoidable corrections, like the change from the first to third person, and the changing of names. They were therefore rightly author's corrections and why should the author not pay for them? I think we began wrong by making no charge in the case of excess corrections on the "Angel," which amounted to seven hundred dollars, so that this charge came to you as a surprise.- And the truth is that many authors do resent being charged for such corrections because they cannot be got to consider them in advance. But if the author does not pay for this cost, after the publisher has paid the 20% allowance himself, the publisher will have to pay that too. Why should he have to do it?

As to the other matter you speak of, your freedom to do whatever you think is to your best interests in business, nobody could ever deny it, and I have often said that we did not. I certainly would not wish you to make what you thought was a sacrifice on my account, and I would know that whatever you did would be sincerely believed to be right by you,- as I know that you sincerely believe the contentions you make in this letter to me, to be right. I have never doubted your sincerity and never will. I wish you could have felt that way toward us.

Always yours,

<u>Max</u>

TLS, 2 pp., PUL
TW's personal letterhead, 865 First Avenue, New York City

April 23rd, 1936

Dear Max:

I got your letter this morning and I just want to write you back now to tell you that everything is settled so far as I am concerned, so let's forget about it.

Now that you have told me that you would restore my old royalty of 15%, I want to tell you that I don't want it and want to stick to the contract I signed. That goes for all my other obligations as well. I really made up my mind to this yesterday, and that was the reason I called you up last night and went around to see you.

I wanted to tell you and I am afraid I didn't succeed telling you very well that all the damn contracts in the world don't mean as much to me as your friendship means, and it suddenly occurred to me yesterday that life is too short to quarrel this way with a friend over something that matters so little. But I do want to tell you again just how genuinely and deeply sorry I am for boiling over the way I did the other night. We have had fireworks of this sort before and I am afraid it may occur again, but every time they do, I say something to a friend that is unjust and wrong and sweat blood about it later. So just help me along with this by forgetting all about it, and let's look forward to the future.

I suppose it is a good thing for me to have had this experience in the last year but there is something a little grotesque and tragic in the fact that the success I wanted and looked forward to having as a child, should have brought me so much trouble, worry, bewilderment and disillusion, but I am going to try to add the whole experience to the sum of things I have found out about all through my life and I hope that I will be able to make use of it, instead of letting it make use of me.

I see know what a terribly dangerous thing a little success may be because it seems to me the effort of an artist must always aim at even greater concentration and intensity and effort of the will where his work is concerned and anything that tends to take him away from that, to distract him, to weaken his effort is a bad thing.

I am now started on another book. I need your friendship, and support more than I ever did, so please forget the worst mistakes I have made in the past and let's see if I can't do somewhat better in the future.

Sincerely,
Tom

FROM: John Hall Wheelock   *TLS, 2 pp., PUL*

June 9, 1936

Dear Tom: I enclose translation of a letter from your German publisher, Rowohlt, which may be of interest to you.

We have taken care of the sending of the copies of "The Story of a Novel," of the principal reviews of your books, of photographs, and are returning all the German reviews which they had loaned to us. We have advised them that "Look Homeward Angel" and "Of Time and the River" have been or will be published in Czechoslovakia, Norway, Sweden, Holland and France—this is in answer to their query.

There is nothing left for you to attend to but the matter of the contract for

"From Death to Morning" which is now in your hands, to do with as you think best.

Don't bother to return this translation, as I have several copies. I hope the work goes along well, dear Tom.

With best wishes,

As ever,

<u>J.H.W.</u>

To
Mr. Thomas Wolfe,
865 First Avenue,
New York City.

∽

Postcard of the Pariser Platz, PUL
Berlin

Aug 7, 1936

Dear Max: I've had a good trip—seen all my old friends here—and lots of new people—Also newspaper interviews, drawings, etc—The town is crowded with Olympic visitors, and the Germans have done their job beautifully—Wonderfully cool and clean after NY—Tom

∽

CC, 2 pp., PUL

Aug. 19, 1936

Dear Tom:

I got your postcard yesterday. I had somehow thought of you as beyond the reach of communication, but Miss Nowell had got a letter asking her to send you some books, so it must be that you will receive anything that is forwarded.

I had a postcard from Mabel in North Carolina, wherever Fred is, the ten or fifteen words of which sounded cheerful and spoke highly of the ice cream Fred is concerned with.

There isn't much news to give you except that your royalty report shows a balance of something over seventeen hundred dollars,- which is not due but can be had if you want it.

I have been so busy since you left, even on weekends, that the time has gone fast. If you were hereabouts I would try to persuade you to take a vacation with me in Quebec,- above the hay fever line where you could probably work very well, and we could see the old city and voyage on the St. Lawrence. But I do not want to go up there alone, and Louise cannot because of preparations for the wedding. The girls got back, and what they said of Scotland made it seem wonderful even though I had always thought it must be.

Don't stay away too long.

Always, yours,
[Maxwell Perkins]

∽

TO: *Maxwell Perkins*   *Postcard of Alpbach mit Galtenberg, PUL*

Alpbach, Germany
Aug 26, 1936

I climbed that big mtn. (the highest one) yesterday It damned near finished me but I did it—It makes all of your New Eng. mtns, look like toad-stools. This is a beautiful country and good people—on way back to Munich and Berlin today—Will sail next week if I can get passage

∽

TO: *Maxwell Perkins*   *Postcard of the guard at Wachtruppe am Brandenburg Tor,*
Berlin, PUL
Late August 1936   *Berlin*

We can never learn to march like these boys.
—And it looks as if they're about ready to go again.

∽

TO: *Maxwell Perkins*   *Postcard of the beach at Le Havre, PUL*
September 1936   *Le Havre, France*

This picture was made last year here in Fr and is called The Hour of the Bath They did not have good [*three words indecipherable*] this time

∽

TO: *Irma Wyckoff*   *ALS, 1 p., PUL*
New York City

Dear Miss Wyckoff:

From now on will you please address and send any mail that may come for me to 865 First Avenue, New York City?[1]

Sincerely,
Thomas Wolfe

Oct 5, 1936

1. It had been TW's custom to go to Scribners regularly for his mail. This letter marks a clear break in his relations with the firm.

~

FROM: *John Hall Wheelock*   *TLS, 4 pp., Harvard*

October 8, 1936

Dear Tom:

I want to thank you with all my heart for the splendid letter you have written me about my book.[1] It is a letter that a writer would be proud and happy to receive from any source, but coming from yourself it is precious beyond words.[2] The feeling that your overgenerous praise is undoubtedly, though unconsciously, influenced by our friendship—is "tainted by friendship," in the words of a certain critic—doesn't make it any less welcome. You couldn't have said anything that would please me more than the words you write about finding a man, rather than merely an author, in these poems. I feel that I could have made the book less vulnerable to detailed criticism,

and more perfect from the point of view of a selection merely, by omitting a number of the poems which, nevertheless, I felt were needed to give the rounded impression of a human being and his life.

As for your remark about your indebtedness to me for some image, phrase or rhythm, I can only smile and attribute that, too, Tom, to your desire to make me happy, and to your generous imagination, for, much as I should like to claim the honor, I cannot really feel that I am entitled to it.

The younger school of reviewers have already reduced me to mincemeat: notably in the <u>New</u> <u>Yorker</u>, wherein I am informed that it is "démodé" to write about love and that the religious emotions of awe and reverence are just a lot of tripe. The kind of love poetry which is written to-day, and is therefore of course the best, is along the lines of

"I had an aunt

Who loved a plant

But you're my cup of tea."

Another reviewer states that the book is worse than nothing, that it is positively evil. Here is one of the Harvard boys writing about the sea and about dawn in the city, while his fellow human beings are starving to death—a poet who seems unfamiliar with the dialectic of materialism and of the whole proletarian ideology. I'm trying very hard to look at this criticism impartially and to find out just how much of it is true and applicable, but it's difficult even at so early an age as fifty to dislocate your mind sufficiently to make these readjustments. Another reviewer tells me that the book is "a good example of a certain kind of genuine poetic feeling." I wonder how different kinds of genuine poetic feeling there are? I am also told that I should write with more "violence, venom, and scorn," and yet it would be difficult, perhaps, to maintain these emotions on all subjects.

But all this is beside the point. I wanted to thank you, Tom, for your letter, which means a great deal to me and has left a glow in my heart.

As ever,
Your friend,
Jack

To
Mr. Thomas Wolfe,
865 First Avenue,
New York City.

1. *Poems* 1911–1936 (New York: Scribners, 1936).
2. Wheelock's book and letter unlocated.

TLS, 2 pp., PUL
TW's personal letterhead, 865 First Avenue, New York City

November 12, 1936

Dear Max:

I think you should now write me a letter in which you explicitly state the nature of my relations with Chas Scribners' Sons. I think you ought to say that I have <u>faithfully</u> and honorably discharged all obligations to Chas Scribners' Sons, whether financial, personal or contractual, and that no further agreement or obligation of any sort exists between us.

I must tell you plainly now what you must know already, that, in view of all that has happened in the last year and a half, the differences of opinion and belief, the fundamental disagreements that we have discussed so openly, so frankly, and so passionately, a thousand times, and which have brought about this unmistakable and grievous severance, I think you should have written this letter that I am asking you to write long before this. I am compelled by your failure to do so to ask you, in simple justice, to write it now.

I think it is unfair to put a man in a position where he is forced to deny an obligation that does not exist, to refuse an agreement that was never offered and never made. I think it is also unfair to try to exert, at no expense to oneself, such control of a man's future and his future work as will bring one profit if that man succeeds, and that absolves one from any commitments of any kind, should he fail. I also think it is unfair that a man without income, with little money, and with no economic security against the future, who has time and again, in the past, refused offers and proposals that would have brought him comfort and security, should now, at a time when his reputation has been obscured, and when there are no offers and little market for his work, be compelled to this last and sorrowful exercise of his fruitless devotion. And finally, I do not think that life is a game of chess, and if it were, I could not be a player.

I have nothing more to say here except to tell you that I am your friend and that my feeling toward you is unchanged.

Sincerely yours,
Tom Wolfe

⟿

ALS, 1 p., Harvard
MP's personal Scribner letterhead, New York

Tuesday Nov. 17th, 36

Dear Tom:—I haven't time to write today,—we have a meeting that often lasts till five + my late P.M. + evening are full too. I can say this though,—I never knew a soul with whom I felt I was in such fundamentally complete agreement as you. What's more, + what has to do with it, I know you would not ever do an insincere thing,- or any thing you did not think was right. I don't fully understand your letter but I'll answer it as best I can. You must surely know though that any publisher would leap at the chance to publish you.

Always Yours
Maxwell Perkins

You have with us at present a balance of over $2000 all but about $500 of which is overdue.

Max

⟿

ALS, 2 pp., Harvard
MP's personal Scribner letterhead, New York

Nov 18th 1936

Dear Tom:—With this is a more formal letter which I hope is what you want. This is to say that on my part there has been no "severance." I can't express certain kinds of feelings very comfortably, but you must realize what my feelings are toward you. Ever since Look Homeward Angel your work has been the foremost interest in my life, + I have never doubted for your future on any grounds except, at times, on those of your being able to control the vast mass of material you have accumulated + have to form into books. You seem to think I have tried to control you. I only did that when you asked my help + then I did the best I could do. It all seems very confusing to me but, whatever the result I hope you don't mean it to keep us from seeing each other, or that you won't come to our house.

<u>Max</u>

Perkins's initial response to Wolfe's announcement on 12 November 1936 that he intended to leave Scribners. (Houghton Library, Harvard University).

CCS, 3 pp., PUL

Nov. 18, 1936

Dear Tom:

You ask me to explicitly state the nature of your relations with Charles Scribner's Sons. To begin with, you have faithfully discharged all obligations to us, and no further agreement of any sort exists between us with respect to the future. Our relations are simply those of a publisher who profoundly admires the work of an author and takes great pride in publishing whatever he may of that author's writings. They are not such as to give us any sort of rights, or anything approaching that, over that author's future work. Contrary to custom, we have not even an option which would give us the privilege of seeing first any new manuscript.

We do not wholly understand parts of your letter, where you speak of us as putting you in a position of denying an obligation that does not exist, for we do not know how we have done that; or where you refer to 'exerting control of a man's future,' which we have no intention of doing at all, and would not have the power or right to do. There are other phrases in that part of your letter that I do not understand, one of which is that which refers to us as being absolved from any commitments of any kind "should the author fail." If this and these other phrases signify that you think you should have a contract from us if our relations are to continue, you can certainly have one. We should be delighted to have one. You must surely know the faith this house has in you. There are, of course, limits in terms beyond which nobody can go in a contract, but we should expect to make one that would suit you if you told us what was required.

Ever sincerely yours,
MEP

TLS with holograph postscript, 1 p., Harvard

Nov. 20, 1936

Dear Tom:

I thought I might as well send you the enclosed check since it has been drawn, together with a statement. About five hundred dollars more will be due in February, together with whatever else has accumulated in sales since the first of last August,- which may be a considerable sum.

Always yours,

Max

I wish I could see you but I don't want to force myself on you.
MP.

FROM: *John Hall Wheelock*   *TLS, 2 pp., Harvard*

November 28, 1936

Dear Tom:

Mr. H. M. Ledig, of Rowohlt Verlag in Berlin, writes me, enclosing copy of a new write-up of your books which takes up two whole pages of the <u>Buchhändler Börsenblatt</u>, the official book-trade organ of Germany. He wants you to know of the efforts they are making to increase the sale of your books there and he thinks you might be interested to see what overwhelmingly enthusiastic notices both books have received in the German press. No writer since Goethe has had such notices in Germany. I am therefore enclosing a copy of the write-up, together with a translation.

Mr. Ledig also says in speaking of you, "Please tell him that we are going to write him soon, and give him our love."

Don't bother to acknowledge this, dear Tom. I know that you read German quite fluently, but I thought you might like to have an English copy for your file.

I hope the work goes forward well and that you aren't wearing yourself out at it.

As ever, dear Tom, with best wishes,

Your friend,
Jack

To
Mr. Thomas Wolfe,
865 First Avenue,
New York City.

&

FROM: *Charles Scribner III*   *CC, 1 p., PUL*

Dec. 2, 1936.

Dear Tom:

Enclosed is the form of letter which Mr. Cook[1] suggests that you send him. As a matter of fact you could sign and date this copy and mail it on at once, if you cared to. I do not think you can make any mistake in signing the letter and I believe it will save both complications and expense. As soon as I hear from Cook again I will let you know.

Sincerely yours

To
Thomas Wolfe, esq.,
835 First Avenue

1. Alfred A. Cook, lawyer retained by Scribners to represent TW and the firm in the libel suit brought by Marjorie Dorman, TW's Brooklyn landlady. She asserted that TW libeled herself and her family in "No Door" in *From Death to Morning*. TW reluctantly

settled the lawsuit in early 1937 for $2,850; TW paid half the settlement and legal expenses totalling $5,590. See Charles Scribner III to TW (19 January 1938).

TLS with holograph postscript, 27 pp., PUL[1]
TW's personal letterhead, 865 First Avenue, New York City

December 15, 1936

Dear Max:

I am sorry for the delay in answering your three letters of November 17th and 18th. As you know, I have been hard at work here day after day and, in addition, have recently been beset by some more of the legal difficulties, threats and worries which have hounded my life for the last year and a half. And finally, I wanted to have time to think over your letters carefully and to meditate my own reply before I answered you.

First of all, let me tell you that for what you say in your own two personal letters of November 17th and November 18th I shall be forever proud and grateful. I shall remember it with the greatest happiness as long as I live. I must tell you again, no matter what embarrassment it may cause you, what I have already publicly acknowledged and what I believe is now somewhat understood and known about in the world, namely, that your faith in me, your friendship for me, during the years of doubt, confusion and distress, was and will always be one of the great things in my life.

When I did give utterance to this fact in print - when I tried to make some slight acknowledgment of a debt of friendship and of loyalty, which no mere acknowledgment could ever repay - some of my enemies, as you know, tried to seize upon the simple words I had written in an effort to twist and pervert them to their own uses, to indicate that my acknowledgment was for a technical and professional service, which it was not, to assert that I was myself incapable of projecting and accomplishing my own purpose without your own editorial help, which is untrue.[2] But although such statements as these were made to injure me, and perhaps have done me an injury, I believe that injury to be at best only a temporary one. As for the rest, what I had really said, what I had really written about my debt to you, is plain and unmistakable, clearly and definitely understood by people of good will, who have a mind to understand. I would not retract a word of it, except to wish the words were written better, I would not withdraw a line of it, except to hope that I might write another line that would more adequately express the whole meaning and implication of what I feel and want to say.

As to those statements which were made, it seems to me malevolently, for what purpose I do not know, by people I have never met - that I had to have your technical and critical assistance "to help me write my books," etc, - they are so contemptible, so manifestly false, I have no fear whatever of their ultimate exposure. If refutation were needed, if the artist had time enough or felt it necessary to make an answer to all the curs that snap at him, it would not take me long, I think, to brand these falsehoods for the lies they are. I would only have to point out, I think, that so far from needing any outside aid "to help me write my books," the very book which my detractors now eagerly seize on as my best one, the gauge by which the others must be mentioned, and itself the proof and demonstration of my subsequent decline, had been utterly finished and completed, to the final period, in utter isolation, without a word of criticism or advice from any one, before any publisher ever saw it; and that whatever changes were finally made were almost entirely changes in the form of omission and of cuts in view of bringing the book down to a more publishable and condensed form. That book, of course, was "Look Homeward, Angel," and I believe that with everything else I ever wrote, the process was much the same, although the finality of completion was not so marked, because in later books I was working in a more experimental, individual fashion and dealing with the problem of how to shape and bring into articulate form a giant mass of raw material, whose proportions almost defeated me.

The very truth of the matter is that, so far from ever having been unsure of purpose and direction, in the last five years at any rate I have been almost too sure. My sense of purpose and direction is definite and overwhelming. I think, I feel and know what I want to do; the direction in which, if I live and if I am allowed to go on working and fulfill myself, I want to go, is with me more clear and certain than with any one that I have ever known. My difficulty has never been one of purpose or direction. Nothing is more certain than this fact, that I know what I want to do and where I want to go. Nothing is more certain than the fact that I shall finish any book I set out to write if life and health hold out. My difficulty from the outset, as you know, has never been one of direction, it has only been one of means. As I have already said and written, in language that seems to be so clear and unmistakable that no one could misunderstand it, I have been faced with the problem of discovering for myself my own language, my own pattern, my own structure, my own design, my own universe and creation. That, as I have said before, is a problem that is, I think, by no means unique, by no means special to myself. I believe it may have been the problem of every artist that ever lived. In my own case, however, I believe the difficulties of the problem may have been increased and complicated by the denseness of the fabric, the dimensions of the structure, the variety of the plan. For that reason I have, as you know, at times found myself almost hopelessly enmeshed in my own web.

In one sense, my whole effort for years might be described as an effort to fathom my own design, to explore my own channels, to discover my own ways. In these respects, in an effort to help me to discover, to better use, these means I was striving to apprehend and make my own, you gave me the most generous, the most painstaking, the most valuable help. But that kind of help might have been given to me by many other skilful people - and of course there are other skilful people in the world who could give such help, - although none that I know of who could give it so skillfully as you.

But what you gave me, what in my acknowledgment I tried to give expression to, was so much more than this technical assistance - an aid of spiritual sustenance, of personal faith, of high purpose, of profound and sensitive understanding, of utter loyalty and staunch support, at a time when many people had no belief at all in me, or when what little belief they had was colored by serious doubt that I would ever be able to continue or achieve my purpose, fulfill my "promise" - all of this was a help of such priceless and incalculable value, of such spiritual magnitude, that it made any other kind of help seem paltry by comparison. And for that reason mainly I have resented the contemptible insinuations of my enemies that I have to have you "to help me write my books." As you know, I don't have to have you or any other man alive to help me with my books. I do not even have to have technical help or advice, although I need it badly, and have been so immensely grateful for it. But if the worst came to the worst - and of course the worst does and will come to the worst - all this I could and will and do learn for myself, as all hard things are learned, with blood-sweat, anguish and despair.

As for another kind of help - a help that would attempt to shape my purpose or define for me my own direction, - I not only do not need that sort of help but if I found that it had in any way invaded the unity of my purpose, or was trying in any fundamental way to modify or alter the direction of my creative life, the way in which it seems to me it ought and has to go - I should repulse it as an enemy, I should fight it and oppose it with every energy of my life, because I feel so strongly that it is the final and unpardonable intrusion upon the one thing in an artist's life that must be held and kept inviolable.

All this I know you understand and will agree to. As to the final kind of help, the help of friendship, the help of faith, the help and belief and understanding of a fellow creature whom you know and reverence, not only as a person of individual genius but as a spirit of incorruptible integrity - that kind of help I do need, that kind of help I think I have been given, that kind of help I shall evermore hope to deserve and pray that I shall have. But if that too should fail - if that too should be taken from me, as so many rare and priceless things are taken from us in this life - that kind of dark and tragic fortitude that grows on us in life as we get older, and which tells us that in the end we can and must endure all things, might make it possible for me to bear even that final and irreparable loss, to agree with Samuel Johnson when he said: "The shepherd in Vergil grew at last acquainted with Love, and found him a native of the rocks."

You say in one of your letters that you never knew a soul with whom you felt that you were in such fundamentally complete agreement as with me. May I tell you that I shall remember these words with proud happiness and with loyal gratefulness as long as I live. For I too on my own part feel that way about you. I know that somehow, in some hard, deep, vexed and troubling way in which all the truth of life is hidden and which, at the cost of so much living, so much perplexity and anguish of the spirit, we have got to try to find and fathom, what you say is true: I believe we are somehow, in this strange, hard way, in this complete and fundamental agreement with each other.

And yet, were there ever two men since time began who were as completely different as you and I? Have you ever known two other people who were, in almost every respect of temperament, thinking, feeling and acting, as far apart? It seems to me that each of us might almost represent, typify, be the personal embodiment of, two opposite poles of life. How to put it I do not know exactly, but I might say, I think, that you in your essential self are the Conservative and I, in my essential self, am the Revolutionary.

I use these words, I hope, in what may have been their original and natural meanings. I am not using them with reference to any of the political, social, economic or religious connotations that are now so often tied up with them. When I say that you a Conservative, I am not thinking of you as some one who voted for Governor Landon,[3] for I can see how an action of that sort and your own considered reasons for doing it might easily have revolutionary consequences. When I say that I am a Revolutionary I know that you will never for a moment think of me as some one who is usually referred to in America as a "radical." You know that my whole feeling toward life could not be indicated or included under such a category. I am not a party man, I am not a propaganda man, I am not a Union Square or Greenwich Village communist. I not only do not believe in these people; I do not even believe they believe in themselves. I mistrust their sincerity, I mistrust their motives, I do not believe they have any essential capacity for devotion or for belief in the very principles of Revolution, of government, of economics and of life, which they all profess.

More than that, I believe that these people themselves are parasitic excrescences of the very society which they profess to abhor, whose destruction they prophesy and whose overthrow they urge. I believe that these people would be unable to live without the society which they profess to abhor, and I know that I could live if I had to, not only under this society but under any other one, and that in the end I might probably approve no other one more than I do this.

I believe further that these very people who talk of the workers with such reverence, and who assert that they are workers and are for the worker's cause, do not reverence the workers, are not themselves workers and in the end are traitors to the worker's cause. I believe that I myself not only know the workers and am a friend of the worker's cause but that I am myself a brother to the workers, because I am myself, as every artist is, a worker, and I am myself moreover the son of a working man. I know furthermore that at the bottom there is no difference between the artist and the worker. They both come from the same family, they recognize and understand each other instantly. They speak the same language. They have always stood together. And I know that our enemies, the people who betray us, are these apes and monkeys of the arts, who believe in everything and who believe in nothing and who hate the artist and who hate the living man no matter what lip service they may pay to us. These people are the enemies to life, the enemies to revolution. Nothing is more certain than that they will betray us in the end.

I have said these things simply to indicate to you a difference of which I know you must be already well aware. The difference between the revolutionary and the "radical," the difference between the artist and the ape of art, the difference between the worker and those who say they are the worker's friend. The same thing could be said, it seems to me, on your own side, about the true conservative and the person who only votes conservative and owns property and has money in the bank.

Just as in some hard, strange way there is between us probably this fundamentally complete agreement which you speak of, so too, in other hard, strange ways there is this complete and polar difference. It must be so with the South pole and the North pole. I believe that in the end they too must be in fundamentally complete agreement - but the whole earth lies between them. I don't know exactly how to define conservatism or the essential conservative spirit of which I speak here, but I think I might say it is a kind of fatalism of the spirit. Its fundaments, it seems to me, are based upon a kind of unhoping hope, an imperturbable acceptation, a determined resignation, which believes that fundamentally life will never change, but that on this account we must all of us do the best we can.

The result of all this, it seems to me, is that these differences between us have multiplied in complexity and difficulty. The plain truth of the matter now is that I hardly know where to turn. The whole natural impulse of creation - and with me, creation is a natural impulse, it has got to flow, it has got to realize itself through the process of torrential production - is checked and hampered at every place. In spite of this, I have finally and at last, during these past two months, broken through into the greatest imaginative conquest of my life - the only complete and whole one I have ever had. And now I dare not broach it to you, I dare not bring it to you, I dare not show it to you, for fear that this thing which I cannot trifle with, that may come to a man but once in his whole life, may be killed at its inception by cold caution, by indifference, by the growing apprehensiveness and dogmatism of your own conservatism. You say that you are not aware that there is any severance between us. Will you please tell me what there is in the life around us on which we both agree? We don't agree in politics, we don't agree on economics, we are in entire disagreement on the present system of life around us, the way people live, the changes that should be made.[4]

Your own idea, evidently, is that life itself is unchangeable, that the abuses I protest against, the greed, the waste, the poverty, the filth, the suffering, are inherent in humanity, and that any other system than the one we have would be just as bad as this one.[5] In this, I find myself in profound and passionate conflict. I hold no brief, as you know, for the present communist system as it is practiced in Russia today, but it seems to me to be the most absurd and hollow casuistry to argue seriously that because a good Russian worker is given a thicker slice of beef than a bad one, or because a highly trained mechanic enjoys a slightly better standard of living and is given more privileges and comforts than an inferior mechanic, the class system has been reestablished in Russia and is identical[6] with the one existing in this country, whereby a young girl who inherits the fortune of a five-and-ten-cent store king is allowed to live a life of useless, vicious idleness and to enjoy an income of five million dollars annually while other young girls work in the very stores that produce her fortune for ten dollars a week.[7]

It is all very well to say that the artist should not concern himself with these things but with "life." What are these things if they are not life - one of the cruelest and most intolerable aspects of it, it is true, but as much a part of the whole human spectacle as a woman producing a child. You, better than any one, have had the chance to observe during the past year how this consciousness of society, of the social elements, that govern life today, have sunk into my spirit, how my convictions about all these things have grown deeper, wider, more intense at every point. On your own part, it seems to me, there has been a corresponding stiffening, an increasing conservatism that is now, I fear, reached the point of dogged and unyielding inflexibility and obstinate resolve to try to maintain the status quo at any cost.[8]

Since that is your condition, your considered judgment, I will not try to change it, or to persuade you in any way, because I know your reasons for so thinking and so feeling are honest ones. But neither must you now try to change me, or to persuade me to alter or deny convictions which are the result of no superficial or temporary influence, no Union Square-Greenwich Village cult, but the result of my own deep living, my own deep feeling, my own deep labor and my own deep thought.

Had I given full expression to these convictions in "Of Time and the River" I believe it would have been a better book.[9] You do not think so. But I will say that these feelings, these convictions, are becoming deeper and intenser all the time, and so far from feeling that the world cannot be changed, that it cannot be made better, that the evils of life are unremediable, that all the faults and vices at which we protest will always exist, I find myself more passionately convinced than ever of the necessity of change, more passionately confirmed than ever in the faith and the belief that the life and the condition of the whole human race can be immeasurably improved. And this is something that grows stronger with me all the time. It has been my lot to start life with an obedient faith, with a conservative tradition, only to have that faith grow weaker and fade out as I grew older. I cannot tell you all the ways in which this came about, but I think I can indicate to you one of the principal ones.

I was a child of faith. I grew up in the most conservative section of America, and as a child I put an almost unquestioning belief and confidence in the things that were told me, the precepts that were taught me. As I grew older I began to see the terrible and shocking differences between appearance and reality all around me. I was told, for example, in church, of a Sunday morning, that people should love one another as their brothers, that they should not bear false witness against their fellow-man, that they should not covet their neighbor's wife, that they should not commit adultery, that they should not cheat, trick, betray and rob their fellows. And as I grew older and my knowledge of life and of the whole community increased, until there was hardly a family in town whose whole history I did not know, I began to see what a shameful travesty of goodness these lives were. I began to see that the very people who said on Sunday that one should not bear false witness against his neighbors bore false witness all the time, until the very air was poisonous with their slanders, with their hatreds, their vicious slanderings of life and of their neighbors. I began to see how the people who talked about not coveting their neighbors' wives did covet their neighbors' wives and committed adultery with them. I saw how the minister who got up and denounced a proposal to introduce a little innocent amusement in the Sunday life of the people - a baseball game or a moving picture show,—upon the grounds that it not only violated the law of God but was an imposition on our fellow-man, that we had no right to ask our fellows to do work on Sunday, had, at that very moment, two sweating negro girls in the kitchen of his own home, employed at meagre wages to cook his Sunday dinner for him. I saw how the wife of the town's richest man would go in for what was called social work and lecture the poor little shop-girls of the Y.W.C.A., telling them that no decent girl would take a drink, would stay out after nine o'clock at night, would tolerate the company of a young man without a chaperone - while her own daughter, unreproved, unchecked and licensed, was the heroine of five hundred fornications, was even at that moment lying in a state of drunken stupor in the embraces of another young town parasite.

Well, it is an old, old story, but to me it was a new one. Like every other boy of sense, intelligence and imagination, whoever first discovered these things for himself, I thought I was the first one in the world to see these things. I thought that I had come upon a horrible catastrophe, a whole universe of volcanic infamy over which the good people of the earth were treading blissfully and innocently with trusting smiles. I thought I had to tell this thing to some one. I thought I had to warn the world, to tell all my friends and teachers that all the goodness and integrity and purity of their lives was menaced by this snake of unsuspected evil.

I don't need to tell you what happened. I was received either with smiles of amused and pitying tolerance or with curt reprimands, admonitions to shut up, not to talk about my betters, not to say a word against people who had won a name and who were the high and mighty ones in town. Then slowly, like some one living in a nightmare only to wake up and find out that the nightmare is really true, I began to find out that they <u>didn't</u> mean it, they didn't mean what they said. I began to discover that all these fine words, these splendid precepts, these noble teachings had no meaning at all, because the very people who professed them had no belief in them. I began to discover that it didn't matter at all whether you bore false witness against your neighbor, if you only said that one should not bear false witness against his neighbor. I began to see that it didn't matter at all whether you took your neighbor's ox or his ass or his wife, if only you had the cunning and the power to take them. I began to see that it did not matter at all whether you committed adultery or not, so long as it did not come out in the papers. Every one in town might know you had committed it, and with whom, and on what occasions, the whole history might be a matter for sly jesting, furtive snickerings, the lewd and common property of the whole community, and you could still be deacon of the church provided you were not sued for alienation of affection. I began to see that you could talk of chastity, of purity, of standards of morality and high conduct, of loving your neighbor as yourself, and still derive your filthy income from a horde of rotting tenements down in niggertown that were so vile and filthy they were not fit to be the habitation of pigs. You could talk to a crowd of miserable, over-worked and under-paid shop-girls about their moral life and the necessity of chastity even though your own daughter was the most promiscuous, drunken little whore in town. And it didn't matter, it didn't matter - if you had the dough. That was all that mattered.

I discovered very early that people who had the money could do pretty damn near anything they wanted to. Whoredom, drunkenness, debauchery of every sort was the privilege of the rich, the crime of the poor. And as I grew older, as my experience of life widened and increased, as I first came to know, to explore, to investigate life in this overwhelming city, with all the passion, the hope, the faith, the fervor and the poetic imagination of youth, I found that here too it was just the same. Here too, if anything, it was more overwhelming because it was so condensed, so multiplied. Here too, if anything, it was even more terrible because the privileged city classes no longer pretended to cloak themselves in the spurious affirmations of religion. The result has been, as I have grown older, as I have seen life in manifold phases all over the earth, that I have become more passionately convinced than ever before that this system that we have is evil, that it brings misery and injustice not only to the lives of the poor but to the wretched and sterile lives of the privileged classes who are supported by it, that this system of living must be changed, that men must have a new faith, a new heroism, a new belief, if life is to be made better. And that life can be made better, that life will be made better is the heart and core of my own faith and my own conviction, the end toward which I believe I must henceforth direct every energy of my life and talent.

All this, I know, you consider elementary, and I agree with you. It is. These evidences of corruption in the life around me which I have mentioned to you, you consider almost childishly naive. Perhaps they are. But if they are, the anterior fundamental sources of corruption which have produced them are certainly neither childish nor naive. You have told me that you consider the life of a Smith Reynolds,[10] the vicious life of a young girl who, without ever having done a stroke of work herself, is privileged to enjoy an income of two million, or five million, or ten million a year, only a trifling and superficial manifestation and of no importance. With this, of course, I am in utter opposition. If these people, as you say, are only flies upon the tender of a locomotive, they are locomotive flies, and the locomotive that produced them should be scrapped.

I have gone into all this, not because these bases of contention are even fundamental to you and me, but because they are indicative of all the various widening channels of difference that have come up between us in recent years. Just as my own feeling for the necessity for change, for essential revolution in this way of life, has become steadily deeper and more confirmed, so too have you, hardened by the challenge of the depression, deeply alarmed by the menace of the times to the fortune of which you are the custodian[11] - not for yourself, I know, for you yourself I truly believe are not a man who needs material things, but alarmed by the menace of these times to the security and future of five young and tender creatures who, protected as they have been, and unprepared as they are to meet the peril of these coming times, are themselves, it seems to me, the unfortunate victims of this very system you must now try to help maintain - you have accordingly become more set and more confirmed in your own convictions.[12] With these personal affairs, these intimate details of your fine family, I have no intention to intrude save where it seems to me to have resulted in a bias that challenges the essence of my own purpose and direction.

What I really want to say to you most earnestly now is this: there has never been a time when I've been so determined to write as I please, to say what I intend to say, to publish the books I want to publish, as I am now. I know that you have asserted time and again that you were in entire sympathy with this feeling, that, more than this, you were willing to be the eager promoter and supporter of this intention, that you were willing to publish whatever I wanted you to publish, that you were only waiting for me to give it to you. In this I think you have deceived yourself. I think you are mistaken when you say that all you have waited for was the word from me, that you would publish anything I wanted you to publish. There are many things that I have wanted you to publish which have not been published.[13] Some of them have not been published because they were too long for magazine space, or too short for book space, or too different in their design and quality to fit under the heading of a short story, or too incomplete to be called a novel. All this is true. All this I grant. And yet, admitting all these things, without a word of criticism of you or of the technical and publishing requirements of the present time that make their publication impracticable, I will still say that I think some of them should have been published. I still think that much of the best writing that a man may do is writing that does not follow under the convenient but extremely limited forms of modern publication. It is not your fault. It is not Scribner's fault. It is just the way things are. But as I have been telling you, the way things are is not always the way, it seems to me that things should be; and one fact that has become plain to me in recent years and is now imbedded in my conviction, is that in spite of the rivers of print that inundate this broad land, the thousands of newspapers, the hundreds of magazines, the thousands of books that get printed every year, and the scores of publishers who assure you that they are sitting on the edges of their chairs and eagerly waiting, praying, that some one will come in with a piece of writing of originality and power, that all they are waiting for, all they ask for, is just for the opportunity of discovering it and printing it, the means of publication are still most limited for a life of the complexity, the variety, the richness, the fascination, the terror, the poetry, the beauty and the whole unuttered magnificence of this tremendous life around us, the means of publication are really pitifully meager, ungenerous, meanly, sterilely constricted.

Which brings me now to an essential point, a point that bears practically and dangerously on every thing that I have heretofore said to you.

About fifteen years ago, as you know, an extraordinary book was produced which startled the whole critical and publishing world. This book was the Ulysses of James Joyce. I know that you are well aware of the history of that book, but for the sake of the argument I am presently to make, let me review it again for you. Ulysses was published, if I mistake not, in 1921.[14] I have been informed dozens of times in the last few years by reputable and well-known publishers, including yourself, that they are eagerly waiting a chance to produce a work of originality and power, that they would produce it without question, without modification, if it were given to them. What are the facts concerning Ulysses? Was it published by Chas Scribner's Sons?[15] No, it was not. Was it published by Harper's, by Macmillan's, by Houghton-Mifflin, by one of the great English houses? It was not. Who published it then? It was published privately, obscurely, by a woman who ran a book shop in Paris.[16] And at first, as you know, it was treated by most critics as kind of literary curiosity - either as a work of deliberate pornography or as a work of wilfully complicated obscurity, of no genuine value or importance, save to a little group of clique adepts. And as you know, the book was taken up by clique adepts every-where and used, or rather misused, in their customary way, as a badge of their snob-bish superiority. But in addition to both these groups there was also a third group, I think, a very small group composed of those people scattered throughout the world who are able to read and feel and understand and form their own judgment without prejudice of the merits of a powerful and original work. It seems to me that almost the best, the most fortunate thing in life - in a writer's life at least - is that these people do exist. A great book is not lost. It does not get done to death by fools and snobs. It may be misunderstood for years. Its writer may be ridiculed or reviled or betrayed by false idolatry, but the book does not get lost. There are always a few people who will save it. The book will make its way. That is what happened to Ulysses. As time went on, the circle widened. Its public increased. As people over-came their own inertia, mastered the difficulty which every new and original work creates, became familiar with its whole design, they began to understand that the book was neither an obscene book nor an obscure book, certainly it was not a work of wilful dilettante caprice. It was, on the contrary, an orderly, densely constructed creation, whose greatest fault, it seems to me, so far from being a fault of caprice, was rather the fault of an almost Jesuitical logic which is essentially too dry and life-less in its mechanics for a work of the imagination. At any rate, now, after fifteen years, Ulysses is no longer thought of as a book meant solely for a little group of lit-erary adepts. The adepts of this day, in fact, speak somewhat patronizingly of the work as marking "the end of an epoch," as being "the final development of an out worn naturalism," etc., etc. But the book itself had now won an unquestioned and established place in literature. Its whole method, its style, its characters, its story and design has become so familiar to many of us that we no longer think of it as diffi-cult or obscure. It seems no more difficult that Tristram Shandy.[17] For my part, I do not find Ulysses as difficult as Tristram. Certainly it is no where near as difficult as The Ring and the Book.[18] Moreover, Ulysses can now be published openly in this country, sold over the counter as any other book is sold, without fear of arrest or action by the law. And at the present time, as you know, it is being sold that way, in what is known as "large quantities," by one of your fellow publishers. This man told me a year and a half ago that the sale up to that time, I believe, was something like 30,000 copies.[18] Ulysses, therefore, has made its way not only critically but commercially as well. These are the facts. I do not recall them in order to accuse you with them. I know you did not have the opportunity of publishing Ulysses. Perhaps no other well-known publisher, either in England or America, had that opportunity. I suppose furthermore that at that time it would have been impossible for any rep-utable publisher to have published that book openly. But the fact remains it did get published, didn't it - not by Scribner's, not by Houghton, not by any known pub-lisher in England, but privately, by a little obscure bookseller in Paris.

And the reason your associates, the Modern Library, Inc., can now publish this book; in large quantities, openly, and derive a profit from it now, is because some private, obscure person took the chance fifteen years ago - took the chance, I fear, without the profits.

What, then? You say you are waiting eagerly to discover a manuscript of originality and power. You say that you are waiting eagerly to publish a manuscript of mine, that you will publish anything I want you to publish. I know you believe what you say, but I also think you deceive yourself. I am not going to write a Ulysses book. Like many another young man who came under the influence of that remarkable work, I wrote my Ulysses book and got it published too. That book, as you know, was Look Homeward, Angel. And now, I am finished with Ulysses and with Mr. Joyce, save that I am not an ingrate and will always, I hope, be able to remember a work that stirred me, that opened new vistas into writing, and to pay the tribute to a man of genius that is due him.

However, I am now going to write my own Ulysses. The first volume is now under way. The first volume will be called The Hound of Darkness, and the whole work, when completed, will be called The Vision of Spangler's Paul.[20] Like Mr. Joyce, I am going to write as I please, and this time, no one is going to cut me unless I want them to.[21] Like Mr. Joyce, and like most artists, I believe, I am by nature a Puritan. At any rate, a growing devotion to work, to purpose, to fulfillment, a growing intensity of will, tends to distill one's life into a purer liquor. I shall never hereafter - I hope that I have never heretofore - but I shall never hereafter write a word for the purpose of arousing sensational surprise, of shocking the prudish, of flaunting the outraged respectabilities of the middle-class mind. But I shall use as precisely, as truthfully, as tellingly as I can, every word I have to use, every word, if need be, in my vocabulary, every word, if need be, in the vocabulary of the foulest-mouthed taxi driver, the most prurient-tongued prostitute that ever screamed an obscene epithet. Like Mr. Joyce, I have at last discovered my own America, I believe I have found my language, I think I know my way. And I shall wreak out my vision of this life, this way, this world and this America, to the top of my bent, to the height of my ability, but with an unswerving devotion, integrity and purity of purpose that shall not be menaced, altered or weakened by any one. I will go to jail because of this book if I have to.[22] I will lose my friends because of it, if I will have to. I will be libeled, slandered, blackmailed, threatened, menaced, sneered at, derided and assailed by every parasite, every ape, every blackmailer, every scandalmonger, every little Saturday-Reviewer of the venomous and corrupt respectabilities. I will be exiled from my country because of it, if I have to. I can endure exile. I have endured it before, as you well know, on account of a book which you yourself published, although few -among them, some of the very ones who betrayed me then either by "silence or evasion now try to smile feebly when I speak of exile, but it was the truth and may be true again. But no matter what happens I am going to write this book.

You have heard me talk to you before. You have not always been disposed to take seriously what I say to you. I pray most earnestly that you will take this seriously. For seven years now, during this long and for me wonderful association with you, I have been increasingly aware of a certain direction which our lives were taking. Looking back, I can see now that although Look Homeward, Angel gave you pleasure and satisfaction, you were extremely alarmed even then about its publication, and entertained the hope - the sincere and honest hope directed, I know, to what you considered my own best interests - that the years would temper me to a greater conservatism, a milder intensity, a more decorous moderation. And I think where I have been most wrong, most unsure in these past seven years, has been where I have yielded to this benevolent pressure. Because I think that it is just there that I have allowed myself to falter in my purpose, to be diverted from the direction toward which the whole impulsion of my life and talent is now driving me, to have failed there insofar as I have yielded to the modifications of this restraint. Restraint, discipline - yes, they were needed desperately, they are needed badly still. But let us not get the issues confused, let us not again get into the old confusion between substance and technique, purpose and manner, direction and means, the spirit and the letter. Restrain my adjectives, by all means, discipline my adverbs, moderate the technical extravagances of my incondite exuberance, but don't derail the train, don't take the Pacific Limited and switch it down the siding towards Hogwart Junction. It can't be done. I'm not going to let it happen. If you expected me to grow conservative simply because I got bald and fat and for the first time in life had a few dollars in the bank, you are going to be grievously mistaken. Besides, what is there longer for me to fear? I have been through it all now, I have seen how women can betray you, how friends can sell you out for a few filthy dollars, how the whole set-up of society and of justice in its present form permits the thief, the parasite, the scavenger, the scandal-monger to rob, cheat, outrage and defame you, how even those people who swear they are your sincerest and most enduring friends, who say they value your talent and your work, can sink to the final dishonor of silence and of caution when you are attacked, will not even lift their voices in a word of protest or of indignation when they hear you lied about by scoundrels or maligned by rascals. So what am I now to lose? Even the little money that I had, the greater part of it, has now been taken from me by these thieves and parasites of life. Well, they can take it, they can have it, they have got it. They can take everything I have, but no one henceforth shall take from me my work.

I am afraid of nothing now. I have nothing more to lose except my life and health. And those I pray and hope to God will stay with me till my work is done. That, it seems to me, is the only tragedy that can now stay with me.

The other day you were present when we were having an interview with a distinguished member of the legal profession.[23] I wonder what was going on in your mind when you saw that man and when you looked at me. When you saw that man, secure in wealth, in smugness, in respectability, even though all these authorities had come to him from his accursed profession, from shuffling papers, peering around for legal crevices, seeking not for truth or justice but for technical advantages. When you heard this man ask me if I had lived in certain neighborhoods, in certain kinds of habitation, if I ever drank, etc., and when you heard him cough pompously behind his hand and say that although he of course had never led "that sort of life" he was - ahem, ahem - not narrow-minded and understood that there were those that did. Understand? Why, what could he understand of "my kind of life"? He could no more understand it than a dog could understand the books in his master's library. And I have been forced to wonder of late, after some of the sad events of this last year, how much of it you understood. What I am trying to tell you, what I am forced to say, because it is the truth, is that I am a righteous man, and few people know it because there are few righteous people in the world.

But from my boyhood, from my early youth, I have lived a life of solitude, industry, consecration. I have cost few people anything in this world, except perhaps the pains of birth. I have given people everything I had. I think that I have taken from no one more than I have given them. Certainly, I suppose that not even my bitterest enemies have ever accused me of living or working or thinking about money. During the time that you yourself have known me you have had ample demonstration of that fact. I known you have not forgotten them, and I hope that if anything should happen to me, if I should die, as indeed I have no wish to do, there would be some one left who had known me who would say some of these things I know to be true.

Please understand, that I neither intend nor imply any criticism of you, or of your friendship when I say these things. I know you are my friend. I value your friendship more than anything else in the world, the belief that you, above all people, respected my work and found happiness in being able to help me with it has been the greatest spiritual support and comfort I've ever known. I think further that if I ever heard you slandered or defamed or lied about I would assault the person who defamed you. But I know that that is not your way.[24] You believe that silence is the best answer, and perhaps you are right. At any rate, I want you to know that as long as I know you are my friend to the very hilt, to the very last, if need be, and I hope it never need be, to your own peril and security, that is all that matters. And that is the way I feel about you.

I do not know if you have always been aware of how I felt about these things, of what a naked, fiercely lacerated thing my spirit was, how I have writhed beneath the lies and injuries and at times, almost maddened to insanity at the treachery, the injustice and the hatred I have had to experience and endure, at what a frightful cost I have attained even the little fortitude I have attained. At times, particularly during the last year or two, the spectacle of the victim squirming beneath the lash has seemed to amuse you.[25] I know there is no cruelty in your nature. I do suggest to you, however, that where one is secure in life, when one is vested with authority, established in position, surrounded by a little world of his own making, of his own love, he may sometimes be a little unmindful of the lives of people less fortunate than himself. There is an unhappy tendency in all of us to endure with fortitude the anguish of another man. There is also a tendency among people of active and imaginative minds and temperaments who live themselves conventional and conservative lives to indulge vicariously their interest in the adventures and experiences of other people whose lives are not so sheltered as their own. And these people, I think, often derive what seems to be a kind of quiet, philosophic amusement at the spectacle of what is so falsely known as the "human comedy." But I might suggest to such people that what affords them quiet entertainment is being paid for by another man with blood and agony, and that while we smile at the difficulties and troubles in which an impulsive and generous person gets involved, a man of genius or of talent may be done to death.

I suppose it is very true to say that "every one has these troubles." I do think, however, that a man in my own position, of my own temperament, whose personality seems to penetrate his work in a peculiarly intimate way, so that he then becomes the target for intrigues and scandals of all sorts - such a man, I say, may have them to an exaggerated degree and through no essential fault of his own. Certainly, I do not think he could expect to be protected wholly from them. Certainly no one has the right to expect that his own life will be wholly free from the griefs and troubles that other people have. But I think a man who has not injured other people, who has not interfered with other people's lives or solicited their intrusion, has a right to expect a reasonable and decent amount of privacy - the reasonable and decent amount of privacy that a carpenter, a truck driver or a railroad engineer might have.

At any rate, in spite of all these things, I shall push forward somehow to the completion of my work. I feel that any more confusion or uncertainty might be ruinous to my purpose. There has been too much indecision already. We postponed the completion and publication of the October Fair, with some intention, I suppose, of showing the critics and the public I could create in a different vein, in a more objective manner than I had yet done. We also deferred completion and publication of The Hills Beyond Pentland. I know you said you were willing to go ahead and publish these books. You have always assured me on that point. But I did feel that your counsel and your caution were against their publication now.[26] I believe you may have allowed your apprehensions concerning who and what I might now write about at the period I had now reached in my writing to influence your judgments. I don't like to go into all this again. The thing that happened last summer, your reaction to the manuscript Miss Nowell brought to you while I was in Europe, and your own comment as expressed to her in a note which she sent to me and which said, after she had cut all the parts you objected to in the manuscript out of it, that "the only person it can now possibly hurt is Thomas Wolfe," was to me a shocking revelation.[27] I am not of the opinion now that the manuscript in question was one of any great merit. I know that I've done much better work. But the point, as I told you after my return from Europe, the point that we discussed so frankly and so openly, was that your action, if carried to its logical conclusions and applied to everything I write from now on, struck a deadly blow at the very vitals of my whole creative life.[28] The only possible inference that could be drawn from this matter was that from now on, if I wished to continue writing books which Charles Scribner's Sons were going to publish, I must now submit myself to the most rigid censorship, a censorship which would delete from all my writings any episode, any scene, any character, any reference that might seem to have any connection, however remote, with the house of Charles Scribner's Sons and its sisters and its cousins and its aunts. Such a conclusion, if I agreed to it, would result in the total enervation and castration of my work - a work which, as I have told you in this letter, I am now resolved must be more strong and forthright in its fidelity to purpose than ever. Again, in this whole situation there is a display, an almost unbelievable vanity and arrogance. It was first of all the vanity and arrogance that would lead certain people to suppose that I was going to "write about them," and then the vanity and arrogance of people who said that, although it was perfectly all right for me to write about other people "in humble walks of life," it was an unpardonable affront to all these important high-toned personages to be "written about" freely and frankly by a low scribbling fellow,[29] who is good enough no doubt to supply a publisher of manuscript, to give employment to his business, to add prestige to the reputation of his firm, but who must be put in his place when he overstepped the bounds of human sanctity.

Now, in the first place, as I told you before, whoever got the idea that I was going to write about him or her or them anyway? And in the second place, whoever got the idea that I was not going ahead and write as I damned pleased, about anything I wished to write about, with the complete freedom to which every artist is entitled, and that no one in the world is going to stand in the way of my doing this? I am certain at the present time not interested in writing about Chas Scribner's Sons or any one connected with Chas Scribner's Sons. It has at the present time no part of my creative plan or of my writing effort. And as you know very well, I don't "write about" people. I create living characters of my own - a whole universe of my own creation.[30] And any character that I create is so unmistakably my own that anyone familiar with my work would know instantly it was my own, even if it had no title and no name.

But, to go back to this simple, fundamental, inescapable necessity of all art, which I have patiently, laboriously, coherently explained a thousand times, in such language that no one misunderstand it, to all the people in this country, to all the people who, for some strange and extraordinary reason, in America and nowhere else that I have ever been on earth, keep harping forever, with a kind of idiot pertinacity, upon the word "autobiography" - you can't make something out of nothing. You can either say that there is no such thing as autobiographical writing or you can say that all writing is autobiographical, a statement with which I should be inclined to agree.[31] But you cannot say, you must not say that one man is an autobiographical writer and another man is not an autobiographical writer. You cannot and must not say that one novel is an autobiographical novel and another novel is not an autobiographical novel. Because if you say these things, you are uttering falsehood and palpable nonsense. It has no meaning.

My books are neither more nor less autobiographical than War and Peace. If anything, I should say that they are less, because a great writer like Tolstoi, who achieves his purpose, achieves it because he has made a perfect utilization of all the means, the materials at his disposal. This Tolstoi did in War and Peace. I have never yet succeeded in doing it completely and perfectly. Accordingly, Tolstoi is a more autobiographical writer than I am, because he has succeeded better in using what he had. But make no mistake about it, both of us, and every other man who ever wrote a book, are autobiographical. You are therefore not to touch my life in this way. When you or any man tries to exert this kind of control, to modify or shape my material in an improper way because of some paltry personal, social apprehension, you do the unpardonable thing. You try to take from the artist his personal property, to steal his substance, to defraud him of his treasure - the only treasure he has, the only property and wealth which is truly, inexorably, his own.

You can take it from him, but by so doing you commit a crime. You have stolen what does not belong to you. You have not only taken what belongs to another man, but you have taken what belongs to him in such a way that no one else can possibly claim ownership. No one owns what he has as does the artist. When you try to steal it from him he only laughs at you, because you could take it to the ends of the earth and bury it in a mountain and it would still shine straight through the mountain side like radium. You couldn't hide it. Any one on earth could find it and would know at once who the proper owner was.

That is what this final argument is about. I'm not going to be interfered with on this score. I get my material, I acquire my wealth as every artist does, from his own living, from his own experience, from his own observation. And when any outer agency tries to interpose itself between me and any portion of my own property, however small, and says to me "hands off," "you can't have that particular piece there," some one is going to get hurt.

You told me when I discussed these things with you in October, after my return from Europe, that you agreed with me, that in the last analysis you were always with the man of talent, and that if the worst comes to the worst you could resign your executive and editorial functions. Well, don't worry, you'll never have to. In the first place, your executive and editorial functions are so special and valuable that they can not be substituted by any other person on earth. They could not be done without by the business that employs them. It would be like having a house with the lights turned out. Furthermore, no one is going to resign on my account. There are still enough people in the world who value what I do, I believe, to support me freely, heartily and cheerfully, with no sense that they are enduring martyrdom on my account. So if there is ever any situation that might indicate any future necessity for any one to resign anything on my account, that situation will never arise, simply because I won't be there to be resigned about.[32]

This business about the artist hurting people is for the most part nonsense. The artist is not here in life to hurt it but to illuminate it. He is not here to teach men hatred but to show them beauty. No one in the end ever got hurt by a great book, or if he did the hurt was paltry and temporary in comparison to the immense good that was conferred.

Now, at a time when I am more firmly resolved than ever before to exert my full amount, to use my full stroke, to shine my purest and intensest ray, it is distressing to see the very people who published my first efforts with complete equanimity, and with no qualms whatever about the possibility of anybody getting "hurt," begin to squirm around uncomfortably and call for calf-rope and whine that their own toes are being stepped upon, even when nothing has been said, nothing written.[33] They have no knowledge or declaration of my own intention except that I intend in my own way to finish my own book. What are you going to do about it? You say you are not aware that there have been any difficulties or any severance. If these things I have been talking about are not difficulties, if this is not a threatened severance of the gravest nature, I should like to know what you consider difficult and what severance is? We can not continue in this irresolute, temporizing "Well now, you go ahead for the present - we'll wait and see how it all turns out - "

manner. My life has been ravaged, my energy exhausted, my work confused and aborted long enough by this kind of miserable, time serving procrastination. I'm not going to endure it any longer. I'm not going to pour my sweat and blood and energy and life and talent into another book now, only to be told two or three years from now that it would be inadvisable to publish it without certain formidable deletions, or that perhaps we'd better wait a few years longer and see "how everything turns out."

We stalled around this way with October Fair, until all the intensity and passion I had put into the book was lost, until I had gone stale on it, until I was no longer interested in it - and to what purpose? Why, because you allowed your fond weakness for the female sex to get the better of your principle, because you were afraid some foolish female, who was inwardly praying for nothing better than to be a leading character in a book of mine, and who was bitterly disappointed when she was not, might get her feelings hurt - or that the pocketbook of the firm might get touched by suits for libel. Well, there would have been no suits for libel. I never libelled anybody in my life. Certainly, there was no remote danger of libel in The October Fair, but because of our weakness and irresolution the news got around that we were afraid of publication for this reason. The lying rumor was spread around in the column of a filthy gossip-writer, and the result now is that we have a libel suit on our hands from a person who was never libelled, who doesn't have a leg to stand on, but who is willing to take the chance and make the effort to get something because we were not firm and resolute in the beginning.[34]

Let's make an end of all this devil's business. Let's stand to our guns like men. Let's go ahead and try to do our work without qualification, without fear, without apology. What are you willing to do? My own position is now clear. I have nothing to be afraid of. And my greatest duty, my deepest obligation now is to the completion of my own work. If that can not be done any longer upon the terms that I have stated here, then I must either stand alone or turn to other quarters for support, if I can find it. You yourself must now say plainly what the decision is to be, because the decision now rests with you. You can no longer have any doubt as to how I feel about these matters. I don't see how you can any longer have any doubt that difficulties of a grave and desperate nature do exist.

I can only repeat here what I have told you before, that the possibility of an irrevocable and permanent severance has caused me the greatest distress and anguish of the mind for months, that if it occurs it will seem to me like death, but that whatever happens, what I have said and written about the way I feel towards you will remain.

I'm going South in a few days for the first time in seven years. It is a tremendous experience for me. Those seven years to me have been a lifetime. So much has been crowded into them - exile and vituperation from my own country, modest success and recognition, then partial oblivion, years of struggling and despairing, to conquer a new medium, to fashion a new world, partial success again, added recognition, partial oblivion again. It seems to move in cycles. Now I'm up against the same grim struggle, the same necessity for new discovery, new beginning, new achievement, as before. It will be strange to be back home again. I had but recently met you when I was there last. I was unknown then, but within a few weeks after my visit home a storm of calumny and abuse broke out that made me long for my former oblivion. Now that storm apparently has died down. They are willing to have me come back. So much has happened in those seven years. I've seen so many people that I know go down to ruin, others have died, others have grown up, some have lost everything, some have recovered something. People I knew well I no longer see. People who swore eternal love are now irrevocably separated. Nothing has turned out as we thought it would turn out. Nothing is the way we thought it was going to be. But Life, I now begin to see, moves in a great wheel, the wheel swings and things and people that we knew are lost, but some day they come back again. So it is a strange and wonderful event for me to be going back home. I knew so little of the world and people then, although I thought I knew so much of them. Now I really think I know a little more about the world and people than I knew then, and I think all of us understand a little more about one another.

I'm sorry this letter has had to be so long. It seemed to me there had to be some sort of final statement. I hope, now the statement has been made, the problem is more clear. I send all of you now all my best wishes for Christmas and for a New Year which I hope will bring to all of us an accomplishment and fulfillment of some of those things we most desire.

Meanwhile, with all friendship, all good wishes,

Sincerely yours,

Tom Wolfe

—Max, this is not a well-written letter, but it is a genuine and honest one. If you still have any interest in me, please attend to what I say here carefully!

P.S. New Orleans, Jan 10, 1937: I have with held this letter as long as possible. I had hoped against hope not to have to send it. But now, after the shocking events of the past two weeks since I left NY—Mitchell's letter conveying the blackmail threats of Dooher[35]—the growing peril of my situation in a mesh of scoundrelism—and your own telegram [36]—the increasing ambiguity and caution of your own statements—I have read the letter through again and decided that it _must be sent_. In spite of its great length there is much more to say—but let this stand now for a record![37]

1. The letter has marginal comments, lines, and underlines presumably made by MP; they have been noted.

2. In "Genius Is Not Enough" (*Saturday Review of Literature*, 25 April 1936), a review of *The Story of a Novel*, Bernard De Voto wrote: "The most flagrant evidence of his incompleteness is the fact that, so far, one indispensable part of the artist has existed not in Mr. Wolfe but in Maxwell Perkins. Such organizing faculty and such critical intelligence as have been applied to the book have come not from inside the artist, not from the artist's feeling for form and esthetic integrity, but from the office of Charles Scribner's Sons" (4).

In a 13 November 1935 letter to Wolfe putative biographer John Terry, MP wrote: "The article or review by De Voto was the most important in its effect upon Tom's relation with me. It was that that set him to believe he must prove that I was not necessary to him. And I think that that was at the very root of our trouble" (UNC). See *Always Yours,*

Max: Maxwell Perkins Responds to Questions about Thomas Wolfe, ed. Alice R. Cotton (n.p.: Thomas Wolfe Society, 1997).

3. Alf(red) Landon, governor of Kansas and the 1936 Republican presidential nominee.

4. There are two vertical lines in the left margin at the end of this paragraph.

5. Vertical lines in left margin along the first three lines of this paragraph.

6. This word is underlined and there is a mark in the left margin.

7. Reference to Barbara Hutton, heiress to the Woolworth fortune.

8. There is a vertical line in the left margin along the last three lines and "S Q."

9. Vertical line and "T R" in left margin.

10. Heir to the Reynolds tobacco fortune; his wife, Libby Holman, was arrested for but not convicted of his murder.

11. MP's wife, Louise, came from a wealthy family.

12. MP had five daughters. There is a question mark in the left margin opposite reference to his daughters.

13. Question mark in the left margin opposite this sentence.

14. *Ulysses* was published in 1922 by Shakespeare & Co. of Paris.

15. "Not offered" written in left margin.

16. Sylvia Beach (1887–1962), proprietor of Shakespeare & Co.

17. Novel by Laurence Sterne (1713–1768) published in 1765.

18. Poem by Robert Browning (1812–1889) published in 1868–1869.

19. In 1933 Bennett Cerf and Donald S. Klopfer, partners in Random House, successfully contested the American ban on *Ulysses*.

20. TW's proposed book about a writer's conflict with his publishing house. Portions of the story are in *The Web and the Rock* and *You Can't Go Home Again*.

21. Vertical line and arrow in left margin opposite this sentence.

22. "Publisher" written in left margin.

23. Cornelius Mitchell.

24. Arrow and "NO" written in the left margin.

25. Question mark in the left margin.

26. Vertical line in the left margin opposite preceding three sentences.

27. "No More Rivers," a short story based on Scribners editor Wallace Meyer. MP was openly concerned about TW's announced intention to use Scribner material that had come from MP in conversation. The cut version of "No More Rivers" was published posthumously in *Beyond Love and Loyalty* (Chapel Hill: University of North Carolina Press, 1983). The full version has never been published.

28. Vertical line and "No" in the left margin opposite beginning of this sentence.

29. Vertical line and question mark in left margin opposite this and preceding sentence.

30. "Yes but" in left margin.

31. Vertical line in left margin opposite first fourteen lines of this paragraph.

32. Vertical line and question mark in the left margin opposite last four lines of this paragraph.

33. In margin "Meyer Bridges Chapin," names of Scribner employees Wallace Meyer, Robert Bridges, and Joseph Hawley Chapin.

34. Vertical line in left margin opposite entire paragraph and "I did not tell." TW is referring to Walter Winchell in the *New York Daily Mirror*, 21 September 1936.

35. TW had allowed Muredach Dooher to act as his agent in selling the typescript of *Of Time and the River* to rare book dealers. TW mistakenly consigned Dooher unpublished manuscripts. After canceling his agreement with Dooher, TW sued Dooher for

return of the material; Dooher countersued, demanding an agent's fee for the unsold material.

36. MP's telegram unlocated.

37. TW sent a carbon copy of this letter to his friend Hamilton Basso with a handwritten postscript: "I've gone upon the record here—this is not perhaps the whole story—but in a general way it says some things I feel had to be said. I am leaving this copy of the letter in your care and, if anything should happen to me, I leave it to your discretion what should [be done] with this letter" (Hamilton Basso Papers, Yale University).

TLS with holograph postscript, 9 pp., PUL[1]
TW's personal letterhead, 865 First Avenue, New York City

December 23, 1936

Dear Max:

I have already written you a long answer to your two personal letters of November 17th and November 18th which you should have received by the time you receive this.[2] Now, before I go away, I want to write an answer to your formal business letter of November 18th, in which you state the relations that now exist between myself and Charles Scribner's Sons.

First of all, let me thank you for acknowledging that I have faithfully and honorably discharged all obligations to you and that no further agreement of any sort exists between us with respect to the future. Then I want to tell you that I am sorry you found parts of my letter obscure and did not wholly understand them. I am sorry, because it seemed to me that the letter was clear. But if there has been any misunderstanding to what I meant, I shall try to clarify it now.

You say you do not wholly understand the part where "you speak of us as putting you in a position of denying an obligation that does not exist, for we do not know that we have done that." Well, what I said in my letter was "I think it is unfair to put a man in a position where he is forced to deny an obligation that does not exist, to refuse an agreement that was never offered and never made." That is a little different from the way you put it, but I thought it was clear, but if further explanation be needed, I can tell you that what I meant to say, by "I think it is unfair to put a man in a position where he is forced to deny an obligation that does not exist" is simply that no one has a right in my opinion to mix calculation and friendliness, business caution with personal friendship, financial astuteness with personal affection. The artist can not do that. Where his friendship, affection and devotion are involved, he cannot say "I think the world of all of you but of course business is business and I shall make such publishing arrangements as shall be most profitable to me." That is what I meant by "I think it is unfair to put a man in a position where he is forced to deny an obligation that does not exist." For, although you have acknowledged that no obligation does exist, after two years of delay since the publication of "Of Time and the River" no concrete proposal has ever been made to me concerning any novel or novels which were to follow it. I have waited in vain, with

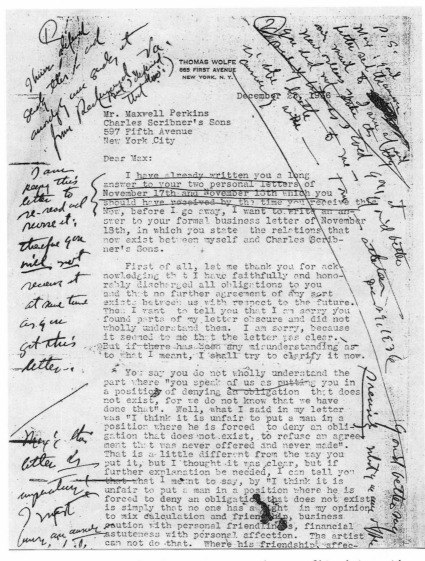

Wolfe's annotated copy of his letter summarizing the state of his relations with Perkins and the House of Scribner. Wolfe mailed the letter on 10 January 1937 (Princeton University Library).

growing anxiety and bewilderment for such proposal to be made until the matter has now reached a point of critical acuteness which compelled me to write you as I have written you and say "I think it is unfair to put a man in a position where he is forced to deny an obligation that does not exist."

As to the next phrase, "to refuse an agreement that was never offered and never made," I think the meaning of that phrase is now sufficiently clarified by what has been already said.

To proceed: You say you also do not wholly understand the part of my letter where I refer to "'exerting control of a man's future' which we have no intention of doing at all, and would not have the power or right to do." What I said was "I think it is also unfair to try to exert, at no expense to oneself, such control of a man's future and his future work as will bring one profit if that man succeeds, and that absolves one from any commitments of any kind, should he fail." I thought that sentence was clear too. But if you require additional explanation I can only say that what I meant was that I did not think it fair again to play business against friendship, to accept the loyalty and devotion of an author to the firm that has published him without saying precisely upon what terms and upon what conditions you are will-ing to publish him in the future. In other words, if I must be still more explicit, I am now in the undeniable position of being compelled to tell people who ask me who my publisher is, of saying that my publisher is Charles Scribner's Sons, While Charles Scribner's Sons on their part, without risk, without involving criticism of any sort, are undeniably in the position where they are able to tell any one that they are my publishers, provided they want to be, but are not my publishers if they do not want to be.

You continue in your letter by saying "there are other phrases in that part of your letter that I do not understand, one of which is that which refers to us as being absolved from any commitments of any kind 'should the author fail.'" I do not see why you should have found this statement obscure or puzzling, but if you did I think that what I have already said in this letter precisely and exactly defines my meaning.

You continue by saying "if this and these other phrases signify that you think you should have a contract from us if our relations are to continue, you can cer-tainly have one. We should be delighted to have one. You must surely know the faith this house has in you. There are, of course, limits in terms to which nobody can go in a contract, but we should expect to make one that would suit you if you told us what was required."

I think it is now my turn to be puzzled. I do not wholly understand what you mean when you say "we should expect to make one"—(a contract)—"that would suit you if you told us what was required." This really seems almost too good to be true. I have never heard of an author before being able and privileged to tell a pub-lisher "what was required" in the terms of a contract. I cannot believe that is a prac-tice of the publishing business. Authors do not dictate terms of a publisher's contracts. The publisher states the terms himself, and the author accepts them. For my part, so far as my relations with Scribner's are concerned, I have always accepted what was offered to me instantly and without question. It seems now a delightfully unexpected, overwhelming privilege to be suddenly told that it is now up to me to state "what is required" in the way of a contract.

Well, then, if I am to be allowed this privilege, may I ask for information on these specific points? When you say in your letter that "our relations are simply those of a publisher who profoundly admires the work of an author and takes great pride in publishing whatever he may of that author's writings" - in what sense and meaning am I going to understand the word "may"? I hate to quibble about words, but since you have yourself found it difficult and hard to understand phrases and sentences in my own letter which seem absolutely clear to me, it seems to me that the interpretation of even a little word like "may" - may be important. Neither of us surely is so ingenuous as to believe that this statement means that Scribner's is eagerly waiting my gracious permission to publish any and all manuscript that I may choose to give to them. We both know that such an interpretation as this would be ridiculous. We both know that in the past six or seven years I have written several million words of which Scribner's has published approximately seven or eight hundred thousand. We both know that you have seen and read millions of words of my manuscript which have never been published, which you rejected for publication flatly, or whose publication you advised against. We both know that I not only accepted your advice gratefully but that I also accepted your decision without question, even though it sometimes caused me grievous disappointment when I found that something I had thought good and worthy of publication was not thought good or worthy of publication by the person in whose judgment and critical authority I had and still have unqualified belief. We both know that there was never a time, there has never been a moment since I first walked into your office eight years ago when I have been in a position to hand you a piece of manuscript and arbitrarily demand that you publish it. The right of selection has always been yours. The right of rejection has always been yours. The right to say what you would or would not publish has always, and to my mind, properly, been finally and absolutely your own privilege. It seems manifest therefore that what you mean by the word "may" as used in your sentence must be interpreted as what you "may see fit" to publish. To this interpretation I have certainly never objected, but now that this misunderstanding and the danger of possible misinterpretation has arisen, I must ask you, secondly, if you won't try to specify, insofar as you are able, what it is you may see fit to publish of mine. I understand, of course, that there are obvious limits to what a publisher may be expected to publish - limits imposed by law and custom. But within those limits, how far are you willing to go?

You say in one of your personal letters that you "have never doubted for my future on any grounds except, at times, on those of being unable to control the vast mass of material I have accumulated and have to form into books." Alas, it has now become evident that this is not the only difficulty. It is not even any longer a fundamental one. As I have explained in my long letter to you, no matter how great a man's material may be, it has its limits. He can come to the end of it. No man can exceed his own material - it is his constant effort to surpass it, it is true - but he cannot spend money when he has not got it, he can not fish coin from the empty air, he cannot plank it down across the counter when his pockets are empty. No man has more than his one life, and no man's material is greater than his one life can absorb and hold. No man, therefore, not even the artist, can become the utter spendthrift with what he has. It is spitting straight in the face of fortune, and in the end he will get paid back for his folly. You say you have been worried about my being able to control my vast masses of material. May I tell you that in the past year one of my own chief and constantly growing worries has been whether I shall have any material left that I could use if you continue to advise against my present use of it, or if these growing anxieties and perturbations in the year past as to what I should use, as to what I should write about, continued to develop to the utter enervation and castration of my work. Therefore, having as you do some approximate knowledge, a far better one than any one else, at any rate, of the material at my command, can't you try, in view of all these doubts and misunderstandings, to specify what you think you may be able to publish and how much of it.

Third, at about what time would you now desire and expect to publish it, if I fulfilled my work in time? I know that I have been grievously at fault in meeting publication dates heretofore, but you know too it has not been through lack of effort or of application but rather through the difficulties imposed by my own nature and my imperfect understanding of the writer's art and the command of the tools of my profession. Nevertheless, and in spite of all these imperfections on my part, I should like to get some fairly definite notion of when it is you next expect to publish me, if ever. The reason that I am so earnestly and seriously concerned with this is that in former years, before the publication of "Of Time and the River," you did show the greatest anxiety on this score. You were constant in your efforts to spur me on, to get me to complete and finish something for publication. Now, although almost two years have gone by since the publication of my last long book, you no longer show any anxiety whatever and, so far as I can judge, no immediate interest.

Finally, if you do want to publish another book of mine, if you can try to tell me what it is you think you want to publish, what you will be able to publish, and when you would like to publish it, what, finally and specifically, are these terms of which you speak?

You say "there are, of course, limits in terms to which nobody can go under contract, but we should expect to make one that would suit you if you told us what was required." I suppose, of course, that when you say that there are "limits in terms to which nobody can go in a contract" you mean that there are limits in terms beyond which no one can go. I understand this perfectly. But what, specifically, are these limits? What, specifically, are these terms?

Now I'm awfully sorry, Max, to have to try your patience with another long letter, and I am sorry if I seem to quibble over words and phrases, but I really do not think I quibble, since all these matters are of such vital and immediate concern to me and since we both have seemed to have trouble understanding sentences and phrases in each other's letters. I have gone to extreme lengths in this one to make everything I say as clear as possible. I shall be on my way South when you get this letter. I intend to be in New Orleans New Year's day, but since I am still uncertain whether I shall stay with friends or in a hotel, I suggest that you write me, if you have time and feel like writing, in care of General Delivery.

Meanwhile, until I hear from you, or until I see you again, with all my best and friendliest greetings to everyone at Scribners,

Sincerely yours,

Tom Wolfe

P.S. I am writing you this from Richmond. Frankly, I think we are at the end. I am sending this to you now—I should have sent it to you long ago, in view of the agony, the despair, the utter desolation this thing has cost me—but I <u>must</u> send it to you now. As to the other letter—the enormously long letter I wrote in answer to your two (over) personal ones I—I shall hold on to it a day longer—re-read it—perhaps make little revisions here and there—anything! anything!—to try to temper the sorrow and the grief of this final decision into which I—God knows—have been compelled without even the power of saying whether I wanted it or not. You must answer this straight!³

Additional P.S.—As to your statement that anyone would <u>want</u> me—that, as you must <u>now</u> know, is not true. I am almost penniless this suit for libel has appeared with almost sinister immediacy in the last month or two—I have turned down <u>for-tunes</u>—$10,000 is a fortune to me, and you knew of <u>that</u> one at once.—the one that was made over two years ago when I was <u>really</u> penniless, and when you asked me to tell you what the offer was. I am broke—I have lost everything—I do not think we can go on—Who, then, are these <u>eager</u> publishers?—Answer at once please! Tom

> *[Margin notes from first page]*
> ① I have deferred sending this, and accordingly am sending it from Richmond, Va. (But I deferred that too!)
> ② P.S. Max: You'd better send the answer air mail to New Orleans—I am afraid you did not take this thing seriously but as I told you, it is like death to me—You'd better answer by wire—Tom—Atlanta, December 29, 1936.
> You'd better say precisely what you can offer. Atlanta, December 29, 1936.
> Max: This letter is imperative. I must have an <u>answer</u>—a definite one—at once!

1. The first page of this letter has a holograph note by TW around the margins: "I am keeping this letter to re-read and revise it; therefore you <u>will not</u> receive it at same time as you get this letter."

2. TW underlined the first sentence of this letter.

3. "straight" is underlined four times.

AL, 4 pp., Harvard
The Jefferson Hotel letterhead, Richmond, Virginia

[Handwriting and notes indicating placement on letter suggest that this is TW's copy for his own records of the postscripts he wrote on his letter sent from Richmond dated 23 December 1936.]

P.S.

I am writing you this from Richmond. Frankly I think we are at the end. I am sending this to you now. I should have sent it to you long ago—in view of the agony, the despair, the utter desolation this thing has cost me—but I must send it to you now. Also the other letters—the enormously long letter I wrote in answer to your two (one same <u>one</u> next page?) personal ones—I shall hold[1] on to it a day longer—re-read it—perhaps make little revisions here and there—anything! anything!—to try to temper the sorrow and the grief of this final decision into which I—God knows—have been compelled without even the power of saying whether I wanted it or not—you must answer this straight![2]

(on front side) lefthand <u>above</u> what has been written)

Additional P.S.—As to your statement that anyone would <u>want</u> me—that, as you must <u>now</u> know is false.—I am almost penniless, this suit for libel has appeared with almost sinister immediacy in the last month or two—I have (at top of page) turned down fortunes—$10,000 is a fortune to me, and (right margin) you knew of <u>that</u> one at once—the one that was made over two years ago when I was <u>really</u> penniless, and when you asked me to tell you what the offer was—I am broke: I have lost everything. I do not think we can go on—who then are these eager publishers— Answer at once—please—Tom

P.S. Max: you'd better send the answer that I want to New Orleans—I am afraid you did not take this thing seriously but as I told you it is like death to me—you'd better answer by wire—Tom—Atlanta—Dec 29—1936—Youd better say <u>precisely</u> what <u>you</u> can offer
(Atlanta—Tom)[3]

1. TW wrote "not in letter" above this line.
2. "straight" is underlined three times.
3. Last paragraph written on the front and back of an unaddressed envelope.

John Hall Wheelock in 1951 (Pach Brothers).

TO: *Maxwell Perkins*   *Wire, PUL*
7 January 1937, 8:19 a.m.   *New Orleans*

HOW DARE YOU GIVE ANY ONE MY ADDRESS
                        THOMAS WOLFE.

TO: *Maxwell Perkins*   *Wire, PUL*
9 January 1937: 3:16 a.m.   *New Orleans*

WHAT IS YOUR OFFER
                        THOMAS WOLFE HOTEL ROOSEVELT.

Wire draft, 1 p., PUL
Jan. 9, 1937

Mr. Thomas Wolfe
Hotel Roosevelt
New Orleans, La.

If you refer to book we shall make it verbally when you return as arrangements will depend on your requirements stop Gave no one your address but suggested two possibilities to your lawyer who thought it important for you to communicate

Maxwell Perkins

ALS, 10 pp., PUL
New Orleans

Sat Jan 9, 1937

Dear Max: I'm sorry I telegraphed you as I did. And I don't even know now exactly what I telegraphed you. But maybe you can understand a little when I tell you that all this worry, grief, and disappointment of the last two years has almost broken me, and finally this last letter of Mitchell's was almost the last straw, I was desperately in need of rest and quiet—the letter destroyed it all, ruined all the happiness and joy I had hoped to get from this trip—the horrible injustice of the whole thing has almost maddened me. I can understand none of it any more—first the Boyd thing, then Mrs Bernstein and the [   ] of last year, then the libel suit, then this latest blackmail threat of Doohers—most of all your own attitude—Max, I simply can't understand: you yourself urged—not only urged but indignantly insisted that I take action against Dooher at a time when I was practically decided to let these scoundrels take what they could rather than let them take my life—my work—my talent. Now, you speak of paying him off—you told me only a few weeks ago that you would pay the $500 and be done with it—this after insisting at first that I take action, recover the mss. and that there should be no compromises—In God's name, what is your meaning? Are you—the man I trusted and reverenced above all else in the world—trying, for some mad reason I can not even guess—to destroy me? How am I going to interpret the events of the past two years? Don't you want me to go on? Don't you want me to write another book? Don't you hope for my life—my growth—the fulfillment of my talent? In Christ's name, what is it, then? My health is well nigh wrecked—worry, grief, and disillusionment has almost destroyed my talent—is this what you wanted? And why?—As for Mr Mitchell I have given up trying to fathom his motives or his reasoning? When I last saw him a few weeks ago, it seemed to me that our course was clear—that we were in entire agreement—that the evidence against Dooher was complete and overwhelming At this time he gave me Dooher's offer of compromise for $500 and Morrisons letter suggesting settlement at that figure.[1] My own feeling was absolutely against such a settlement, particularly since the offer was couched in such ambiguous and obscure phrases that it was impossible to know just what I was going to get in return for my money—I understood that Mr Mitchell felt this way, too, and that it would be improper to agree to such a settlement—In addition, I wrote him a very long and very clear letter about the proposal of settlement and Mr Morrison's own attitude, pointed out numerous ambiguities in phrasing, and said that I wanted to go ahead and compel Dooher if I could to return the mss., but that Mr Morrison's attitude was depressing—it was hard to go on with a vigorous attack when one's own legal representative was so lukewarm—and in favor of yielding to a preposterous offer of settlement—At the time of my conversation with Mr Mitchell he also mentioned Dooher's threat to publish "Salacious matter" from the mss. I told Mr Mitchell that this threat was blackmail pure and simple—and, regardless of the proposal of settlement, it would be the height of folly to yield to such a threat now, Well, the result is that this latest letter from Mitchell instead of saying what <u>we</u> are going to do, is an apprehensive account of Dooher's blackmail threats from beginning to end. In addition to the publication of the alleged "salacious matter," he is going to aid and abet the libel suit of the Brooklyn woman, and "stir up" libel suits in North Carolina. As for the statement that I opened a trunkful of mss and told him to help himself, this is just a lie. If he has all the other mss, he stole them—took them without my knowledge and consent when I was not looking—how, in what way, I do not know. And you—where are you, Max? Have you too become terrified at these threats of libel suits? Are you going to advise me to yield to the blackmail menaces of this scoundrel simply because the interests of Scribners might be involved? What are we going to do? This thing is like death to me? Have we really reached the end? I fear desperately we have—it is all so tragically sad—and as for that powerful and magnificent talent that I had two years ago—in the name of God is that to be lost utterly, destroyed under the repeated assaults and criminalities of this blackmail society under which we live. <u>Now</u> I know what happens to the artist in America. <u>Now</u> I know what must be changed. <u>Now</u> truly, henceforth and forever after, I shall work with all my strength for revolution—for the abolition of this vile and rotten system under which we live—for a better world, a better life—And you? You are in very many ways the best person I have ever known, the person for whom I have had the greatest reverence and devotion—but in some few ways, perhaps, I am a better man than you. Forgive me these wild telegrams—even if we have now come to the end of our publishing connection—a connection for which I have sacrificed everything—a connection that is now being severed when I have nothing left, when no one wants me—for God's sake let us try to save our belief and faith in each other—a belief and faith that I still have—that I hope you have not lost. I would to God I were a better man—but I will not cease trying to be a better one—and for you I cannot bear to see you just a good but timid man: I am in deadly peril, but right or wrong, I want you to go into battle with me—I see you as the noble captain, strong and faithful, at no matter what the cost right to the end—I have no right to ask it, but you must be the great man that I know you are—Don't give up the ship. I am leaving here tomorrow I think—some friends are taking me to the country in an effort to get me some quiet at rest—I hope to be in North Carolina in a few days—

although now, feeling as I do—I [   ] the approval of my friends. But if you want to write me, you might address the letter in care of Mr. Garland Porter, The Atlanta Georgian, Atlanta. But whatever you do—unless it is something involving the serious sickness or death of a member of my family don't give my address to anyone: I'm in a wretched state and I've got to get on my feet before I come back to N.Y.

Meanwhile Sincerely,

Tom Wolfe

P.S. I was worn out yesterday when I wrote this. Today I feel a little better—and I am assured now of my course—Further words, arguments, entreaties are useless. We are either at the end or we shall go on, I am sending two letters which I wrote some weeks ago and which, hoping against hope: I have withheld. These letters in a general way put the story of my relations to you and Scribners upon the record. There's nothing in either of them that can do you any harm. But in case anything happens to me, I am sending duplicates to a friend. I think this is proper.

1. Presumably Mitchell's associate.

ALS, 4 pp., Harvard
MP's personal Scribner letterhead, New York

Jan 13th '37

Dear Tom:- I just got your long letter + have only glanced through it, so that I can't yet properly answer it.—The other came yesterday. I am dashing this off now to make clear two things.

My belief is that the one important, supreme object is to advance your work. Anything in furtherance of that is good + anything that impedes it is bad. What impedes it especially is not the great difficulty + pain of doing it,—for you are the reverse of lazy. You work furiously—but the harassment, the torment of outside worries. When you spoke to me about the settlement, it was, + had been before, very plain that this suit was such a worry, that it was impeding you in your work. It was only because of that that I gave the advice I did. I thought, then get rid of it, forget it, + clear the way more for what is really important supremely.—Now this blackmail talk puts a new face on that matter altogether.

As to my own self: I stand ready to help if I can whenever you want. You asked my help on Time + the River. I was glad + proud to give it. No understanding person could believe that it affected the book in any serious or important way,—that it was much more than mechanical help.—It did seem that the book was too enormous to get between covers. That was the first problem. There might be a problem in a book such as prohibited the publication of Joyce for years in this country. If you wished it we would publish any book by you as written except for such problems as those which prohibit,—some can't be avoided but I don't foresee them. Length could be dealt with by publishing in sections. Anyhow, apart from physical or legal limitations not within the possibility of change by us we will publish anything as you write it.

I simply want to quickly to put these points before you. You are not a private character though. No one whose work has been published, + has roused the interest + admiration of thousands of people can be that in the sense that a carpenter or truck driver are. To lose that kind of privacy is a consequence of important writing. In this case the writing is so important that it has to be done,- +, I know, at great cost to you

Yours,
Max

⤳

ALS, 1 p., Harvard
MP's personal Scribner letterhead, New York

14 January 1937

Dear Tom:- I've read your letter carefully. I think it's a wonderful letter. I have no quarrel with any of it,—except that you have greatly misunderstood some things I must explain.—But what a task you've put me to to search myself—in whom I'm not so very much interested any more— + give you an adequate answer. Your position is right. I understand it + agree with it.

Always yours,
Max

⤳

CCS, 6 pp., PUL

Saturday, January 16, 1937

Dear Tom:

In the first place I completely subscribe to what you say a writer should do, and always have believed it. If it were not true that you, for instance, should write as you see, feel, and think, then a writer would be of no importance, and books merely things for amusement. And since I have always thought that there could be nothing so important as a book can be, and some are, I could not help but think as you do. But there are limitations of time, of space, and of human laws which cannot be treated as if they did not exist. I think that a writer should, of course, be the one to make his book what he wants it to be, and that if because of the laws of space it must be cut, he should be the one to cut it:- and especially with you, I think the labour and discipline that would come from doing that without help or interference would further the pretty terrible task of mastering the material. But my impression was that you asked my help, that you wanted it.- And it is my impression too, that changes were not forced on you (You're not very forceable, Tom, nor I very forceful) but were argued over, often for hours. But I agree with you about this too, fully,

and unless you want help it will certainly not be thrust upon you. It would be better if you could fight it out alone—better for your work, in the end, certainly;- and
what's more, I believe you are now in a position to publish with less regard to any
conventions of bookmaking, say a certain number of pages almost, whether or not
it had what in a novel is regarded as an ending, or anything else that is commonly
expected in a novel. I believe the writer, anyway, should always be the final judge,
and I meant you to be so. I have always held to that position and have sometimes
seen books hurt thereby, but at least as often helped. "The book belongs to the
author."

I certainly do not care nor does this house—how revolutionary your books are.
I did try to keep you from injecting radical, or Marxian beliefs into "Time and the
River" because they were your beliefs in 1934 and 35, and not those of Eugene in
the time of the book.- So it did not seem that they could rightly belong in the book.
If they could have, then the times could not be rightly pictured, I thought. It must
be so-Still, you were then and always conscious of social wrong and that is plainly
in the book as you then saw it. There was the Astor story.[1] What was told was not
heard by Eugene. It was second-hand, and second-hand material—something told,
not heard and seen—is inferior to first-hand. If cutting had to be done, ought that
not to be cut? I know your memory is a miracle, but it seems as if you must have
forgotten how we worked and argued. You were never overruled. Do you think you
are clay to be moulded! I never saw anyone less malleable.- And as for publishing
what you like, or being prevented from it, apart from the limitations of space, you
have not been, intentionally. Are you thinking of K 19?[2] We would have published
it if you had said to do it. At the time I said to Jack: "Maybe it's the way Tom is.
Maybe we should just publish him as he comes and in the end it will all be right."
But if we had, and the results had been bad at the moment, would you not have
blamed me? Certainly I should have bitterly blamed myself. I do not want the passage of time to make you cautious or conservative, but I do want it to give you a
full control—as it has done in the case of great writers in the past—over your great
talent.- And if you can stand the struggle it will. But you must struggle too, and perhaps even more than in the writing, in the shaping and revising.- That might be the
hardest thing of all to your nature. You have so much in you that the need with you
is to get it uttered. Then to go back and polish and perfect seems petty, and goes
against your nature, I guess.

Tom, you ought not to say some of the things you do,- that I find your sufferings amusing and don't take them seriously. I know something of them. I do try to
turn your mind from them and to arouse your humor, because to spend dreadful
hours brooding over them and in denunciation and abuse on account of them,
seems to be only to aggravate them. It does no good. You have to suffer to write as
you do, and the slings and arrows that strike you from outside madden you the
more because you instinctively know that all that matters is your work and so why
can't you be left to do it. I understand that. Have you seen me amused by other people's sufferings? You know that was unjust.

Then comes the question of your writing about the people here. I don't want
to discuss it, because I agree that you have the same right to make use of them as of

anyone else in the same way, and if there is an argument on it the whole thing may be bedevilled as was "October Fair" after Mrs. Bernstein protested.-(And by the way, wasn't it up to me to tell you of her visits? She went out saying I was her enemy. I conceded nothing to her.) But when I spoke of resigning after we published- and the moment I inadvertently said it I told Miss Nowell she must not repeat it, and she said she would not- I did not mean I would be asked or wanted to resign. That would never happen on any such ground. But it isn't the way you think, and it's up to you to write as you think you should.- Your plan as outlined seems to me a splendid one too. I hope you will get on with it now.

There remains the question of whether we are in fundamental agreement. But it is no question if you feel it is not so. I have always instinctively felt that it was so, and no one I ever knew has said more of the things that I believed than you. It was so from the moment that I began to read your first book. Nothing else, I would say, could have kept such different people together through such trials. But I believe in democracy and not in dictators; and in government by principles and not by men; and in less government if possible rather than more; and that power always means injustice and so should be as little concentrated as is compatible with the good of the majority; and that violence breeds more evils than it kills; and that it's better to sizzle in the fryingpan until you're sure your jump won't take you into the fire; and that Erasmus who begged his friend Luther not to destroy the good in the Church because of the bad in it, which he thought could be forced out with the spread of education, was right, though not heroic, and the heroic Luther wrong.- and that Europe is the worse for his impetuosity today. I don't believe that things can't improve. I believe that the only thing that can prevent improvement is the ruin of violence, or of reckless finance which will end in violence.- That is why Roosevelt needs an opposition and it is the only serious defect in him. I believe that change really comes from great deep causes too complex for contemporary men, or any others perhaps, fully to understand, and that when even great men like Lenin try to make over a whole society suddenly the end is almost sure to be bad, and that the right end, the natural one, will come from the efforts of innumerable people trying to do right, and to understand it, because they are a part of the natural forces that are set at work by changed conditions.- It is the effort of man to adjust himself to change and it has to be led,- but the misfortune of man is that strong will almost always beats down intelligence, and the passionate, the reasonable. I believe that such as you can help on change, but that it ought to be by your writings, not by violent acts. I believe that wealth is bad but that it should not be confiscated, but reduced by law, and in accordance with a principle, not arbitrarily and in passion;- and if it is done in passion and violence the result will be a new privileged class made up of delegates of the man or the oligarchy that has seized the power. But it may be that the great underlying changes will dictate Communism as the best society for most people.- Then we ought to have it; but if we can evolve into it gradually how much better (though I know many on both sides say that is impossible) than if we go in by revolution and civil war. At least let us try the way of evolution first.- It seems to me that our Civil War and many of the great convulsions were caused by extremists on both sides, by those too hot-headed to wait for natural forces to disclose their direction, when the inevitable outcome could no longer be resisted. I do not believe the world can ever be perfect, of course,- though it might in a sense approximate a political and economic perfection if conditions ceased from changing so that a long enough time was given to deal with known and permanent factors.- But this is getting to be too much of a philosophy of history or something, and I don't think it has anything to do with fundamental agreement. I had always felt it existed- and I don't feel, because you differ with me, however violently, on such things as I've said above, that it does not, necessarily. It is more that I like and admire the same things and despise many of the same things, and the same people too, and think the same things important and unimportant,- at least this is the way it has seemed to me.

Anyhow, I don't see why you should have hesitated to write me as you did, or rather to send the letter. There was mighty little of it that I did not wholly accept and what I did not, I perfectly well understood. There were places in it that made me angry, but it was a fine letter, a fine writer's statement of his beliefs, as fine as any I ever saw, and though I have vanities enough, as many as most, it gave me great pleasure too—that which comes from hearing brave and sincere beliefs uttered with sincerity and nobility.

> Always yours,
> MEP

1. Unidentified.
2. TW's short novel named for a railway sleeping car was scheduled for publication in 1932 but withdrawn by Scribners; see *K-19: Salvaged Pieces*.

⌒

FROM: *J. F. Tallon*[1]

> *TLS, 1 p., Harvard*
> *Charles Scribner's letterhead*

> February 2, 1937

Dear Mr. Wolfe:

We are obliged to report to the Treasury Department all payments for salaries, royalties, etc., when such payments amount to $1,000. to a single person or $2,500. if married.

We are, accordingly, reporting amount paid to you during 1936 as $13,628.34. We trust you will find this in agreement with your records.

> Yours very truly,
> CHARLES SCRIBNER'S SONS.
> J.F. Tallon

1. Scribner bookkeeper.

FROM: *Charles Scribner III*   *TLS with holograph postscript,*
                                                     3 pp., Harvard

Feb. 18, 1937.

Dear Tom:

I found after you telephoned last evening that all of the stenographers had gone home, so I could not write to you at the time and as I had a number of friends in my apartment last night there was no chance to do it at home. I tried to get you on the telephone but you were out.

You can feel assured that we have no option or moral claim on any of your future books. We would like to continue as your publishers as we have every faith in your work and feel certain that you are due to write even finer books than those which we have published. On the other hand if you find that the connection with us is not to your liking I certainly do not wish to press you to continue.

With regard to the present libel suit we agreed at luncheon to go fifty-fifty on this and if you agree to settle it for not over $2,500. (Cook hoped it would be nearer $1,500.) we would divide that and Mr. Cook's fee, so neither of us ought to be out more than about $1,500. This arrangement would not constitute any obligation on your part to continue with us if you decide to do otherwise. The more I think of it the more certain I am that it would be the wise thing to get this out of the way, for your own peace of mind. I fully appreciate the fact that you do not wish to be held up but it would certainly take a lot of time and money to fight it out. If you decide, however, that you would rather not settle I am perfectly prepared to back you in seeing it through to a finish.

Personally I am and always will be very fond of you and count you as a friend whether I act as your publisher or not. Whatever you decide will always have my best wishes.

Very sincerely
Charles Scribner

To
Thomas Wolfe, esq.
P.S.

Max has just told me that you telephoned him asking to put off the decision another day. I hope this will not be the case and that you will let me know by telephone later. I promised Cook a decision and if we fight we have a hard week's work ahead right away.

Charlie

Wire draft, Harvard.

c. February 1937

Dear Max Perkins
    Does Scribners Want My Next Book? Please Answer immediately.
    Thomas Wolfe

〜

Wire: night letter, 1 p., PUL

NEWYORK NY JUN 30 1937
CROSS,[1] CHAS SCRIBNERS SONS
  597 5 AVE NYK
PLEASE SEND ROYALTY STATEMENTS AND ROYALTY CHECKS ON
ALL MY BOOKS OTEEN NORTHCAROLINA MISS NOWELL REPORTS
HAVING RECEIVED COMMISSION ON STORY OF A NOVEL WHICH
CAME OUT MORE THAN YEAR AGO I HAVE NEVER RECEIVED MY
MONEY FOR THIS DO NOT REMEMBER RECEIVING ROYALTY STATE-
MENTS OR ROYALTY CHECKS IN MORE THAN YEAR AM SURE YOU
CAN CORRECT THIS IMMEDIATELY ANSWER AT ONCE SINCERELY
    THOMAS WOLFE

    1. Robert Cross, Scribner bookkeeper.

〜

TLS with holograph postscript, 2 pp., Harvard
July 16, 1937[1]

Dear Tom:
    I read your piece, "'E" in the New Yorker with delight and I thought it was very
artfully composed.- It could not have been better.[2]
    I hope everything is going well with you,- that you are really getting a rest,
which I do not think you have really had since I first knew you. I don't think there
is much rest in travelling in Europe, and a rest is certainly what you needed. You
escaped some terrific weather by going when you did, and the heat is still holding
up, according to Miss Wyckoff—but there has been lots of rain too, and fog, and
everything unpleasant and sticky.
    You may find Marjorie Rawlings[3] in your neighborhood before the summer is
over. She is just leaving New York for Florida. Scott got his Hollywood job and left
Asheville almost the moment he arrived there for Los Angeles.[4] So now if he can
only maintain his recent record, with this new work, he may have finally turned his
corner.

Remembrances to your mother, Fred, and the Wheatons if you see them.

Always yours,

Max

I had them send you a royalty report to date, + it showed a debit.—But I hope this may somehow be disregarded, + if you need money overlook it. After all, we publish Wecter + Kang this summer + they're both promising[5] M.P.

Louise has been up in Milford for 2 weeks with Mrs. Pat Campbell,[6] Stella, her lap dog, Moonbeam + a theatrical troupe.—I think she's pretty fed up on the thespian temperament.

I've been seeing a lot of Kang, staying here late + working with him on his proof,- + then a planter's punch at the Chatham. I'm really getting to know him at last + he's mighty good company.

1. TW was in New York during February–May 1937 but discontinued his custom of coming to the Scribner Building, although he visited MP at his home.

2. "'E, A Recollection," *The New Yorker*, 17 July 1937.

3. (1896–1953), novelist and Scribners author. She published *The Yearling* in 1938.

4. Fitzgerald had been staying in the Asheville area during 1936 and 1937. MGM interviewed him in New York in June 1937.

5. *The Saga of American Society: A Record of Social Aspiration 1607–1937* by Dixon Wecter; *East Goes West: The Making of an Oriental Yankee* by Younghill Kang.

6. Distinguished English actress and drama teacher.

TLS, 2 pp., UNC
August 13, 1937

Dear Tom:

I am sending you your royalty report, though it is of course very like the one MissWyckoff sent you soon after you went South. She's away now on vacation, and I had to forward a letter I know contained a bill for your apartment. I suppose you got it alright.

I could tell you about lots of happenings hereabouts, but they are just the kind of things that I guess you were fed up on,- when you went away. So I won't.

Louise's theatrical ventures didn't accomplish much for her, but it did give her a good rest. Milford turned out to be a very pretty town. I went over there once, but Mrs. Patrick Campbell didn't turn out to be very pretty, between us.

We have a new grandchild, and Bert[1] seems very well. I was mighty worried this time, but it all turned out rightly,- except in the matter of sex. Name, Jane.

The girls on the cruise are now in England and we have scarcely heard at all from them, but we have heard indirectly that although Mima's[2] father and mother forbade her, and got Louise to forbid our girls, to go to Moscow, they nevertheless did go.- And since they are apparently well and there wasn't any trouble, I am glad they did.

Always yours,
Max

P. S. The news from Scott is of the very best and he is paying his debts week by week.

MP

1. MP's daughter, Bertha Perkins Frothingham.
2. Friend of the Perkins sisters.

⸺

TO: *Fred Wolfe*   *TLS, 3 pp., UNC*

Nov. 1, 1937

Dear Fred:

I can tell you, at any rate, that Tom is all right, and that if your mother or any-one wants to write to him, and will send the letter in care of Elizabeth Nowell, 114 East 56th Street, New York City, (his agent), it will get to him within a day or two. He has left his apartment on First Avenue, and has been living in different hotels until he finds a place to settle, I understand.- He has also turned his back on me, and Scribners, and so I have not seen him at all, though I would very much like to. I never could understand about all the trouble, but I hope in the end it will smooth out, at least so far as personal relations are concerned.

Thanks ever so much for writing and telling me how things are going. I sup-pose the ice cream business is only at low ebb because of the season of the year, and that it will come up again in the Spring.- Anyhow, I hope the fruit may have the desired effect on the cash register.

Won't anything ever bring you to New York again? If it does, you must come and see us all. Everyone remembers you very well in my family,- which now is smaller because two daughters are married,- and there are two grandchildren and another in prospect. It is really getting larger, therefore, though smaller in the house.

Please give my remembrances to Mrs. Wheaton and her husband, and to your mother when you see them. I never saw your sister but once, in Washington. She often intended to come up to New York, and I would have jumped at the chance to talk to her if she had.

I do not know how much of a reader you are, but I thought you might like a Texas story we have just published, or the pictures at any rate, and so I am sending "Gone to Texas."[1]

Always yours,
Maxwell Perkins

1. By John Thomason

TO: Julia Wolfe   *CC, 2 pp., PUL*

Nov. 5, 1937

Dear Mrs. Wolfe:

I wrote Fred some days ago about Tom, who I know is well and is working, although I have not seen him. He gave up his apartment on First Avenue and hasn't yet found another. At present he is living in some hotel but I do not know which. The quickest way for you to reach him would be to write in care of his agent, Elizabeth Nowell, 114 East 56th Street.

I just had a fine long letter from Fred in which he says that it is not impossible he may come to New York.- If he does, he will have a warm welcome from all of my family, for all of them took to him at sight. I hope he may turn up.

As we have had a number of authors in and about Asheville lately, I have often heard news of you and all your family,- from people like Hamilton Basso,[1] for instance. Scott Fitzgerald is now in Hollywood paying off his very large debts quickly and conscientiously.- And I hear he is very well again.

Hoping that everything goes well with you all, I am,

Always yours,
[Maxwell Perkins]

1. Basso (1904–1964), novelist and Scribners author who lived near Asheville. He and TW were warm friends.

TLS with holograph postscript,[1] 10 pp., PUL
New York City

November 19, 1937

Dear Max:

My brother Fred has just written me, enclosing two letters that you wrote to him and to my mother, and a copy of a letter he wrote to you.

I want to go upon the record right now about several things. You told Fred that I had turned my back on you and Scribners. You told Miss Nowell that I had been going around town talking about you. And you told Basso that you were afraid now I was going to "write about" you and Scribners, and that if I did this you would resign and move to the country. I think that if you have said or felt these things you have been unjust and misleading. But what is a whole lot more important to me, I think they may have had an effect upon our friendship, which is the thing that matters to me most, and which I am willing to do anything I can to preserve.

Now, I am going to answer these specific things at once. In the first place, I did not "turn my back" on you and Scribners, and I think it is misleading and disingenuous for anyone to say this was the case. The facts of the matter are that the misunderstanding and disagreement between us had grown in complexity and difficulty for the past two years, and perhaps longer, and you and everybody else there at Scribners have known the situation as well as I. Furthermore, you have known for at least a year, and I think longer, that the possibility of this severance in our relations was a very real imminent one and we have talked about the situation many times. More than this, Charlie Scribner wrote me a letter last spring, at the time of the libel suit, and told me that although he would be sorry to lose me he would not try to hold me, if I wanted to go, and that I was free to go. Further, you told me once last winter to go, if I wanted to, but not to talk about it any more. Later you came to see me in my apartment on First Avenue and told me to go if I wanted to, but that the important thing was that you and I be friends. That is exactly my own position now. Finally, you have known for at least three months, since August, that my going was no longer a possibility, but an actual fact. You told Miss Nowell that I had communicated with various publishers and you asked her if it was true that I had signed up with Little, Brown & Company. It was not true.

Now that's the record. It is absurd for any one now to pretend that he is surprised, and that it has all come suddenly and is news to him.

You said in your letter to Fred that you could never understand about all this trouble, and that is the way I feel, too. But I do know that we both understood very definitely, and over a long period of time, that there was trouble, and I think it would be misleading and untruthful for either of us to say that he had absolutely no conception what it was all about. We did have a conception, and a very clear conception, too. There are so many things about it that are still puzzling and confusing to me, although I've spent a good part of the last year, and the better part of the last four months trying to think it out. But there are certain things that you knew and that I knew very clearly, and without going into the whole painful and agonizing business all over again, which we threshed out so many hundred times, beginning with Of Time and The River and continuing on with The October Fair and what I was going to do with it, and on to the book of stories and the Story of a Novel, and the lawsuits and the lawyers culminating in our final disagreement about the libel suit, the proper course to be taken, and the possible implications of the whole thing concerning my whole future life and work and the use of my material - there has been one thing after another, which we talked about and argued about a thousand times, so how can either of us truthfully say now that he has absolutely no idea what the misunderstanding is about.

You know that as a man and as a writer, I had finally reached a state of such baffled perplexity that I no longer knew what to do, what to try to accomplish and finish next, or whether, if I did finish and accomplish something I could ever have any hope under existing circumstances, of getting it published. You know and I know that beginning with Look Homeward, Angel, and mounting steadily there has been a constantly increasing objection and opposition to what I wanted to do, which phrased itself in various forms, but which had the total effect of dampening my hope, cooling my enthusiasm, and almost nullifying my creative capacity, to the work that I had projected, to the use I should make of my material, and even in some cases going so far as to oppose my possible use of material on personal rather than on artistic grounds. I am not trying to put all the blame for this on someone else, either. I know that I have often been unfair and unjust, and difficult to handle, but I do think that all this difficulty came out of these troubles I have mentioned. I felt baffled and exasperated because it really seemed to me I had a great creative energy which was being bottled up, not used, and not given an outlet. And if energy of this kind is not used, if it keeps boiling over and is given no way of getting out, then it will eventually destroy and smother the person who has it.

So that is why I think you are wrong when you tell my brother Fred and other people that I have turned my back on you and Scribners, and you don't know why. I am not going to do anything to carry on the debate of who left who - or whose back was turned, but I do know that there was no agreement of any sort between us concerning future work, no contract, and no assurance except perhaps that if I did something that satisfied you and that avoided the things you were afraid of, you would publish me. But, at the very least, under those same conditions any other publisher in the land would publish me, and I can't see that a connection is much of a connection when all the risk and obligation is on one side and there is none whatever on the other. This condition has persisted and developed for at least two years and I have said nothing to anyone about it outside of Scribners until very recently. If you are going to tell people that I turned my back on you and walked out on you, why don't you also tell them that three years ago when I didn't have a penny and was working on Of Time and The River I was approached by another publisher and offered what seemed to me a fortune. You know that I not only called you up and informed you of the matter instantly just as soon as it happened, but even asked you if I should even meet and talk to the people and that with great fairness you told me that it was certainly my right to meet and talk with them and listen to what they had to offer and then submit the offer to you and Scribners and give you a chance to meet it or to say you couldn't. You know when I did meet and talk with these people and heard their offer and rejected it on my own accord,[2] and told you all about it, I never once asked you or Scribners to meet the offer, although most writers apparently, and even publishers, would have considered that entirely fair and business like. So if you are going to say now that I walked out on you, why not tell some of the rest of the story too, and admit that I not only never tried to hold you up about anything, but never made approaches to anybody else, and rejected all that were made to me, even when I didn't have a cent. That is just the simple truth and I think in justice to me you ought to say so. But there is no use trying to go through all of this again, we have talked about it so many times, and both of us may be partly right and partly wrong, but how can either of us deny now that a situation has existed for months which had got into such a hopeless complex snarl, that at the end there was absolutely no way out of the mesh except by cutting it. That is the truth, and you know that is the truth. You have understood for a long time that it is the truth and that it existed, and I think you are now unjust to me if you pretend to anyone that you did not know it was the truth.

About your statement to Miss Nowell that I was going around "talking about you" in an injurious sense, I want to assure you that there is not an atom of truth in it. In the first place, I do not "go around"; I am not a gossip monger; I have no stories about any one to trade around. I am afraid that most of the gossip has come from the other side of the fence. You know better than I do that the profession in which you are employed and the circles in which you have to move are productive of rumor and much false report. I would injure myself before I injured you, but grim justice here compels me to remind you that those who live by the sword shall perish by the sword, and those who contemplate too often the play of the serpents fangs and find the spectacle amusing must run the risk some day of having those swift fangs buried in their own flesh.

I want to tell you now, if there were any further need of my going on the record, that if I have ever spoken about you to any man or woman, no one could have possibly construed my speech and meaning in any other way except in such a way as did you honor. And that was not only true when you were my publisher, but it is even more true now when you are my publisher no longer.

Fred told you in his letter that he had never heard me speak of you in any way except in such a way as to plainly indicate the affection and respect I felt for you. And I can assure you that has been true not only with Fred, but with everybody else; and not only in Asheville this summer but in New York since I returned to it in September, and if anyone has really given you any different idea, he has either deliberately lied or wickedly, wilfully and maliciously twisted or perverted something I said out of its context and its plain meaning for some bad purpose of his own. You owe me nothing, and I consider that I owe you a great deal. I don't want any acknowledgment for seeing and understanding that you were a great editor even when I first met you; but I did see and understand it, and later I acknowledged it in words which have been printed by your own house, and of which now there is a public record. The world would have found out any way that you were a great editor, but now, when people solemnly remind me that you are with an air of patiently enlightening me on a matter about which I have hitherto been unaware, I find it ironically amusing to reflect that I myself was the first one publicly to point out the fact in such a way that it could not be forgotten, that I, as much as any man alive, was responsible for pulling the light out from underneath the bushel basket, and that it is now a part of my privilege to hear myself quoted on every hand, as who should say to me: "Have you read Wolfe?"

About the rest of it, I came up here in September and for two full months I saw no one and communicated with no one except Miss Nowell. During all this time, I stayed alone and tried to think this whole thing out. And I want to tell you that one reason I now resent these trivialities and this gossip is that this may be a matter which is only important enough to some people to be productive of false and empty rumor or nonsensical statement, but to me it has been a matter of life and death. I can only tell you straight from the heart that I have not had anything affect me as deeply as this in ten years and I have not been so bereaved and grief stricken by anything since my brother's death. To hear, therefore, that at a time when I have eaten my heart out thinking of the full and tragic consequences of this severance with people with whom I have been associated for eight years, who printed my first work, and for whom I felt such personal devotion - the thing that chiefly was worrying you was the tremendous question of whether I am going to "write about you" and whether you could endure such a calamity is enough to make me groan with anguish.

I cannot believe you were very serious about this when there were so many more important and serious things to think about. But, if it will relieve your mind at all, I can tell you "writing about you" is certainly no part of my present intention. But what if it was, or ever should be?

What possible concern either as friend or editor, ought you to have, except to hope that if I ever "wrote about" you, I would write about you as an artist should, add something to my own accomplishment, and to the amount of truth, reality, and beauty that exists. This I thought was your only concern when you considered Look Homeward, Angel, and not whether it was about possible persons living in a specific little town. This I thought was also, with one or two reservations, your chief concern with Of Time and The River. This, I think, has been less and less your concern ever since - with the October Fair, with perturbations about other work that I have projected since, and finally with the crowning nothingness of this. I don't know how or why this thing has come about - or what has happened to you - but I know my grief and bewilderment have grown for two years and are immense.

Like you, I am puzzled and bewildered about what has happened, but in conclusion can offer this: - that maybe for me the editor and the friend got too close together and perhaps I got the two relations mixed. I don't know how it was with you, but maybe something like this happened to you too, I don't know. If this is true, it is a fault in both of us, but it is a fault that I would consider more on the side of the angels, than the devil's side.

I think, however, that what is even more likely to be a fault in modern life is when the elements of friendship and of business get confused, and when there is likely to be a misapprehension on the part of one or both of the parties as to which is which. I won't pretend to be naive about business or to tell you that the artist is a child where business matters are concerned. The artist is not a child where business is concerned, but he may seem to be so to business men, because he is playing the game with only one set of chips, and the other people are sometimes playing the game with two sets of chips. I don't want you to understand by this that I think playing the game with two sets of chips is always wrong and wicked and playing the game with one set of chips is always right. I do not think so. But I do think that when the players sit down to play, each of them ought to know what kind of game is being played - with one set of chips or two. I think this is important, because I think most of the misunderstanding comes from this. To give you a simple hypothetical example, which, let us say, I invented for purposes of illustration, and which I assure you certainly does not dig into the past or concern my relations with my former publishers: a publisher,[3] let us say, hear's an author is without a publisher and writes him. It is a very nice and charming letter, and says that the publisher has heard that the writer no longer has a publisher and tells him, if that is the case, he would like to see him and to talk to him. He goes on further to say that everybody in his office feels as he does personally about the work that he has done and about the work that he is going to do, and that it would be a privilege and an honor to publish him.

Do I suppose that this letter is hokum and that it is only a part of a publisher's formula when approaching any author. By no means. I think the publisher is sincere and honest and means what he says.

But to proceed with this hypothetical case: The author replies to the publisher that it is true he is without a publisher, but that he is in a great state of perplexity and puzzlement about his work, about a great amount of manuscript involving the material of several books and the labor of several years, and about what he is going to do next. He tells the publisher that what he needs most of all first is someone of editorial experience and judgment he can talk to. He tells him further that he is not at all sure that the work he has in mind would be the kind of work the publisher of this house would care to publish. But he asks the man if he wants to talk it over and find out what the situation is.

The upshot of it is the publisher telephones and comes to see him right away. They go out to dinner together, they have a good meal and some good drinks, and they talk the situation over. The publisher tells the author again how he and his house feel about the author's work and repeats and emphasizes his warm interest. The author then lays the matter before the publisher, tells him so far as he can, the problems and the perplexities that have been bothering him about his work and his manuscript. The publisher then asks which part of this manuscript the author thinks is nearest to completion. The author tells him and the publisher says where is the manuscript. The author tells him that the manuscript is packed up and in storage, and the publisher asks the author to get it out and show it to him. The author replies that he would like to, but that he is living in a small rented room and that the bulk and magnitude of the manuscript is such that it would be impossible to get it out and work on it in his own place. The publisher replies that in the offices of his company there is loads of space, and that he would be delighted if the author would make use of it. He can move his manuscript here and be free to work without disturbing anyone.

The author agrees to this proposal, and before they part the publisher addresses the author by his first name.

Now, so far so good: This hypothetical story must have a very familiar sound to you and you must agree as I do that so far everything is fine. Both parties are not only sincere and mean everything they say, but both sides are also playing with one set of chips.

Now to proceed: in a day or two, the publisher calls up again and tells the author that a young man in his publishing house is free and would be very glad to help the author move the manuscript that very afternoon. The author agrees to this, meets the young man and together they go to the storage warehouse, get the manuscript and bring it back to the publisher's office, where it is left. The next day, the author goes to the publisher's office, the crates and boxes of manuscript have been opened up, everything is ready, and the author sets to work. The publisher comes in, jokes about the size and bulk of the manuscript, repeats again his eagerness to see it and his desire to get at it as quickly as possible, and asks the author if he may call him by his first name, Jim. The author replies that this is his name and that he would be delighted if the publisher called him Jim. The publisher is catching a train in a few minutes, the two men shake hands very warmly, just before he leaves the publisher says: "Oh, by the way," and hands the author an envelope. When the author asks him what the envelope is, the publisher says it is nothing, just an acknowledgment that he has received the manuscript and to put it away among his papers. The author sticks the envelope into his pocket without looking at it. That night, however, in his room he sees the envelope upon his table and opens it: It reads as follows, "Dear Jones - this is to acknowledge that we have received one large packing case of manuscript, nine pasteboard cartons, and two valises, which are now stored in our offices. In view of the possible value of this material, we wish to inform you that this house can assume no responsibility for it, and that you leave it here entirely at your own risk."4

Now, what is the truth about this situation? Is the publisher wrong? By no means. Apparently, he is justified in writing such a letter by all the standards of good business practice, and it would be hard to find a business person who would say that he was anything except exactly right. Furthermore, the publisher may have acted as he did out of a scrupulous observance of what seemed to him the rules of business fairness and honesty. Nevertheless, the author cannot help remembering that the publisher asked if he could call him Jim when they were having drinks together over the dinner table, but calls him Jones when he writes a business letter. The author also cannot help remembering when the publisher talked to him over the dinner table, he told him it was not the money he hoped to make out of the author's books or the sales he hoped the books would have that concerned him principally, but rather the pride he would have in publishing the author's works, the privilege and the honor it would be to publish them, regardless of any commercial advantages that might accrue. He has told the author also that he can rest assured that if he comes to his house, he need not worry about the economic future, that no matter whether his next book sold or not, the house was a house which would stand by its authors through disappointments and vicissitudes and was willing to back its faith with its support. Furthermore, I believe that the publisher was sincere and meant what he said.

But the author is puzzled, and I think he has a right to be puzzled. Any business man would tell you the publisher was right not only about what he said over the dinner table, but right also when he wrote the letter about who should assume the risk and responsibility for the manuscript. The author can understand both conversations, but what he cannot understand is both conversations together. What he objects to is "Jim" over the dinner table, and in editorial relations, but "Jones" where business is concerned. From my own point of view, the author is right. The publisher did not tell him that it was going to be Jim in friendship and in editing, but Jones in business. He led the author to believe, with his talk of faith and belief and support and the privilege and the honor of publishing the author, that it was going to be Jim all the time.

Now, from my own point of view, Max, I think the publisher was wrong. I know that many people will not agree with me and will say that the publisher was right, that it was business, and that he was justified in everything that he did. I do not think so, and I think that much of the misunderstanding between publishers and authors comes from just this fact. I think the trouble comes when one side is playing with one set of chips, and the other side with two. Please understand that I am not accusing the side that plays the two of dishonesty or of unscrupulous practices. But I do think they are wrong in not making it clear at the beginning, the kind of game they are playing. And I have used deliberately a trifling and relatively unimportant example to illustrate my meaning. When you multiply this examples by scores by much more important and vital examples, and when Jim finds that it is always Jones when a question of business advantage, of profit or loss, is concerned, when Jim finds that friendship and business are not equal and balance each other, but that business always gets the upper hand when a question of advantage is concerned, then there is likely to be trouble.

I want to say also that I think Jim was wrong in the very beginning when he allowed his personal feelings to get so involved that he lost his perspective. I think Jim was wrong in that he based his publishing relationship too much on friendship, on feelings of personal loyalty and devotion, no matter at what cost to himself. I think in doing this Jim was unfair to himself and unfair to his publishers. I think that perhaps the best publishing relation would be one in which Jim felt friendship and respect and belief for his publishers, and they for him, but in which neither side got too personally involved. In the end, it is likely to involve too great a cost of disillusionment and grief and disappointment for someone, perhaps upon both sides. Please believe that I have offered this not by way of criticism of anyone, but just as possibly throwing some light upon a confused and troubled problem.

Now I am faced with one of the greatest decisions of my life and I am about to take a momentous and decisive step. You are no longer my publisher, but with a full consciousness of the peril of my position, and the responsibility of the obligation I am now about to assume, I want to feel that you are still my friend, and I do feel that in spite of all that has happened. I feel that you want me to go on and grow in merit and accomplishment, and do my work; and I believe that you would sincerely wish for my success and high achievement, and be sorry for my failure, no matter who became my publisher. I believe other people there at Scribners feel the same way. You said a year ago that the important thing, regardless of who published me is that we remain friends. That expresses my own feeling now, and I am writing to tell you so and to tell you that I hope it is the same with you. This letter is a sad farewell, but I hope also it is for both of us a new beginning, a renewal and a growth of all the good that has been.

You told Fred that I had not been to see you but that you would like to see me. I want to see you, but I do not think that now is the right time. I think you ought to see by now that I am not "sore" at anybody, but I am sore inside, and I want to wait until things heal. And my whole desire now is to preserve and save, without reservation, without any rankling doubt or bitterness, the friendship that we had, and that I hope we shall forever have. This is about all that I can say. I have felt pretty bad, and for a time my eyes went back on me but I am wearing glasses when I work now, and am now back at work again. If I can keep on working, without interruptions and the costly experiences of the last two years, I think everything may yet turn out all right.

You don't need to answer this letter. I wrote it to you just to go upon the record, to tell you how things really were, and let you know what was in my mind and heart. I hope that I have done so.

With all good wishes to you, to Louise, and the children, and to Scribners,

Sincerely yours,

Tom Wolfe

I am your friend, Max, and that is why I wrote this letter—to tell you so. If I wrote so much else here that the main thing was obscured—the only damn one that matters—that I am your friend and want you to be mine—please take this last line as being what I wanted to say the whole way through—Tom

[TW's record copy of his holograph postscript written on his CC of the letter]

Max, I am your friend, and I have written this letter to tell you that I am—This is the only damn thing that matters—to let you know that I am your friend, and I hope that you are mine—and if I have written so much else that this is obscured— that I am your friend—then please take this last line as being what I was trying to say through the whole letter—Tom

1. This letter also survives in a five-page single-spaced typed draft dated 18 November 1937.
2. Charles A. Pierce, an editor at Harcourt, Brace may have approached TW, but was not authorized to do so by Alfred Harcourt.
3. Robert N. Linscott of Houghton Mifflin. TW deposited papers with the publishing house in anticipation of a contract.
4. TW's account reflects his experience with Houghton Mifflin and editor Robert N. Linscott.

ALS, 3 pp., Harvard

MP's personal Scribner letterhead, New York

Nov. 20th '37

Dear Tom:—I am your friend + always will be, I think, + it grieved me deeply that you should even have transacted the little business that needed to be done through an intermediary instead of face to face.—But it made no difference otherwise + I hope we may soon meet as friends. Of course I had to tell Fred + others, when they asked me about you what the situation was. It was humiliating + had to be faced. I could not properly, even by silence, let it be assumed that things were as they had been. I told Fred truly too when I said I did not understand about it. I don't,—but that need make no difference between us, + I wont let it on my side. Miss Nowell should never have told you of my concern as to your writing about <u>us</u>—it was not <u>me</u>—though I think her motive was a kind one. I know the difficulty of your problem + I never meant this point to come up to confuse you. But don't you see that serious injury to this house + to my long time association here, for which I was responsible, would make me wish to be elsewhere? I hate to speak about this, but I can't have you misunderstand it.

I've missed you, + felt badly about it. I want to hear you tell of all you saw in the South sometime. I'm sorry about your eyes. Anyone who reads + writes so much must wear glasses though.—The worst thing about them is that they are always getting lost, but in the end one masters even that.

Anyhow I'm glad to have seen your hand writing again

> Always yours
> Max

❧

CC, 1 p., Harvard
New York City

December 7, 1937

Dear Max:

I wish I could come to the party you are giving to Mrs. Colum on Friday afternoon, but I do not believe I will be able to make it. I am working here every day now and the young lady who is working for me stays until 5:30. Also, I have already made arrangements with someone for dinner at six on Friday.

I wish you would tell Molly Colum that I am sorry that I could not come, and thanks very much for inviting me. I am looking forward to reading her book.[1] I hear she mentions me and, of course, I am grateful for her interest. This is all now.

With best wishes and hopes of seeing you some time soon.

> Sincerely yours,
> [Thomas Wolfe]

Mr. Maxwell Evarts Perkins,
246 East 49th Street,
New York CIty.

1. *From These Roots: The Ideas That Have Made Modern Literature* (New York: Scribners, 1937).

❧

TLS, 3 pp., PUL
New York City

December 27, 1937.

Dear Max:

I have had a talk at last with Mr. Ralph Lum, who is now representing me in that Dooher manuscript case over in New Jersey, and I am glad to say that at last it looks as if something is going to get done, and that I have a man on the job who knows how to do it. He told me the present state of affairs, outlined the situation very clearly, and asked me if I would get in touch with you to see if there was any help you could give us. I told him that I knew you would be glad to, if there was anything you could do, so to put the whole thing briefly, here is the way things stand now: the case comes up in the Court of Chancery in Jersey City early in February, and Mr. Lum seems to think it will go right through in an hour or two. He told me that I would recover my manuscripts - those that are left - and that disposes of this end of it. About the other end, Mr. Lum did not seem to be worried very much, and apparently does not believe Dooher has much of a case. In fact, he said that Dooher had gone so far with his contentions and allegations that he might find himself in a precarious and dangerous situation, if he attempts to press them. He is suing me for the sum, I believe, of $2600 - which Mr. Lum said might just as well be $26,000 - basing his suit apparently on the contention that I owe him the money for his services as a "manuscript appraiser" - whatever that may mean - and for his services as a manuscript agent.

Dooher contends that a verbal agreement or contract existed between us, that there were no witnesses present to the agreement and that it is what is known as "an unlimited agreement" - which means that I gave him complete and absolute authority over all of my manuscript, without reservation of any sort, to do with as he saw fit, from now on, henceforth, and forever after. This, of course, as you know, is preposterous - and Mr. Lum believes it will seem to be preposterous to the Chancellor when the case comes up before him. If Dooher really contends this, I suppose it will simply come down to the question of his word against mine, but Mr. Lum feels that if I can now enlist the aid of some other people - yourself, Chester Arthur,[1] Ruder,[2] the manuscript man, or anyone else who might have dealt with Dooher, or been present at conversations that I had with him - it would help.

I told Mr. Lum that the only part you had in the matter was that of a friend and adviser, but that you had been present on several occasions when I talked to Dooher, and I thought you would be able and willing to say that from your own observation, and what you yourself saw and heard, there was no suggestion of "manuscript appraising," unlimited agreements, etc, but that rather my whole connection with Dooher was entirely provisional and tentative, and that I was simply letting him "try the market" with certain pieces of manuscript to see what luck he had and what came of it. This, of course, as you know, is just exactly what happened, but I do think, Max, if you could say so - that is, tell Mr. Lum that that was your understanding of the situation from what you saw of it, it would help us.

I am just as sorry as I can be to have to trouble you again about this thing, or about anything else. But I do believe we are beginning to see light at last, and I know you have always wanted me to get this thing settled and thought I ought to see it through. I agree with you absolutely, and Mr. Lum not only agrees, but he says that it is imperative now that I see this through, and I think you will feel so more strongly than ever when I tell you the kind of answer Dooher has made: You remember he wrote some threatening letters to my former lawyers in New Jersey, revealing to them certain alleged obscene phrases and expressions which he threatened to make public if we continued with the suit. Of course, for some astounding reason I could never fathom, the first set of attorneys over there were thrown into a panic by this threat. As you and I both know, the threat is ridiculous: I have now seen the alleged words and phrases, and I think it may perhaps make you smile that most of them have already been printed in Look Homeward, Angel, anyway. Nevertheless, it was intended to be an ugly threat, and Mr. Lum thinks on that account that I must go through with this thing now - I don't think I am violating his confidence when I quote him to this effect: "The way to answer blackmail is to answer it" - which is a statement I know you thoroughly agree with. What Dooher has done in his answer is this: he apparently tries to get around the legal responsibility in which he may be involved by saying in his "Answer" that he cannot exactly describe the following manuscripts except by these phrases, which he happens to remember - "_____ _____ _____ _____ _____" - then follows, of course, a list of the alleged obscene phrases. As Mr. Lum says, he is skating on pretty thin ice. Beyond that, it's pretty ugly, isn't it?

Anyway I wanted to describe the situation to you, because I thought you would be interested to know how matters now stand, and also to ask you if you won't call Mr. Lum up, or write him and contribute anything you can by way of additional information that might help us. I think you understand the whole situation now, and will see what Mr. Lum is driving at. And honestly, Max, I hate like hell to bother you, but I do think this is one of those cases where people ought to stand together if they can, not only for personal or friendly reasons, but just because it's taking a stand in favor of the human race. But anyway, I am your friend as I told you in my letter, and I know that whatever you do will be all right.

I hope you have had a good Christmas and I send you all my best wishes for this coming year. By the way, Martha Dodd just called up, and in behalf of all of us I gave her the hearty welcome of the American nation. I told her that old man Dodd from a diplomatic point of view might not be a good ambassador, but he was something a whole lot better than that - a good man and a good American, that we were proud of him. She told me to go out and get today's World-Telegram, because she had written a piece about the Nazis. If she can write, she certainly ought to have material for a tremendous book.

Goodbye for the present, Max. I hope that I shall see you soon. And forgive me for troubling you this time. With all good wishes,

Sincerely,

Tom

1. TW's neighbor at 865 First Avenue.
2. Barnett Ruder, New York rare-book and manuscript dealer.

TLS, 3 pp., Harvard
Scribner letterhead

Dec. 28, 1937

Dear Tom:

Of course I shall do anything possible to help in the Dooher matter, and I am glad it is going forward. But all I know is what you told me,- that you once said to Dooher when he proposed that he might sell manuscripts for you, to go ahead. I know too that there was a general understanding that Dooher was not to sell without putting the matter before you in each instance, but I cannot remember how I know this,- that is, whether Dooher ever said that this was the case before me or not. I know that he did, until relations were broken off, bring each proposal to you. Anyhow, I shall do what I can, and will write Mr. Lum to that effect.

I think you told me that when you told Dooher to go ahead there were people present. Was Hoagland there?[1] I should think if he were, that his statement that all you said was in a general sense, and that no kind of permanent agreement was made, would help a great deal.- Though it might be hard on Hoagland to have to act against even such a brother-in-law.

I got a postcard from your mother in Miami, and a Christmas card from Fred and the Wheatons. I drink a lonely glass of ale every night in Manny Wolfe's while waiting for the paper.- But you couldn't go there now anyway because they broadcast, and the man who runs the show has a way of calling upon any celebrated person present to come up and say something. I should think it would frighten all the celebrities away, but maybe they fix it in advance. We really had a mighty good Christmas, but we missed you.

Always yours,
Max

1. Clayton Hoagland, writer for the *New York Sun* and TW's friend. TW had asked him to mediate his dispute with Dooher, but Hoagland declined.

FROM: Charles Scribner III　　　　　　　　　　　*ALS, 3 pp., Harvard*
December 1937　　　　　　　　　*Dew Hollow, Far Hills, New Jersey*

Sunday

Dear Tom—

I was delighted to get your Christmas card yesterday. Many times I had thought of dropping you a line to ask if you would dine with me and my family again as we always enjoyed having you. It seemed to me a bit embarrassing however as having learned that you were deciding on another publisher I was naturally reluctant on doing anything that might be misinterpreted as being inspired from business motives rather than from personal friendship.

Well, I may well be a bum publisher and am personally very willing to own up to that—but I have always flattered myself that there was something more between us than merely a business connection therefore when you came back to town I was rather hurt until I got your card yesterday.

Now that I hear you have definitely gone with another house I am hoping that we can discuss Love - Marriage and whatnot + whatnot again over a drink—to hell with all books!!!

Many good wishes for the New Year from Me + Mine

Sincerely

Charles Scribner

Excuse spelling - grammar etc. it was a tough Christmas in the country.

TO: *Charles Scribner III*   *CC, 1 p., Harvard*

December 29, 1937.

Dear Charley:

I can't tell you how happy I was to get your letter. Believe me, nothing was further from my intention in not writing or seeing any of you before than hurting the feelings of people who mean so much to me. As I told Max in the letter I wrote him, the reason I didn't come around was for no other reason except to think things out for myself, and to try to spare everybody pain, including myself.

Whatever happiness I had this Christmas was mixed in with a lot of sadness, too. Without going into the past, hashing it all up again, trying to thread back through the whole tangled snarl - like Max, I am still confused about so many things - just let me tell you that I think you are not only the finest publishers, but among the finest people I have ever known. Whatever comes of all of this, I know we will be friends; and now that I am committed to a new and for me very lonely and formidable course, that knowledge gives me the deepest comfort.

Some time soon, I look forward to seeing you again. Meanwhile, with affectionate greetings to you and all of your family, and with all good wishes for the coming year,

Sincerely,

[Tom Wolfe]

Mr. Charles Scribner, Jr.
Dew Hollow
Far Hills, New Jersey.

FROM: Charles Scribner III   *TLS, 2 pp., Harvard*

January 19, 1938.

Dear Tom:

I have been having quite a time with our cashier's department straightening out the report that they are obliged to make to the United States Government on Form 1099 regarding the money that you received from us in the year 1937. They were going to put it on a cash basis showing $3,089.45, which would include the payments made by us in settling the libel suit, as well as commissions.

This does not make sense to me, so I have told them to report $1,864.05, which is the actual royalty, plus the $250. paid by the Magazine, earned by you during the year.

I have regarded the payments on the libel suit charged against your account as a loan, as it was a direct obligation of which we voluntarily paid one-half ourselves, this half not being shown on the statement. Max was uncertain as to whether we agreed to carry this amount as against royalty to be earned in the future, but in any event this was done before we had any idea that we would not continue as your publishers.

The royalties earned, including the statement I have had made up to January 18, 1938, subtracted from the deficit on your account leave a debit balance of $826.38. In the course of a year and a half this amount will probably be met by the royalties on the books we published and I do not wish to embarrass you by pressing you to pay the debit balance owing to us, at this time, if you cannot conveniently do so. On the other hand if you have the money that you can spare it would seem just as well to wind this up, and as I understand you will probably receive during the year a considerable payment of your new book, it might work out better for you from the income tax point of view. I am not a lawyer and cannot advise you but it would seem as if you could charge off the expenses in the settlement of the libel suit against your income tax.

I hope you agree with me now that you did the sensible thing in settling this suit, as you are now free to go ahead with your work without interruption, whereas you would otherwise be tied up with us for an indefinite time in fighting the thing out at probably a considerably larger cost and all of the payment would have fallen on your shoulders.

Sincerely yours
Charles Scribner

To
Thomas Wolfe, esq.
Hotel Chelsea
222 West 23rd Street

January 21, 1938
114 E. 56th Street
New York, New York
c/o Miss Eliz. Nowell

Dear Charlie:

I have your letters of January 18th together with the royalty statements, and the various disbursements for legal fees, settlements, etc., with the deficit which is still owing.

Yes, I do have money enough now to make good the deficit you mention, but I am going to ask you if it will be agreeable to you to let the deficit wait for the present, until I get a clearer notion of the state of my finances, or possibly until additional royalties from my books are sufficient to wipe the deficit out. I did get an advance from Harpers but I signed a contract with them, but I have been hoping that that advance would relieve somewhat the strain of financial and economic worry which I have felt and that, for a change, I might regard the given sum of money with some assurance as my own, and not as a kind of public drawing fund for lawyers and various other people who have made very free with it during the past two or three years. Of course, I don't want to inconvenience you a bit, and I want to pay up every penny of my debts to everyone, but if this deficit could be deferred for the time being, I should appreciate it. I have one more law suit on my hands- the last one, I hope- which is coming up for trial in New Jersey in February. I don't know how much it is going to cost, but as you know, litigation is never cheap. I hope now this is the end of it, after all the unhappy experiences of the last two or three years. I hope also that you are right in believing that I will be free now to do my work in peace without interruption, and that the settlement we made in the case last year was a good one in that it helped to achieve this result. I don't know: I know that you did what you thought was right, and I know also how sincerely I regret having involved you, however innocently, in a matter such as this. But it still seems to me, from a standpoint of ideal justice, at any rate, that to have to buy the privilege of doing one's work and earning one's living by the payment of hush money to anyone who chooses to use the law as the means of annoying and coercing one, is a heavy price to pay, and furthermore a very dangerous and risky one, since I cannot be convinced that a dog once baited with a hunk of meat will be permanently appeased, but finding getting easy will come yelping at the heels again. It's not your fault, and it's not mine either: it seems to be the way of the world. But it's a bad way, and a wrong way, and I for one am all for changing it.

But I hope this is the end of all that trouble now, that this new year will be a good year for you and me in every way. If what I have proposed about the deficit is not satisfactory to you write and let me know. But I hope you can see your way clear to arrange the matter as I have suggested. Meanwhile, with all good wishes,

Sincerely
Tom Wolfe

TLS, 1 p., Harvard
Scribner letterhead

Jan. 29, 1938

Dear Tom:

If I am to be in court on February 8th when your case comes up, ought I not to check up with you first,- as to dates, etc.? Ten minutes would do it. Your lawyer implied I was not to be called on, but was only intended to help to overawe Mr. Dooher so I will try to look awful.- But his lawyer might call me, and I ought to get oriented.

Yours,
Max

⤺

TLS, 4 pp., PUL

114 E. 56th Street
New York, New York
c/o Miss Elizabeth Nowell
February 2, 1938

Mr. Maxwell E. Perkins
c/o Charles Scribner's Sons
597 Fifth Avenue
New York, New York

Dear Max:

I thought I would just send you for your own convenience this memorandum, to help out the notes you made last night: your first meeting with Dooher, as I recall it, was in February 1935, a week or two before the publication of "Of Time and the River." I think you saw him two or three times then, and we talked the manuscript business over: at any rate, at this time I allowed him to take part of the written manuscript of "Bascom Hawke" and "try the market." He came back in a day or two and told us he had received an offer for the manuscript and mentioned a considerable sum of money, $250——perhaps even $500, or more. I was just on the point of going to Europe in a day or two and the book was about to be published, and your reaction to the offer, as I recall, was that it was a very good one and that if my manuscript was really worth this much perhaps it would be wiser not to break it up at the time, but to keep it intact, and to wait until the publication of my book for further developments. To this Dooher readily agreed, returned the manuscript, and there the matter rested until late the following autumn.

I think you next saw Dooher in December 1936, when he again established connections with me. Sometime in December 1935, as I recall it, I let him take three or four items of manuscript, again to try the market, and early in January

1936, as I recall it, he informed me that he had received a lump offer for all the items I had let him have involving a considerable sum of money, $675, I believe.

This deal, which was with Ruder, fell through when Ruder later objected to the price he had first offered: I thereupon recalled the items I had let Dooher have, he was very crestfallen and agitated about his failure and thought I was dismissing him, but I cheered him up, told him I had confidence in him, and advised him to try something simpler and less ambitious in his next attempt. He agreed to this very eagerly, and upon his own suggestion, I let him have a single item, which was my own copy of "Of Time and the River," with notations and corrections in my own handwriting in the margins of the book.

Dooher took this out and got an offer of $125 from Ruder immediately, and came back to Scribner's and informed us- you and I- of the offer which we both thought was a good one. Accordingly, I gave Dooher my permission to complete the sale, this was done. In a few days, after I had waited, at your suggestion, to make sure that Ruder's check was good, I allowed Dooher to have two or three more small items, which he again immediately sold to Ruder for a lump sum of $125: the date of the checks for the two sales being January 13, 1936 and January 17, 1936 respectively.

Dooher then asked me about the typed manuscript for "Of Time and the River," and I believe said he could sell it very readily to Ruder: I asked you about it, you said it was in the Scribner safe, I gave Dooher a written order authorizing you or someone at Scribner's to let him have the manuscript, and Scribner's gave him a large wrapped package of manuscript which we all thought was the typed manuscript, printer's version, of "Of Time and the River."

In a few days Dooher informed me that Ruder had made an offer for it- I forget the price but it seemed to be a good one- he said the manuscript was in a very confused state, that Ruder and his assistants were collating the material, and that only a small portion of the material really was what we had thought it to be- namely, the printer's version of "Of Time and the River." When I asked him what the remaining portion of the manuscript was he replied indifferently that he did not know, that it apparently consisted of manuscript that had never been published.

When I informed you of this, you expressed surprise and wondered what the manuscript could be, and we both instantly agreed that I should recall the manuscript at once, find out what it was, and assure myself that I had typed copies of it. I instructed Dooher to this effect at once: he took it in very bad grace and protested about the amount of work that Ruder and his assistant had done in collating the material. I assured him that I was recalling the manuscript only to assure myself what it was and that I had copies of it. Dooher went away and brought the manuscript back; and it was at this point that the row broke out, and that I dismissed him as my agent.

I think this gives you a pretty clear idea of the whole business from first to last, and I hope it will refresh your memory on certain points.

I think the point you made last night was a very important one- namely, that before I went to Europe in 1935 I gave you, in written form the power of attorney, and that this power of attorney vested in you, among other things, the power to deal with Dooher and any offers he might receive for manuscripts at your own discretion and as you thought best.

I am awfully glad you brought that up Max, because I thought I had remembered everything, and had given Mr. Lum a full record of everything. Now I am writing him to tell him about this power of attorney which I had forgotten.

As you say, the power of attorney indicates pretty conclusively that Dooher had no final authority with the manuscript whatever, and it would seem to me refutes his claim that he had such authority. Moreover, as I recall the matter now- and I ask you to refresh your own memory on the subject- the power of attorney, giving you this discretionary power, was made at Dooher's own suggestion, his argument being, that if I were away in Europe and he received an advantageous offer for any of my manuscript, he would be strapped and unable to act unless I vested authority in someone here who would have the power to act for me and make decisions in my behalf.

I think this clears up everything, so far as you are concerned. I hope they do not have to use your testimony at all, but if they do, I think this may be an important point, so I am writing to inform Mr. Lum about it without further delay. I will call you up in a day or two to make arrangements with you about going over to Jersey City.

It was good to see you last night, and I hope we can see each other more often now. Meanwhile, until I talk to you again,

Sincerely

Tom

P.S. Max, I am adding this postscript just after having written Mr. Lum a letter in which I told him about the power of attorney. The more I think about it, the more important it seems: I told Mr. Lum that if he could arrange to get Dooher on the stand, and get him to testify that this alleged verbal agreement, at which no witnesses were present, giving him unlimited authority, was made between us prior to March 2, 1935, it seems to me that your own testimony about the power of attorney which I gave you might be conclusive in refuting his claims. It seems to me that the only answer he could then make would be that he did not know about the power of attorney, was not aware of its existence, and that it was made without his knowledge or consent. But plainly this is not the case: my whole clear and definite recollection of the matter now is not only that the power of attorney was made and given to you with Dooher's knowledge, but that it was done largely at his own instigation and suggestion, upon the grounds that if he did receive advantageous offers for some portions of my manuscript during the time I was abroad there ought to be someone here who had authority to act for me, to give consent, or to make decisions concerning the manuscript in my behalf: and in your capacity as my editor and my friend, and the person who knew most about my work and about my manuscript, you were the one who ought to have the power of attorney. I am just about as absolutely clear and certain on all of this as anyone can be about something he remembers. I certainly think there is no doubt whatever that Dooher knew about the power of attorney, and I hope your own recollection of the matter coincides with mine.

T.W

⌒

TLS, 2 pp., Harvard
Scribner letterhead

Feb. 4, 1938

Dear Tom:

I think that is an important point too, and to substantiate it, I am sending herewith the power of attorney which you ought to revoke anyway.- I think you can do that by just destroying it—and also a letter I have unearthed from Dooher. This letter indicates that he thought he was to apply to me during your absence to discuss a sale.- And there could be no point in his discussing it unless he knew that I was authorized to authorize him either to make the sale or to refuse to. Better send these on to the lawyer.

I have been haunted by your story about the girl Ann and her mother and the ruined house down there in Virginia.[1]

Always yours,
Max

1. Unlocated.

⌒

TO: *Charles Scribner, III* *TLS, 1 p., PUL*

114 East 56th Street
New York, New York
c/o Miss Elizabeth Nowell
February 14, 1938

Mr. Charles Scribner, Jr.
c/o Charles Scribner's Sons
597 Fifth Avenue
New York, New York

Dear Charlie:

· I am sorry to have delayed answering your letter of January 19th so long, but, as you know, I have been wrestling with a law suit- the last I pray I may ever have- and doing my level best to help the lawyer and protect myself against a series of legal outrages that included practically everything except arson. As you know, I won the case, or at least it will seem as if I won it until I begin paying the lawyer bills.

Now, about your own letter and your suggestion that I pay you now the deficit which stands against my account in your books: I have thought this over very carefully, and I want to ask you to let the deficit remain unpaid for the present, and to allow it to be absorbed, as you suggest it can be, by future sales of my books which you publish.

Yes, it is true, that I did receive a considerable advance from Harper's, but it was money which I hope to keep, so far as possible, for my own use, to support me until I get another piece of work done. The lawyers are already swarming around, flapping their wings and emitting blood thirsty caws, and if I am going to begin the new year in the same way as the two or three before it, paying out large sums of money in suits and settlements and lawyers' fees, the advance is not going to stretch too far. So, if you understand my position, I should prefer it if you will agree to let the deficit be paid off by further and, I hope, continued sales.

I hope you are right when you say that settlement of the libel suit has left me free to do my work in peace. At any rate, I shall now find out. The experience of the past three years has been a very costly one, in time, in energy, and in money: I can only hope now that I may derive some future profit from it. Please let me know if my proposal here about the deficit is agreeable to you. Meanwhile, with all good wishes,

Sincerely,
Tom Wolfe

⤳

FROM: Charles Scribner III   *TLS, 2 pp., Harvard*

Feb. 15, 1938.

Dear Tom:

I am glad to learn that you have one more trouble behind you. Max told me about the trial. Let us hope that you will not run into any further libel suits. Anything to do with lawyers is always expensive and unpleasant.

I am willing to allow your obligation on the suit we had to run along for the time being, although it is not customary to carry such accounts for an author for whom you are no longer acting as publisher, and our contract, which is similar to that of other publishers and agents, calls for a settlement on the part of the author for any suits of this kind which may be brought.

I hope that you are making good progress with your book. I have been amused at reading parts of the book by your old friend Mrs. Bernstein, though it is rather heavy going if one attempted to read it from beginning to end.[1]

With best wishes

Sincerely yours
Charles Scribner

1. *The Journey Down* (New York: Knopf, 1938), Bernstein's autobiographical novel of her relationship with TW.

TO: *Charles Scribner III*   *CC, 4 pp., Harvard*

114 East 56th Street
New York, New York
c/o Miss Elizabeth Nowell

February 18, 1938

Dear Charlie:

I don't want to inconvenience you a bit, and if you say the deficit has got to be paid now I will pay it. My only point was that since my books made almost twenty-three hundred dollars last year, according to the royalty statement you sent along with the letter, I therefore felt they would naturally be expected to make good the eight hundred dollar deficit within a reasonable time.

I notice that you refer in your last letter to the deficit as an "obligation on the suit." Well, I am not going to argue with you about the suit. I never have. I told you last year how I felt, and I still feel the same way. I am sorry as hell that you got involved in it through something I had written which you published. But as you know and I know, and as the lawyers knew, I did not libel anyone.

You say in your letter you hope I do not have any more libel suits, and I second the motion with all my might. But I do not know what you or I or any man can do about people suing you. It is a racket, a part of a great organized national industry of shaking-down- in my case, of being shook- and you and I and every other decent citizen ought to do everything we can to stop it. And the only way to stop it is to fight it, because it lives by threat and flourishes on submission. As long as we submit it will continue to flourish.

I think that when a writer willfully, deliberately and maliciously writes something for the purpose of insulting and injuring a living person, or a dead one for that matter, he ought to be punished for it. But I do not think he ought to be punished for being honest and decent and doing his work, and having been unfortunate enough, maybe, to attract some public notice and get his name in the press. And you know that is what happened. You are yourself an honest and a decent man, and you know as well as I do that it was a shake-down. I am not going to harp upon it any more, but you have mentioned the thing several times in your letters, and I have got to tell you what I told you a year ago. I think we should have fought it out.

I want you to know, and I am sure you do know, that there is not an ounce of resentment in my heart, and that particular thing is all over now. But we should have fought it out. I do not think it is sticking to the real point to talk about publishers' contracts, and what the clause of the contract says concerning libel suits, and who is to be responsible for them.

The point is, it seems to me, that a publisher ought to stick to a writer and fight with him when he knows that that writer is loyal and honest, has injured no one in his writing, and is being unfairly taken advantage of, and, believe me, Charlie, I am not saying this because I have any rankling memory of the past. I just hope that I will profit by the experience, and I also hope that in the future publishers and writers will stick together and fight for each other in matters of this sort. For, as any decent person knows that is the only thing to do. When you publish a man, when you put the imprint of your name upon a man's book, you are for him, and not against him. I think you have always been for me, and what is more I think you always will be, no matter who is my publisher. But I think that in that particular matter we were wrong in not fighting it, and furthermore I think we were licked before we started, because our own lawyers cost so much that we were practically forced to settle to protect ourselves against our own lawyers' bill if we went on. Frankly, so far as I can see we would have done as well if we had had Abie Glickstein[1] and paid him fifty bucks. In the end, the three floors of office space in the Chase National Bank, the magnificent private offices, regiments of slick-looking assistants, etchings of Abraham Lincoln, etc., did not mean a damn thing except trouble and money: it was a sorry job.

I know you took it on the chin on account of something that I wrote, but Charlie, all that suit proved to me was that a man might write "The cat has whiskers" and then get sued for libel by an old maid in Keokuk. I am sorry as hell you had to be involved, but I still think we should have fought it out. You took it on the chin to the extent of about three thousand bucks, but so did I- and maybe you have got some idea of how much three thousand bucks is in my young life. It is just about ten per cent of all the money I ever earned from the beginning out of writing. Those facts are correct, and people tell me I am a well-known writer.

So the only reason I am harping on it is not because I have got an atom of soreness or resentment in me: you did what you thought was right, but I am only saying that if guys like you and me do not stick together and fight it out sometimes when people try to shake us down, it is not only going to be too bad for writers, but too bad for publishers too. And that is that: I have spoken my little piece and I know you will take my word it, I am not sore. I am your friend.

And now about the eight hundred dollar deficit: if you say I have got to pay it now, I will pay it. But honestly I do not think you are running much of a risk in letting it run on, in view of the fact that the work of mine which you publish earned almost three times that much last year. But if you do feel that it ought to be paid now, it seems to me that a simple and decent arrangement of the matter would be one in which we square the whole account, and you relinquish to me the rights of my books which you publish.

Frankly, I think you ought to do it. They are my books, they belong to me because I created them and because they mean something to me they cannot mean to anyone else: I would like to see you and talk to you about this, and I think we could reach an agreement that would be satisfactory to both of us, and which would clear the whole situation up in such a way that the deficit would not only be wiped out, but you would also be relieved of all the risks and responsibilities attendant on suits, publication, and keeping the books in print.

And now that is all in a business way, but I am sorry to have to protract the discussion of a matter which must already have grown tedious to you. For my own part I can only repeat what you said to me in your fine letter of Christmas, when you heard that I had definitely gone with another house- it has always seemed to me that there has been something more between us than a business connection and, as you say, friendship is considerably more important.

I know that you will always hope for my success, and that if my next book is a good one there will be no one in the world more genuinely pleased about it than you. For that reason, I am grateful for the kind inquiry you make in your last letter about the progress I am making. I see no reason now that the legal difficulties which have beset my life for the last three years have been settled I should not get ahead with my work very rapidly. I have collected an immense amount of material and done an immense amount of writing, and the scheme and pattern of the book is all clear. An immense labor still remains to be done, but I believe it is worth doing, and naturally I hope that the result will be one that all of us can be proud of.

I know there may be some pretty dark times ahead, times when I may almost lose hope, but when I do I shall always remember the letter you wrote me a year ago, when you told me that I was free to go if I liked, but that whatever happened you would be my friend, and you expected me to go on and grow and prosper in my work, as time went on. Naturally, I can only hope that you are right, and the knowledge that you feel that way will always be a source of comfort and inspiration to me. I still have that letter and shall always treasure it as a token that no matter who publishes me, or what business connections I form, I shall always have your friendship. And I still hope that some night when you have nothing else to do, and feel like having a drink, you will call me up.

Meanwhile, with all good wishes to you all,

Sincerely,

[Thomas Wolfe]

Mr. Charles Scribner, Jr.
c/o Charles Scribner's Sons
New York, New York
TW/GJ

1. Invented name.

⌒

FROM: Charles Scribner III   *TLS, 2 pp., Harvard*

February 24, 1938.

Dear Tom:

I shall be delighted to give you a call next week and see if we can arrange to have a drink together and talk things over. I do wish to say one thing, however, to square our position with what you have written in your letter.

I told you not once but several times that I was perfectly prepared to go ahead with you in fighting out the libel suit, if that was what you wished to do. The lawyer advised that the cheapest and safest way was to settle and personally I was inclined to agree with him, as did Morris Ernst,[1] but I distinctly left the final decision to you.

I do not like any idea of being blackmailed any more than you do but if you look into the libel law you will see that the case might easily have gone against us, especially before a Brooklyn jury who would be inclined to sympathize with the girl who was evidently hard up and who was quite obviously referred to. The law itself may be unjust but it is still the law and its interpretation is not always in the most competent hands. Apart from this your work would have been subject to interruption for the next three years and as things worked out you would be tied up in this case to a company who were no longer your publishers.

I would also like to say a word on the other point you raise with regard to our giving up to you the publishing rights on your books. I do not believe that you have thought through the whole of the partnership relationship which you say should exist between author and publisher and which I am completely in accord with you in principle. When the libel suit came up we waived at once our contract rights as publishers to dump the entire cost of the suit and any damages that might result on you as the author and agreed to go into it fifty-fifty, as we felt we had entered a more or less permanent relationship. When you asked, I naturally advised you as to how I felt about going on with the suit, but you are mistaken if you take it that I attempted to dictate to you. Now with regard to the books published, it is true that they are your creation, but we made a mutual agreement to invest our money as publishers in making the plates, printing them and selling them, your share being in the enterprise the royalty we agreed to pay on sales, and our share being any profit we might realize after our investment was met and the cost of printing, selling and royalty had been deducted. We like your books and are proud to have them on our list, and as long as we do our part in keeping them in print and selling them, we have a right to continue with them and to make our share of the profit from their sale. We do not wish to sell our rights, but if this should come about, it would then be up to any publisher who might take them over to buy out our rights, and they would have to pay a damn high price as I have every faith that they will go on selling for years.

All this seems as if I were giving you a business lecture but I am not trying to rub in any rights or wrongs - only to make our position clear. When we have drinks between us it will be much pleasanter to talk business if there is anything left we need to discuss, apart from the joys of life.

With every good wish

Very sincerely
Charles

1. Prominent lawyer specializing in publishing and First Amendment cases.

TLS, 1 p., PUL

Hotel Chelsea
222 West 23rd Street
New York, New York

February 28, 1938

Dear Max:

I am going to see "The River"[1] this week. Met the man who made it in New Orleans last winter and he told me all about his work.

You ought to see a picture called "Peter the First"[2] if it is still on. It is a Russian film and you cannot understand what they say but there is running dialogue in English underneath. The acting is wonderful, no Hollywood stuff but the kind of vitality and sincerity they get into their writing. Also saw "Tom Sawyer"[3] a movie now running at Radio City. It was not as good as it might have been, but it brought back the book to me and is worth seeing.

Go see "Peter the First" if it is still running anywhere and I will go to see "The River." But a half hour about the Mississippi is not enough: it ought to be a full length film.

Yours,
Tom

1. 1937 documentary movie written and directed by Pare Lorentz.
2. 1937, directed by Vladimir Petrov.
3. *The Adventures of Tom Sawyer* (1938), produced by David O. Selznick and directed by Norman Taurog.

TO: Fred Wolfe[1]   *TLS, 2 pp., UNC*

July 25, 1938

Dear Fred:

I don't know how things may be, but if you have the time and don't think I am asking too much, I wish you would drop me a letter, or anyhow a postcard about old Tom. I haven't been able to find out anything that one could depend upon, but I know he must have been mighty sick, and maybe still is. Could you let me know? I wanted to write to him, but Miss Nowell thought it would be better not to, that it might bother him. And perhaps he is not in any shape to read letters anyway. I would be ever so grateful to have some word from you. I only know that he has been ill for some time, and with pneumonia, and that a few days ago he was thought to be coming safely out of it.- But then later word from Miss Nowell was much less reassuring. I hope everything will go well.

Always yours,
Maxwell Perkins

1. Letter addressed to "Fred Wolfe c/o Dr. E. C. Ruge, 1424 Fourth Ave., Seattle, Washington." During a trip west, TW was hospitalized with pneumonia.

TLS, 3 pp., UNC
Scribner letterhead

August 9, 1938

Dear Tom:

I could not really find out how things were going with you for a long time,- except through Miss Nowell, whose information did not seem very satisfactory. But then I found Fred was out there, and wrote him a letter at the address I got from Miss Nowell, and he wrote me a fine answer, and I was mighty grateful. And then it turned out that Ham Basso was making inquiries on his own, and had learned various things from Asheville and also from where you are.[1]– So I gather that now you are recuperating in good style, and I thought you might like to hear same of the gossip.

As I am once more a commuter, as I was born, and always should have been, I do not get around so much.- But whenever I do go to any of the old places like Cherio's or Chatham Walk, or Manny Wolf's, everybody asks for you.- The old captain at the Chatham the other day told me that whenever you came back, there would be a warm welcome awaiting you. I did not tell him you were sick, but I did tell Cherio, who was very much disturbed and wanted all sorts or messages to go to you.- And I told that Joe, or whatever his name is who used to be a sailor, at Manny Wolf's. He always has asked about you with great interest.

I like being back in New Canaan. Louise has become somewhat of a landscape gardener, and we have hemlocks in front and at the side of the house.- And she has made a sort of an 18th century grove around a diminutive fish pond created from an old washtub painted blue. I could not see how it could turn out well, but it really did.- It would make you think of those grottoes and groves that Horace Walpole used to write letters about such as Pope indulged in. Then our place not being large enough for a deer park, she thought she would improve the landscape with a couple of kids.- I mean real kids. And she bought them somewhere on the Merritt Highway, but they did not turn out very well in the end. They are not very clean animals, and so she took them back just after I had got quite attached to them. We have had quite a household there.- I do not know that I ever told you about Zippy's[2] son,- a very fierce looking baby who might well bring trouble to the world, with the nose and chin of a Caesar, and flat ears,- and red hair! Douglas,[3] by the way, is painting a portrait of the daughter of Mrs. Bernstein.[4] I forget her name. He says she has a perfect 18th century face and he has a good sketch of her and means to do her at full length, monocle and all. Douglas tried to rent, and finally borrowed, for they refused to take money for such sacred precincts, the studio of that old Rogers who made the Rogers groups.[5]— You ought to go into that studio and see some of the groups there that never got into the market, and one that did, and some not finished. It is so near to the house that it is mighty convenient. I hope we are done with New York for good and all, but I think Louise aims to be in for two or three months anyhow.- But not in the house. Zippy and Bert and their families pretty well fill it up.- And Peg[6] too is beginning to work on next Monday at Bergdorf Goodman (thanks to Mrs. B) and will probably live there if I can keep her from taking an apartment.- I should be glad to have her take an apartment with some other girl, but I hate to have her cooking and ironing and taking baths and doing all those things that seem so dangerous for women when there is nobody about to help her if she catches on fire or falls down. But she points out to me that men haven't the authority they used to have over women over twenty-one.

Everything is looking up in business, and apparently should for another year. It was pretty bad six months ago, or even less, and we were most fortunate in having "The Yearling." We have just printed beyond 200,000, and it seems as if it were going to go much further. Then it will in the end be a juvenile, which is the best thing that could happen to a book after its first year or so. But the success was largely spoiled for Marjorie—what a world this is!—because she got sick with some obscure trouble that is still more or less unfathomed and may be bad. But maybe not too. We had an operation in the family but it came so quick, and was over so soon, that though it was quite serious, we hardly noticed it.- It was Peg and she took it beautifully and is now all recovered.

Darrow is having a fine time with his cook book,- a book after his own heart. All kinds of campaigns are going on about it, and it looks as if it might be a kind of corner stone before we are done with it which might not be for a good many years. And we have a very notable dark horse in the stable to bring out in the early Fall.[7]

I do not know whether you knew that Jack's mother died, and he was very lonely and cast down, and later on I was very much worried for fear he might commit the folly (at his age) of getting married.- Particularly when the poetess who aroused my anxiety got him to go up to see the Cloisters[8] and in those surroundings told him that she had almost resolved to go into a convent.- But nothing more than that has happened so far, and Jack is a well-balanced and cautious gent.

All the people hereabouts are just as you used to know them, though Weber has grown a little heavier, and all of them were mightily concerned about your illness.- But honestly, Tom, it may well be the best thing that ever happened to you, for it will give you a fresh start after a good rest.

Always yours,
<u>Max</u>

1. Seattle, Washington.
2. MP's daughter Elisabeth Perkins Gorsline.
3. Elisabeth's husband, Douglas W. Gorsline, illustrated the 1947 edition of *Look Homeward, Angel.*
4. Edla Bernstein.
5. After the Civil War John Rogers (1829–1904) mass-produced inexpensive sculptures representing idealized social gatherings, e.g., "Checker Players" and "Neighboring Pews."

6. MP's daughter, Louise "Peggy" Perkins.
7. Probably *Dynasty of Death* by Taylor Caldwell.
8. Museum in New York City.

〰

ALS, 1 p., UNC
MP's personal Scribner letterhead

Mid-August 1938

Dear old Tom:- I'm mighty sorry you've been ill + now you've won out so well for God's sake take care for a while + get really strong again.—If you do, this bad business may well turn out to have been a good one. You've needed rest ever since I've known you + your recuperation should give it to you, + you'll come to you work a refreshed + new man. I'm writing you a letter in type because my hand is so illegible.—But I wanted to tell you how happy I was to know that you were getting well

Always yours,
<u>Max</u>

〰

ALS, 4 pp., Harvard
Providence Hospital letterhead, Seattle, Washington

Aug 12,
1938

Dear Max: I'm sneaking this against orders—but "I've got a hunch"—and I wanted to write these words to you.

—I've made a long voyage and been to a strange country, and I've seen the dark man very close; and I don't think I was too much afraid of him, but so much of mortality still clings to me—I wanted most desperately to live and still do, and I thought about you all a 1000 times, and wanted to see you all again, and there was the impossible anguish and regret of all the work I had not done, of all the work I had to do—and I know now I'm just a grain of dust, and I feel as if a great window has been opened on life I did not know about before—and if I come through this, I hope to God I am a better man, and in some strange way I can't explain I know I am a deeper and a wiser one—If I get on my feet and out of here, it will be months before I head back, but if I get on my feet, I'll come back

—Whatever happens—I had this "hunch" and wanted to write you and tell you, no matter what happens or has happened, I shall always think of you and feel about you the way it was that 4th of July day 3 yrs. ago when you met me at the boat, and we went out on the cafe on the river and had a drink and later went on top of the tall building and all the strangeness and the glory and the power of life and of the city were below[1]—Yours Always

Tom

1. After TW's death MP wrote about the Fourth of July episode TW described; MP may have intended this material for his article "Thomas Wolfe" published in the *Harvard Library Bulletin* (Autumn 1947), pp. 267–77, but it was not included:

> Once, some three months after the triumphant publication of "Of Time and the River" Tom landed from a steamer on a blazing hot Fourth of July, and I met him. For all his good times abroad, his over-whelming reception in Germany, no child could have been more happy to be home, more eager to see all of New York at once. And that afternoon and night we did range from the floating restaurant on the East River at 55th Street, to the roof of the Prince George Hotel in Brooklyn where the whole shining city and the harbor were spread out. In the course of our wanderings we passed a doorway somewhere near Tenth Street close to Third Avenue. Tom caught me by the shoulder, swung me round and pointed to the top of a house. "There," he said, "is where a young man, six years ago began to write his first novel in an attic." And he added eagerly, "Let's go up and see it." But when we got to the top floor under its low ceiling and Tom knocked, and then rattled the door, no one was within. Meanwhile I was looking out a rear window, I saw that by going up one fire escape and down another, you could enter the so-called attic. I said, "Tom if we want to see the eyrie where the young eaglet mewed his mighty youth we can do it," and we did. Maybe it was burglary but the window was open and the statute of limitations must now obtain. There it was that he had begun to write "Look Homeward, Angel" and it was an attic but a comfortable one, and in the spacious dimensions of Thomas Wolfe himself.—*Dictionary of Literary Biography Documentary Series Volume 16: The House of Scribner, 1905–1930,* ed. John Delaney [Detroit: Bruccoli Clrak Layman/Gale Research, 1997], p. 330).

TLS, 3 pp., Harvard
Scribner letterhead

Aug. 19, 1938

Dear Tom:

I was most happy to get your letter, but don't do it again. That is enough, and will always be valued. And I remember that night as a magical night, and way the city looked. I always meant to go back there, but maybe it would be better not to, for things are never the same the second time. I tried to find you some good picture books, and found three good in their way. But maybe I shall find something better. I'll keep my eyes open for it.

Everyone hereabouts is greatly concerned over your illness, and that means many people who do not even know you too. Don't get impatient about loss of time. You don't really lose time, in the ordinary sense.- Even six months would not

Phone East 1340

PROVIDENCE HOSPITAL
17TH AVENUE AND EAST JEFFERSON STREET
SEATTLE, WASH.

Aug 12;
1938

Dear Max: I'm stealing this against orders — but "I've got a hunch" — and I wanted to write these words to you.

— I've made a long voyage and been to a strange country, and I've seen the dark man very close; and I don't think I was too much afraid of him, but so much of mortality still clings to me — I wanted most desperately to live and still do, and I thought about you all a 1000 times, and wanted to see you all again, and there was the impossible anguish and regret of all the work I had not done, of all the work I had to do — and I know now I'm just a grain of dust, and I feel as if a great window has been opened on life I did not know about before — and if I come through this, I hope to God I am a better man, and

The last letter (Houghton Library, Harvard University).

Phone East 1340

PROVIDENCE HOSPITAL
17TH AVENUE AND EAST JEFFERSON STREET
SEATTLE, WASH.

in some strange way, I can't explain
I know I am a deeper and a wiser
one — If I get on my feet out
of here, it will be months before I head
back, but if I get on my feet, I'll
come back
— Whatever happens — I had this "hunch" and wanted
to write you and tell you, no matter what
happens or has happened, I shall always think
of you and feel about you the way it was
that 4th of July day 3 yrs. ago when you
met me at the boat, and we went out
on the Café on the river and had a drink
and later went on top of the Hotel Multby.
and all the skyscrapers and the glimpse of
the power of life and of the city we saw — Yours always,
Tom

be important. Even if you were really relaxing, as they call it, all that time, you would be getting good from it, even as a writer.- I hope you will manage to do it too.

I am expecting to go up with Louise tomorrow to Windsor, for over Sunday, mostly to see my mother, and to see my uncle who has now passed ninety, and is in better shape than he was ten or twelve years ago. He was next to the oldest in that family of twelve, just barely too young for the Civil War to which his older brother ran away, from Yale, and joined the cavalry and got his health destroyed by it, but I think Uncle Ally would have come through that all right. I do not think though, that he is going to cheer me up about the state of the nation and the prospects for the human race. He foretold the downfall of 1929, but said that he did not expect anyone to listen to him. And they didn't.

I could send you some good books to read, but I don't think you will want to do any reading for yet awhile. What you ought to do is to realize that by really resting now, you are in fact actually gaining time, not losing it.

Always yours,

Max

&

FROM: *Fred Wolfe*
11 September 1938

Wire, 1 p., PUL
Baltimore, Maryland

MAXWELL PERKINS
246 EAST 49 ST
PLAN OPERATING ON TOM TOMORROW MORNING FEEL YOUR PRESENCE WOULD HELP IF YOU CAME TONIGHT COME TO MARBURG BUILDING RECEPTION ROOM HOPKINS
FRED W WOLFE.

&

TO: *Fred Wolfe*

File copy of telegram, 1 p., PUL

SEPTEMBER 15, 1938

FRED WOLFE
512 NORTH BROADWAY
BALTIMORE
MARYLAND
DEEPLY SORRY   MY FRIENDSHIP WITH TOM WAS ONE OF THE GREATEST THINGS IN MY LIFE   GIVE MY LOVE TO MABEL AND YOUR MOTHER   I ADMIRED YOU ALL SO MUCH   ONE CAN SEE HOW TOM CAME BY HIS GREAT QUALITIES
MAXWELL PERKINS

Perkins in his office during the Forties. He claimed that wearing a hat helped his deafness.

Appendix 1

Undatable Letters

ALS, 1 p., Harvard

Tom—

Here's the book + just what you want, I guess

<u>Max</u>

Michael Strange[1] just called up.—Busy till Wednesday. Can you go then for tea at 5:30?

1. Pseudonym for poet and actress Blanch Oelrichs Thomas Barrymore Tweed (1890–1950); in 1940 Scribners published her autobiography, *Who Tells Me True.*

TO: John Hall Wheelock *ALS, 1 p., PUL*

Dear Jack: Max told me you are off on your vacation—I haven't got your address handy, so I'm sending this to Scribner's for forwarding—I just want to wish you as happy and successful a vacation as anyone can have. I know how you love the sea. So I hope you have splendid days and all the sun and swimming that you like. And I hope you forget those everlasting proofs and all the books you edit and soak in the solar energy until you come back. Goodbye, for the present, Jack—I hope this may be the best holiday you ever had—Tom Wolfe

Appendix 2

Unmailed Wolfe Letters

TO: *John Hall Wheelock*
Early September 1929

AL draft, 3 pp., Harvard

My Dear Jack: May I not say to you—now that several days have passed, and I have had time sufficiently to observe the contents of the noble and magnificent volume which you sent me—that you must be accounted among the poets who have lived and died—but <u>always</u> lived—upon this earth, and that I know no other words to pay to you the homage—and the tribute that you so gloriously deserve? May I not add further the acknowledgement, which for the first time in the reading of these pages I became wholly aware of, that again and again I find how much—how greatly—how inestimably—in word, in phrase, or, what is more important, in the whole and entire emotion of the spirit—I have taken from your poems feelings, rhythms, and the impulse of entire movements,—for my own work.

TO: *John Hall Wheelock*
Early September 1929

AL draft, 3 pp., Harvard

Dear Mr Wheelock: I like to write, rather than to speak, the things I feel and believe most deeply—I think I can say them more clearly that way, and keep them better.

In the last few months, when I have come to know you, I have observed again and again the seriousness with which you would deliberate even the smallest changes in my book. As time went on I saw that this slow and patient care came from the grand integrity of your soul. Consequently, when you presented me with a book of your poems on the day when we had finished our work together on my novel, this simple act was invested with an importance and emotion which I can not describe to you now—every one of the subtle and rich associations of your character went with that book of poems, I was profoundly moved, profoundly grateful, and I knew that I would treasure this book as long as I live.

When I got out on the street I opened it and read your inscription to me and the magnificent lines that follow it.[1] In this inscription you speak of me as your friend. I am filled with pride and joy that you should say so. I am honored in knowing you, I am honored in having you call me friend, I am exalted and lifted up by every word of trust and commendation you have ever spoken to me.

You are a true poet—you have looked upon the terrible face of Patience, and the quality of enduring and waiting shines in every line you have written. The poets who are dead have given me life; when I have faltered I have seized upon their strength. Now I have by me living poetry and a living poet, and in his patience and in his strong soul I shall often abide.

I have now read all the poems in your book—I think I have read them all several times. But true poetry is a rich and difficult thing—we invade it slowly, and slowly it becomes a part of us. I have read few books as often as three or four times, but there are poems I have read three or four hundred times. I do not presume therefore to offer you a glib criticism of poems I shall read many times more—and I do not presume to think you would be seriously interested in my feeling. But there are some of your poems that are already communicated to me—I dare to say entirely—and that have become a part of the rich deposit of my life.

I wish to say that Meditation seems to me one of the finest modern poems I have ever read—modern only in being written by a man now living. When I read this poem I had that moment of discovery which tells us plainly that we have gained something precious—it has now become a part of me, it is mixed with me, and some day, in some unconscious but not wholly unworthy plagiary, it will come from me again woven into my own fabric.

1. Wheelock inscribed *The Bright Doom* (1927) to TW with lines from his poem "Noon: Amagansett Beach":

> for
>   Thomas Wolfe
> in friendship and admiration—
> "Loneliness—loneliness forever. Dune beyond dune,
>   Stretches the infinite loneliness—pale sand and pale sea-grass,
> Pale beaches, mile upon mile. In the immensity of noon
>   A hawk moves upon the wind. Clouds darken and pass."
>   John Hall Wheelock
>   August 26,
>   1929
> (Harvard).

ALS, 4 pp., Harvard

August 1930

Dear Mr Perkins: We create the figure of our father, and we create the figure of our enemy. The figure of my enemy I created years ago: he is a person, he has a name, he is an inferior thing, he has no talent, but I made of him my Opponent: it is this person who will always appear to cheat you of what you most desire: he is nothing, he has no life save that you gave him, but he is there to take all you want away from you. Thus, if you love a woman, and your Opponent is millions of people, thousands of miles away, he will come to trick her from you. He is there like a fate and a destiny. He is nothing, but he is all the horror and pain on earth. This has happened to me.

Where are you? Are you crawling out of it? Send me my money or send me my ticket home. Send me your friendship or send me your final disbelief. I will tell you this very plainly; I do not think I am a good venture for Chas. Scrib. Sons I think I may be done for utterly. I think you may now get out of it profitably. If anything's left, send it to me, and break our pub. relations

Tom Wolfe

Incomplete AL, 8 pp., Harvard
c. October 1930   *London*

Dear Mr Perkins:—I did not know how long it had been since I had written you, or sent that cable from the Black Forest, until I got your cable the other day. When you are alone for a long period, Time begins to make an unreal sound, and all the events of your life past and present are telescoped: you wake in the morning in a foreign land thinking of home, and at night in your sleep you hear voices of people you knew years ago, or sounds of the streets in America. The changes in time also help this feeling of unreality—I am writing you this a ten oclock at night in London, for a moment I think of what you maybe doing at the same time at ten o'clock, and then I realize it is only five oclock in New York, and that you are probably at Scribners just before going home.

I think of you a dozen times a day, and I think all of you are in my mind like a sand of living radium deposit whether I am consciously thinking of you or not. My longing for America amounts to a constant ache: I can feel it inside me all the time like some terrible hunger that can not be appeased. It will always be the same: the other night after listening to miles and miles of the silliest talk by English people about America—it was not a nation, but a raw mass of different peoples; Americans were incapable of real feeling, only sentimentality; the country was a matriarchy, the women ruled it; the Americans were incapable of love, with all the rest of it, including the machine age, Puritanism, Rotarians, etc—I could listen to no more of it and I told them, I think without passion and I know with utter conviction on my part, that to anyone who had ever known America as I have known it, no life in Europe, no life anywhere, can ever seem very interesting. It surprised and angered them, for they saw I meant it, and they had never expected to hear anything like this. People here, especially Mr Reeves at Heinemann, have been very kind to me—I have not done much going out, but I get a good many invitations.— I am resuming here after several days—it has become for some reason terribly difficult for me to write letters: the more I am away from home, the more I miss seeing a few people, the harder it seems to write to them—it has always been this way. I think the reason is that I have really got started at length, I stay alone in my place here a great deal (I will tell you about it later), I go through periods of the most horrible depression, weariness of spirit, loneliness and despair, but then I think about the book for long stretches and work on it. Only, in God's name, is there not some way to find peace and kindliness in this world to do one's work without paying so bitterly for human relations.

I have cut almost everything away from me, and if I do not get my work done now I do not know what I shall do: there is nothing else left for me—Surely to God it does not have to be made so cruelly and needlessly difficult I must now tell you plainly certain things—much more plainly than I have ever been able to tell them to you in person—but if I can not tell them to you, who in God's world am I to talk to? I shall try never to cause you any distress or embarrassment—my great fear now is that I will cause you disappointment by failure to do the work you expect me to do. I must tell you now very plainly that you occupy an immense place in my belief and affection:—please do not think I am exaggerating, and please do not be at all embarrassed by this statement—I think it is very unfair to you for me to feel this way, I have no right to place the burden of this feeling on any man, but I think you have become for me a symbol of that outer strength

Late December 1930

Incomplete, AL 2 pp., Harvard
London

The hour of going for the mail was a nauseous experience, I lived all through the day in apprehension of it; if there was news it was bad, and if there was none, it was worse; and once, after the worst of these death threats there was a silence of over a month or six weeks, during which I have put in the most dreadful hours of my life—I was sick with the thing, and once I lay on my back for two days, palsied and unable to move, to dress myself, or to take food. This, so help me God, is the everlasting truth: my great vitality and physical power is wrecked, I can neither eat nor sleep, I am as close to physical collapse as I have ever been—but I shall not collapse, and I shall work.

Late December 1930

Incomplete AL, 36 pp., Harvard
London and Paris

Dear Mr Perkins: I suppose you have by now an enormous letter I wrote you about two weeks ago—it was filled with work and woes; I want to write you this short one to tell you my plans and intentions—First, it is only three or four days before Christmas, I have the satisfaction of feeling completely exhausted with work for the moment: my mind is tired and I can not sleep very well. I am going to keep it up until Christmas, then I am going to Paris for four or five days, and I am going to do nothing but sleep, eat, and drink the best food and wine I can get. Then I propose to come back here and work till I drop for about six weeks until I know I can bring the first part in consecutive chapters or in draft back home. Then I propose taking 3d class on the fastest boat I can find—the Bremen or Europa—so that I'll be in New York in 5 or 6 days after sailing. Then I should like to proceed <u>immediately</u> (this is the hard part) to a place <u>where I can get to work again.</u> I have told you that my new book is haunted throughout by the Idea of the river—of Time and Change. Well, so am I—and the thing that is eating at my entrails at present is when can I have this formidable work ready. You have been wonderful not saying anything about time, but I feel you would like to see something before next Fall—I dont make any promises but I'll try like hell: I am distressed at the time I spent over personal worries, excitement over the first one, and fiddling around, but its no good crying about that now—I think this came as fast as it could, now I've got it all inside me, and much of it down on paper, but I must work like hell. The thing that is good for me is almost <u>total</u> <u>obscurity</u>—I love praise and flattery for my work, but there must be no more parties, no more going out—I must live in two rooms somewhere until I hate to leave them: I want to see you and one or two other people, but I want to come back without seeing anyone in New York for several weeks <u>except</u> <u>you</u> and <u>one or two others:</u> don't think I'm talking through my hat, it's the only way I can do this piece of work and I must do it in this way.

Now about the place to work—this is a hell of a lot to ask you, but I don't want you to do it if you can get someone else to do it—try to help me if you can. I don't know whether it is good to live in New York now, my present obsession is that I am going within the next few years to get married and live somewhere in America in the country or in one of the smaller cities—in Baltimore, or in Virginia, or in the Pennsylvania farm country or in the West—but I have no time to go wandering all over American now (my book by the way is filled with this kind of exuberance, exultancy and joy—I <u>know</u> if I can make people feel it they will eat it up: I hope to God the energy is still there, this homesickness abroad has made me feel it more than ever—I mean the richness, fabulousness, exultancy and wonderful life of America—the way you feel (I mean the young fellow, the college kid, going off on his own for the first time) when he is rushing through the night in a dark pullman berth and he sees the dark mysterious American landscape rolling by (Virginia, say) and the voluptuous good looking woman in the berth below stirring her pretty legs between the sheets, the sound of the other people snoring, and the sound of voices on the little station platforms in the night—some man and woman seeing their daughter off, then you hear her rustle down the aisle behind the nigger porter and they knock against your green curtain—it is all so strange and familiar and full of joy, it is as if some woman you loved had laid her hand on your bowels—then the wonderful richness and size of the country, the feeling that you can be rich and famous, that you can make money easily, the wonderful soil—sometimes desolate and lonely looking as you found the parts of North Carolina you visited, yet that same earth, Mr Perkins, produces enough pungent and magnificent tobacco to smoke up the world, and from that same clay come the most luscious peaches, apples, melons, all manner of juicy, pungent and wonderful things—I was thinking of it in Switzerland this summer—how incredibly beautiful Switzerland is—the story-book lakes,

the unbelievable mountains, the lush velvety mountain meadows—and how desolate and ugly North Carolina would seem to a European—and yet Switzerland is a
kind of fake—horribly dull food, dull stunted little fruits and vegetables, dull
grapes, dull wine, dull people—and horrible dead sea fish that comes from those
lovely Alpine lakes: Switzerland for all its rich grand beauty can not produce anything 1/10 as good or pungent as North Carolina tobacco, melons, peaches, apples,
or the wonderful ducks, turkeys, and marvellous fish along the lonely desolate N.C.
coast—And that is America—the only country where you feel this joy, this glory,
this exuberance—the thing that makes the young fellows cry out and squeal in their
throats—these poor dull tired bastards with their terrible soft wooly steamy dreary
skies—do you think <u>they</u> can ever feel this way. They may sneer at us, hate us, revile
and mock us, say we are base and without beauty or culture—but no matter how
much they call on their dead glories, their Shakespeares, Moliéres, Shelleys—you
know there can be no lying, no hocus-pocus about their beastly, damnable dreary
air—they cant argue about that, they have to breathe it, and it will rot and decay
anyone after a time—just as bad food, bad housing will do it. I feel pity and sorrow
for them—the plain truth is that the lives of most of their people are dreary compared to ours—they have to go to American movies for amusement No, they cant
have the feeling we have in Autumn when the frost comes and all the wonderful colors come out, and you hear the great winds at night and the burrs plopping to the
ground and the far off frosty barking of a dog, and the wonderful sound far off of
an American train on the rails and its whistle

The people of North Carolina are like that wonderful earth—they are not little dull dreary Babbitts: I am going to <u>tell the truth</u> about these people and By God
it is the truth about America, I don't care what any little worn out waste lander,
European or American, or anyone else says, I <u>know what I know</u>: the people in
North Carolina have these same wonderful qualities as the tobacco, the great juicy
peaches melons apples, the wonderful shad and oysters of the coast, the rich red clay,
the haunting brooding quality of the earth—they are rich, juicy, deliberate, full of
pungent and sardonic humor and honesty, conservative and cautious on top, but at
bottom wild, savage, and full of the murderous innocence of the earth and the
wilderness—do you think this is far fetched? Scott F.G. did and ridiculed the idea
that the earth we lived on had anything to do with us—but don't you see that 300
years upon this earth, living alone minute by minute in the wilderness, eating its
food, growing its tobacco, being buried and mixed with it gets into the blood, bone,
marrow sinew of the people—just as breathing this dreary stuff here has got into
these dull, depressed, splenetic and despondent wretches who have to breathe it:
how in God's name can anyone be pigheaded or stubborn enough to deny it. You
are a New Englander and quieter about it but every American has this exultant feeling at times—the way snow comes in New England and the way it spits against your
window at night and the sounds of the world get numb, you are living like a spirit
in wonderful dark isolation: my bowels used to stir with it, and once I got off the
Fall River boat after a night of storm and snow in the dark water of the Sound, and
the wind and powdery snow were blowing and howling at dawn, everything was

white and smokey wonderful grey, and there was the train for Boston in the middle of it, black, warm, fast, and all around the lonely and tragic beauty of New England (yes! and <u>another</u> good looking woman in the stateroom next to me coming up on the boat)—this is glory and wonder, and I shall not be ashamed to tell all of it—What else is homesickness, loyalty, love of country than this—each one of the million moments of your life, the intolerable memory of all the sounds and sights and feelings you knew there. I shall neither try to defend or condemn anything—it is in me, all of it, I shall tell of the cruelty and horror, murder and sudden death, the Irish cop, the smell of blood and brains upon the sidewalk along with everything else—it is all part of my story, and I <u>know</u> it <u>is time</u>, and so do you, it is also glorious and exultant and nowhere else in the world can they feel this way: if I tell about it as it is, in all its magnificence and joy, how can it fail to be good? I do not say that I can, but we shall see.

All this was a parenthesis: to get back to the question of lodgings—once you mentioned in conversation, also in a letter, the possibility of finding a place out in your part of the country: in a talk you spoke of boarding houses and said there were some good ones. But I will never get along in a boarding house—I must have two rooms where I can be absolutely free, tramp about and work all night, and sleep all day if I want to. You can't do this with peace of mind in a house with other people. An apartment house, or rooms in a business b'l'd'g that's deserted at night is more in my line. Also I must have a gas stove where I can cook bacon and eggs and make all the coffee I want. If I can get this out in the country it would be fine: I notice they are building apartment houses out in the country now—Bronxville, etc—the idea is not bad I should like to be either out your way—or else I have thought of Brooklyn—somewhere where I can look at the wonderful river—I think of Brooklyn because people will not bother you or come to see you there so much:—all I need is two rooms, one to sleep in, one to work in, a little kitchen or kitchenette, and a gas stove—also a showerbath or bath: don't you think I could get this in some modet place for $60 or $70 a month. I want to be quiet, and I want to see either the earth (that is out your way) or the river. Could something be done about it, also, in view of the present hard times couldn't I get something without signing a year's lease—say for three or six mos, or month by month, with a privilege of staying on if I want to. Sinclair Lewis wrote me two nice letters—he said Vermont is the most beautiful and cheapest place in the country—maybe I could go there in the hot weather. If you dont know of anything yourself could you speak to someone who does? There's a boy named Kizenberger (or something like that) down with Miss Devoy in the Art Dep—he seemed a fine friendly competent fellow: do you think he could help us. It is a lot to ask but it would be a Godsend if I could have a place waiting for me when I came back and not lose time. I do not want to lose at the outside over <u>one</u> month of the <u>nine</u> months that elapse between Jan. 1 and next October—whether on steamers, trains, hunting rooms, or anything else: I'll stand by any arrangement you can make—just see if it's quiet and they'll let me work, eat, and sleep as I please. Will you please write me about this and tell me if it can be done?

—Paris, Dec 29 1930—I have come to Paris for two or three days before New Year's—and I am going to finish the letter here. I was damned tired and had brain fog but already I am nervous and restless and feel impatient to get back to the book. I have brought the big ledgers in which I write and I keep fooling with it here, although I ought not to, I think—I have got the desperate feeling about it and think I may come through to something—Now here is the plan: I may be here another day or two until New Years, then I go back to London, and write like hell until the flesh can do no more for six or eight weeks. Then America again, and a quiet place of my own to work, and I will show you something complete (a complete book and story but not the whole of The October Fair—the part called Antaeus) sometime during the summer. It is bound to be good if I can be hopeful and exultant while I write it: when I am that way I can do anything—tonight I am afraid. I am afraid of no one person, no thing, I am afraid of fear, desolation, and the nauseous sickness and horror of the guts that comes from unknown fear—Paris gives me that feeling, I can hardly bear to go to the Left Bank for fear I shall see some of these God damned life hating, death loving bastards: but I did go yesterday, because one of them had been phoning me in Paris last week and I had promised to look them up here. I refer to Mrs Jean Gorman, the wife of Herbert[1]—I refer to that prettied up and malignant cutter, and my prophetic soul told me it was a frame up of some sort—one of 3 things; well it turned out to be all three: one was to pry in to my supposed history with someone I knew in London, another into my supposed New York history, another—how much had it written on my book, what was it about, when would it be ready. When I got there they had the gang lined up—on one side someone who knew a friend in New York, on another side someone who knew a person in London—they volleyed and thundered—From the right "I believe you know so and so in London—she is my cousin"—from the Left "I believe you know so and so in New York—she is related to me" Then the sly looks and snickers— God, it makes me vomit! Then the prize bitch, Mrs G. spoke of your friend Mrs Colum, who is here—I want to see her if I can see her away from these Scandal-mongering apes and baboons. This is Paris and I loathe it! They are here to work— Jesus Christ! none of them has ever worked here: I am here to eat and drink and sleep and I shall stay to myself and do it. For God's sake, don't think I am mad with suspicion and distrust—I have never hated or in the end suspected a good person, but I know that my exultancy is right, that the sense of joy and glory is true and just, that the richness, glory, beauty, wonder and magnificence of America—the feel of the wind, the sound of snow, the smell of a great American steak—By God, these are real things and true things, and these people are liars and cheap swindlers. But if I am going to get this glory and faith and exultancy into my book I must feel it myself: and I do feel it most of the time, only when I meet these people my heart turns rotten, and my guts are sick and nauseous, after the book is written I will be afraid of nothing—but now I am afraid of anything that gets in the way: that is why I want to see you and one or two others and no one else when I come back—I should like to go with you to that 49th St speakeasy and have a few drinks of Amer-ican gin and one of those immense steaks—then I should like to talk to you as we used to: these seem to me to be mighty good times, and that speakeasy was a fine place—I have remembered it and put it in my book.

Mr Perkins, no one has ever written a book about America—no one has ever put into it the things I know and the things everyone knows—it may be grandiose and pompous for me to think I can, but for God's sake let me try. Furthermore it will be a story, and I believe a damned good story—you know what you said to me over a year ago about the book that might be written about a man looking for his father and how everything could be put into it—well you were right: don't think that I gave up what I wanted to do, only I had this vast amount of material and what you said began to give shape to it. I have gone through the most damnable torture not merely rewriting but in re-arranging, but now I've got it, if I can get it down on paper. The advantage of your story is not only that it is immensely and profoundly true—namely, all of us are wandering and groping through life for an image outside ourselves—for a superior and external wisdom to which we can appeal and trust—but the story also gives shape to things: Coleridge said that Ben Jonson's play The Alchemist had one of the three finest plots in the world—(the other two were Oedipus and Tom Jones) and Coleridge mentions as the wonderful virtue of The Alchemist the fact that the action could be brought to a close at any point by the return of the master (the play as I remember concerns the tricks of a rascal of a servant palming himself off as the master on a world of dupes and rogues)—well, so in this story, the action could be brought to a close by the son finding his father—I have thought over the Antaeus myth a lot, and it seems to me to be a true and beautiful one; it says what I want about man's jointure to the earth whence comes his strength, but Antaeus is also faithful to the memory of his father (Poseidon) to whom he builds a temple from the skulls of those he vanquishes. Poseidon, of course, represents eternal movement and wandering and in a book where a man is looking for his father what could be more true than this?—About Sinclair Lewis: it was a wonderful thing for him to do and I wrote and told him so—he also wrote me two letters, and said he would try to see me over here—I hope it sells a few copies of the book—thanks for using it and advertising it—but I am a little worried by it also: the Great American Writer business is pretty tough stuff for a man who is on his second book—and I hope they won't be gunning for me: also, I have begun to come to a way of life—I meant what I said about obscurity—its the only thing for me, otherwise I'm done for: I want to write famous books, but I want to live quietly and modestly. Also, I am determined to resist in my own heart any attempt to make or be made the great "I Am," of anything. If I tell myself that I am not anybody's "I Am"—but only a fellow who is going to stick relentlessly to the things he has seen and known, to say the things he has to say as honestly and beautifully as he can, to realize that is all he has, and that if it has any value it is because other people have felt these things or will feel their truth—Why, then, if I stick to this and work like hell, I don't believe they can hurt me seriously either when they praise me or turn against me. Don't you think this is the only wise and honest way to work and live?

Now, finally—about the book again. If I have been incoherent and chaotic it has been from haste and not from lack of certainty—as well as I can tell you quickly and in this small space this is what my book is about: First, it is a story of a man who is looking for his father—this gives it plan and direction, and it also expresses a fundamental human desire—the story of a man's love for a woman is told with the utmost passion and sincerity and sensuousness in one part of it, together with all the phenomena of lust, hunger, jealousy, madness, cruelty and tenderness—but the idea that the two sexes are from different worlds, different universes, and can never know each other is implicit, and the father idea—the need for wisdom, strength and confession, with the kinship and companionship of one's own kind and father, hangs over the story all the time: under this story structure are the ideas of the fixity and eternity of the earth and the beauty of man's life

1. Herbert Gorman (1893–1954), critic and biographer; he was an early explicator of James Joyce's writings.

<table>
<tr><td>Late December 1930</td><td style="text-align:right">Incomplete AL, 4 pp., Harvard
London</td></tr>
</table>

Dear Mr Perkins: It is three o'clock in the morning in London as I write you this. I suppose that means it is about ten o'clock the evening before in America—in New York or New Canaan—or whatever wherever you happen to be at this moment. I am working, and I shall work through the night until eight o'clock tomorrow morning, when my charwoman will come and get me breakfast, and the shops will open down below and people will begin to come through in the street. I am haunted by the strange mystery of time, I can not forget it for a moment, and it gets into everything I do. I think of all the forgotten moments of our lives and of all the forgotten people, and lost sounds, and I wish to God it were possible to hear just five minutes of the life of five hundred years ago—the sounds in the streets of London, the voices of the people, and what they said, the sounds of their feet. But much stranger and farther off than that is the time of just a generation or two ago!

I have been thinking of America in all its aspects and at all times and it seems that I know everything that ever happened there. I am a part of its enormous and everlasting innocence, its eternal wistfulness. Fools sneer and snicker at this, but it is only the truth: I think of them in a thousand of their moments—the young men gathered at the corner under the lamps at night when the songs that they sang were Sweet Adaline and Love me and the World is mine, the improvised quartets and the people sitting on the front porches in the summer nights listening and saying it was mighty pretty; the glib pert travelling man with the gift of gab and a "good line" talking to the yokels at their commercial hotel, while they drink in his guff with open mouths: the young fellows taking their girls for a "buggy ride," the livery stable, the livery man, the nigger stable boys, the smell of the wooden floors and horse dung, the stamp of the hooves on the wooden floors, and the loafers playing checkers and talking about the baseball scores in the livery stable office. And I think of

Ben in all his aspects: I see him in early October on the raised scaffold in the windows of the Asheville Citizen: it is the time of the World Series and the Philadelphia Athletics are playing someone—Ben is in his shirtsleeves, and he has neat armbands to hold them up, a pair of earphones is clamped to his head, a cigarette dangles from his lips, he is getting the plays from the Associated Press man as fast as they come in, he is irritable and scowling and calls for the cardboard squares with the plays, players, and hits which a man below is passing to him and which he constantly replaces on the scoreboard: Ben's stomach is all sunken in and his trousers hang upon his hip bones, he has a belt with a silver buckle and his initials on it: outside there is a big crowd—Old Man Oates is rooting at the top of his voice for the Athletics, and the old nigger with the fog horn voice from the military school keeps yelling "Comeawn—Mistah Bak-uh, Come awn—Mistah Collins" (naming his favorite players) and all the crowd laughs

Late December 1930

*Incomplete AL, 4 pp., Harvard
London*

If ever a man deserved to succeed with his work, it is I. For six months there have been scarcely five consecutive moments when my mind has been free from the most cruel pain and worry; there has not been an hour or a minute of that time that I have not drawn my breath in weariness and labor, of the reason for all this you know something; I have told you something of that madness of passion that for five years rooted itself deeper and deeper into my heart like a terrible growth, and I knew how hard it was going to be to conquer and exterminate this sickness, and I was prepared for this; but you do not know, because I could not foresee and tell you, the means that have been taken to keep me in this horror, the lies and threats that have been written and cabled to me. The letters signed with blood, and the cables which threatened death and suicide and asked me if I would accept the responsibility—and my final horror and despair now that I am told by the woman's own sister that these messages were not even dignified by any appearance of feeling—that they were callously and vilely sent to me by a person flushed and insolent with success, health, and new adventures. During all this time, when I have lived in almost complete solitude, and when I needed the help of a friend more than any time of my life, there has been written or cabled to me not one word of genuin love and kindness, not one word of calmness or hope which would let me know that this woman I have loved so dearly was also my friend, and would now help me, with her superior wisdom, tranquillity, and strength to get not only my own life, but I thought hers, too, under some better control. I did not believe that these frantic threats would actually be carried out, but I did believe they were sent to me by a woman in the greatest pain and distress, and there was always the horrible ghastly feeling that there might be some atom of conviction in them, and that in some desperate moment she would attempt to injure herself.

Incomplete AL, 8 pp., Harvard
London

Late December 1930

your friend, Mr Brooks. When the lover sees the figure of his mistress against this background; it is as if a man had found a lovely flower growing from a dunghill (as I believe a lovely flower <u>could</u> grow there), or as if a man found a healthy and beautiful plant growing out of the rotten green scum of a poisonous marsh. The lover looks at the lovely and beautiful face of his mistress, it seems delicate and good and gentle, her words are sweet and full of faith and love—she will love him + noone but him until death, she will always be faithful, his distrust of faith are killing her, etc—and then he sees her among a society of notorious paederasts, opium takers, lesbians, adulterers, fondling old men and slimy young ones, he sees her in the beautiful world of literary and theatrical whores and whoremasters, in the world of five minute loves and two month fidelities, in the world of the public pawing and frigging frolics—and although he is constantly told, in the argot now fashionable, that so-and-so is "a very grand person" and terribly misunderstood, that "so-and-so has something very fine and lovely in him or her in spite of all the things they say"— etc—he begins to doubt the lovely flower face, the innocent looks and words, the protestations of Forever! I have even had some commerce with one lady, who is a rich, young, and handsome Widow, and who is celebrated among her friends as a "Very Good Person," etc, and further as one of those faithful-unto-death wives who "went almost mad" when her husband died and "who has never got over it." The lady has got out a couple of volumes of memorial verse, she broods upon her husbands death all the time, and one of the volumes is prefaced by an <u>In Memoriam</u> poem written by her husbands friend, a fashionable T.S. Elioter, with whom she had gone to bed not two months after her true loves death:—they stood in the cold winds of March in the little New Eng. graveyard, these two grief stricken friends, before the worms had got even a good toe hold on the husband's carcass, and that night the Elioter was taken to the holy places—he did his poem which is bitter, fastidious, elegant, in the Eliot manner—and when the lady heard it she said it was just too beautiful and she wept; and they went to bed together sobbing and f—ing as if their dear little hearts would break—they were doing it for "purity," you see, out of memory for poor John, and not because of any desire for base personal gratification. Since that time, the lady has remembered John in many other beds and places: she prefers to remember him with poets of the T.S. Eliot school who have been well spoken-of by her friends, she will even remember him with baser fry of novelists, etc, who have been well spoken of, although she would not think of remembering him with Hugh Walpole or Cabell. When she gets ready to remember John with a young poet, she invites him into her parlor, she says it is too hot and pulls off her dress, after that she says she cannot bear to see you suffer so, poor boy! If that is what you want, take me, for God's sake, take me! I have nothing to offer you, but if it makes you happier, take it." So then they get into bed together, the lady and the Bard, on which she begins to behave very strangely—she moans and tosses about on the boy, and shakes her black hair tragically calling out "John! John! O darling, where are you? Why have you left me?" etc—at which the Bard whose name is not John but Henry gets alarmed and tries to crawl out—but the lady wont hear of this, she's too noble and big-hearted, she clutches him moaning: "No, no! Poor boy! If I give you any comfort take me, take me!" Then she looks at him with a strange tragic look, saying: "You're in bed with a dead woman. Don't you know that? My heart is dead, buried in the grave?

Late December 1930
Incomplete AL, 4 pp., Harvard
London

that is due me. Please don't do it if it is too much trouble, but if these people are trying to get money from me I can not afford to lose, I wish you would . You could then let me have the money as I need it, but they would not be able to touch it. I wish to God I could enjoy a little peace. (over)

I live alone here and	Tom Wolfe
work—my feeling	75 Ebury St
for America is like	London
an ache—I'll come	
back only when I know	

I've really got it well on the way—can you find me place in country

[new page]
Please do not hesitate to do this thing if it is necessary. I am not wronging or cheating anybody—I tell you this is the damnedest swindle that these men are perpetrating![1] For God's Sake, let's not allow them to triumph and gloat over righteousness without a struggle.

I am so homesick at times that its like the Black Death, and in addition to dentists, I get cables and letters from New York that wreck me. But so help me God, I believe I'm going to do this book, and that it will be good. You're the only person I've got left to look to—I can not help it if people in comfortable homes, with friends and family, would sneer at such an utterance—but I am a complete exile and solitary on the face of the earth: it is the Simple God's truth. I want to write you about the book—I think its all bound together now, and an idea hovers over the whole thing that thrills me. You gave me the idea once, and I have never forgotten it

---

1. TW proposed that Scribners bank his royalties and pay him a salary, in order to prevent claimants from attaching his earnings.

Incomplete AL, 6 pp., Harvard
Late December 1930   *London*

Dear Mr Perkins: I will not be beaten because I cannot be beaten. These puny bastards in New York and elsewhere who think I've been counted out by the old country-boy-who-comes-to-the-wicked-city hoakum are going to get a little surprise: I'm prepared to do a prodigy of work—I'll do such work for years to come as will make Anthony Trollope look sick by comparison[1]—the stuff is in me and it's bound to come. The only days on which I am beaten are those days on which I don't work; so for God's Sake help me to get settled without loss of time back in the Old Country.

My sore raw spot is simply the names of half a dozen people: the only way at present I can meet this problem is to stop people immediately when these names appear in any conversation—this is going to be difficult and get me in trouble but at present I shall follow this plan ruthlessly—I shall often be wrong and make myself ridiculous before many decent people, but I shall also thwart a number of cunning little bastards who failing to hurt one in himself try to get at him through something to which his feeling or affection has been attached. No one can hurt one in himself if he's all right in himself, and I am, or will be, all right.

Don't think this is simply another mania—the people like Madame B.[2] who deal in poison would call it a mania, but the real and final truth behind what I say is shown by people like this same woman—and there are many!

I have been to the offices of the N. German Lloyd[3]—the Europa leaves for America Feb 26 and gets there 4′ days later. If I take her, as I plan, I shall be back by March 3[d], and I want to be at my book again March 10.

I have really got now the passion for work—I mean I can work daily until I drop I have making all kinds of combinations and changes, but now I've got it on the rails, I think, even the titles. Do you know what I think my next book is going to be called, if you think it is publishable—Well, of course it is going to be called The October Fair, but that is the name of <u>three</u> books. I have fooled tentatively with many subtitles, such as <u>Antaeus</u>, <u>Faust and Helen</u>, etc—but it seems to me that one kind of good title ought to describe the book, and I have found one that I think is a grand title, and I hope you do it, too, although you may not like it at all. The title is <u>Love</u> <u>and</u> <u>Hunger</u> (part of The October Fair)

1. Prolific 19th-century British novelist.
2. Madeleine Boyd.
3. German ship line.

Incomplete AL, 4 pp., Harvard

Paris Feb. 20, 1931
Dear Mr. Perkins: Your cable saying you were writing came to me some time ago in London. I suppose your letter will be there when I go back. I have been away a

week; went to Holland and came back by Paris, and am staying here for two days. I worked until I left; since then I have done little.

I want you to forgive me for writing you all these long winded letters, filled with my troubles. Since then I have had time to think things over. It was wrong of me to write you as I did. You can do nothing. I must help myself now—nobody can help me. When I was a child I used to hear men say of some one: "He let wimmen and licker get him." I have let that happen to me, and now I must try to get the best of both of them. I do not know if I can, but I will try. I am thirty years old.

The woman, I think, is utterly, horribly bad—the thing's I have heard and know are like a nightmare; it is inconceivable that I could go on for years with a picture of her that had no relation to the truth; in my brain now I curse her, but in my heart I love her.

The thing is with me always. When I sleep it goes on. I am poisoned. The thing is like a poison; it is in my brain and heart, and it has tained my blood.

TO: *Charles Scribner III*   *ALS, 4 pp., Harvard*
12 November 1936

Dear Charles:

I have upon this present date written a letter to Maxwell Perkins in which I told him that the firm of Charles Scribners Sons are no longer, for any publication save those which have been previously been published by Charles Scribner's Sons, my publisher. It is a painful and chastising experience to renounce an agreement that does not exist, an understanding for the future that, however undefined, was mine alone, and in my mind alone; but in order that there may be no misunderstanding of my purpose, or of the meaning of this letter, I do state here and now that you are no longer my publisher—that you will never again be my publisher for anything that I may ever write; that I hearby renounce, adjure, abrogate, deny, and terminate any requests, claims, offers, inducements, obligations, commitments, or persuasions which you have made formerly, shall make now, or in the future make.

Faithfully and Sincerely Yours
T. Wolfe

                                                    AL draft, 3 pp., Harvard
12 November 1936   *New York*

Dear Max: I think you must write me a letter now in which you say: "Dear Tom: You are no longer connected with the firm of Charles Scribners Sons. You have discharged your contractual duties to us faithfully and honorably, you are under no contractual duties of any kind soever to us, we have been proud to publish your past works and we now release you from the only bond that holds you—the bond of your own loyalty, generosity, and devotion from a future connection with

Yours sincerely
Charles Scribners Sons

Presumed draft for longer letter, 3 pp., Harvard

Late November 1936

Dear Max: I acknowledge receipt of your three letters—your two personal letters of Nov. 17, 1936, and Nov. 18, 1936; and the business letter of Nov. 18, 1936, which accompanied your second letter.

First of all, as to the business letter—the answers you make, and the questions you raise.

You say "there are, of course, limits in terms, to which nobody can go in a contract, but we should expect to make one that would suit you if you told us what was required"—

I will tell you "what is required." You say that "there are, of course, limits in terms to which nobody can go in a contract—"

I should like to know what these "limits" are—and especially whether you really mean that you cannot go "to" them, or that you mean you cannot go beyond them.

In other words, what, specifically, are these "limits": what are your terms.

Incomplete AL, 8 pp., Harvard

Late November 1936

Dear Max: I have your letters—your two personal ones, and the business one and I am glad to get the acknowledgment that I asked for. First of all, in reference to your typed letter, the one that represents the position of the Scribner firm: I am sorry if you had any difficulty in understanding anything in my own letter: You say "we do not wholly understand parts of your letter," and I will try to explain them to you. First, you say you do not understand the part where "you speak of us as denying an obligation that does not exist, for we do not know that we have done that" Now Max, what I said in my letter was this: "I think it is unfair to put a man in a position where he is forced to deny an obligation that does not exist, to refuse an agreement that was never offered and never made"—I am sorry if you found this obscure or hard to understand, because all I meant to say here was that I thought it was unfair to put a man in a position where he was forced to deny an obligation which did not exist, refuse an agreement that had never been offered and that had never been made

Upon examining this statement again, I find it to be a plain and simple statement of blunt fact, and I hope this explanation makes that portion of the letter clear.

You say that "we should expect to make one that would suit you if you told us what was required

I find this simply amazingly, perfectly beautiful. Since when, have authors had the glorious—(and I think,—<u>just</u>)—privilege of telling their publishers what, in terms of contract, was "required"

—You added,—(somewhat thriftily, I thought)—that "there are, of course, limits in terms to which nobody can go in a contract, but we should expect to make one that would suit you if you told us what was required

—Now, Max, it seems to me that all this is beside the point.

AL draft, 17 pp., Harvard

Late November 1936

Dear Max: I am writing to tell you that I have at last taken the step of communicating formally to other publishers the severance of my relations with Charles Scribners Sons. It is true that no formal relation between us existed, and that both you and Charlie have told me I was free to go. But I think the relation existed in our minds, at any rate, and for me—I believe for you, as well,—it existed in the heart.

If any apprehensions concerning my letter to the publishers may exist in the minds of any of you—and I know they will not exist in yours—let me assure you at once that I spoke of my former publisher in such a way as left no doubt as to my own earnestness and sincerity, or as to my own belief in the integrity and high [capability] of your house. No one could read that letter without understanding that the necessity for this severance is a matter of deep and poignant regret to all of us *[These last four words are at the head of otherwise blank page.]*

I am sick and tired, but I believe that I shall rise again, as I have done before: . . . . I know that for a time now the world will say that you and I have fallen out, that the great sounding-board of rumor and malicious gossip that echoes round and round the granite walls of this little universe, the city, will frame its hundred little stories and that all of them, as usual, will be false.

—I know that they will say this and that—

well, <u>let</u> them say.

That is honestly the way I feel now.

The editorial relation between us, which began—it seems to me—so hopefully, and for me so wonderfully, has now and lost its initial substance. It has become a myth—and what is worse than that, an untrue myth—and it seems to me that both of us are victims of that myth. You know the terms of the myth well enough:—it was venomously recorded by a man named De Voto in The Saturday Review of Literature during this past summer—And the terms of the myth are these:—that I cannot write my books without your assistance, that there exists at Scribner's an "assembly line" that must fit the great dismembered portions of my manuscript together into a semblance of unity, that I am unable to perform these functions of an artist for myself. How far from the truth these suppositions are you know yourself better than any one on earth. There are few men—certainly no man I have ever known—who is more sure of <u>purpose</u> than myself. There are many many men, of course, who are more sure of <u>means</u>—but that assurance, with such men, is just a small one—with me, it is a hard and [thorny] one, because my means must be my own.

I know that you will not be uncandid enough to deny that these differences and misunderstandings have become profound and fundamental. *[Four lines on an otherwise blank page.]*

Plainly may I tell you that I think that looking like a plain man, you are not a plain man; that speaking like a simple man, you are not a simple man; that speaking in words and phrases that as time went on enchanted and assured me by their simplicity and innocent directness, so that they seemed to be the very character of your soul, I do not now believe that they were so!

In fact, I now believe you are not a plain man—you are an un-plain man I do not believe you are a simple man—you are an un-simple man

I do not believe your words

I impeach your motives and your conduct: may I tell you frankly, plainly, that I do not believe they have achieved and maintained always the quality of unconditioned innocence, faith, good will, and simple and direct integrity that you have always claimed for them

The fault, I think, is here: that having so much that belonged to humankind, you lacked—or you with-held—what makes us one

And therefore I renounce you, who have already, for so long a time, renounced me and got so safely, with no guilt or wrong, so freely rid of me.

ALS fragment, 3 pp., Harvard

Late November 1936

. . . . and I am writing therefore now to tell you that I am, upon the date of these words, dissolving a relationship that does not exist, renouncing a contract that was never made, severing myself, and of my own accord, a bond of loyalty, devotion, and self-sacrifice that existed solely, simply, and entirely within my own mind, and to my own past grief of doubt, my present grief of sorrow, loss, and final understanding.

With infinite regret, my dear Max, with the deepest and most genuine sorrow, with an assurance—if you will generously accept it—of my friendship for yourself

Faithfully And Sincerely

Yours -
Thomas Wolfe

AL fragment, 1 p., Harvard

Late November 1936

I understand that you have been afraid that some day I might "write about" you. Well, you need not be afraid any longer The day has come—and I am writing about you. Your fears have been realized—I think you will find that your fears, like most fears, have been exaggerated.[1]

1. TW wrote an unpublished story, "The Fox and the Lion," in which Foxhall Edwards is clearly based on MP. Other TW writings about Foxhall Edwards and the James Rodney publishing company appear in *The Web and the Rock* and *You Can't Go Home Again.*

AL fragment, 3 pp., Harvard

Late November 1936

This is one of the saddest and most melancholy occasions of my life. To say now that I have "thought about" this thing, or "arrived at certain conclusions" would be ludicrous. I have not thought about the thing—I have sweat blood about it; I have carried it with me like a waking nightmare in the day time, and like a sleeping torment in the night. I have not "arrived" at my conclusions; I have come to them through every anguish that the brain, heart, nerves, and soul of man can know—and I am <u>there</u> at last. I can't go on in this way: it is a matter of the most desperate uncertainty whether I can go on at all. For seven years I have been increasingly aware of the seepage of my talents, the diminution of my powers, the dilution of my force—and I can not go on.

AL fragment, 2 pp., Harvard

Late November 1936

I am therefore asking you to send me at once an unqualified and unequivocal statement to this effect: that I have discharged all debts and all contractual obligations to the firm of Charles Scribners Sons, and that I am no longer under any obligation to them whether personal, financial, or contractual *[two words]* I want you to make this statement in your own language, but according to the terms I have mentioned, if you think them just!

AL fragment, 1 p., Harvard

Late November 1936

In the name of honesty and sincerity, I can write no more than here I have written: in the name of justice and of fairness you can, and will, write no less,

∽

AL fragment, 1 p., Harvard

Late November 1936

I beg and request you to send me at once, without intervention of personal conversations or telephone call this letter that I am asking you to write.

∽

Incomplete AL, 1 p., Harvard

December 1936

Dear Max: I am writing to tell you that I have written and mailed a letter to various publishers in which I

∽

AL fragment, 1 p., Harvard

December 1936

I suggest this—that you make your offer—and name unequivocally the highest possible sum that you are prepared to pay as an advance. I shall then submit this offer to other publishers, and see if they are willing to meet it.

∽

ALS fragment, 1 p., Harvard

December 1936

Novel Why Do You Not Make Royalty Statements And Send Money On This And Other Books

Respectfully
Thomas Wolfe

AL fragment, 1 p., Harvard

December 1936

Dear Max: I am returning South, where I was born, for the first time in seven years, and before I [go], I want to write in answer [to] the letters which you wrote a month ago.

⌒

AL fragment, 1 p., Harvard

December 1936

I can't tell you how much I appreciate your interest in my new book. The knowledge that I have your affectionate and kind regard in what I do means more to me than I can here express. When you wrote me last Spring that I was free to go wherever I wished, and that wherever I went

And the fact that your letters have the same friendly tone as they had then makes my sense of obligation all the greater.

⌒

ALS, 10 pp., Harvard
Roosevelt Hotel letterhead, New Orleans

Early January 1937

Cornelius Mitchell has written me an astounding letter in answer to one I wrote him in Dooher matter. I had supposed the evidence against Dooher to be complete and overwhelming but now instead of telling me what we are going to do he tells me of fantastic threats that Dooher is making and requests my instant return to New York This I unconditionally refuse to do I have come here for a rest of which I was in desperate need, this amazing letter has caused me the most intense distress, I have been hounded by this shameful business for a year and a half now— and it has got to stop! I am an honorable man and an artist—and the crucial thing <u>now</u> is that my work and talent are being destroyed. Mitchell says he got my address here from you. In the name of God, knowing the state of health and utter exhaustion I was in when I left New York, how could you do it? Max, I have begun to lose faith in your power to stick or to help when a man is in danger, I know now that I must fight this whole horrible business out alone—the whole vicious complex of slander, blackmail, theft, and parasitic infamy that menaces and usually destroys the artist under this accursed and rotten system that now exists in America. You are going to get out from under when you see me threatened with calamity—but, in the name of God, in the name of all the faith and devotion and unquestioning belief I have had in you—if you can not help me, for Christ's sake, do not add your own influence to those who are now trying to destroy me. Under <u>no</u> conditions, save the death or serious illness of a member of my family,—do not give my address hereafter to anyone. Before I come back to that black and vicious horror again, I must restore myself—I shall fight to the end, but for Christ's sake have manhood now not to aid in the attack until I can try to mend a little in energy and health

Tom Wolfe

❧

The following drafts and fragments relate to TW's 7–9 January 1937 communications with MP. The handwriting suggests that TW wrote these documents when drunk.

Early January 1937   *AL wire draft, 2 pp., Harvard*
                                        Roosevelt Hotel letterhead, New Orleans

Mr Maxwell Perkins

Was simply astounded to know you gave Mitchell my address—I told you to give no one at Scribners my address—As result of your giving Mitchell my address when no one else would take them on—my health has been impaired

❧

Early January 1937   *AL wire draft, 1 p., Harvard*
                                        Roosevelt Hotel letterhead, New Orleans

Maxwell Perkins
Chas Scribner Sons,
N.Y.C.

Was astounded and horrified to know you gave Mitchell my address—I told you to give no one my address

❧

Early January 1937   *AL wire draft, 1 p., Harvard*
                                        Roosevelt Hotel letterhead, New Orleans

Cornelius Mitchell has written me a letter which blackmail disturbed my peace, [   ] my money, and ruined my happiness—He [   ] that address for

❧

Early January 1937   *AL fragment, 2 pp., Harvard*
                                        Roosevelt Hotel letterhead, New Orleans

Mitchell—says I must now return NY for I have of course as impossible and Mitchell with the threats continued in his letter has destroyed my health and the pleasure of my trip My health and talent are now [   ]. You can answer this telegram as a bidder for my body but not as a [   ] You that is must send letter [   ] from you

⌒

Early January 1937   *ALS fragment, 1 p., Harvard*
Roosevelt Hotel letterhead, New Orleans

me that you too are in the destruction plot I do not believe it—
    <u>What may you</u>
      You may [   ] here
                                    Wolfe

    P.S.
    and must

⌒

Early January 1937   *AL wire draft, 1 p., Harvard*
Roosevelt Hotel letterhead, New Orleans

Mr. M. E. Perkins

Was simply astounded at C/Mitchell's letter—I thought had been settled all was over but now it is All else I told you to give no one my address and you gave it

⌒

Early January 1937   *AL fragment, 1 p., Harvard*
Roosevelt Hotel letterhead, New Orleans

On your advisal I took the suit. I look to you for explicit and unequivocal answer at once

⌒

Three drafts of this letter survive: a thirteen-page manuscript dated 15 July 1936; an undated five-page revised typescript; and an incomplete one-page retyping. With these drafts is a 2–page note by Edward C. Aswell:

> Tom gave me this letter in Dec. 1937, because he said it could explain the nature of his severance with Scribners. It was written in the early part of that year, and was intended at the time as an approach to several publishers who might be interested in his work As I recall what Tom told me, the letter was never sent. Instead, Tom phoned several publishers from Asheville when he went there in the summer of 1937.

TO: *All publishers*
March 1937

Unmailed TL with holograph revisions,
5 pp., Harvard

Gentlemen:

I am the author of four published books, of which two are novels, one, a book of stories, and one, a short volume about my experience as a writer. Since I am no longer under any obligation, whether financial, contractual, or personal, to any publisher, I am writing to inquire if I could talk to you about my future work.

In order that there may be nothing in this letter capable of misinterpretation, I want to state here with the utmost candour my reasons for writing you. First of all, I want to say most earnestly that I am not approaching any publisher at the present time in an effort to secure good terms and get a contract, but in the genuine hope that this letter will reach some person of critical judgment and understanding who will be interested - and disinterested - enough to listen to my story, allow me to lay the matter before him, with all its difficulties and complexities, and then, if he can, give me the benefit of his advice.

This would involve the discussion of unpublished manuscript that runs into millions of words, and projects for work that will occupy me for years. I realize that to ask for advice and guidance of this sort from people that I do not know, when I have at the present time no completed work to offer for examination, is a strenuous and perhaps unwarranted demand upon the generosity of a stranger, but necessity of the gravest kind has compelled me to this course as being the only one that is now left open to me.

May I say here that so far as my relations with my former publishers are concerned, they have been characterized from beginning to end on both sides by feelings of the deepest affection and respect. I have been fortunate in having for my publishers a firm which not only enjoys a public and professional standing of the highest order but which, in all its dealings with me has been eminently just and fair. Moreover, the nature of our relationship has been so peculiarly intimate and personal that no one can possibly know, better than myself, the gravity of the step I am now taking, or the peril with which it is charged.

For seven years or more I have enjoyed the friendship of an editor of extraordinary character and ability, who at a time when I needed help desperately, when I was trying to learn how to write, when I was involved with gigantic masses of material and struggling with a task of such magnitude that at times I almost gave up in despair, stood by me and gave me without stint not only the benefits of his great technical and editorial skill but also the even more priceless support of his faith and belief, a spiritual sustenance of the grandest and most unselfish kind. To this man I owe a debt of gratitude so deep and lasting that I feel I can never repay it, or never sufficiently testify to it by anything I say or write. And the prospect of this severance of our relations - professionally, at any rate - not only with this man but with many other people in that house, is for me not only a prospect of the utmost gravity, but it is like having to face the [prospect] of making a new, and perhaps disastrous, beginning in my life.

But I can see no other course before me. For months now, perhaps for a year, or more, there has been a steady widening of the ground between us, a difference of opinion, of conviction, of belief, even a spiritual severance that is so profound and grave that it touches the very heart of my life and work, and if I remain I see no prospect before me but the utter enervation of my work, my final bafflement and frustration as an artist.

I should like to say here further that the necessity which compels me to write this letter is, I believe, understood and appreciated thoroughly by my former publishers, has been examined and discussed so thoroughly in the conversation and correspondence of several months that there is now nothing more to say on either side, except that this necessity is a matter of the most genuine and profound regret to each of us.

Now, I can only say, with utter candour, that I hope that I am prepared to do the best work of my life, but that, if I am to do any work at all, I can now do it only by making no compromise of artistic integrity, by making rather the most full, free, honest, and final use of my talents and of my materials that I have ever made.

Finally I should like to say that these differences, I believe, were inevitable and inescapable, that they have been honorably and honestly arrived at on both sides, and that the feeling of friendship and respect between my publishers and myself is as deep as it always was. I believe that they would confirm me in all I say.

To have to write in a formal letter, and at such length, explanations of such intimate and personal concern to myself and other people, is a painful and difficult task. But it seemed to me that, circumstances being what they are, to write less explicitly than I have might lay open to misinterpretation not only my own position but my relations to other people whose conduct has been generous and high.

As I have no wide acquaintance in the publishing profession I have taken this means, as difficult as it is, as being the only one by which I could state my problem and establish contact with someone who might help me. Accordingly, I have addressed this letter to several publishers.

But, so far as possible within these limitations, I hope that the contents of this letter will be treated as personal and confidential.

Sincerely Yours

I believe that I am now engaged upon the most important book that I have ever written. But the book is far from complete: a great task is before me. Now I should like to talk to some editor of critical understanding and judgment, for the purpose of laying the matter before him, with complete frankness and with all the difficulties and perplexities it entails.

If there is such a person in your house who is willing to give me an evening's time, with no commitments on either side, I should be grateful for his courtesy in doing so. I can be reached at this address, and any evening after March twenty-fifth would be convenient.

Appendix 3

Maxwell Perkins's Biographical Observations on Thomas Wolfe

On 14 March 1935 MP provided Lawrence Greene of the Philadelphia Evening Public Ledger *with replies to questions submitted by Greene for a syndicated article on TW; the questions have not been located. The article was not published in the* Ledger. *MP stipulated in a cover letter that his name was not "to appear in connection with the article" (PUL).*

CC, 6 pp., PUL

1. I also enclose a brief statement of some of the facts of Mr. Wolfe's life, which will complete the answer to this question. He began to write for publication about three years before the publication of "Look Homeward Angel" which appeared in 1929. Before that he had written two plays but neither one was ever produced although those to whom they were submitted did discern the great talent of the man. Probably the play form is too precise and sharply limited for his sort of expansive genius.

2. The members of Mr. Wolfe's family have always been extraordinarily loyal to him. The book was based upon his own life, and the characters in "Look Homeward" though never literally transcribed, of course, were based upon the members of his family. So many intimate things, such as the death of his brother Ben, were in the book that it no doubt was painful reading for members of the family, but there was never any rift between him and them. They rejoiced in the great success of the book. He is in touch with them all the time, even though they live at a distance, and often goes to see them, or sees them when they come to New York. They are a most loyal family, and an affectionate one.

3. Mr. Wolfe is about six feet six, and proportionately broad and strong. He is so striking in appearance that people look at him wherever he goes. When he is troubled or indignant his brow resembles that in the popular picture of Beethoven, clouded and frowning. His face is very mobile and expressive more often of humorous penetration than anything else. He talks almost in the way in which he writes,- most eloquently and humorously, using much less slang or profanity than most conventionally educated men.

He dresses conservatively but has trouble on account of his size, in getting fitted and he is careless about his appearance so that his waistcoat and the tops of his trousers do not always meet. He invariably wears a black felt hat. He smokes cigarettes and as his books indicate, enjoys eating and drinking, and all of what is known of the good things of life.

He writes voluminously, and with great rapidity. He keeps many notebooks. Going abroad, he left four crates of manuscript books as large as a large office desk in the keeping of his publishers.

4. "Look Homeward Angel" was brought to Scribners by an agent who exacted the promise that every word of it would be read. It was about 500,000[1] words long. It had been declined by a number of other publishers, and the author had given up all hope of its publication. It immediately excited the Scribner editorial staff. Mr. Wolfe was in Europe. As soon as he returned, the work of reducing its size was begun. The list of the books which he plans, as well as the ones which he has published, is given in the front of the book.[2] The next book will be presumably approximately as long as this one which runs to 500,000 words. After that there are three others in prospect, the length of which cannot now be estimated.

Mr. Wolfe writes with a pencil, in a very large hand. He once said that he could write the best advertisement imaginable for the Frigidaire people since he had never been able to make the usual uses of a frigidaire, but had found it exactly the right height to write on when standing, and with enough space for him to handle his manuscript on the top. He writes mostly standing in that way, and frequently strides about the room when unable to find the right way of expressing himself. He has almost no sense of time, and therefore a schedule is a thing that never could exist for him. He has frequently been two hours late for an appointment with his editor, and it is doubtful if he has ever been on time. The dimensions of everything, physical and abstract, are too small for him.

5. The sale in the year following the publication of "Look Homeward Angel" was probably not more than 12,000 copies. The book was not reviewed by the prominent reviewers, though it received many very enthusiastic reviews from those to whom it was given by the papers. Its sale in the years following has more than doubled the sale of the first year,- which is most unusual in these days. It is now in the Modern Library, and selling extremely well there. Evidently the book will sell for many years,- no one could guess at how many.

6. The story about Thomas Wolfe jumping off the train is substantially true.[3]

His great curiosity leads him, at times when he is not working hard, to prowl around the city all night long, in the markets along the waterfronts, on the bridges, in the saloon, observing and listening, and studying. Many of the people whom he rates as friends are waiters in restaurants all over the city. He has often turned up here when the office opened in the morning, after walking about the city all night alone. On the night before he sailed for Europe he was to dine at the house of some friends. The hostess, knowing his ideas of time were unreliable, asked him to be there at half past six, thinking he might then be at seven.[4] He arrived at eight and rushed in full of apologies, to say that he had been delayed because he had tried to deliver the manuscript of "October Fair" at the offices of his publishers but that their building had been closed. He begged that he might leave it in his friends' house. The lady, expecting a sizable package that could be put away in a bureau drawer, immediately agreed. He disappeared into the street. There were sounds of bumping and thumping, and finally he and a taxicab driver rolled in a huge wooden box, too heavy to lift, which to the lady's dismay blocked up the entire hall. The man of the house, observing the exhausted state of the driver, brought him a cocktail. Everyone drank cocktails from the top of the crate, and Wolfe asked the taxi man his name. He said it was Good Luck. This overjoyed Mr. Wolfe who thereupon insisted upon his drinking another cocktail.[5]

7. His next book will be a book of stories running in length to 150,000 words. That will be published in the fall of 1935. Presumably the following book will be published the following fall, or possibly in the spring of 1936. It is already complete, but needs to be revised and no doubt will also contain many additions to what now exists.[6]

8. There is hardly anything he is not interested in. His curiosity is omnivorous. He wants to know about everything and will sit up any night as long as anybody else will do it, talking. The questions of the depression, of communism, etc., are greatly in his mind at present. He has a passion for trains and boats. Painting is something that he has never studied, but has an extraordinary understanding for and sympathy with. He never forgets a picture and can describe most of the famous masterpieces in the museums of Europe.

It is difficult to deal with the question about the autobiographical in his writing. The writings of a great novelist are in some considerable degree autobiographical.- He always creates out of what is seen, and in fact, the best novels of almost every great novelist, like "David Copperfield," "Pendennis," Tolstoi's "War and Peace" etc., are very close indeed to autobiography, but everything in them is different from what it really was, has been transmuted in passing through the imagination of the writer. It is this way with Thomas Wolfe. None of the people are literally as he presents them, nor are any of the happenings. They are the basis out of which he creates a world. Wolfe's books certainly are more autobiographical than "David Copperfield" but the difference is only one in degree. Wolfe is really doing what every great novelist has done. His materials are taken from what he has seen and what has happened to him, but they are all transmuted in the imagination. Presumably his later books will be of that same sort.

9. It is difficult to answer this question precisely since reviews have been published all over the country in every sort of medium,- in critical articles between the publication of "Look Homeward Angel" and of "Of Time and the River." He has published some eight or ten stories in Scribner's, The Virginia Quarterly Review, the Modern Monthly, the Mercury, and will soon have one published in Harper's Bazaar.

I do not think any articles about him alone have been published in any magazine, but he has been referred to in many of them on literary matters.

10. Mr. Wolfe is not very much influenced by the opinions of critics. His writings have run contrary to the tendencies in recent literature, and he has no intention of bending himself to current fashions or popular trends. He is not, however, satisfied with his work by any means,- far from it. His writing is done as the result of an enormous struggle, and his desire is to express things so difficult of being grasped and comprehended within any measurable scope that he perhaps never

could be satisfied. He has a sense of America as utterly different from any other country, and wrestles with the effort to express that.- America never has been comprehended and put into a synthesis of thought as England has, or any other nation which is old. This vast, lonely, inchoate continent which yet has got a stamp of unity upon it, and even upon its conglomerate people, is one of the things he wants to utter. Only a giant and a poet could do it,- but he is both a giant and a poet. He never could be called a "Patriot." There isn't a trace of Chauvinism in him. He rages against much that is American. He loves Europe too, and has written beautifully of it in "Of Time and the River" and elsewhere. But he feels the Americaness of this nation as it is today, when an East Side Jew, or Greek, or a northwestern Scandinavian, or a New England Portuguese, are really Americans now and not what their previous nationality would indicate. It is this vast people who inhabit America and the great physical America itself that he wants to give voice to.

11. He is not married, and never has been.

1. The actual length was closer to 275,000 words.

2. *Of Time and the River.*

3. On 26 January 1932 TW intended to accompany MP one evening to his editor's home in New Canaan, Conn.; but TW decided to remain in the city and jumped off the train as it was leaving Grand Central Station and severely injured his arm.

4. The hostess was Louise Perkins.

5. MP also recounted this anecdote in "Thomas Wolfe," *Harvard Library Bulletin* (Autumn 1947): "Tom and I and the taxi man carried it in and set it down. Then Tom said to the man, 'What is your name?' He said 'Lucky.' 'Lucky!' said Tom—I think it was perhaps an Americanization of some Italian name—and grasped his hand. It seemed a good omen. We three had done something together. We were together for that moment. We all shook hands. But for days, that huge packing case blocked our hall until I got it removed to Scribner's" (270).

6. Scribners did not publish TW's third novel; *The Web and the Rock* (1939) was published posthumously by Harper.

A photocopy of the following Maxwell Perkins document with his manuscript revisions was found by Matthew J. Bruccoli in 2000 with a file of F. Scott Fitzgerald material. The original has not been located.

Perkins was responding to a series of questions, but the circumstances are unknown. No published use of this material has been identified. Perkins's answers were written in 1940 or later, as indicated by the mention of You Can't Go Home Again. *Richard S. Kennedy has pointed out an error in section 11: The passage in "The Hills Beyond Pentland" where "George Webber and his Uncle sit on a hillside" appeared in* The Web and the Rock, *not in* You Can't Go Home Again.

1. I think the passage referred to at the end of "You Can't Go Home Again" shows conclusively that Tom had come to a belief in continued life after death. This was presumably written some eight months before his death too, and it is very curious and I can't explain it. I had hardly seen Tom for a year or more. Before that time,

when I saw him constantly, I never knew him to show any sort of belief in a future life, nor to have any formulated religious views. In a vague and general way, there is a sort of religious feeling conveyed in his novels.- But I always did think that Tom was the kind of a man who should have been in some sense religious, and in fact would have been. In truth all this searching for a father, was searching for God even though it was never realized by Tom himself,- at least until that final year. I attach a copy of the letter which was the last thing he ever wrote. It was written in pencil on the very day that his illness took its fatal turn, and when it still appeared that he was getting well. I think that by inference this throws light on the question you ask.

2. Thomas Wolfe was not in the least political-minded, and still less was he economically minded. I think he never voted for any ticket but the Democratic,- which is the ticket all North Carolinians vote for anyhow. He was radical only in a personal way,- and in fact writers have almost all been radicals in that sense. That is, they are more sensitive to injustice and inequalities than other people who accept the conventions of society generally as being as inevitable as the law of gravitation. "The Angel" and all his books show his rebellion against social injustice, but he subscribed to no program to remove it. At one time I think he came pretty close to joining the Communist party, but in truth he could not have done it, for it was not in his nature. He had wholly turned away from Communism a year or so before his death.

3. All of the Wolfe family, except perhaps one, are people of amazingly strong emotions and one of the strongest of all is that of loyalty to each other, to the tribe. But not one of them can get along comfortably with any other because of the characteristics that come out in Tom's novels. Fred, for instance, who is Luke in the novels, is one of the most likable people in the world, but he has the characteristics ascribed to him, and they would drive Tom crazy. The mother's interminable talk, which is good except in being interminable, was as represented in Eliza. That too would drive Tom, and all the other children, wild. Still, they all had a tremendously strong family feeling toward each other. When we were working here on "The Angel", and well into the revision of it, I suddenly fully realized that these people— though transmuted in Tom's imagination—were the members of his own family. I was horrified, and showed it in my expression, and Tom wriggling in his chair from embarrassment, said: "But you don't understand. I think these people are great people." In other words, he knew that he would give them pain, but in a sense he was celebrating them. They were great characters, he thought, and important. They are astonishing people too in their own qualities.

4. His family did not understand his wanting to be a writer. I think Eliza's view as shown in the early part of "Of Time and the River" was probably typical, except perhaps for Mabel, i.e. Helen. She is extremely intelligent. She would have read his books except that, as she told me, they gave her too much pain. She couldn't bear to read "The Angel". I don't really think any of the other members of the family understood very well what a book was. And I doubt if any of them really read any of his books, and certainly not with much understanding.

His family though, did realize—and I think it was greatly to their credit—that Tom was unusual, and I don't think that his mother or sisters, at any rate, begrudged him any of the money that was given him. Possibly the boys felt a little bit of jealousy, as has sometimes been suggested.

As a matter of fact, his family are none of them miserly at all. His mother wanted to acquire property, and it seems to me that she was parsimonious for the sake of getting money to do it with. I do think, in fact, Tom was unfair in his representation of his family,- except that of course he was writing a novel, and was making them something different from what they actually were. But Tom did have a sense of being abused, which seems to be a characteristic of mountaineers. He did think that he had been unfairly treated, and once just before the publication of "Of Time and the River" I said to him that I thought he had been amazingly well treated by his family, and favored, and that it was remarkable that they, living shut in there in the mountains, should have realized his unusual qualities and given him special opportunities.- And he said then, "I am just beginning to see it that way." I do think Mrs. Wolfe was unfairly treated if Eliza is to be taken as a literal portrayal of her. She did have that instinct for keeping everything, storing it up, but so did Tom himself, and he was very free with money.

6. Wolfe's emotions ran away with him, and to great lengths, especially when his work was in any way involved. But on those occasions when he was objective, he showed unusual intellectual power. On the whole, however, he was governed by emotions.

7. He was often amazingly unreasonable, and his anger was sometimes uncontrollable. He was sometimes very cruel indeed, and apparently with little reason,- as when he told an unhappy writer who had got to his fifties and had begun to realize he amounted to little, that the trouble with him was he had thought himself a great writer, and found he was no good at all. He said very cruel things to many people,- but one realized that the reason was generally that he was himself so tormented as to somehow have to release his emotion against something. That those who knew him realized this is shown by the very remarkable fact that although he wronged many, every one of them forgave him. For instance, the original of Mrs. Jack, and the original of Jerry Alsop.[1]

Someone once characterized him as having in him an archangel and ten thousand devils. All the devils in the world cannot cancel an archangel. This expressed the feeling people always had that he was a towering and a noble being. But yet there were in him the ten thousand devils, too.

8. I do not think James Joyce was ever a great idol of Tom's. Or that any contemporary writer was anything like that. He was at one time somewhat under the influence of Ulysses, as appears in "The Angel" but Tom's feeling for him was very far indeed this side idolatry. He knew many writers including Fitzgerald, Hemingway, Marjorie Rawlings, James Boyd, Sherwood Anderson, etc. But I don't think he ever read any of them to any extent. He certainly felt that the talent in him made him vastly more important than they.- And yet there was nothing of conceit in Tom, nor vanity. I tried to explain this in one of the pieces I sent you. He read the old books greatly. One of the chief influences on him was DeQuincey. He had, I think, read the whole of Burton's "The Anatomy of Melancholy". One of his favorite poems was "The Ancient Mariner".

9. Tom had almost no sense of humor when he was concerned with his work,- and this was most of the time. When he wasn't, he was a most humorous man.

10. Tom never was expelled from college. He had often told me of the hazing incident as something that happened before he went to college. It made a great impression on him, but he wasn't, I am practically positive, concerned in it.- And I don't fully understand why he put that part into the book, especially in that part of it. One could have understood his putting it into the narrative of George Webber's college days, or of Eugene's.

11. What was to have been "The October Fair" is now "Of Time and the River" and the second half of "The Web and the Rock", that is, the love story part. "The Hills Beyond Pentland" was never written, except in part, and those parts are in "You Can't Go Home Again",- for instance, the place where the boy George Webber and his uncle sit on a hillside, I think, and his uncle tells him about the family. All that Thomas Wolfe wrote was moved around by him and by others in the process of publishing. There are things even in the last two books which were written far back. The incident of the two boys watching Jeb Stuart's troops go through Pennsylvania, which is told as a remembrance of the dying Gant in Baltimore, was originally the very beginning of "Look Homeward Angel". None of Tom's writings were ever lost. If some fragment was not used in one book, it was used in another, and that would always have been true.- But very little of "The Hills beyond Pentland" was ever written.

12. I think it highly probable in fact I should think certain, that Tom Wolfe did really pick his father up when intoxicated.

13. Mrs. Wolfe did, through her boarding house, accumulate enough to buy property both in Asheville and in Florida. At one time if she had sold at the current prices, she would have had a fortune of $500,000, so Tom said. Unfortunately she was buying in a boom and she did not sell, and her values went to practically nothing, and left her in debt. Mr. Wolfe was in fact more successful. He invested also in realestate somewhat, and on his death he left $100,000.

1. Aline Bernstein and John Skally Terry.

Appendix 4

Errors and Inconsistencies in the
Published Text of *Look Homeward, Angel*

Maxwell Perkins was a notably bad proofreader who delegated this chore to his secretary, Irma Wyckoff, or to other editors. John Hall Wheelock was primarily responsible for proofing Look Homeward, Angel; *he was a better proofreader than Perkins but shared Perkins's lack of concern about textual errors. Wolfe read the proofs for* Look Homeward, Angel *(see Wolfe/Wheelock letters for July 1930); but his marked galleys do not survive. Many of the cruces in* Look Homeward, Angel *originated in Wolfe's lost setting-copy typescript for "O Lost."*

Louis N. Feipel made a hobby of proofreading published books. None of the errors or inconsistencies that he noted in Look Homeward, Angel *was emended.*

TLS, 12 pp., PUL

One Hanson Place, Brooklyn, New York,
June 23, 1930.

Mr. Thomas Wolfe,
    c/o Charles Scribner's Sons
      New York, N. Y.

Dear Sir:

    I enjoyed reading your book, "Look Homeward, Angel"; and while doing so I made note of certain points about its editing, typesetting, and proof-reading (subjects in which I specialize), with the following results, which may be of interest to you.

(?) Misprints or Editorial Lapses

threshhold (p.180)	? should be	threshold
ilk (184)	? "	silk
alloted (285)	? "	allotted
ærial (297)	? "	aerial [as on p.295 ff.]
staioned (506)	? "	stationed
glueily (167)	? "	gluily [as on p.109]
hussey (104)	? "	hussy

gorsey (223)	?	"	gorsy
domey (462)	?	"	domy
Prosperine (277)	?	"	Proserpine
Smollet (422)	?	"	Smollett
goins-on (288)	?	"	goin's-on
jews-harp (333)	?	"	jew's-harp <u>or</u> jews'-harp
Rhode's Scholar (397)	?	"	Rhodes Scholar [as on p.487]
pine comb (88)	?	"	pine cone
oats sack (47)	?	"	oat sack [as on p.519]
at the Hilliards (173 ff.)	?	"	at the Hilliards'
the...minutia of her transaction (440)	?	"	...minutiae...
in the...pullman (457)	?	"	...Pullman [as on pp. 417, 601]
the mounting and triumphal greek which described the moment (308)	?	"	...Greek...
His calloused feet (514)	?	"	...callused...
calloused palm (516)	?	"	...callused...
devoured a chest full of dime novels (156)	?	"	...a chestful of... cf. ladelfuls of oysters (187)
the thousand phantom shapes that beaconed (473)	?	"	...beckoned cf. all groups were beckoning him (488)
the blue great cup of the hills seem closer (95)	?	"	...seems...
neither Eliza nor Gant were at any pains to... (112)	?	"	...was at any pains...
when his heart or head were deeply involved (116)	?	"	...was deeply involved
all the devices...sunk so deeply... (103)	?	"	...sank... cf.He sank his fingers in...(331) The...words...sank...(392)
he had, more than any of the family (120)	?	"	...more than any other member of the family
although each felt dumbly that they had come...(129)	?	"	although both...
and especially necessary that she feel her efforts had gone unappreciated (133)	?	"	...had not gone unappreciated

Orthographic Inconsistencies

whisky (23 ff.)	<u>vs.</u> whiskey (303 ff.)
story [floor] 76 ff.	storey (407)
good-by (53 ff.)	good-bye (352)
darkey (132 ff.)	darkies (157 ff.)

moneyed (104)   monied (573)
snicker (291 ff.)   snigger (298 ff.)
fantasy (86 ff.)   phantasy (56 ff.)
chitlins (74)   chitlings (174)
plowed (156) plowman (324)   plough (487)
gaily (145 ff.) gaiety (64 ff.)   gayly (338)
slily (93 ff.)   slyly (65 ff.)
                  dryly (60 ff.) spryly (98) shyly (272)

unshakable (5) likable (121)   unnameable (575)
corseted (285) uncorseted (266)   corsetted (146 ff.)
jacketed (330)
uncarpeted (408)
buffeted (232) coroneted (197)
recognize (369 ff.)   criticise (238)
realize (379 ff.) economize (531) &c.

plumtree (9 ff.)   <u>vs.</u> plum-tree (165 ff.)   <u>vs.</u> plum tree (15)
                   apple-tree (455)   apple tree (68)
                   chestnut-tree (451)   cherry tree (39 ff.) &c.
grapevine (181)   grape vine (16)
roseleaf (186)   dock-leaf (452)   mine leaf (85)
                                oak leaf (88) &c.
lilystalk (4)   lily stipe (618)
fingernail (198 ff.)   toe-nail (176)
goathoof (95)   mule-hoof (6)
horseback (374)   horse-back (161)
horsehead (172)
cornfield (173)   daisy-field (85)   coal field (144)
flowerbed (329)   flower-bed (466)   lily bed (28 ff.)
farmland (605)   mountain land (8)
pineland (191)   flower land (71)
                                waste land (215 ff.)

inksmell (112)   ink-smell (166)
                   fern-smell (85)   brine smell (86)
                   paint-smell (99) &c.
                   flower-scent (599)   sherry scent (84)
                   hen-stench (99)   orchard scent (167)
                   sun-stench (97 ff.)   cod scent (511) &c.
drugstore (258)   drug-store (102 ff.)   drug store (421)
bedroom (557 et passim)   bed-room (431 ff.)
poolroom (146)   pool-room (243)
washroom (329)   wash-room (64 ff.)
warehouse (197 ff.)   ware-house (100)
barnyard (3 ff.)   barn-yard (99)
soupkitchen (315)   soup-kitchen (66 ff.)

washtub (505)	wash-tub (294)	
bathtub (325)		
workclothes (101)	work-apron (67)	choir apron (452)
armband (515)	arm-band (429)	
neckband (289 ff.)		
wineglass (109)	wine-glass (492)	
gravestone (99)	grave-stone (579)	grave slab (507)
ashcan (272)	oil-can (78 ff.)	
banknote (228 ff.)	bank-note (304)	
churchbell (597)		church bell (84 ff.)
		school bell (50)
spearhead (351)	spear-head (35 ff.)	
calfskin (485)	calf-skin (61 ff.)	
hillflank (173)	cheek-flank (348)	hill flank (324)
footstep (557 et passim)	foot-step (320)	
footfall (520)	foot-fall (322 ff.)	
nightmare (225)	night-mare (135)	
scrollwork (305)	scroll-work (161)	
cornbread (174 ff.)	corn-bread (68)	
horseplay (99)	horse-play (327)	
hellhound (64)	hell-hound (280)	
counterman (171 ff.)	counter-man (563 ff.)	counter man (338)
barman (284)	bar-man (23)	
countryman (249)		country woman (26 ff.)
saddlemaker (243 ff.)	saddle-maker (146)	
streetwalker (483)	street-walker (532)	
heartbreaker (409)	heart-breaker (361)	
speechmaking (487)	speech-making (426)	
backroom (287)	back-room (371)	back room (130 ff.)
backyard (98 ff.)		back yard (54 ff.)
undershirt (183)	under-shirt (297)	
afterthought (30)	after-thought (82)	
cutpurse (3)	cut-purse (193)	
passersby (416 ff.)	passers-by (607 et passim)	
horsewhipped (244)	horse-whip (233)	
outthrust (315)	out-thrust (404)	
rekindle (95)	re-kindling (63)	
rebirth (557)	re-born (521)	
repaid (126)	re-shaded (552)	
restacked (185)	re-tying (124)	
recapture (557) &c.		
adroop (133)	a-bed (538)	
aprowl (113)	a-search (548)	
aplot (162)		
acoming (211)	a-going (441)	a comin' (9)

a-rolling (440) &c.

birdlike (14 ff.)   bird-like (29)

childlike (516)   child-like (470)

hangdog (10)   hang-dog (34 ff.)

otherworldly (174)   other-worldliness (238)

finespun (456)   fine spun (380)

                 firm-planted (86)

                 high-strung (364)

                 tight-folded (490)

                 soft-spoken (418)

bigboned (243)   big-boned (201)

highboned (173 ff.)   high-boned (359)

smallboned (182)

straightlipped (173)   thin lipped (93)

whiteheaded (97)   broad-minded (468)   thin rinded (187)

truehearted (108)

greenscummed (97)

fullblooded (238)

millionfooted (95)

flatfootedly (132)   flat-footedly (174 ff.)

silkshod (286)   silk-shod (362)

hillborn (412)   hill-born (369 ff.)

rundown shoes (98)   run down (355 ff.)

                 worn-out eyes (358)   broken down
                                                              prizefighter (159)

                 worked-on (478)   laughed at (116)

hardworking (354)   hard-working...Genevieve (146)

uphill (327)   up hill (75)

downhill (437)   down hill (97)

upstairs (26 ff.)

downstairs (34 ff.)   down stairs (168 ff.)

uptown (471)   up-town (327)

                 down-town (317)

undersea (passim)   under sea (560)

off shore (367)   under ground (101)

overnight (475)   over night (282)

tax-collector (12 ff.)   <u>vs.</u>   tax collector (312)

paper-carrier (73 ff.)   paper carrier (294)

cotton-farmer (258)   cotton farmer (152)

cattle-drover (8)   tobacco farmer (404)

ball-player (252)   croquet player (429)

school-teacher (210 ff.)   cotton grower (184)

soda-jerker (46 ff.)   stone cutter (4)

snake-eater (56) &c.   mill owner (148) &c.

playing-field (202)   playing field (421)
sleeping-porch (183 ff.)   sleeping porch (141 ff.)
lodging-house (405)   lodging house (152 ff.)
boarding-house (8 ff.)   playing court (322)
sitting-room (14)   hunting lodge (8)
puddling-iron (85)   carving knife (69 ff.)
examining-board (529)   examining board (533)
earning-power (194)   purchasingpower (103)
spending-money (113) &c.   earning capacity (196) &c.
window-shade (186 ff.)   window shade (79)
window-pane (91 ff.) &c.
lard-bucket (295)   lard bucket (185)
milk-bottle (167 ff.)   medicine bottle (183)
beer-bottle (332)
coffee-pot (559)   coffee urn (172)
shoe-box (444) ice-box (168) &c.   shoe box (155)
paper-bag (299)   cartridge belt (106)
telephone-pole (593)   telephone pole (329)
cricket-bat (269)   bean plate (173) &c.
car-shed (75) cow-shed (329) &c.   carriage shed (182 ff.)
lunch-room (123 ff.)   lunch room (113)
press-room (168 ff.)   press room (170)
rest-room (188) &c.
grocery-store (43 ff.)   grocery store (146)
cigar-store (576)   paint store (158) &c.
burial-ground (101)   burial ground (507)
seed-time (86)   harvest time (3) &c.
wedding-day (104)   wedding trip (16)
wedding-cake (104) &c.
paper-boy (561)   paper boy (304)
delivery-boy (187)   delivery boy (46 ff.)
day-coach (359)   day couch (152)   day labor (515)
side-porch (269)   side porch (41 ff.)
side-steps (42)   side entrance (77)
side-openings (56) &c.
porch-swing (290 ff.)   porch rocker (366) &c.
kitchen-light (470)   kitchen table (493) &c.
travelling-man (259)   travelling man (365)
                                        sailing vessel (3) &c.
water-mote (456)   water mote (429)
step-edge (449)   step edge (463)
                                        porch edge (268)
shirt-tail (395)   coat sleeve (544)
                                        coat lapel (488) &c.
pine-needle (85)   pine bough (188) &c.

lily-pad (85)
cherry-blossom (88)
peanut-shell (486)   orange rind (84)
stair-rail (26)   stair rail (285)
                                       porch rail (323 ff.)
station-curbing (256)   station curbing (538)
                                       station platform (457)

horse-teeth (381)   horse teeth (171)
beast-eye (450)   gypsy eyes (323)
snake-eye (422)
fiend-face (431)   mummy face (588)
boy-face (220)   peasant face (410)
beast-body (62)   phantom shape (473)
cat-form (303)   scissor legs (394)
animal-squeal (301)   spectre moan (15)
fiend-voice (295 ff.)   child look (291)
cat-warmth (222 ff.)   earth strength (222)
cat-speed (182) &c.   kangaroo walk (238) &c.
morning-light (207) &c.   morning light (509)
                                       morning sleep (307) &c.

frock-coat (601)   frock coat (171)
grass-widow (462)   grass widow (285)
leather-chair (75)   leather chair (85)
                                       wicker chair (312)

screen-door (332)   screen door (247)
mission-chair (441)   mission settle (494)
kidney-bean (123)   kidney bean (170 ff.)
mince-pie (165)   mince pie (172 ff.)
apple-pie (123)   apple tobacco (63)
pork-sausage (189)   currant jelly (274 ff.)
bread-sandwich (85) &c.
stomach-ache (279)   belly ache (172)
flicker-dance (486)   shadow dance (384)
crackle-dance (75) &c.
spear-forest (62)   pine woods (152)
mill-town (148)   cotton town (152)
junction-town (7)   home town (394)
                                       mountain town (108 ff.) &c.
gas-stove (540)   gas range (246)
                                       oil lamp (202)
pork-chop (68)   pork chop (199)
hog-chitlins (74)   hog chitlings (174)
tobacco-juice (62)   tobacco juice (284 ff.)
corn-whisky (529)   corn whisky (170)
wood-smoke (84 ff.)   cigarette smoke (297)

pine-sap (85)

organ-music (552)   organ music (105)

bird-song (207 et passim)   siren song (319)

centaur-cry (419)   whisky laughter (23)

bird-cry (451) &c.

war-enchantment (351)   war excitement (533)

boy-life (314)   boy life (232)

                                     group life (527) &c.

wood-fire (75)   wood fire (320)

coal-fire (222 ff.)

coal-mine (441)   gold mine (248)

oil-well (441)

fisher-boy (319)   farmer boy (270)

Double-Standard (415)   double file (205)

                                     double pneumonia (537)

middle-forties (401)   middle years (600)

                                     middle ground (139)

half-hour (548)   half hour (50 ff.)

half-fare (53)   half fare (154)

half-dollar (518)   half price (226)

half-pint (311) &c.   half can (63)

quarter-million (240)   half million (197)

quarter-strength (76)   quarter share (239)

good-nature (573)   good nature (119)

good-humor (133 ff.)   good humor (50)

good-will (117 ff.)

real-estate (509 ff.)   real estate (382 ff.)

high-horse (531)   high chair (69)

dark-room (85)   first aid (188)

soft-drink (142)   live stock (215)

spare-ribs (188)   public house (3)

sweet-pickle (85)

son-of-a-bitch (405)   son of a bitch (172)

man-of-all-work (566)   jack of all trades (107)

master-of-ceremonies (567)   coat of arms (332)

life-in-death (331)

So-and-so [a person] (312)   so and so [a person] (114)

lima-beans (68)   lima beans (231)

Coca-Cola (168)   Coca Cola (271)

three-quarters (541)   three quarters (372)

four-fifths (482) &c.

fashionably-dressed men (188)   deeply scalloped wings (13)

                                     newly organized bank (195) &c.

well-built woman (109) &c.   well brushed coat (9)

well-shaped...head (182)   well brushed garment (101) &c.
well-lined belly (61)   well chosen pieces (196)
well-filled purse (196) &c.   &c.
well-brushed (421)   well kept (148)
well-behaved (198)   well born (35)
well-mannered (147)   well bred (35)
well-liked (317) &c.   &c.
half-unbuttoned (76)   half buried (369)
half-masked (182)
half-shown (291) &c.
half-empty (47)   half full (167 ff.)
half-awake (243) &c.
smoking-hot (85)   blazing hot (54)
screaming-mad (89)   cursing mad (302)
waddling-fat (607)   roaring drunk (157)
dull-brown (213)   dull green (228)
light-brown (405)   dead white (481)
rotten-ripe (34)   tearful bright (311)
drowsy-warm (208)
far-faint (521 ff.) &c.
sloe-black eyes (55)   jet black hair (10)
coal-black (46)
high-school numerals (405)   high school days (146)
     high school position (321)
green-silk garter (285)   gray silk hose (304)
     pink silk hose (372)
     gray flannel nightgown (183)
     red brick residence (41) &c.
half-dozen words (317) &c.   half dozen vegetables (316)
nine-o'clock...bell (50)   Sunday morning air (137)
Good-night (437 ff.)   Good night (31)
Good-morning (443 ff.)   Good morning (171)
Good-evening (264)   Good evening (29 ff.)
     Good day (102 ff.)
     Good afternoon (9)
the bringer-home of packed   the rooting up of their...home (129)
  ice-cream (116)   the snuffing out of a young life (235)
     laying on of hands (339)
you have drunk my heart's-blood you would drink my heart's blood (280)
  (287)
fattening upon my heart's-blood
  (431) &c.
with his curious old-man's   knotted fiercely by his old man's scowl (165)
  look (58)

the long yellow skull's-head
   of Coker (541)
      &c.

the sturdy child's body of his infancy
lengthened (115)
a thin devil's grin (299) &c.

Fair Grounds (55)

Fair grounds (57)

public Square (100)

public square (8 ff.)

market Square (100)

market square (306)

on Upper Valley [Street] (185)

upper Valley Street (184)

east Pine Street (185)

Church Street (336 ff.)

Lisle street (311)

Woodson Street (492) &c.

East India Tea House (84)

East India tea-house (56)

The Sluder Building (271)

the Singer building (271)

The Gruner Building (339) &c.

the Baptist Church (275 bottom)

the Baptist church (275 middle)

the Episcopal church (327)

Civil War (366)

Civil war (8)

Revolutionary war (8)

Christmas Day (90)

Christmas eve (491)

Coca-Cola (168 ff.)

coca-cola (354)

Mr. So-and-so (312)

so and so [a person] (114)

Poor White (100)

poor white (97 ff.)

Mountain Grill (174)

mountain grill (102 ff.)

Redskin (333)

redskin (271)

Mid-Westerner (466)

Mid-western (334)

Maenad (456)

maenad (286)

bacchic (386)

Bacchic (286 ff.)

negress's (433)

negress' (289)

Lord a' mercy (408)

Lord a'mercy (349)

The Lord a' mercy (312)

          he'd a-caught the rabbit (34)

trousers pocket (31)

trousers' leg (363)

the ninety seconds treason (455)

only five years' difference (454)

big 'uns (72) tall 'uns (507)

younguns (33)

little 'un (223)

cracklin' (74)

cracklin (85)

Saint Louis [Mo.] (51 ff.)

St. Louis [Mo.] (70 ff.)

pebble-dash [in roman] (77)

pebbledash [italic] 71

Other Debatable Orthographic Forms

hack-man (24)
junk-man (197)
press-man (563)
stove-pipe (74)
ware-room (100 ff.)
cross-bow (326)

foundry-man (46)
hill-man (359)
hill-top (60 ff.)
horse-hair (84)
arm-pit (222)
even-tide (328)

lumber man (148 ff.)
bird-man (517)
wood-cut (61)
honey-suckle (84)
church woman (282)
honey-dew (342)

cockle-burr (453)	horse-shoe (460)	room-mate (480)
thunder-bolt (498)	arm-chair (501)	wax-work (570)
pass-word (622)	mid-day (68 ff.)	dead-head (299)
whipper-snapper (312)	re-union (457)	nitro-glycerin (525)
break-neck (40)	lamb-like (251)	pre-natal (298 ff.)
sub-normal (481)	a-grin (572)	tell-tale (340)
sing-song (556)	see-sawed (117)	boo-hooing (485)

The leading orthographical authorities say that the foregoing should be written in the completely-consolidated one-word form.

fighting cock (3)	rocking chair (304)	watermain (87)
watercloset (194)	shirtsleeve (243)	hell fire (333)
eyeshade (405 ff.)	makeup (168)	culs de sac (127)
swaybacked (311)		

They likewise say that the foregoing should be hyphened.

cannoncracker (177)   They say further that this should be written as two distinct words.

lumber yard (17)	laughing stock (132)	summer house (367)
warpaint (106)	lawnmower (183)	seamoss (183)
drayhorse (270)	bearcat (409)	rosewater (464)
fullback (591)		

The dictionary-forms for the foregoing, while not themselves in agreement, nevertheless differ from those cited.

anti-climatic (387)	? should be	anticlimactic
seasteak (76)	? "	sea-steak
prisonhouse (143)	? "	prison-house
chippyhouse (146)	? "	chippy-house
fireflame (228)	? "	fire-flame
boneframe (236)	? "	bone-frame
nosewing (490)	? "	nose-wing
shirtsleeved (77 ff.)	? "	shirt-sleeved
earthstained (186)	? "	earth-stained
roseflushed (190)	? "	rose-flushed
housebroken (230)	? "	house-broken
seasunken (276)	? "	sea-sunken
hillbound (423)	? "	hill-bound
bluebordered (265)	? "	blue-bordered
thin gloved (203)	? "	thin-gloved
high mettled (325)	? "	high-mettled [cf.low-pitched, 473]

milky white (223)	?	"	milky-white
sensual looking (290)	?	"	sensual-looking
long drawn out (344)	?	"	long-drawn-out
land ownership (66)	?	"	land-ownership
second baseman (252)	?	"	second-baseman
first baseman (355)	?	"	first-baseman
pitch darkness (259)	?	"	pitch-darkness
a dollar-and-a-half (120)	?	"	a-dollar-and-a-half
three twenty-five (170)	?	"	three-twenty-five
sold like hot cakes (257)	?	"	...hot-cakes
oaten-stop (95)	?	"	oaten stop
tow-sack (211)	?	"	tow sack
Middle-West (315 ff.)	?	"	Middle West
sotto-voce (386)	?	"	sotto voce
four and fifty years (59)	?	"	four-and-fifty years
a peach and apple cobbler (68)	?	"	a peach-and-apple cobbler
fish and oyster man (187)	?	"	fish-and-oyster man
truck and livery business (252)	?	"	truck-and-livery business
a five and ten cent store (315)	?	"	a five-and-ten-cent store
an ice-cream and candy-store (527)	?	"	an ice-cream-and-candy store
a red, white and blue band (240)	?	"	a red-white-and-blue band
five and ten-dollar bills (196)	?	"	five- and ten-dollar bills
five and ten-cent pieces (200)	?	"	five- and ten-cent pieces
the mean three-and-four-story brickbuilt buildings (76)	?	"	the mean three- and four-story brick-built buildings
food products company (152)	?	"	food-products company
life insurance policy (194)	?	"	life-insurance policy
cash register salesman (378)	?	"	cash-register salesman
pale blue eyes (332)	?	"	pale-blue eyes
right hand corner (334)	?	"	right-hand corner
			cf. plain-clothes men (154)
all right people (355)	?	"	all-right people
hotels de luxe (189)	?	"	hotels de-luxe or hotels de luxe
wild-goose chase (315 ff.)	?	"	wild goose-chase
the little ticking sounds (509)	?	"	the little ticking-sounds
we've all got to go some time (10)&c.	?	"	...sometime
a joy he thought he had lost forever (12) &c.	?	"	...for ever
lima-beans (68)	?	"	Lima beans
the tropics (86)	?	"	the Tropics
fig-newton (142)	?	"	Fig Newton
biblical (153)	?	"	Biblical
hamburger steak (229 ff.)	?	"	Hamburger steak
limburger cheese (332)	?	"	Limburger cheese
Whitstone hotel (337)	?	"	Whitstone Hotel

oxford shoes (405)	?	"	Oxford shoes
pre-Raphaelite (472)	?	"	Pre-Raphaelite
a Luini madonna (472)	?	"	a Luini Madonna
Jeremiad (101)	?	"	jeremiad
Bright's Disease (154)	?	"	Bright's disease
He played Casino (611)	?	"	...casino
melée (62)	?	"	mêlée
suede (304 ff.)	?	"	suède
long striped apron (101) &c.	?	"	long, striped apron &c.
six weeks' jailbird (70)	?	"	six-weeks jailbird
seven weeks' journey (71)	?	"	seven-weeks journey
a two days' visit (425)	?	"	a two-day visit
Goddam it! (226)	?	"	Goddamn it <u>or</u> God damn it

Missyllabications

buc-kles (234)	? should be		buck-les
uncontroll-ably (406)	?	"	uncontrol-lably
pill-ioned (423)	?	"	pil-lioned
grim-ace (439)	?	"	gri-mace
sprink-ling (464)	?	"	sprin-kling

Miscellaneous

Are the following as you intended them, or should we possibly emend them as indicated?

eave (28)	? should be		eaves
U. B. Freely (180)	?	"	U. P. Freely
elasticly (181)	?	"	elastically
pigs' knockles (189)	?	"	pigs' knuckles
Münchener dunkels (276)	?	"	Münchener Dunkles
he would summons her by ringing (276)	?	"	...summon...
The rich plums lay bursted on the grass (68)	?	"	...lay burst...
Red plums...will fall bursted on the loamy warm wet earth (165)	?	"	...burst...
his fragile unfurnished body (112)	?	"	his frail...body
he became fragile (115) &c.	?	"	...frail
their tall keels looked over on the street behind the sea walls (156)	?	"	their tall sterns...
men drank from glacéd tall glasses (162)	?	"	...from iced tall glasses
he lay the night-long through within his berth (162)	?	"	...the night long within...<u>or</u> the night through within...

He would perhaps have had difficulty in constructing a page of Latin prose and verse (220)	?	"	...in construing a page... cf. to construe a passage in Homer (312)
he griped his hand affectionately around the boy's arm (322)	?	"	he gripped...
He fastened his brutal gripe... into the boy's thin arm (324)	?	"	...grip...
And from even deeper adyts of his brain there swam up...(330)	?	"	...adyta... or ...adytums...
the lost and secret adyts of his childhood (550)	?	"	...adyta... or ...adytums...
as if it was cold (171) &c.	?	"	as if it were cold cf. as if he were...(507) &c.
the little fat girl (462)	?	"	the fat little girl [as on same page]
the little particular markings (510)	?	"	the particular little markings
a little sallow woman (358)	?	"	a sallow little woman cf. dusty little shop (11) &c.
little tinkling fountains (193)	?	"	tinkling little fountains cf. creaking little fence (100) crawling little fire (77) unpleasant snarling little cat (234)
the little latticed veranda (40)	?	"	the latticed little veranda
the little moated castle (52)	?	"	the moated little castle
little wasted shell (58)	?	"	wasted little shell
a little crippled man (162)	?	"	a crippled little man
little grated blinds (193)	?	"	grated little blinds
little orphaned children (284)	?	"	orphaned little children
a little furtive-faced boy (96)	?	"	a furtive-faced little boy
little gray-haired man (370)	?	"	gray-haired little man cf. battered little dresser (305) hunted little animal (89) stricken little face (58)

What determines your variant usage, as exemplified in the following?

six feet four (5)	vs. six foot four (526)
six feet three (223)	
a hysterical (156)	an hysterical (484)
He lit a cigarette (532)	He lighted a cigarette (passim)
these images that burnt in him (192)	his powerful clairvoyance...burned inward
they burnt the soles of his feet (226)	back across the phantom years (191)
stared out the window (6)	look out of the window (117)

looking out the window (53)
She looked out the window (227)

What do the following terms mean? Are they coinages of yours? I do not find them
in my dictionaries.

octopal (? pertaining to an octopus)
    in the slow octopal movements of her temper (18)
        a diver twined desperately in octopal feelers (300)
ripstink   in the gaseous ripstink (99)
gabular (? pertaining to a gable)
    in gabular appearance (127)
coprous (? resembling copper)
    in the beautiful coprous olive of the skin (182)
esymplastic   in the esymplastic power of his imagination (201)
fluescence; fluescent
    in a soft dark fluescence of appearance (234) &c.
cut-bank (72); bull-milk (73); mountain grill (passim); brier moth (216);
    sandclay (258); yard-pot (302).

Why do you prefer the obsolete "shamefast" (71 ff.) to "shamefaced"?

Is not "but stumbling from exhaustion, the command to return was horrible" (519)
    a case of what the purists call "dangling participle"?

What is the point to the allusion to Brooklyn in "They stood quietly, frightened, in
    that strange place, waiting to hear the summons of his voice, with expectant
    unbelief, as some one looking for the god in Brooklyn" (420)? (And should not
    "as" be "like"?)

                    Sincerely yours,
                    Louis N. Feipel [signature]
                    Louis N. Feipel [typed]

Appendix 5

Scribners Alteration Lists for *Of Time and the River*

These alterations were made in later printings.

TS, 1 p., PUL

Stamped FEB 18 REC'D

Printer: Make these corrections in the plates of "Of Time + the River" and <u>return</u> this <u>list</u>

Ed[1]

Page	29,	line	9,	"moist" should be "most"
"	52,	"	14,	change "the bare path" to "bare paths" (omit "the")
"	89,	"	3,	"elemental" should be "eternal"
"	89,	"	14,	"numerous" should be "murmurous"
"	89,	"	18,	put comma after "twisted"
"	89,	"	3	from bottom, question mark instead of period.
"	92,	"	7	" " Change "board" to "hoard"
"	94,	"	20,	Change "one of most" to "one of the most"
"	186,	"	1,	"my" should be "his"
"	187,	"	13	from bottom, Change "oevah" to "ovah"
"	189,	"	7,	Change "youh" to "yoah"
"	189,	"	24,	" "my" to "his"
"	200,	"	2	from bottom, Change "scowly" to "scowling"
"	274,	"	5	from bottom, Change "strange" to "shining"
"	308,	"	9,	Subborn should be "stubborn"
"	317,	"	16,	Change "Posillippo's" to "Masillippo's"
"	338,	"	6	from bottom, "my" should be "his"
"	400,	"	23,	Change "aptly" to "everything" and "eagerly" to "anything"
"	402,	"	4	from bottom, Change "rush" to "urge"
"	404,	"	9,	Change "sweet" to "secret"
"	464,	"	18,	"Uncertitude" should be "incertitude"
"	466,	"	2,	Omit "him"
"	466,	"	2	from bottom Change "me" to "Eugene"
"	487,	"	3	" " " "I have ever seen" to "he had ever seen"

"	519,	"	20,	"	"	"	"ah" to "so"
"	627,	"	14	from bottom, Change "ploddy" to "plodding"
"	678,	"	11	"	"	Change "character" to "diameter"
"	771,	"	10	from bottom, Change "strong" to "stormy"
"	861,	"	21,	"light hunched" should be "eight hundred"

1. In MP's hand.

∽

TS, 1 p., PUL

Feb. 25, 1935

Correction for "Of Time and the River" - Wolfe
Page 398, line 1, change "John" to "Gene"

∽

TS, 2 pp., PUL

March 6, 1935

Corrections for "Of Time and the River" - Wolfe

Page	76,	Line	11,	"will" should be "with"
"	98,	"	16,	comma after "We've got a bet on"
"	149,	"	7,	uhearted should be unhearted
"	184,	"	6	from bottom, for Louse read Louise
"	193,	"	16	" " for dulness read dullness
"	204,	"	4	" " for Jordan read Sluder
"	205,	"	3	for Jordan read Sluder
"	243,	"	6	from bottom, omit "The boy never saw him again"
"	248,	"	21,	for engines read energies
"	250,	last line for looket read looked
"	343,	line 8 from bottom, for t-t-t-trouble read trouble
"	350,	"	15,	for into the fire read into the air
"	304,	"	10,	for weavings read hazards
"	367,	"	21,	for landing into read ending up in
"	343,	"	8 from bottom, for Frankly read F-f-f-frankly
"	397,	"	2 " "	for "Wy-wy-wy— read "Wy—
"	397,	"	2 " "	for frankly read f-f-f-frankly
"	398,	"	1,	for John read Gene
"	498,	"	13 from bottom, for Here read Where
"	499,	"	23,	for transmitted read transmuted
"	499,	"	5 from bottom, for resins read resinous
"	506,	"	7,	omit of

"	521,	"	14 from bottom, for <u>that</u> read <u>this</u>
"	543,	"	8, for <u>pint</u> read <u>pound</u>
"	545,	"	2, for <u>envy</u> read <u>error</u>
"	545,	"	10, for <u>beings</u> read <u>kings</u>
"	545,	"	22, for <u>leonic</u> read <u>leonine</u>
Page	545,		line 6 from bottom, for <u>bad</u> read <u>hard</u>, and for <u>volume</u> read <u>violence</u>
"	545,	"	5 " " for <u>marked</u> read <u>masked</u>
"	546,	"	5 " " for <u>beard</u> read <u>head</u>
"	549,	"	6, for <u>dullness</u> read <u>darkness</u>
"	549,	"	19, for <u>loneliness</u> read <u>loveliness</u>
"	576,	"	14, beginning, "spoke with a crisp" is a mistake. This line should read: "about the background, Madge . . . . I think you're wrong: I'd like to
"	578,	"	8, hyphen missing after <u>turn</u>, at end of line
"	588,	"	14 from bottom, for <u>ever-long</u> read <u>ever-living</u>
"	591,	"	8, for <u>lusts</u> read <u>lasts</u> and for <u>all-causing</u> read <u>all-consuming</u>
"	595,	"	6 from bottom, for <u>day</u> read <u>clay</u>
"	596,	"	7 " " for <u>straw-blade</u> read <u>straw-pale</u>
"	598,	"	14, for <u>measure</u> read <u>menace</u>
"	671,	"	7 from bottom, for <u>there</u> read <u>them</u>
"	673,	"	20, for <u>Light</u> read <u>Lift</u>
"	716,	"	5, for <u>He</u> read <u>Eugene</u>
"	794,		omit last sentence, "He never saw her again"
"	853,		line 3, for <u>tune</u> read <u>time</u>
"	855,	"	4, for <u>on</u> read <u>in</u>
"	855,	"	5, for <u>Sunday</u> read <u>Society</u>
"	870,	"	1, for <u>loved</u> read <u>lived</u>
"	903,	"	3 from bottom, for <u>foundered</u> read <u>founded</u>
"	910,	"	5 " " for <u>Oh</u> read <u>O</u>

TS, 1 p., PUL

March 19, 1935
Corrections for "Of Time and the River"

Page	572,	line	8 from bottom, Change "into dainty" to "into a dainty"
"	572,	"	7 " " Change "stools" to "stool"
"	586,	"	23,24,25, Omit beginning "No one knows" through "—about", making line read: "gravely, 'Mums needs me. Mums and Pups'—he said, etc."
"	586,	"	26, Make paragraph beginning "For a moment"

TS, 1 p., PUL

April 8, 1935

Additional corrections

Wolfe's "Of Time and the River"

Page 54, line 5, question-mark (?) at the end of this sentence should be a period (.).

Page 126, line 12 from bottom, <u>laughted</u> should be <u>laughed</u>.

Page 380, line 9, <u>subborn</u> should be <u>stubborn</u>.

Page 466, second line from bottom, <u>me</u> should be <u>Eugene</u>.

Page 243, second line from bottom, <u>three</u> years should read <u>two</u> years.

Page 309, line 19, <u>third</u> should read <u>second</u>.

Page 361, line 6 from bottom, <u>two years</u> ago should read <u>one year</u> ago.

TS, 1 p., PUL

c. Spring 1935

Memorandum for Mr. Zimmerman[1]

<u>Wolfe - "Of Time and the River"</u>

On page 903, 3rd line from bottom, "as if she were fixed and founded there".

This read correctly in page proof, but the printer, for some reason, changed it in foundry proof to read "as if she were fixed and foundered there," and inquired in the margin, "Is this O.K.?"   I marked on foundry proof: "No - should read founded".

I note that in the book it is printed "foundered". Please see that the correction is made on the plates.

1. Memo probably by John Hall Wheelock. Zimmerman was an employee at the Scribner Press.

Background Readings

Berg, A. Scott. *Max Perkins: Editor of Genius*. New York: Dutton, 1978.

Donald, David Herbert. *Look Homeward: A Life of Thomas Wolfe*. Boston: Little, Brown, 1987.

Field, Leslie A., ed. *Thomas Wolfe: Three Decades of Criticism*. New York: New York University Press, 1968.

Johnston, Carol. *Thomas Wolfe: A Descriptive Bibliography*. Pittsburgh: University of Pittsburgh, 1987.

Kennedy, Richard S. *The Window of Memory: The Literary Career of Thomas Wolfe*. Chapel Hill: The University of North Carolina Press, 1962.

Nowell, Elizabeth. *Thomas Wolfe: A Biography*. Garden City, N.Y.: Doubleday, 1960.

Perkins, Maxwell. *Always Yours, Max*. Ed. Alice R. Cotten. N.p.: Thomas Wolfe Society, 1997.

———. *Editor to Author*. Ed. John Hall Wheelock. New York: Scribners, 1950.

———. "Scribner's and Thomas Wolfe." *Carolina Magazine* 68, no. 1 (October 1938): 15–17.

———. "Thomas Wolfe." *Harvard Library Bulletin* 1, no. 3 (Autumn 1947): 269–77.

Wolfe, Thomas. *Look Homeward, Angel*. New York: Scribners, 1929.

———. *Of Time and the River*. New York: Scribners, 1935.

———. *From Death to Morning*. New York: Scribners, 1935.

———. *The Story of a Novel*. New York: Scribners, 1936.

———. *The Letters of Thomas Wolfe*. Ed. Elizabeth Nowell. New York: Scribners, 1956.

———. *The Letters of Thomas Wolfe to His Mother*. Ed. C. Hugh Holman and Sue Fields Ross. Chapel Hill: University of North Carolina Press, 1968.

———. *The Notebooks of Thomas Wolfe*. 2 vols. Ed. Richard S. Kennedy and Paschal Reeves. Chapel Hill: University of North Carolina Press, 1970.

Wolfe, Thomas, and Elizabeth Nowell. *Beyond Love and Loyalty*. Ed. Richard S. Kennedy. Chapel Hill: University of North Carolina Press, 1983.

Index

Adams, Franklin Pierce (F.P.A.), 144, 147n. 9

The Adventures of Tom Sawyer (movie), 267

Aiken, Conrad, 39

Aldington, Richard, 38, 50

Anderson, Maxwell, 178n. 2

"An Angel on the Porch" (Wolfe), 12n. 1

Antaeus, or A Memory of Earth (Wolfe), 36–37, 39n. 3, 41–42, 44–47. *See also* Wolfe, Thomas: and Antaeus myth

Arlen, Michael, 38, 39n. 5

Arthur, Chester, 252

Asheville, N.C., 284; Wolfe's visit to, 28. *See also* Wolfe, Fred; Wolfe, Julia

Aswell, Edward C., 163n. 1, 181n. 1, 301

Babbitt, Irving, 14

Basso, Hamilton, 223n. 37, 242, 268

Baum, Vicki, 84n. 3

Benét, William Rose, 34, 35n. 3

Beowulf, 46

Berlin, Wolfe in, 159–63, 165

Bernstein, Aline, xviii, 28n. 2, 47n. 2, 73, 78–83, 93, 148n. 9, 172n. 3, 173–74, 231, 236, 262, 268, 289, 293, 311n. 1

Bernstein, Edla, 269n. 4

Beyond Love and Loyalty (Wolfe and Nowell), 222n. 27

Bible, 51

Bogan, Louise, 34

Book-of-the-Month Club, 29n. 1

Boole, Ella, 113

Bowler, Ruth Colburn, 134

Boyd, Ernest, 89

Boyd, James, 40, 43, 65

Boyd, Madeleine, 54, 58, 67, 79, 90, 116, 292; lawsuit filed by, 163, 169n. 1, 171, 172, 173–74, 231; and *Look Homeward, Angel,* 3, 4–5, 8, 9, 22, 24, 29n. 1, 70n. 2

Boyd, Thomas, xvi, 20, 24

Bridges, Robert, 222n. 33

The Bright Doom (Wheelock), 280n. 1

Brooks, Van Wyck, 52, 79, 99

Brown, John Mason, 92

Bruccoli, Matthew J., 308

Breughel, Pieter, 166

"The Bums at Sunset" (Wolfe), 173

Burnham, David, 39n. 1

Burton, Robert, 310

Byron, George Gordon, Lord, 159, 160

Caldwell, Erskine, xvi

Caldwell, Taylor, xvi, 270n. 7

Calverton, V. F., 188

Campbell, Alan, 178n. 3

Campbell, Mrs. Patrick, 240

Cerf, Bennett, 222n. 19

Chacey, Donald V., 112n. 1, 112–13

Chamberlain, John, 133, 134n. 1

Chapin, Joseph Hawley, 222n. 33

Charles Scribner's Sons. *See* Scribner, House of

Charvat, William, xv

"The Child by Tiger" (Wolfe), 47n. 4

Churchill, Winston, xvii

Cohn, Louis Henry, 89

Coleridge, Samuel Taylor, 287

Colum, Mary, 64–65, 75, 84–85, 251, 286

Colum, Padraic, 64–65, 84–85

Comstock, Anthony, 75

Cook, Alfred A., 203, 238

Copeland, Charles Townsend, 53

"Cottage by the Tracks" (Wolfe), 184n. 1

Cross, Robert, 141, 150n. 1, 239

The Damnation of Theron Ware (Frederic), 91

Dangerfield, George, 154n. 3

"Dark in the Forest, Strange as Time" (Wolfe), 123–24

Darrow, Whitney, 55, 59, 73, 82, 90, 93, 100, 150n. 1, 269

Dashiell, Alfred, xvi, 9, 11, 23, 42, 43, 82, 95, 116

Davenport, Marcia, xvi

"Death, the Proud Brother" (Wolfe), 103, 107n. 3, 109, 176, 181–82

De Quincey, Thomas, 310

De Voto, Bernard, xx, 187, 221n. 2, 295

Dodd, Martha, 159, 160, 163, 253

Donne, John, 27, 28n. 2

Dooher, Muredach, 221, 222–23n. 35, 231–32, 251–53, 254, 258–61, 299

Dorman, Marjorie, 203–4n. 1

Dos Passos, John, 64

Doubleday, Frank Nelson, 76

Dunn, Charles F., 35

"'E, A Recollection" (Wolfe), 239

Ecclesiastes, 51

Eliot, T. S., 63, 75, 290

Emerson, Ralph Waldo, 162

Ernst, Morris, 265

"The Face of the War" (Wolfe), 183

Fadiman, Clifton, 146, 148n. 11

"The Far and the Near" (Wolfe), 183

A Farewell to Arms (Hemingway), 10n. 3

Faulkner, William, 148n. 10

Feipel, Louis N., 313

Ferber, Edna, 176

Fitzgerald, F. Scott, xvi, xvii, xxii, 34, 49, 54, 239, 240n. 4, 241, 242, 284, 308; and Thomas Wolfe, xxii, xxiii, 40, 43, 57–58, 67, 70n. 3, 74

Fitzgerald, Zelda, 40, 49

Flaubert, Gustave, xxii

"For Any Man Alive" (Wolfe), 110–11

Forman, Henry James, 157

"The Four Lost Men" (Wolfe), 120n. 1, 123, 126n. 2

"The Fox and the Lion" (Wolfe), 297n. 1

France, Wolfe's letters from, 39–42, 131

Frederic, Harold, 94n. 5

Freeman, Douglas Southall, xvii

Frere-Reeves, A. S., 38, 40, 50, 51, 76, 126n. 1, 136, 139, 140, 281

From Death to Morning (Wolfe), xx, 96, 126n. 2, 127, 155, 156, 157n. 2, 172, 176–78, 181–82, 183–84, 196, 203–4n. 1; dedication of, 184–85; dust jacket for, 186

Frothingham, Bertha Perkins ("Bert"), 85, 240, 269

Frothingham, Jane, 240

Galantière, Lewis, 144, 148n. 9

Galileo, 40

Galsworthy, John, xvi, 34, 53, 139

Germany, Wolfe's travels in, 159–65, 197

Goethe, Johann Wolfgang von, 160, 162, 164

Gold, Michael, 144, 147n. 9

Gordon, Caroline, xvi

Gorman, Herbert, 75, 286

Gorman, Jean, 286

Gorsline, Douglas W., 268, 269n. 3

Granich, Irving. *See* Gold, Michael

Greene, Lawrence, 305

Guggenheim Foundation, 120–21n. 1

"Gulliver, the Story of a Tall Man"
(Wolfe), 156, 166n. 1, 183

Hale, Nancy, xvi
Hall, Bolton, 100
Harcourt, Alfred, 250n. 2
Harper, House of, xxi
Hart, Henry, 144, 147n. 9
Harvard University, 14
Heinemann, Ltd. (publisher), 34, 50,
76, 124, 126n. 1, 154
Hemingway, Ernest, xvi, xxii, xxiii, 51,
64, 65, 102, 128n. 1, 167
Herrmann, John, 97n. 1
The Hills Beyond (Wolfe), 115n. 2
Hitler, Adolf, 161–62, 172
Hoagland, Clayton, 254
Hogarth, William, 150
Holden, Raymond, 34
Holman, Libby, 222n. 10
Hoover, Herbert, 85
The Hound of Darkness (Wolfe),
179–80, 214
Hurston, Zora Neale, xvi
Hutton, Barbara, 222n. 7

Jack, Peter Munro, xviii
James, Will, 49
Jelliffe, Belinda, 168, 169n. 4
Jelliffe, Smith Ely, 169n. 4
Johnson, Samuel, 206
Jones, James, xvii
Jonson, Ben, 287
Joyce, James, 212–14, 310

Kang, Younghill, 65, 116, 240
Keats, John, 20, 56
Kennedy, Richard, 308
Kirstein, Lincoln, 144, 148n. 9
Klopfer, Donald S., 222n. 19
"K-19" (unpublished novel) (Wolfe),
100, 101, 105, 107n. 1, 123n. 1,
235

Landon, Alf, 207

Lardner, Ring, xvi
Lawrence, D. H., 167, 173n. 2
Ledig, H. M., 203
Lemmon, Elizabeth, 125n. 1, 168
Lewis, Sinclair, 64, 72, 76, 133, 134n.
1, 165, 185, 285, 287
Linscott, Robert N., 250n. 3, 250n. 4
Litvinoff, Ivy, 84n. 6
London, Wolfe in, 62, 83–84, 136,
138–41, 142
Look Homeward, Angel (originally titled
"O Lost") (Wolfe), xvii, 85, 98,
117, 147n. 9, 195, 205, 214–15,
246, 271n. 1, 306; contract for,
6–7; dust jacket for, 30; earnings
from, 88; English publisher of, 22,
24, 34, 50, 54; English reviews of,
49, 50, 52–53, 54, 55, 56, 57n. 1;
errors in, 48, 313–27; German
reviews of, 108, 114–15, 117–19;
Sinclair Lewis's remarks on, 64, 72,
76; Modern Library edition, 125;
Perkins's initial interest in, 3–5;
Perkins's acceptance of, 8–9;
Perkins's suggestions for, 11, 16, 18,
21, 27; proofing and final revisions
of, 11–28; reviews of, 31; Swedish
reviews of, 114, 115n. 1; Wolfe's
note to the reader, 1–3, 4–5, 27
Lorentz, Pare, 267n. 1
"The Lost Boy" (Wolfe), 178
Luhan, Mabel Dodge, 173, 174, 175
Lum, Ralph, 251–53, 254, 260

Mackaye, Percy, 114
Maine, Wolfe's letters from, 9–25, 88
Marquand, J. P., xvi
Maugham, Somerset, 139
Maurois, André, 72
McMurry, Frank M., 28n. 1
Melville, Herman, 53
Mencken, H. L., 36, 75
Meyer, Wallace, 35, 222n. 27, 222n. 33
Mitchell, Cornelius, 168, 171, 172n.
3, 174, 221, 231, 299–301

Moby-Dick (Melville), 53

Moe, Henry Allen, 120n. 1

Morley, Christopher, 144, 147n. 9, 185

Munich, Wolfe in, 4

Nathan, Robert, 144, 147n. 9

The New Yorker, 239

"No Door: A Story of Time and the
Wanderer" (Wolfe), xx, 107n. 3,
109–10, 116, 203–4n. 1

"No More Rivers" (Wolfe), 222n. 27

Norwood, Robert, 98

Nowell, Elizabeth, xv, 94n. 7, 109n. 1,
156, 173, 174, 196, 217, 236, 239,
241, 242, 244, 267, 268

The October Fair (unpublished novel)
(Wolfe), 39n. 3, 51, 67–69, 88,
93n. 1, 94n. 7, 105–6, 162, 163n.
1, 172, 217, 220, 236, 246, 286,
292, 306–7, 311

Of Time and the River (Wolfe), xviii,
xix, 39n. 3, 42n. 3, 93, 106,
124–25, 131, 163n. 1, 181, 195,
209, 222–23n. 35, 244, 246, 259,
309, 310, 311; advertisement for,
135; alterations charges for, 189,
192, 194; announcement for, 122;
Czechoslovakian publisher of, 171;
dedication of, 128, 129, 130; dust
jacket for, 132; English reviews of,
175, 176n. 1; errors in, 143–44,
147n. 5, 149, 329–32; Perkins's
suggestions for, 121, 123, 233–34,
235; reviews of, 131, 133–34,
148n. 11, 148n. 12, 154–55, 167;
success of, 136, 153–54, 156, 173

"O Lost," xvii, 3n. 1, 3n. 2, 5n. 2, 8,
10n. 1, 12n. 4, 84n. 1. See also
Look Homeward, Angel

Olson, Alma Luise, 115n. 1

Paris, Wolfe in, 40, 137, 141–42

Parker, Dorothy, 177, 178n. 3

Paterson, Isabel M., 144, 146, 147n. 9

Paton, Alan, xvii

Peckham, Richard, 35n. 2

Perkins, Bertha. *See* Frothingham,
Bertha Perkins

Perkins, Elisabeth ("Zippy"), 268

Perkins, Louise, 125, 150, 152–53,
156, 196, 240, 268, 274

Perkins, Maxwell: biographical observations of Thomas Wolfe, 305–11; as
editor, xvi–xx, xxi–xxii; and *Look
Homeward, Angel,* 3–5, 8–9, 11, 13,
16, 18, 21, 27; and *Of Time and the
River,* 128, 129, 130; relationship
with Thomas Wolfe, xv, xvii–xxiii,
29, 32, 34, 204–21, 223–29,
234–37, 242–51, 295–96; and
Wolfe's break with Scribners,
199–202, 242–43, 294–96; Wolfe's
dispute with regarding royalties,
189–95; on women, 84

Perkins, Peggy, 269

Peter the First (movie), 267

Petrov, Vladimir, 267n. 2

Phelps, William Lyon, 166, 167

The Picture of Dorian Gray (Wilde), 91

Pierce, Charles A., 250n. 2

Porter, Garland, 233

"A Portrait of Bascom Hawke" (Wolfe),
94n. 1, 95n. 1, 97, 258

Rascoe, Burton, 97n. 1, 146, 148n. 12,
154–56

Rawlings, Marjorie Kinnan, xvi, xxi,
239, 240n. 3, 269

Raynolds, Robert, 119

Reynolds, Smith, 211

"The Ring and the Book" (Browning),
213

The River (movie), 267

Rogers, John, 268, 269n. 5

Roosevelt, Franklin, 236

Roosevelt, Theodore, xvi

Rose, Carl, 10n. 3

Rowohlt Verlag (German publisher), 165, 195–96, 203
Ruder, Barnett, 252, 259

Salter, Katherine Hayden, 98, 117
Santayana, George, xvi
Schiller, Friedrich von, 160
Schreiber, George, 185
Scott, Evelyn, 166, 167
Scott, Sir Walter, 51
Scribner, Charles, III, xvi, xx, 29n. 1, 136, 138, 194, 203, 238, 243, 254–55, 256, 257, 261, 263–66
Scribner, Mrs. Charles, III, 136, 138
Scribner, House of, xvi; and *Look Homeward, Angel,* xvii; Wolfe's relationship with, xx–xxi, 199–202, 217–18, 223–26, 242–44, 293–97
Scribner's Magazine, 9, 11, 12n. 1, 23n. 1, 94n. 1, 95n. 1, 103, 107, 109, 112n. 1, 114, 120–21n. 1, 123n. 1, 166n. 1
Seiffert, Marjorie Allen, 34, 72
Selznick, David O., 267n. 3
Simonson, Lee, 144, 148n. 9
Soskin, William, 97n. 1
Stallings, Laurence, 178n. 2
Stein, Gertrude, 61, 175
Stevens, Henry David, 123n. 1
The Story of a Novel (Wolfe), xviii, xix–xx, 188, 239; dispute over royalties for, 189–95; dust jacket for, 187; reviews of, 221n. 2
Strange, Michael, 277
Switzerland, Wolfe in, 44, 54, 283–84

Tallon, J. F., 237
Tarr, Ralph S., 28n. 1
Taurog, Norman, 267n. 3
Tender Is the Night (Fitzgerald), 42n. 1
Terry, John, 221n. 2, 311n. 1
Thomason, John, 241n. 1
Tolstoy, Leo, 44, 218
"The Train and the City" (Wolfe), 103

Tristram Shandy (Sterne), 213
Trollope, Anthony, 292
Tweed, Blanch Oelrichs Thomas Barrymore, 277n. 1

Ulysses (Joyce), 212–14, 310

Van Dine, S. S., xvi, 50
Van Doren, Carl, 52
Van Doren, Mark, 144, 146, 147n. 9
Van Vechten, Carl, 79, 81

Wagner, Richard, 160
Walpole, Hugh, 136, 139–40
War and Peace (Tolstoy), 44, 218
Wasson, Ben, 144, 147n. 9
The Web and the Rock (Wolfe), 42n. 3, 163n. 1, 181n. 1, 222n. 20, 297n. 1, 308
Weber, William, 115
"The Web of Earth" (Wolfe), 95n. 1, 96, 97n. 2, 97–98, 116n. 1, 156, 176, 177
Wecter, Dixon, 173, 240
Weinberger, Harry, 163, 172n. 3
Welcome to Our City (Wolfe), 148n. 9
the West, Wolfe's travels in, 168, 169, 179
Wharton, Edith, xvi
What Price Glory? (Anderson and Stallings), 177
Wheaton, Mabel Wolfe, 65, 196, 241
Wheaton, Ralph, 65
Wheelock, John Hall, xv–xvi, xxii, 10n. 1, 114, 133, 138, 230, 269, 313; and *Look Homeward, Angel,* 9–27; poetry of, 198–99, 279–80
Wilde, Oscar, 94n. 5
Wilder, Thornton, 52
William Heinemann, Ltd. *See* Heinemann, Ltd. (publisher)
Wilson, Edmund, 97n. 1
Wilson, Harry Leon, 147n. 1
Winchell, Walter, 222n. 34

Wolfe, Benjamin Harrison, 176, 178, 184–85, 289, 305

Wolfe, Fred, 65–66, 70, 71, 73, 74, 85, 196, 241, 242, 244, 245, 249, 267, 268, 274

Wolfe, Grover, 177n. 4

Wolfe, Julia, 178, 242, 309, 310, 311

Wolfe, Thomas: and Antaeus myth, 36–37, 39n. 3, 41–42, 44–47, 67–69, 104–6, 107, 286, 287; in Asheville, 28; and Aline Bernstein, 78–83, 93; autobiography in writings of, 307; on the Bible, 51; break with Scribners, xv, xxi, 199–202, 242–43, 254–55, 293–97, 302–3; at Colorado Writers' Conference, 158, 169–71; and Communism, 125n. 1, 208, 309; on Conservative versus Revolutionary, 207–11; death of, xxii–xxiii; despair at reviews of *Look Homeward, Angel*, 54, 55, 56; dispute with Perkins regarding royalties, 189–95; and Dooher manuscript dispute, 221, 222–23n. 35, 231–32, 251–53, 254, 257, 258–61, 299; and Scott Fitzgerald, xxii, xxiii, 40, 43, 57–58, 67, 70n. 3, 74; in Germany, 159–65, 197; and Guggenheim Fellowship, 120–21n. 1; homesickness of, 38, 40, 65, 71, 281, 285, 291; illness of, 270–74; libel suit brought against, xx, 203–4n. 1, 220, 228, 231, 232, 238, 256, 263–64, 265–66; money problems of, 59–60, 66–67, 90, 140–41; on morality, 209–11; on North Carolina people, 284; Perkins's biographical observations of, 305–11; on the reading public, 112; relationship with Maxwell Perkins, xv, xvii–xxiii, 29, 32, 34, 204–21, 223–29, 234–37, 242–51, 295–96; short stories of, xx, 12n. 1, 47n. 4, 94n. 1, 95n. 1, 96, 97–98, 103, 108–10, 114, 116, 120, 120–21n. 1, 123–24, 126, 127, 156–57, 172, 176–78, 181–82, 183, 184; on Switzerland, 283–84; unmailed letters of, 279–303; in the West, 168, 169, 179; on writing, 13–14; writing plans after break with Scribner, 302–3. See also *From Death to Morning; Look Homeward, Angel; Of Time and the River; The Story of a Novel; The Web and the Rock; You Can't Go Home Again*

Woodford, John, xxi–xxii

Wordsworth, William, 41

Wright, Willard Huntington. *See* Van Dine, S. S.

Wyckoff, Irma, 157–58, 239, 240, 313

Wylie, Elinor, 35n. 3

The Yearling (Rawlings), 269

You Can't Go Home Again (Wolfe), xxi, 42n. 3, 222n. 20, 297n. 1, 308

Zola, Emile, xxii